T0183323

Lecture Notes in Computer Science   11971

More information about this series at http://www.springer.com/series/7409

Roger Chamberlain · Martin Edin Grimheden ·
Walid Taha (Eds.)

Cyber Physical Systems

Model-Based Design

9th International Workshop, CyPhy 2019
and 15th International Workshop, WESE 2019
New York City, NY, USA, October 17–18, 2019
Revised Selected Papers

 Springer

Editors
Roger Chamberlain 🄳
Washington University
St. Louis, MO, USA

Martin Edin Grimheden 🄳
KTH Royal Institute of Technology
Stockholm, Sweden

Walid Taha 🄳
Halmstad University
Halmstad, Sweden

ISSN 0302-9743   ISSN 1611-3349   (electronic)
Lecture Notes in Computer Science
ISBN 978-3-030-41130-5   ISBN 978-3-030-41131-2   (eBook)
https://doi.org/10.1007/978-3-030-41131-2

LNCS Sublibrary: SL3 – Information Systems and Applications, incl. Internet/Web, and HCI

This Springer imprint is published by the registered company Springer Nature Switzerland AG
The registered company address is: Gewerbestrasse 11, 6330 Cham, Switzerland

Preface

This volume contains the joint proceedings of the Workshop on Model-Based Design of Cyber Physical Systems (CyPhy 2019) and the Workshop on Embedded and Cyber-Physical Systems Education (WESE 2019). The two events were co-located and coordinated for the third time in a row with the goal of exploring opportunities for closer collaboration.

This year, CyPhy 2019 planned from the outset to have post-proceedings to allow authors to incorporate feedback and insights from discussions at the workshop. The workshop received 18 submissions. The Program Committee decided to accept 10 of these papers.

The WESE 2019 workshop received six submissions and contributed three papers to the proceedings.

The Program Committee was large and diverse, consisting of 75 members from 18 different countries. As a step towards closer cooperation, the Program Committee was unified, in that all members served both CyPhy 2019 and WESE 2019. Each paper received at least four reviews, and the vast majority received five or more.

All committee members were required to declare conflicts of interests whenever they arose, and were subsequently not involved in reviewing these papers. Three papers created conflicts for one of the program co-chairs, in which case the same process was applied and in addition the other co-chair handled the submission. Of the three submissions for which there was a co-chair conflict, two were accepted.

In addition, there were two keynotes, the first by Edward Lee entitled "Actors Revisited for Cyberphysical Systems" and the second by Martin Edin Grimheden entitled "What can Embedded Systems education learn from current research and trends in the general engineering education area?".

We would like to acknowledge several individuals who were key to the success of the event, including the Program Committee, authors, keynote speakers, the publicity chair: Abdelhamid Taha, and the organizers of ESWEEK 2019.

December 2019

Roger Chamberlain
Martin Edin Grimheden
Walid Taha

Organization

General Chair (CyPhy)

Walid Taha   Halmstad University, Sweden

Program Committee Chair (CyPhy)

Walid Taha   Halmstad University, Sweden

Program Committee Chair (WESE)

Martin Edin Grimheden   KTH Royal Institute of Technology, Sweden

Program Committee

Houssam Abbas   University of Pennsylvania, USA
Erika Abraham   RWTH Aachen University, Germany
Julien Alexandre   ENSTA ParisTech, France
  dit Sandretto
Ayman Aljarbouh   University of Grenoble Alpes, France
Matthias Althoff   TU Munich, Germany
Henric Andersson   Environment & Innovation, Sweden
Hugo Andrade   National Instruments, USA
Stanley Bak   Safe Sky Analytics, USA
Ferenc Bartha   University of Szeged, Hungary
Saddek Bensalem   University of Grenoble Alpes, France
Sergiy Bogomolov   The Australian National University, Australia
Mirko Bordignon   Fraunhofer IPA, Germany
Manfred Broy   TU Munich, Germany
David Broman   KTH Royal Institute of Technology, Sweden
Manuela Bujorianu   University of Strathclyde, UK
Daniela Cancila   Commissariat à l'Énergie Atomique (CEA), France
Ing-Ray Chen   Virginia Tech, USA
Janette Cardoso   Institut Supérieur de l'Aéronautique et de l'Espace
                            (ISAE), France
Thao Dang   Verimag, France
Alex Dean   North Carolina State University, USA
Rayna Dimitrova   Leicester University, UK
Adam Duracz   Rice University, USA
Sinem Coleri Ergen   Koc University, Turkey
Xinyu Feng   Nanjing University, China
Martin Fränzle   University of Oldenburg, Germany

Jon Wade	Stevens Institute of Technology, USA
Rafael Wisniewski	Aalborg University, Germany
Andreas Wortmann	RWTH Aachen University, Germany
Yingfu Zeng	Rice University, USA
Makal Ziane	Laboratoire d'Informatique de Paris, France

Advisory Committee (CyPhy)

Manfred Broy	TU Munich, Germany
Karl Iagnemma	Massachusetts Institute of Technology, USA
Karl Henrik Johansson	KTH Royal Institute of Technology, Sweden
Insup Lee	University of Pennsylvania, USA
Pieter Mosterman	McGill University, Canada
Janos Sztipanovits	Vanderbilt University, USA
Walid Taha	Halmstad University, Sweden

Contents

Formal Methods

Workshop on Embedded and Cyber-Physical Systems Education

Models and Design

A Modular SystemC RTOS Model for Uncertainty Analysis

Lorenzo Lazzara$^{(\boxtimes)}$, Giulio Mosé Mancuso, Fabio Cremona,
and Alessandro Ulisse

United Technologies Research Center, Rome, Italy
{lorenzo.lazzara,giuliomose.mancuso,fabio.cremona,
alessandro.ulisse}@utrc.utc.com

Abstract. Nowadays the complexity of embedded systems is constantly increasing and several different types of applications concurrently execute on the same computational platform. Hence these systems have to satisfy real-time constraints and support real-time communication. The design and verification of these systems is very complex, full formal verification is not always possible and the run-time verification is the only feasible path to follow. In this context, the possibility to simulate their behavior becomes a crucial aspect. This paper proposes a SystemC modular RTOS model to assist the design and the verification of real-time embedded systems. The model architecture has been designed to capture all the typical functionalities that every RTOS owns, in order to easily reproduce the behavior of a large class of RTOS. The RTOS model can support functional simulation for design space exploration to rapidly evaluate the impact of different RTOS configurations (such as scheduling policies) on the overall system performances. Moreover the model can be used for software verification by implementing specific RTOS APIs over the generic services provided by the model, allowing the simulation of a real application without changing any instruction. The proposed approach enables the user to model non-deterministic behaviors at architectural and application level by means of probabilistic distributions. This allows to assess system performances of complex embedded systems under uncertain behavior (e.g. execution time). A use case is proposed considering an instance of the model compliant with the ARINC 653 specification, which requires spatial and temporal segregation, and where typical RTOS performances are assessed given the probability distributions of execution time and aperiodic task activation.

Keywords: Real-time operating system model · SystemC · Uncertainty quantification · Statistical model checking

1 Introduction

Virtual engineering techniques are increasingly popular in several application domains. Models of the system components (seen as "virtual components") are

© Springer Nature Switzerland AG 2020
R. Chamberlain et al. (Eds.): CyPhy 2019/WESE 2019, LNCS 11971, pp. 3–27, 2020.
https://doi.org/10.1007/978-3-030-41131-2_1

used to assess the behavior and performance of a subsystem unit without the need of a physical prototype. This capability is usually exploited (1) in the specification of the subsystem components to compare different design alternatives and select the best design option; (2) in the verification flow, where the satisfaction of requirements can be assessed on a virtual prototype. This approach allows to start the verification process earlier in the design flow anticipating errors that would otherwise propagate along the chain up to the final implementation [5]. System Level Modeling [11,21] seems to be the only feasible way to face the growing design complexity of modern embedded systems. It allows the modeling of critical embedded platform details at high abstraction levels. This enables faster exploration of the design space at early stages and ease the verification of software integration before having access to the real hardware. However existing System Level Design Languages (SLDL) and methodologies do not support a proper modeling of a full real time operating system at higher abstraction level. The Real-time operating system is a critical software component that orchestrates all the application execution in the embedded platform. Hence almost all the timing properties of the platform are dependent from the RTOS. For this reason in the current paper we aim to fill the gap of the current SLDL proposing a modular SystemC generic real-time operating system model. The proposed RTOS model takes into account different functional aspects, providing real-time scheduling and other typical services necessary for real-time software simulation. The modularity of the proposed model ease the configuration of the possible instances enabling functional simulation for design space exploration. The proposed model also provides the capability to implement specific RTOS services allowing a fast integration of the target platform code for software-in-the-loop (SIL) simulations. The proposed RTOS model also considers stochastic behaviors naturally appearing in the real embedded platforms. For example nowadays the computational platform presents complex features like caching, pre-fetching, pipelining, DMA, and interrupts which allow to improve the performance of the system but can lead to a higher degree of uncertainty. In this scenario the timing characteristic of the system can be very unpredictable and a rigorous and precise timing analysis can be very difficult to conduct [4]. In addition, complex embedded system operates in an environment that is intrinsically non-deterministic. Two kinds of non-determinism can be distinguished in embedded systems [19]: pure non-determinism and probabilistic non-determinism. Pure non-determinism is for example the non-determinism due to the interaction with the environment (sensor data input) that is highly unpredictable. Probabilistic non-determinism is appropriate whenever a statistical representation of the phenomenon well represent is occurrence. We believe that the response time may lie in this category. In the current work we will focus on probabilistic non-determinism allowing a stochastic characterization of the main kernel operations by defining their behavior in terms of probability distributions. The proposed approach is validated considering a data acquisition application running on an RTOS model compliant with the ARINC 653 specification [2]. The standard ARINC 653 aims at support the integrated modular avionic framework providing a strict and robust time and space partitioning environment with the definition of a common API (called APEX) between the software applications and the underlying operating system.

2   Related Works

Different techniques have been proposed for high abstraction level RTOS modeling and simulation. One of the early techniques was presented in [23] which uses a specific RTOS model and simulation engine. It allows an highly accurate simulation but limits the design space exploration and the software verification to the specific RTOS. Approaches based on System Level Domain Languages has been proposed in order to provide a general RTOS model able to simulate different RTOS instances. A fully configurable RTOS model was proposed in [15] which targets a functional model simulation. This work models both the behavior and the time aspects of the RTOS for both singlecore as well as multicore platform architectures. It allows the configuration of the model in terms of HW resources and RTOS functionality, moreover it integrates a timed simulation by inserting back-annotation at different level of granularity. The work described in [17] reports a time accurate RTOS model for POSIX compliant applications. It allows the simulation of application source code integrated into the RTOS model to be simulated with dynamically execution time estimation. The work described in [9] present a customizable RTOS with different modules interacting with each other with the definition of a generic services interface towards the task which ease the integration of various RTOS APIs. The approach presented in this paper is based on SystemC [1] similarly to the one proposed in [9,15,17]. In particular those papers address the case in which the designer is able to configure the RTOS model in terms of different functional aspects like scheduling policies, communication mechanisms and other typical RTOS features. However they do not address the possibility to model hierarchical architectures with multi-level schedulers. This type of architecture are important for safety critical systems (i.e. automotive, avionics) where applications usually execute in a temporal and spatial segregated environment. The work in the [17] provides a POSIX API from which the user can interact and run application code. This is an interesting feature, however this does not allow to model other kind specific RTOS APIs. The annotation mechanism discussed in [14] sec. 2.3 consider an annotation for each line of code through the use of a DELAY function. Our approach of annotation is similiar, we introduce a function which allow to simulate the task physical running time on a CPU with the possibility of stopping the time in order to mimic preemption, the behavior of this function is similiar to the one presented in [24]. The model we propose herein takes into account the variability present in the system providing a framework for uncertainty analysis. Several works have been focusing on the uncertainty characterization and propagation for Embedded Systems. The work in [25] and in [26] mainly focused on a formal software representation of the uncertainty in order to support Model Based Testing (MBT) techniques. The work in the [8] and in [7] instead targeted the formal verification of the application code (written in SystemC) by using affine arithmetic. Although those methods provide a formal framework for the verification under uncertainty, they may not scale well with complex application code. The rest of the paper is organized as follows: in Sect. 3 we introduce the model architecture and we will give more details about the software components. In Sect. 4 we introduce the uncertainty analysis able to run on the proposed RTOS model. Finally in Sect. 6 we will show some experimental results on a typical ARINC 653 data acquisition application. The conclusions and the interesting future work will be exposed in Sect. 7.

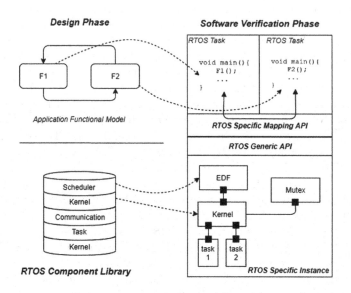

Fig. 1. Conceptual architecture and workflow.

3   Real Time Operating System Model Architecture

In the following section we present the high level model architecture of a SystemC-based System-Level Real-Time Operating System (RTOS) software simulation framework. The main idea behind the proposed approach is the definition of a *Component Library* from which the user can take components and build specific RTOS model instances. The structure of the overall RTOS model can be decomposed in three main parts: the *Generic RTOS Component Library*, *Generic RTOS API* and a *Specific RTOS Mapping API*. A graphical representation of the architecture and a conceptual workflow is depicted in Fig. 1. The generic component library is divided into functional categories i.e. kernel, scheduler, task, communication and synchronization. The user can instantiate a specific RTOS model instance interconnecting specific components from different categories. Components belonging to the same category implement a standard execution interface that allows to easily interchange different blocks with the same interface but with different implementation. This modular approach ease the evaluation of the impact of different implementation choices during the design space exploration. The generic API exposes externally generic RTOS services from all the categories e.g. part of the task management services are exposed in Fig. 2. The specific mapping API focuses on the implementation of specific RTOS services. For example the ARINC 653 and the AUTOSAR specifications detail a specific API (and their semantics) that a real-time operating system should implement. The main purpose of the mapping API is to map the specific services into the generic services. The implementation of a specific API ease the software integration verification phase. As depicted in Fig. 1, our model may enable the validation and the verification of the application at different level of abstraction. For example at the early design stage (e.g. functional model), the generic APIs can be used to validate the preliminary application-RTOS task mapping (top part of Fig. 1). Once the target platform has been selected, the mapping API can be implemented in order to enable software-in-the-loop verification. The interaction between the main components of the system (kernel, scheduler and task) is achieved through SystemC *ports* and *exports* which require the definition of a common interface in order to communicate each other. The interfaces have been defined in a way that they are as much as possible independent from the particular implementation of the services. This architecture allows to decouple the declaration of the system calls (defined at the interface) with their actual implementation in order to guarantee and ease the design exploration by enabling the replacement of a component with another without changing any other component in the overall model. The proposed high-level system architecture is presented in Fig. 2.

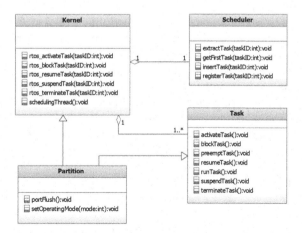

Fig. 2. Simplified system class diagram.

The RTOS model has been integrated into the *Desyre* [5] framework which is a SystemC-based virtual prototyping environment developed at the *United Technologies Research Center*. However the model is based on open standards such as SystemC and IPXACT allowing its integration in any framework which supports those standards.

3.1   Scheduler Model

In all the real-time operating systems the scheduler is in charge of maintaining the correct execution order between the tasks. More formally at each instant in time the scheduler has to decide which is the running task and has to build a queue of available tasks ready to run. Our aim is to model a generic real-time scheduler with different scheduling policies. When tasks are registered within the scheduler, a relative `TaskSchedulingModel` object is instantiated, which contains the scheduling parameters and ID of the task. This approach allows the separation of the task parameters (like period, deadline, wcet, etc.) that are contained in the task class, from the scheduling parameters that are contained in the `TaskSchedulingModel` and which are defined specifically depending on the chosen scheduling algorithm. The ready queue is ordered based on three parameters defined in the `TaskSchedulingModel`. The `priority` is the first level sorting parameter and it depends on the scheduling algorithm used. In order to have a generic priority which would capture both time-dependent scheduling algorithms (e.g. EDF) and fixed priority scheduling algorithms (e.g. FP, RM), this parameter is modeled as a *sc_time* SystemC variable. The priority parameter is used to sort the tasks in ascending order (smaller is the priority value, higher is the scheduling priority) inside the ready queue. If tasks have the same priority value the `insertion time` is used to give higher priority to the oldest tasks in the ready queue, hence following a FIFO sorting principle. The `task ID` is used when modeling an ideal RTOS without system overheads, having therefore the possibility of having tasks with same priority inserted at the same time. The model allows to select among several scheduling policies. *First Come First Served (FCFS)* is implemented exploiting the second level sorting parameter (*insertion time*) to order the tasks in the ready queue. In order to implement the time-sharing preemptive mechanism of the *Round-Robin (RR)* scheduling policy, an event is used in order to trigger the kernel and force a rescheduling whenever a time quantum expires. For *Rate Monotonic (RM)*, when the task is registered within the scheduler, its priority (period) is used to construct the relative `TaskSchedulingModel`. Hence the priority value is assigned only one time (static) and is never changed during execution. In *Earliest Deadline First (EDF)*, since the priority value can not be assigned statically, the task deadline value is retrieved through the interface with the kernel whenever the task is inserted in the ready queue. For *Fixed Priority (FP)*, when the task is registered within the scheduler, its priority is retrieved from a priority-pool inside the scheduler and it is used to construct the relative `TaskSchedulingModel`. The *Partition Scheduler* implements a partition scheduling policy which is a predetermined, repetitive with a fixed periodicity, called *major time frame* (MTF), scheduling algorithm. The scheduling parameters, the major time frame, the offset and duration of each partition window are set during the system configuration. The offset of the partitions is used as a priority in the `TaskSchedulingModel` to sort the partitions in the ready queue, the duration instead is used like the slice time in the RR scheduler, i.e. it defines the next preemption time. Being a time-driven scheduler the interaction with the kernel is similar to that described for the RR. This kind of partition scheduling is used in all the RTOS systems compliant with the ARINC 653 standard. An example of partition scheduling will be presented in the later sections (see Fig. 7).

3.2 Kernel Model

The RTOS Kernel module models all the typical software mechanism of an RTOS, such as: task scheduling, task interaction and synchronization. The kernel model allow to ensure that the execution of the tasks is serialized following the order of the selected scheduling policy. In order to achieve this behavior, all the tasks wait on specific SystemC events which are only released by the kernel. Hence, during scheduling the kernel retrieves the first task from the ready queue and execute it by triggering its event. If there is not a candidate task (ready list is empty), the kernel just waits until a ready task is available. Each task is associated with a task descriptor class that is a data structure containing all its static and run-time information, i.e. task ID, period, deadline and task state. The interaction between the kernel and the task is performed through the data exposed by the task descriptor. The RTOS model supports both periodic and aperiodic tasks. A periodic task at end of its job will call the task wait cycle method in order to wait for its next release point while an aperiodic task will call the terminate method in order to kill its instance. The *Task State Machine* is the basis of both multi-tasking management and scheduling services in the RTOS kernel model. Typical multi-tasking primitive functions include creating tasks, activating tasks, suspending tasks, blocking tasks, resuming tasks, and terminating tasks. These functions control the state transitions of tasks during their execution. In the Fig. 3 is depicted the RTOS task state machine that has five basic states: `dormant`, `running`, `ready`, `suspend` and `blocked`. During the RTOS execution a task can be at only one state:

- `running`: in a uniprocessor system, only one task can enter this state and execute at each time instant. If the `running` task is preempted, then it enters the `ready` state.
- `ready`: tasks at this state are eligible for execution, but cannot execute immediately as another task is currently at the `running` state. All `ready` tasks are organized in the ready queue by the scheduler according to various scheduling policies. During a rescheduling the kernel retrieve the first task in the ready queue; if this new task is different from the `running` task (if there is one), the `running` task is preempted and the new task is dispatched.
- `blocked`: tasks enter the `blocked` state when accessing an (empty) blocking resource or when they explicitly wait for a timer. Each `blocked` task is organized in a waiting queue relative to the blocking resource. Usually a timeout

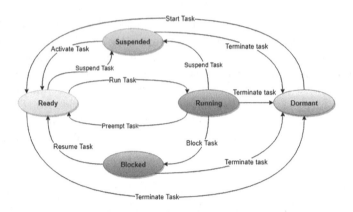

Fig. 3. Task finite state machine.

period can be specified in order to automatically unblock and put in the
ready state the task.
- **suspended**: similarly to the tasks in the **blocked** state, tasks in the **suspended**
state cannot be selected to enter the **running** state. The tasks only enter the
suspended state when the **TaskSuspend()** service is explicitly called. The
task exit the **suspended** state when the resume or activate service is called.
- **dormant**: a task is said to be in the **dormant** state when is created, but has
not yet been started, or when its execution is completed.

Application tasks need to synchronize and share data, in order to cooperate
with each other properly. In the RTOS we can distinguish between *synchronization methods* and *communication methods* where the former is used mainly to
coordinate the execution orders of involved tasks, while the latter can explicitly exchange data between tasks. Unlike the system components previously
described, communication services do not interact with the system through SystemC *ports* and *exports*. The kernel contains a pool of pointers to communication
objects which are discriminated through their communication ID that is assigned
to each communication object when it is instantiated. Modeling remains general
thanks to the introduction of a common generic interface; each communication
object will have a specific implementation of this interface. Communication services are accessed at task level through the interface with the kernel. Inter-task
communication methods are exploited via message passing. The communication
mechanisms can be fully configured in order to have message queues or shared
variables (single instance message), blocking or non-blocking mechanism, queuing policy and other meaningful parameters. The inter-task synchronization can
be achieved through the use of counting semaphores and events. Semaphores
are used to provide controlled access to resource, while events support control
flow between tasks by notifying the occurrences of conditions to waiting tasks.
In order to allow the modeling of temporally segregated RTOS, an extension
of the kernel model has been done to comprehend the concept of a partitioned
RTOS. A partition is a schedulable entity where one or more tasks concurrently

execute; hence, the partition has been modeled, by implementing both the kernel and task interface, as a kernel that can be in turn scheduled. When the partition is selected to run the partition-level scheduler is activated and tasks execute as they are running on a normal kernel. The partition execution can be preempted and in turn if there is a running task, it is also preempted in order to allow the execution of a new partition and the tasks it contains. This run-time behavior is modeled through a SystemC SC_THREAD. As the kernel manages scheduling and communication between tasks, an entity is needed to manage the partitions. The *Supervisor* is a simple kernel that handles partition scheduling and dispatching, as well as inter-partition communication. The supervisor allows the exchange of information between different partitions by means of communication ports. Ports can have different configurations like blocking/non-blocking mechanism, possibility of message queuing with the related queuing policy and direction of transfer. Whenever a partition switch takes place, the outgoing ports, of the currently running partition, are checked for new data available. In case of data transfer the partition inform the supervisor which takes charge of the inter-partition communication transferring data to the destination ports in one or more partitions. The supervisor, together with the partition scheduler, allows to achieve time segregation by limit the processing time assigned to each partition. Whenever the end of a partition time window is reached the supervisor is triggered, it preempts the current running partition and selects the next partition to run. The supervisor and the partitions allow to instantiate an hierarchical RTOS with multiple level of scheduling; moreover each partition can represent a different instance of a RTOS kernel by modifying the attached scheduler or its behavior.

3.3   Functional and Timing Task Model

An important characteristic of the real-time systems is their tight dependency between functional and timing characteristic of the task. It is well known that the correct execution of a real-time application is not only determined by the correct functional output, but it needs to be provided within some time bounds (deadline). It is important then that our RTOS model properly captures both the functional and timing characteristics of the tasks running on top of it. From a functional point of view the proposed RTOS is able to execute the original RTOS task implementation with minor modification (time annotation). This is an extremely useful capability in a verification workflow where the code under test does not need to be modified moving between different validation/verification steps. This is achieved by mapping the generic RTOS APIs to the specific target RTOS services. Indeed when a new real-time operating system (e.g. FreeRTOS [3], DEOS [6], VxWorks [23]) is selected as suitable for the final system implementation, the modeler needs to implement the mapping code between the generic RTOS APIs and the specific RTOS services. An example of this mapping is detailed in Sect. 3.4 for the ARINC 653 specification. An important capability of the RTOS model is also to advance the virtual simulation time corresponding to the virtual execution of the application code. The timing characterization of the tasks is of crucial importance to verify all the timing RTOS performances such as overall tasks schedulability, response time, jitter and so on. There are several approaches to characterize the timing behavior of the task body. A very nice survey on all those techniques can be found in [22]. Out of the scope of the current work is to perform a rigorous execution time analysis of the application code. The main objective however is to be flexible enough to enable most of the timing analysis techniques. We propose a timing task model where the overall execution time is divided into several execution chunks as depicted in Fig. 4a. The zth execution chunk of the jth job instance of τ_i is denoted by $\tau_{i,j[z]}$. The execution time of $\tau_{i,j[z]}$ is denoted by $C_{i,j[z]}$. The total execution time is defined by $C_{i,j} = \sum_{z=1}^{n} C_{i,j[z]}$. In case of fixed execution time among all the task jobs, we remove the index j relative to the task job, e.g. $C_{1,1} = C_{1,1[1]} + C_{i,[2]}$ implies that the second execution chunk $C_{i,[2]}$ is constant for all the jobs. At the end of each execution chunk a time wait function called ConsumeTime() is inserted to emulate real execution time advancing the virtual time. An example of task body code is represented in the Fig. 4b. The wait function can either take a constant time or a stochastic variable allowing stochastic task execution time. The timing information (execution time) can be retrieved using any existing technique. The way we model the timing feature of the task allows a decoupling between the real function implementation code and the execution time. This allows the user to either execute the real application code or leave the task body empty, i.e. definition of *abstract tasks*. An abstract task can be defined at early design stages in order to evaluate real-time performances without considering the functional behavior. Although the user can execute the real application code within an execution chunk, its evaluation must be considered as atomic. The execution of the task body does not advance the virtual time of the simulation. Therefore the application code is always executed at zero virtual execution time, while only the ConsumeTime() will allow the emulation of the computation time. It follows that the granularity of the execution chunks may depend on the specific application, i.e. the insertion of this function at different granularities enables to verify the system at different level of accuracy. The time wait function is not an atomic function and it can be preempted by the kernel. The granularity of insertion of the ConsumeTime() may introduce some approximation in the execution of the code. A preemption by the RTOS kernel can happen almost at any source code instruction (e.g. interrupts). This introduces some complexity on the verification of concurrent systems in presence of shared variables or other synchronization mechanisms. Our preemption model instead only captures the preemption at the level of the ConsumeTime() function missing the relation with the functional source code. A possible mitigation is the insertion of the ConsumeTime() after every code line, although this may increase the simulation time. It is out of the scope of this paper to do a rigorous timing analysis of the code but it is a topic that we will investigate in a future work.

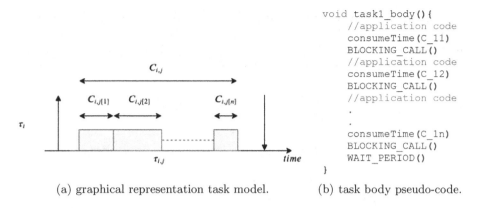

```
void task1_body(){
    //application code
    consumeTime(C_11)
    BLOCKING_CALL()
    //application code
    consumeTime(C_12)
    BLOCKING_CALL()
    //application code
    .
    .
    consumeTime(C_1n)
    BLOCKING_CALL()
    WAIT_PERIOD()
}
```

(a) graphical representation task model.   (b) task body pseudo-code.

Fig. 4. Computational task model.

3.4   ARINC 653 Model Interface

The ARINC 653 standard specifies an *APplication EXecutive*(APEX) interface which provides a list of services consistent with fulfilling integrated modular avionic platform. The main purpose of the standard is to provide a partitioned environment, both spatially and temporally segregated, where one or more avionics applications can independently execute [2]. In order to implement the APEX services, a specific mapping API (static library) has been developed that implements the ARINC 653 specific interface on top of the generic RTOS API. This library can access methods and attributes of the task model and it wraps the low level generic services exposed by the kernel to satisfy the requirements of the APEX API. In order to perform a SIL simulation for a given task set, the tasks are linked with the mapping library enabling the calling of the APEX services directly within the task body. The API for process management are standard RTOS services for task management (start, resume, suspend, stop) which have mostly a direct mapping with the generic services provided by the RTOS model. The communication API are instead a specialization of the low level communication services provided by the kernel. For example the *queuing ports* defined in the ARINC 653 standard for inter-partition communication are mapped to the concept of port defined in Sect. 3.2 and are specialized in order to model a blocking behavior and a message queuing. Instead the sampling ports are specialized with non-blocking behavior and non-queuing mode. The same approach has been used to map the specialized inter-task communication mechanism (i.e. *buffer* and *blackboard*) with the base communication services provided. An RTOS instance compliant with ARINC 653 comprehend a supervisor and one or more partitions. A partition contains one or more tasks which execute in a temporal and spatial segregated environment. The supervisor, together with the partition scheduler, schedules partitions enforcing temporal segregation while the fixed priority scheduler is used to model the partition-level priority based scheduler defined in the ARINC 653 specification. The structure just described is represented in Fig. 5. This particular instance represent a two-level hierarchi-

cal scheduler as required by the standard ARINC 653. The presented workflow
used to integrate the ARINC 653 API is generic. Given a different target RTOS
only the mapping between the specific API and the generic services of the RTOS
model is needed to enable the SIL simulation.

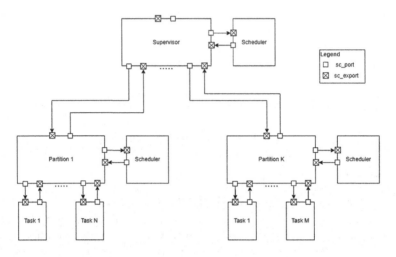

Fig. 5. Specific RTOS model instance compliant with ARINC 653.

4   Uncertainty Analysis

As we introduced before, the modeling of uncertain behavior during the validation and verification of the real-time system is of paramount importance.
Modeling of uncertainties is not only useful to capture the real system operation
but can also be used to model different design aspects at different validation and
verification phases. It can also be used to model unknown platform details at
early design stages. For example the execution time of the application (RTOS
tasks) can be considered uncertain because the processing unit (e.g. CPU) has
not been selected yet at the current design phase. Again the failure probability of
physical components is intrinsically non-deterministic and may generates events
across the platform that will impact the overall system operation. In the current
work we will focus on the probabilistic modeling of the uncertainty affecting real-
time operating system, i.e. all the uncertainty behaviors are modeled in terms
of probability distributions. In particular we will investigate performances under
two main uncertain aspects:

– **Execution time of the task jobs**: this may be the result of the uncertainty
  at lower architectural levels (e.g. RTOS kernel operations), or application specific uncertainty (e.g. branches in the application code due to unpredictable
  events).

- **Activation of aperiodic tasks**: the activation of aperiodic tasks can be the result of an internal functional behavior or can be triggered by an external event generated from the environment.

Although our focus is on the above two aspects, our RTOS model is able to handle more specific kernel aspects. For example the model can be easily extended to explicitly model uncertainty affecting the timing of operations such as context switch between jobs or task queuing. The decision on how detailed should be our uncertainty model is a trade-off between modeling effort and probability distribution complexity. The execution time probability distribution is the results of the correlation of multiple uncertainties affecting several operations in both application, kernel and hardware side. Although it is out of the scope of this work an accurate probabilistic modeling of the uncertainty affecting the system, we are currently providing a framework to enable researcher to approach this problem in a systematic way. In the next section we will focus on the two important analysis: *Forward Uncertainty Propagation* [20] and *Statistical Model Checking* [8]. We will see how those two analysis can be used to verify the performances of the system highlighting how the nominal behavior can drastically change when even a small uncertainty is added to the system.

4.1   Forward Uncertainty Quantification

Uncertainty quantification (UQ) [20] is an interdisciplinary area which addresses the problem of quantifying the impact of the uncertainty present in both complex computational and physical models. Two main research areas can be distinguished:

The *Forward Uncertainty Propagation* [20] focuses on assessing some output performances given a probabilistic characterization of the input. A typical application is the evaluation of low-order moments such as mean or variance of some outputs given the probability distribution of the input.

The *Inverse Uncertainty Quantification* [20] instead focuses on the uncertainty characterization of the input given a set of output measurements. This is generally a more challenging problem then forward uncertainty propagation. Although this area is of extreme importance and complementary to the current work, we will not address this topic in the current work.

In the current paper we will focus only on the forward uncertainty propagation analysis. In particular in the next sections we will address the problem of quantifying, in terms of probability distributions, typical performance metrics for a real-time application. There are several efficient UQ techniques available to perform the uncertainty propagation. All those techniques exploit the model properties in order to be more accurate and reduce computation time. Unfortunately given the nature of our model (computational model without any particular structure) we cannot apply any specific technique and we have to rely on a simple Monte Carlo method.

4.2 Statistical Model Checking

Model checking is a method for algorithmic verification of formal systems, i.e. systems based on a formal model representation. The main objective of model checking is to verify whether a given system model possesses certain properties expressed using a specification logic. These properties are usually specified using temporal logic [12], which is an extension of the propositional logic in order to represent realities that change over time. It uses the classic Boolean logic operators to which temporal connectives are added. An improvement to this method is the *Probabilistic Model Checking* that aim to quantify the likelihood for a stochastic system to satisfy some property rather than giving a boolean flag on a property [16]. When dealing with real-time systems it is also important to monitor the timing behavior of the system (when a particular situation arise), hence the possibility to have timing features in the specification of the requirements is also needed [16]. One major problem with MC-based approaches is the state-space explosion problem [8]. *Statistical Model Checking* (SMC) is an approach that has recently been proposed as an alternative to avoid the state explosion problem of probabilistic (numerical) model checking. The approach can be divided in three macro step: (1) the system under test is simulated, (2) the simulation is monitored in order to retrieve relevant parameters, (3) statistical tools, like sequential hypothesis testing or Monte Carlo simulation, are used in order to decide whether the system satisfies the property or not with some degree of confidence [16]. Statistical Model Checking is a trade-off among testing and traditional model checking procedures. The simulation-based approach is less memory and time consumptive than the formal ones, and it is often the only option. To estimate probabilities, SMC uses a number of statistically independent stochastic simulation traces of a discrete event model [13]. In the next sections we will focus on two main methods for the statistical model checking: Monte Carlo and Hypothesis Testing. The *Monte Carlo Method* in the SMC literature [18] is considered a *quantitative method* and it answers to the following question: *What is the probability p for the model under test to satisfy a logic proposition Ψ?*; The tool returns a simulation trace for the interesting variables with the number of performed simulations and the number of positive simulations, i.e. the number of simulations in which the property Ψ has satisfied. From these two values the probability of satisfying the requirement is obtained. Instead of manually setting the number of simulations, it is possible to use the Chernoff-Hoeffding bound which provides the minimum number of simulations required to ensure the desired confidence level. The implementation of the Chernoff-Hoeffding bound is based on two parameters: the error margin (ϵ) and the confidence bound (δ). The *Sequential Hypothesis Testing* instead is considered a *qualitative approach* and addresses the following question: *Is the probability p for the model under test to satisfy the property Ψ greater or equal than a certain threshold θ?* [18]. The hypothesis testing is used to infer if the simulated execution traces provide statistical evidence on the satisfaction or violation of a property. The test is parameterized by three bounds, α and β and the indifference region IR [18]. In the next section we will see how to take advantage of those methods in order to verify typical RTOS performance metrics.

5   ARINC 653 Application Model: Data Acquisition System

To demonstrate our capability to simulate and verify real-time applications on our RTOS model, we will use a surrogated application targeting an RTOS compliant with the ARINC 653 specification. The sequence diagram of the application is depicted in Fig. 6. It is a simple model of a centralized data acquisition system where all the data are acquired and manipulated on a single computational unit. A task $i \in [0, N]$ in a partition $j \in [A, B, C]$ is represented by τ_i^j. The system is composed by three partitions P_A, P_B and P_C. The partition P_A contains the task τ_1^A that implements all the decision making logic. It is in charge of triggering data acquisition (triggered due to some internal state or due to external events) and based on the manipulated data takes some actions. The task τ_1^A is aperiodic and its execution time is usually variable depending on the sensor measurements and decision making logic. The tasks τ_1^B and τ_2^B in the partition P_B perform a data conditioning and manipulation. Moreover they are in charge of triggering the sensor measurement acquisition from the tasks in the partition P_C. The execution time of the tasks in P_B are slightly variable depending on the amount of data to process at each acquisition event. Tasks in P_C performing the acquisition are usually highly predictable with very short execution time. In our model the generation of the external event is emulated by an aperiodic "artificial" task τ_0^A. The task τ_0^A will trigger the execution of τ_1^A based on a given probability distribution detailed in the next section. The presented base application model can be proportional scaled in order to obtain a more complex system and to analyze the interleaving of the task inside the partitions. In the analysis performed in the next sections we will consider four instances of the model running on the same RTOS. The final system is composed by the task set detailed in the Table 1. The partition has a major time frame of $t_{MTF} = 18$ ms while the time windows have the following configuration $\phi_{A1} = 0$ ms, $\phi_{A2} = 12$ ms, $t_{A1} = 1$ ms, $t_{A2} = 6$ ms, $\phi_{B1} = 1$ ms, $\phi_{B2} = 7$ ms, $t_{B1} = 1$ ms, $t_{B2} = 5$ ms, $\phi_C = 2$ ms, $t_C = 5$ ms where ϕ_{jk} and t_{jk} represent the offset and duration of the k-th time window of the j-th partition. A visual representation of the partition scheduling is presented in Fig. 7. For what is concerns the overall system performances we require that the time elapsed between the data acquisition event (activation of τ_1^A) and the resulting action (end of execution τ_1^A) is not more than 30 ms. This correspond with the response time of tasks in P_A. Of course the tasks in P_A are blocked by all the tasks in the other partitions. The response time of the tasks in P_A will account any delay affecting the tasks in the other partitions.

All the inter-partition communication has been implemented using the *queuing ports*, i.e. each task waits on the queuing port read call until data is available to be manipulated or, if specified, until a timeout expires. Tasks in P_A wait indefinitely on a read call (i.e. until data is available) while task in P_B and P_C have a

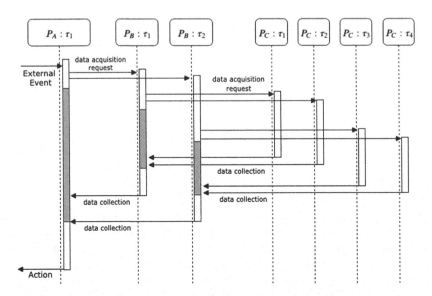

Fig. 6. Application Model - UML-like Sequence Diagram. The grey area represent the task blocking time.

Table 1. Application model task set.

Partition	#Task	Type	Period [ms]	Deadline [ms]	Execution time [ms]
A	4	Aperiodic	-	30	$C^A_{i,[1]} = 0.075;\ C^A_{i,[2]} = 1.075$
B	8	Periodic	18	18	$C^B_{i,[1]} = 0.1;\ C^B_{i,[2]} = 0.55$
C	16	Periodic	18	18	$C^C_i = 0.25$

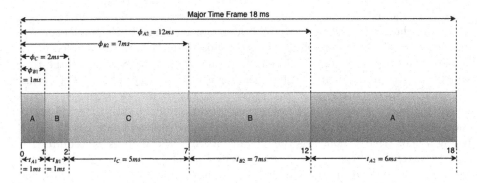

Fig. 7. Partition windows scheduling.

timeout specified within the read call in order not to miss the deadline. Hence, if tasks in P_A don't send the triggering message, the tasks wait only for the specified timeout then waiting for their next release point.

5.1 Application Stochastic Task Model

At the beginning of this section we introduce the task model for all the tasks running on the RTOS model. In the current section we introduce a stochastic variability for some application tasks. In the Fig. 8 is depicted the task model for all the tasks in the application. The tasks in the partition A and B are composed by two execution chunks. The chunks are delimited by the inter-partition communication (possibly blocking calls) involving tasks running on other partitions. The task jobs in the partitions B and C are deterministic and constant during the application execution. The execution time of the generic task instance in B is given by $C_{i,j}^B = C_{i,j[1]}^B + C_{i,j[2]}^B = C_{i,[1]}^B + C_{i,[2]}^B$ where we removed the index j since the execution time is fixed among all the task jobs. The execution of the task jobs running in P_C are constant and given by C_i^C. The execution times for all the tasks are summarized in the Table 1. The tasks running in P_A have a stochastic task model as described below:

- **Uncertain execution time for the task τ_i^A:** The model of the task is represented by two execution chunks. The first one is $C_{1,[1]}^A$ and it is constant for all the job instances. The second chunk $\hat{C}_{1,j[2]}$ is a stochastic variable drawn from a Normal distribution [10], i.e. $\hat{C}_{1,j[2]} \sim \mathcal{N}(\mu = 1, \sigma^2 = 0.25)$. The total execution time for the job instance j is stochastic and it will be the sum of both of the contributions, i.e. $\hat{C}_{i,j}^A = (C_{1,[1]}^A + \hat{C}_{i,j[2]}) \sim \mathcal{N}(\mu + C_{1,[1]}^A, \sigma^2)$.
- **Uncertain activation of the aperiodic task τ_i^A:** As we have seen before, the activation of the task τ_i^A generates a data acquisition event that spreads

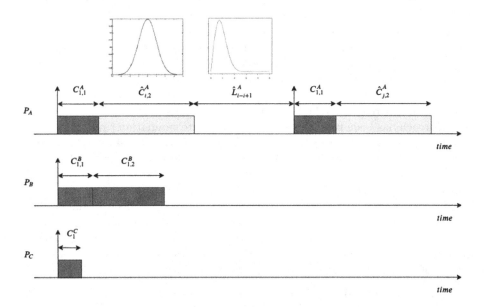

Fig. 8. Application stochastic task model.

across all the system. The probabilistic model is specified in terms of time elapsed between the end of the execution of the task and the next task activation. In the Fig. 8 this value is denoted with L^A_{i-i+1} that is the time elapsed between the end of the execution of the job instance i and the activation of the job instance $i + 1$. This variable is a stochastic variable drawn from a Weibull distribution [10], i.e. $L^A_{i-i+1} \sim \mathcal{W}(\lambda = 4, k = 2)$. Choosing this distribution we consider more likely activation triggered around 3 ms after the end of current job execution ($L^A_{i-i+1} \approx 3$ ms). The distribution considers also more likely event that are not more than 10 ms distant each other, and it penalizes events that are very close each other, i.e. $L^A_{i-i+1} \approx 0$ ms.

6   Results

Given the application described in the Sect. 5, we performed both forward uncertainty propagation and statistical model checking analysis. Although the two analyses are similar, they provide very different insight regarding the model under verification. In particular as we will point out in the next sections the forward uncertainty propagation gives back a global property of the stochastic model. On the other side the SMC predicates on a limited time horizon, therefore nothing can be assessed for the model globally.

6.1   Forward Uncertainty Propagation

As introduced in the previous sections, the main objective of the forward uncertainty propagation is to quantify the impact of any input uncertainty on the output performances. In this case we considered as input disturbance the probability distributions for both the aperiodic task activation and task execution time for all the four tasks in P_A. As output performance we will focus on the response time of the tasks in P_A denoted as $R^A_{i \in \{1,2,3,4\}}$. The main objective is to verify that their value do not exceed a maximum value fixed to $R_{max} = 30$ ms. Although we will focus on the response time our approach is general and can be extended to any relevant RTOS or application performance measure. A qualitative approach has been used to select an appropriate simulation time. It has been tuned in order to exhaustively exercise all the output probability distributions. We selected 1000 s as simulation time frame. A simulation trace for the model has been recorded while the random values for both the Normal and Weibull distribution were generated using the C++ random library [10].

In order to have a reference baseline, the system has been initially simulated in its nominal condition (deterministic simulation) without any stochastic behavior. The nominal case has been designed to satisfy the system requirements. In addition three other different scenarios were simulated considering first the impact of single uncertainties, then the impact of their interaction.

Nominal (Deterministic) Case: In this case the model is purely deterministic. The execution times are fixed equal to the nominal value as detailed in the Table 1. The activation of the aperiodic tasks is triggered at the beginning of the first time window P_{A1}. The values of the response times for the tasks are $R_1^A = 13.075$, $R_2^A = 14.15$, $R_3^A = 15.225$, $R_4^A = 16.03$.

Stochastic Task Execution: During this use case we will consider only the effect of a stochastic execution time for all the tasks in the partition A. The stochastic characteristic is modeled with the Normal distribution as detailed in Sect. 5.1. In the Fig. 9 are reported the histograms of the response times for all the four tasks $\tau_{i \in \{1,2,3,4\}}^A$ with the probability to miss the response time bound, i.e. $\mathrm{P_r}(R_i^A \geq 30\,\text{ms})$. It can be noted that the response time of task with higher priority (R_1^A) have a normal distribution equal to the nominal execution time $\hat{C}_1^A$ since it doesn't suffer the interference from the other tasks. It never violates the $R_{max} = 30\,\text{ms}$ bound, i.e. $\mathrm{P_r}(R_1^A \geq 30\,\text{ms}) = 0$. The lower priority tasks show an interesting behavior. The response time distribution in Fig. 9c and d present two evident distinct peaks (local maxima) separated by a gap. This distribution resemble a bimodal distribution, i.e. a probability distribution with two different modes. The first peak on the left represents the stochastic variability of the response time around its nominal value. The second peak on the right is the result of task activation not triggered inside the P_A time window but in another partition (P_B or P_C) where they are not allowed to execute. This introduce a delay that is equal to the time needed until the next P_A time windows is available again.

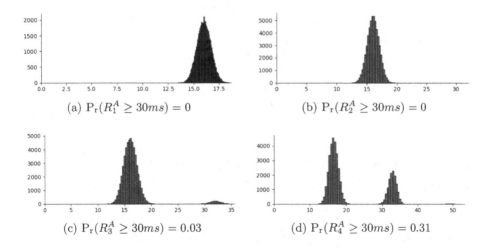

(a) $\mathrm{P_r}(R_1^A \geq 30ms) = 0$ (b) $\mathrm{P_r}(R_2^A \geq 30ms) = 0$

(c) $\mathrm{P_r}(R_3^A \geq 30ms) = 0.03$ (d) $\mathrm{P_r}(R_4^A \geq 30ms) = 0.31$

Fig. 9. Response time histogram for all the tasks in P_A with stochastic execution. In the y-axis we represent the number of occurrences, while in the x-axis the response time in ms.

Stochastic Task Activation: In this case the sequence of activation times for the aperiodic tasks is generated according to a Weibull distribution detailed in Sect. 5.1. The response time histograms of the results are represented in Fig. 10.

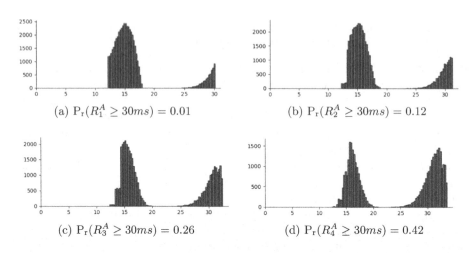

(a) $\mathrm{P_r}(R_1^A \geq 30ms) = 0.01$

(b) $\mathrm{P_r}(R_2^A \geq 30ms) = 0.12$

(c) $\mathrm{P_r}(R_3^A \geq 30ms) = 0.26$

(d) $\mathrm{P_r}(R_4^A \geq 30ms) = 0.42$

Fig. 10. Response time histogram for all the tasks in P_A with stochastic activation. In the y-axis we represent the number of occurrences, while in the x-axis the response time in ms.

It can be noted that the stochastic activation time has a significant impact on the response time showing a bimodal distribution for all the tasks. With random activations, all the aperiodic tasks miss some deadlines (i.e. $\mathrm{P_r}(R_i^A \geq 30\,\mathrm{ms}) > 0$) and not only the lower priority tasks. All the task response times are highly impacted by the application partition scheduling represented in Fig. 7. The distribution of the higher priority task τ_1^A depicted in Fig. 10a is limited by a lower bound ($\approx 12\,\mathrm{ms}$) and an upper bound ($\approx 30\,\mathrm{ms}$). The task τ_i^A is divided in two main execution chunk. During the first chunk the event acquisition is spread across all the system. Once all the data are available (τ_i^B and τ_i^C finish their execution) the second execution chunk can start its execution. When the activation of τ_i^A is triggered within the first partition windows P_{A1}, the execution always ends inside the second time window P_{A2}. The resulting response time, in case of activation in P_{A1} is lower-bounded by $C_{1,[1]}^A + t_{B1} + t_C + t_{B2} + C_{1,[2]}^A = 12.15\,\mathrm{ms}$. The worst case activation generating the worst case response time happens when task τ_i^A cannot finish the execution of the first chunk $\tau_{1,1}^A$ within the time window P_{A1}. In this case the data acquisition event is spread in P_{A2} (when the task is again allowed to execute) and a full time frame must be waited in order to get all the data. The upper bound on the execution time is then approximately $t_{MTF} + t_{B1} + t_C + t_{B2} + C_{1,[2]}^A = 30.075\,\mathrm{ms}$. For the other tasks it is possible to do similar considerations even if the behavior is more complicated due to the possible preemption of the higher priority tasks. Similar observations can be made for the lower priority tasks showing similar "steps" in their distributions (especially for τ_2^A depicted in Fig. 10b and for τ_3^A depicted in Fig. 10c). Those steps are the result of the activation of an higher priority task outside its time window while the lower priority task is activated within its time window, thus managing to complete the execution before the higher priority tasks (since the latter is blocked). This situation is very unlikely so the "steps" in the distributions are small. For τ_2^A the step is only one because it has only one higher priority task τ_1^A, while for τ_3^A the steps are two since it has two higher priority tasks (τ_1^A and τ_2^A) with the second step much lower because in this case both τ_1^A and τ_2^A must have an unfavorable activation value (the product of two probabilities is less than the single probabilities).

Stochastic Task Execution and Activation: In this use case we consider both the execution and activation uncertainties. The distributions are the same considered in the previous use cases. When injecting both uncertainties in the system, the output distributions are similar to the case with only stochastic activation but with the response time covering a wider range of values due to the introduction of variable execution time. By introducing both uncertainties, one would expect a degradation of the system performance by an increasing of deadline miss and an equivalent reduction in the probability to meet the imposed requirement. However the mixing of both uncertainties can lead to a small improvement in the performances as shown in Fig. 11 by the probabilities $P_r(R_i^A \geq 30\,\mathrm{ms})$; compared to the previous case, the tasks τ_3 and τ_4 present a smaller number of deadlines miss, τ_2 performance are almost unchanged and τ_1 is the most impacted. It is interesting to note that a nominal deterministic simulation may not empathize this kind of behaviors vanishing the overall performance assessment.

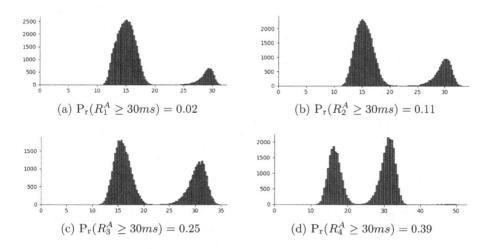

(a) $P_r(R_1^A \geq 30ms) = 0.02$

(b) $P_r(R_2^A \geq 30ms) = 0.11$

(c) $P_r(R_3^A \geq 30ms) = 0.25$

(d) $P_r(R_4^A \geq 30ms) = 0.39$

Fig. 11. Response time histogram for all the tasks in P_A with stochastic execution and activation. In the y-axis we represent the number of occurrences, while in the x-axis the response time in ms.

6.2 Statistical Model Checking

The statistical model checking aims to verify a linear temporal logic targeting a bounded time window, i.e. Bounded Linear Temporal Logic (BLTL). Differently from the forward uncertainty propagation analysis that provided global results, the statistical model checking targets a limited time windows. In our use case we aim to verify the four properties expressed by the BLTL in Eq. 1. The equation expresses the system requirement that: whenever a task τ_i finishes its execution (finish task event $\mathcal{E}_i^f$ is triggered), the resulting response time R_i is always less then a maximum response time R_{max} in the given time window (operator $G_{\leq N}$).

$$\Psi := G_{\leq N}\left((\mathcal{E}_i^f = 1) => (R_i <= R_{max})\right) \tag{1}$$

The time interval was chosen equal to four major time frames, i.e. $N = 72\,\text{ms}$; The maximum response time value was set to $R_{max} = 30\,\text{ms}$.

To perform the statistical model checking analyses we used the Plasma Lab tool. Plasma Lab is a compact, efficient and flexible platform for statistical model checking of stochastic models [13]. All the simulations have been carried out on a workstation with an i7-8850H CPU @ 2.6 GHz and 32 GB of RAM. The Plasma tool makes available different verification algorithms. We focused on two main algorithms: Monte Carlo Method and Hypotheses Testing. The *Monte Carlo method with Chernoff-Hoeffding* was introduced in Sect. 4.2. Plasma implements this method enabling the setting of the error margin ϵ and the confidence bound δ. We selected $\delta = 95\%$ for the confidence and the precision has ranged on 0.1, 0.05, 0.005 requiring respectively 38, 149, 14889 simulations. The SMC analyses were performed on the model with both task execution time and task activation uncertainty. The results are reported in the Table 2 where p represent the

Table 2. PLASMA analysis with Chernoff bound with 95% confidence bound and variable error margin.

Task	Error margin (ϵ)	# Simulations	p	Simulation time [s]
τ_1^A	0.1	38	1.0	20
	0.05	149	0.966	75
	0.005	14889	0.983	7627
τ_2^A	0.1	38	0.921	20
	0.05	149	0.872	75
	0.005	14889	0.881	7627
τ_3^A	0.1	38	0.737	20
	0.05	149	0.772	75
	0.005	14889	0.733	7627
τ_4^A	0.1	38	0.579	20
	0.05	149	0.51	75
	0.005	14889	0.571	7627

Table 3. PLASMA analysis with hypothesis testing bound.

Task	Goal Probability (p)	# Simulations	Estimate Probability (p')	Simulation Time [s]
τ_1^A	0.9	267	0.977	808
	0.7	171	0.982	722
	0.5	127	0.953	331
τ_2^A	0.9	1527	0.887	808
	0.7	258	0.887	722
	0.5	155	0.871	331
τ_3^A	0.9	114	0.719	808
	0.7	1325	0.737	722
	0.5	201	0.786	331
τ_4^A	0.9	76	0.618	808
	0.7	222	0.482	722
	0.5	809	0.571	331

probability to satisfy the BLTL in Eq. 1. It is interesting to note that despite the introduction of a small uncertainty, the performance of the system drops in a significant way compared to the nominal case.

The *Hypothesis Testing* method was introduced in Sect. 4.2. Plasma implements this method enabling the user to set the probabilistic bounds α and β. Also in this case we focused on the response time of the tasks in P_A. This method aims to verify whether the probability to satisfy the LBTL Ψ in Eq. 1 is less than a probability p. We considered three values for the goal probability $p = \{0.9, 0.7, 0.5\}$, while we selected $\alpha = \beta = IR = 0.01$. The results of the analysis are reported in Table 3. The tool returns the probability of satisfying the requirement. The True/False (Green/Red) indicator informs the user if the set probability goal has been respected or not.

7   Conclusions and Future Work

In the current paper we presented a generic modular RTOS SystemC model. The RTOS model has been designed in order to be customized implementing RTOS specific services. This allows the user to run the real application code on top of the model without modifying the original application code targeting a specific RTOS implementation. The proposed model captures the timing info of the application (execution time) by defining a specific API to be added in the application code. Furthermore the model also allows the modeling of uncertain behavior. We presented a use case application where the execution time of the tasks and their aperiodic activation is modeled by mean of probability distributions. The performance analysis of the stochastic application was performed with two different methods: forward uncertainty propagation and statistic model checking. The proposed analyses highlighted how a small uncertainty may introduce a consistent performance degradation. This shows that analyzing the system under uncertain conditions is of paramount importance to a proper verification assessment. Different aspects were not investigated that are of great importance. Claiming generality of the RTOS model is quite difficult since any COT RTOS may implement specific services. Future activity will validate the model against common RTOSes (FreeRTOS, VxWorks, DEOS) and standardized RTOS interfaces as OSEK OS and POSIX. The RTOS model could be enhanced in order to enable the modeling of multicore scheduling. The model can also be improved in order to integrate hardware models (FPGA, FLASH memory, EEPROM, etc.) using transaction level modeling (TLM). This will enable an HW/SW co-simulation in a unified simulation framework. Moreover in order to ease the simulation of application code, techniques for automatic back annotation will be investigated. In addition the performance of real-time systems are affected by uncertainty at different levels such as hardware, RTOS kernel or application. On one side, modeling the uncertainty at all the levels may be time consuming with the estimation of multiple probability distribution. On the other side considering the cumulative distribution of many uncertainties at different levels may move the complexity to fewer distributions with very high modeling complexity. An active research area called Inverse Uncertainty Quantification addresses this issue although, to the best of the authors knowledge, there are not existing works targeting complex embedded systems.

Acknowledgments. This work has received funding from the Clean Sky 2 Joint Undertaking under the European Union's Horizon 2020 research and innovation programme under grant agreement N° 807081.

References

1. Accelera: Core SystemC Language. https://www.accellera.org/downloads/standards/systemc. Accessed Aug 2019
2. Airlines Electronic Engineering Committee (AEEC): ARINC Specification 653 P1. Avionics application software standard interface (2010). rev. 3
3. Barry, R.: FreeRTOS. http://freerots.org. Accessed Aug 2019
4. Buttazzo, G.: Research trends in real-time computing for embedded systems. SIGBED Rev. **3**(3), 1–10 (2006). https://doi.org/10.1145/1164050.1164052
5. D'Angelo, M., Ferrari, A., Ogaard, O., Pinello, C., Ulisse, A.: A Simulator based on QEMU and SystemC for robustness testing of a networked linux-based fire detection and alarm system. In: Proceedings of the Conference on Embedded Real Time Systems and Software, pp. 1–9 (2012)
6. DDC-I: DEOS. https://www.ddci.com/category/deos/. Accessed Aug 2019
7. Grimm, C., Rathmair, M.: Dealing with uncertainties in analog/mixed-signal systems: invited. In: Proceedings of the 54th Annual Design Automation Conference 2017, New York, NY, USA, pp. 35:1–35:6 (2017)
8. Hansen, J.P., Wrage, L.: Verification of real-time systems using statistical model checking. In: AIAA Infotech@ Aerospace, p. 1866 (2015)
9. Huck, E., Miramond, B., Verdier, F.: A modular SystemC RTOS model for embedded services exploration. In: Proceedings of First European Workshop on Design and Architectures for Signal and Image Processing (2007)
10. ISO International Standard ISO/IEC 14882:2017(E): Programming Language C++: Random Library. http://www.cplusplus.com/reference/random/. Accessed Aug 2019

11. Keutzer, K., Newton, A.R., Rabaey, J.M., Sangiovanni-Vincentelli, A.: System-level design: orthogonalization of concerns and platform-based design. IEEE Trans. Comput. Aided Des. Integr. Circuits Syst. **19**(12), 1523–1543 (2000)
12. Lamport, L.: The temporal logic of actions. ACM Trans. Program. Lang. Syst. (TOPLAS) **16**(3), 872–923 (1994)
13. Legay, A., Sedwards, S., Traonouez, L.M.: Plasma lab: a modular statistical model checking platform. In: Margaria, T., Steffen, B. (eds.) ISoLA 2016. LNCS, vol. 9952, pp. 77–93. Springer, Cham (2016). https://doi.org/10.1007/978-3-319-47166-2_6
14. Meyerowitz, T., Sangiovanni-Vincentelli, A., Sauermann, M., Langen, D.: Source-level timing annotation and simulation for a heterogeneous multiprocessor. In: 2008 Design, Automation and Test in Europe, pp. 276–279 (2008). https://doi.org/10.1109/DATE.2008.4484897
15. Mignogna, A., Ferrante, O., Carloni, M., Ferrari, A.: A fully configurable RTOS model for large scale distributed embedded systems simulations based on SystemC. In: Proceedings of Conference on Applied Simulation and Modelling. ACTA Press (2011)
16. Plasma-Lab: Statistical Model Checking. https://project.inria.fr/plasma-lab/statistical-model-checking/. Accessed Aug 2019
17. Posadas, H., Ádamez, J., Villar, E., Blasco, F., Escuder, F.: RTOS modeling in SystemC for real-time embedded SW simulation: a POSIX model. Des. Autom. Emb. Syst. **10**, 209–227 (2005)
18. Quilbeuf, J., Cavalcante, E., Traonouez, L.-M., Oquendo, F., Batista, T., Legay, A.: A logic for the statistical model checking of dynamic software architectures. In: Margaria, T., Steffen, B. (eds.) ISoLA 2016. LNCS, vol. 9952, pp. 806–820. Springer, Cham (2016). https://doi.org/10.1007/978-3-319-47166-2_56
19. Segala, R.: Modeling and verification of randomized distributed real-time systems. Ph.D. thesis, Massachusetts Institute of Technology (1995)
20. Smith, R.C.: Uncertainty Quantification: Theory, Implementation, and Applications. SIAM, Philadelphia (2013)
21. Swan, S.: An introduction to system level modeling in SystemC 2.0. Cadence Design Systems Inc., draft report (2001)
22. Wilhelm, R., et al.: The worst-case execution-time problem - overview of methods and survey of tools. ACM Trans. Embed. Comput. Syst. (TECS) **7**(3), 36 (2008)
23. Wind Rivers Systems: VxWorks. https://www.windriver.com/products/vxworks/. Accessed Aug 2019
24. Zabel, H., Müller, W., Gerstlauer, A.: Accurate RTOS modeling and analysis with SystemC. In: Ecker, W., Müller, W. (eds.) Hardware-Dependent Software: Principles and Practice, pp. 233–260. Springer, Heidelberg (2009). https://doi.org/10.1007/978-1-4020-9436-1_9
25. Zhang, M., Ali, S., Yue, T., Nguyen, P.: Uncertainty modeling framework for the integration level v. 1. Simula Research Laboratory (2016)
26. Zhang, M., Ali, S., Yue, T., Norgren, R., Okariz, O.: Uncertainty-wise cyber-physical system test modeling. Softw. Syst. Model. **18**(2), 1379–1418 (2019)

Multicore Models of Communication for Cyber-Physical Systems

Martin Schoeberl$^{(\boxtimes)}$ (iD)

Department of Applied Mathematics and Computer Science,
Technical University of Denmark, Kgs. Lyngby, Denmark
masca@dtu.dk

Abstract. Cyber-physical systems are systems where the environment interacts with computers (the cyber part) with real-time constraints. Emerging technologies, such as artificial intelligence and machine learning, call for ever-increasing processing power. However, for real-time systems, we need to prove statically that this processing demand can be performed within strict deadlines.

This paper explores a time-predictable multicore architecture for those demanding cyber-physical systems. We explore different models of communication between those multiple cores. We compare the message passing model on top of a network-on-chip with message passing on two forms of shared scratchpad memory.

Keywords: Real-time systems · Multicore communication ·
Time-predictable computer architecture

1 Introduction

Future cyber-physical systems may be in need of higher computing power. One way to increase computing power is to integrate multiple processing cores in a single chip to form a multicore processor. Cyber-physical systems often need to react to the environment within a guaranteed deadline. We call those systems real-time systems. If such a system is part of a safety-critical system, we need to guarantee that all deadlines are met. Such proof includes worst-case execution time (WCET) analysis of individual tasks, analysis of communication time, and schedulability analysis.

Multicore processors used in cyber-physical systems need to support time-predictable computation and communication. As communication via shared main memory supported by a cache coherence protocol is hardly time-predictable, we need other forms of core-to-core communication.

This paper explores different models of communication between processing cores and the hardware support for it. We present forms of shared on-chip memories, links between processor cores, and network-on-chip architectures. In this paper, we include only solutions that are time-predictable, except describing the baseline of a hardly time-predictable shared main memory with cache coherence.

R. Chamberlain et al. (Eds.): CyPhy 2019/WESE 2019, LNCS 11971, pp. 28–43, 2020.
https://doi.org/10.1007/978-3-030-41131-2_2

Shared on-chip memories with a time-predictable arbitration, such as time-division multiplexing, provide an efficient solution for around a dozen cores. For more cores, a distributed communication architecture, such as a network-on-chip, is a better scaling solution.

In this paper, we use the term task as a notion of parts of a program that can execute concurrently. We avoid the term thread, as threads are usually associated with a single form of concurrency: communication via data in shared memory, protected by locks. Tasks need to communicate when working together as an application.

The contribution of this paper is a detailed overview of several communication architectures for a real-time multicore processor. The overview may also serve as a small survey of real-time multicore communication architectures. Furthermore, we picked several architectures and compared them with an evaluation of message passing. Our overall goal is to build time-predictable computer architecture [32] for future demanding cyber-physical systems. Initial ideas on models of communication for multicore processors have been presented in [39].

This paper is organized into 5 sections: Sect. 2 presents the software view of multicore communication. Section 3 is the main section, describing several hardware architectures to support time-predictable multicore communication. Section 4 evaluates several of the presented architectures with a message passing microbenchmark. Section 5 concludes.

2   The Software View

When multiple tasks shall work together towards completing work, they need to communicate in some form. This combination of tasks and forms of communication is also called the "model of computation." The Ptolemy II handbook [30] gives a good overview of those different forms. In the following sections, we focus on three example models of computation and communication.

2.1   Communicating Sequential Processes

One of the first approaches to establish message passing between tasks was Hoare's communicating sequential processes, CSP for short [15]. The CSP concept became popular enough that even a programming language, Occam [23], was developed to include CSP in the language.

Transputers [16, 43], a unique form of processors, where developed to execute Occam programs. Transputers included hardware support for the Occam channels. The idea was to build massive parallel multiprocessors. However, in the mid of the '80s the performance increase of standard processors was still around 50% per year [13], and there was no need for multiprocessor systems. A single task program is easier to develop and test. Dividing an algorithm into multiple tasks that communicate via channels is hard, and errors can lead to hard-to-debug blocking of tasks. Therefore, CSP and transputers did not become a success story.

2.2   Multithreading

Early forms of multiprogramming consisted of using individual programs that communicate. One form of communication was the usage of Unix pipes, where the output of one program is fed as input to another program. A Unix pipe represents a stream with one writer and one reader process. Message passing can easily be built on top of such a stream. A tighter form of communication between programs was the creation of a shared memory space by the operating system. However, those multiple programs still run as individual processes protected from each other by the operating system.

To simplify multiprogramming, the concept of multiple threads of execution in a single process was developed. Those threads share memory and use data allocated on the heap for communication. Those data structures are usually protected by locks [14]. This programming paradigm became especially popular when Java supported threads and locks as part of the core language definition.

A runtime system can map multiple threads to multiple cores in a multicore processor. Also, the communication via shared objects is handled by a cache coherence protocol.

At the time of this writing, multithreading with shared data is the most popular approach to use with concurrent tasks. However, getting the locking of objects right for multithreaded programs is far from trivial. Locking also is a bottleneck for scaling programs for many cores. Therefore, the current trend is to explore message passing again in the form of actors.

2.3   Actors and Message Passing

The concept of actors is currently becoming popular through the Akka[1] toolkit. Akka is a library and runtime to support concurrent and distributed applications. The primary programming model for multiple tasks is actor-based. Akka is written in Scala but can be used from programs written in Java or Scala.

Actors in Akka are the tasks that communicate via message passing. In contrast to CSP, the message passing is asynchronous. Typical Akka programs avoid shared mutable data and locks to protect them.

However, non-constrained asynchronous message passing may lead to buffer overflow and is hardly time-predictable. Stricter forms of communication are, for example, synchronous data flow (SDF) [19]. An SDF actor fires (executes) when all input ports contain their fixed number of tokens. With the fixed number of tokens consumed and produced, buffers are bounded, and for a single core, a statically schedule for the actor firing can be computed.

Recent work extends actors for precise timing in cyber-physical systems [22]. The actors, called reactors in the paper, have strict rules on fire order and mutual exclusion of different reactions. Reactors include the notion of delays and deadlines. Delays allow for physical time to pass, and deadlines are a contract with the environment. WCET and schedulability analysis of reactions can be used to check if all deadlines can be met.

---

[1] Available at https://akka.io/.

3   Communication Hardware

Message passing can be implemented on top of different communication infrastructures. In contrast, the concept of shared objects is usually implemented on top of cache-coherent, shared main memory only. Therefore, message passing is the more hardware *friendly* approach for communication. In the following sections, we discuss several different hardware mechanisms for communication between multiple cores on a chip multicore.

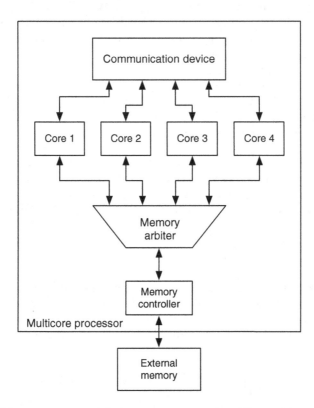

Fig. 1. A multicore processor with the cores connected to (1) an arbiter to the memory controller for the shared, external memory and (2) to the communication hardware.

Figure 1 shows a multicore processor where the cores are connected to (1) external memory via a memory arbiter and (2) to a communication device. That communication device is the topic of this paper, and we discuss variations of it in the following sections.

3.1   Shared Main Memory

The state-of-the-art communication mechanism for multicore processors is shared main memory. Objects are allocated in the main memory, and the access to the objects is protected by locks. As access latency to main memory is in the range of hundreds of processor clock cycles, several levels of cache are introduced. It is not uncommon to include 3 levels of cache, where the 2nd and 3rd levels of cache are shared between the cores. The first level of cache is usually core local. Therefore, when sharing data, these local caches need to be kept coherent with a cache-coherent protocol. As this cache coherence protocol is an all-to-all communication, it scales only to a few tens of processor cores.

However, the main issue with shared memory backed up by a cache coherence protocol is that it is barely time-predictable. The WCET analysis of tasks needs to include an analysis of which memory blocks are in the cache and in which caches. WCET analysis is further complicated by the fact that on a multicore, we have true concurrency where individual tasks influence the occupancy of the shared caches. This problem would need a WCET analysis that includes all tasks in the system. We are not aware of any WCET analysis tool (except niche research experiments) that supports multiple tasks and multiple levels of caches, including the cache coherence protocol. The industry standard WCET tool aiT [12] supports single tasks only. We quote from AbsInt's website:[2]

> aiT computes an upper bound of the WCET of a task. A task must be a sequentially executed piece of code, i.e. there must not be any threads, parallelism, or external events. aiT assumes no interference from the outside. Effects of exceptions, interrupts, DRAM refreshes, input/output, timers and other processors or co-processors are not reflected in the predicted runtime and have to be considered separately, e.g. via quantitative analysis.

However, we are aware that realistic applications and their data are too large to fit in on-chip memory. Therefore, some code and data need to be loaded into external memory. To provide time-predictable access to external memory, we propose to use a time-division-multiplexing (TDM) arbiter for the memory accesses [35].

3.2   Network-on-Chip

Network-on-chip (NoC) technology [6] is an alternative to cache coherence based inter-core communication. A NoC is a distributed architecture, and therefore the provided bandwidth scales well with the number of cores. A NoC connects cores (also called processing elements in NoC literature) to a network of routers. In most cases, one router serves one core. The routers are connected in a network, where mesh and torus are the most common organizations.

A NoC itself does not yet provide a communication mechanism. Between the core and a router, the network interface (NI) provides an interface to the network. NoCs are used for a wide variety of traffics: serving cache coherence traffic, access to a memory controller and external memory, streaming between

---

[2] https://www.absint.com/ait/features.htm.

cores, message-passing between cores, and access to remote on-chip memories. The NI determines what kind of traffic is supported.

Many routers (and NIs) are optimized for the average case performance with buffers and dynamic arbitration at each router. Those NoCs are hardly time-predictable. For real-time systems, two mechanisms are popular: rate control at the injection site or TDM arbitration at the routers.

Rate control, also called traffic shaping, limits the number of packets injected into the NoC. Network calculus [4,5,18] is used to compute bounds on buffer sizes and bounds on latencies. The Kalray multicore processor [7] is especially designed to support time-predictable message passing with rate control in the sender and no further flow control within the NoC [8].

With a static schedule performing TDM arbitration in the NoC routers, there is no traffic conflict, and the worst-case message latency can be statically computed. Æthereal [9] is such a NoC that uses TDM where slots are reserved to allow a block of data to pass through the NoC router without waiting or blocking traffic. Slot tables with routing information are contained in the routers, and no arbitration or link-to-link flow control is required. Instead, credit-based flow control is applied for end-to-end control, saving buffer space between links. aelite, a light version of Æthereal, only offers guaranteed services resulting in a simpler router design [11].

The Argo NoC [17] is another NoC that uses TDM based arbitration of resources. Compared to Æthereal, Argo also uses the same TDM schedule in the NI [42] to time-multiplex the NI resources. The Argo NI offers TDM-based DMA transfer of data from the local memory across the NoC and into the local memory of another core. Argo supports a global asynchronous, local synchronous system with an asynchronous router design and mesochronous (same clock source, but variable upwards bounded skew allowed) NIs.

While Æthereal uses TDM at the routers, it uses buffers with flow-control in the NIs. In contrast, the Argo NoC [17] uses TDM for the arbitration in the routers *and* at the NI [42], resulting in an end-to-end TDM schedule. S4NOC [36, 37] is a TDM based NoC, simpler than Argo, with FIFO buffers as NI. We use S4NOC in the evaluation section.

The Real-Time Capable Many-Core Model proposes many cores with a static switched NoC with TDM-based arbitration [24]. The project also proposes avoiding shared memory altogether and supporting timing analysis by using a fine-grained message passing NoC [25].

Paukovits and Kopetz use a time-triggered NoC for the time-triggered system-on-chip (TTSoC) architecture [28]. The main difference to other NoC designs is the absolute time format, which is *not* directly related to the clock frequency. The macro tick is a power of two fraction of a second and the basis for the TDM slotting. The idea behind this time format is a good integration with off-chip versions of time-triggered networks.

When comparing TDM arbitration with rate control and network calculus [31], TDM arbitration results in shorter worst-case latencies while network calculus leads to higher bandwidth. However, using TDM for arbitration leads to simpler routers and network interfaces than supporting dynamic arbitration and buffering NoC.

3.3 Shared Scratchpad Memory

While NoCs can provide a high bandwidth communication path, their usage is more elaborated. I.e., messages need to be setup and explicitly sent to other cores. An alternative is to use on-chip memory, also called scratchpad memory (SPM), that is shared between several cores. For a small number of cores that memory can be shared by all the cores. However, with an increase in the number of cores, this solution does not scale. Therefore, several shared on-chip memories can be shared only by a subset of the cores. These subsets can be disjoint, as in the Kalray processor, to form clusters, which are connected by a NoC. Alternative, these sets can overlap to provide a communications path between neighboring cores.

The Kalray manycore processor [7] is specially designed for time-critical computation. The processor is organized in 16 clusters of 16 cores. Each core within a cluster is connected to a shared SPM, consisting of 16 independent memory banks. By carefully selecting the allocation of data and access to the memory banks, access can be time-predictable [2].

We have implemented a shared SPM in the T-CREST processor [40]. We use TDM based arbitration, which results with a single cycle SPM in a maximum access time of n clock cycles for n cores. We found that a shared SPM scales up to nine cores when implemented in an FPGA. We use our shared SPM in the evaluation.

3.4 Scratchpad Memory with Ownership

Access latency to a shared SPM is a few clock cycles, way less than access to main memory. However, often, the SPM is not used by all cores, and the TDM arbitration wastes memory bandwidth. For example, in a producer/consumer setting, only a single core writes into the SPM and when finished a different core reads from the SPM. For this setup we introduce the notion of ownership [40]. A core *owns* an SPM for some time, uses it to compute write data into it, and then transfers the ownership to a core that consumes the data. When tasks agree on the ownership of the SPM, there is no need for arbitration. The core has exclusive access to the owned SPM with short (single cycle) access time. This mechanism allows fast transfer of bulk data.

For double-buffered communication and several communication channels, we introduce a pool of SPMs with ownership. Different cores can acquire SPMs out of this pool and after usage, either transfer the ownership to another core or put it back into the pool of free SPMs. This pool of SPMs scales up, similar to a shared SPM, to about nine cores in an FPGA. Beyond that number of cores, the SPM pools need to be clustered.

3.5 Distributed Shared On-Chip Memory

Combining core-local SPMs with a NoC leads to a distributed shared on-chip memory. Each core is attached to local memory and to a NoC that supports access to a local memory of a remote core. A standard solution for remote read and writes is to use two NoCs: one to support writes and read requests and a second to deliver the response for the reads.

Epiphany is a high-performance energy-efficient manycore processor [27] that uses distributed on-chip memory. Epiphany is intended as an accelerator processor for real-time embedded systems. Two versions, a 16-core chip, and a 64-core chip have been taped out. The multicore processor Epiphany uses a distributed memory architecture. Each core contains 32 KB of local memory that is mapped into a global address space. The processors contain no caches. Access to the memory of a remote core is performed over a NoC. The NoC is organized as a mesh and favors writes over reads, as writes are posted writes where the processor does not need to wait for the write to finish. Packets are single word long, and routing is performed in a single cycle per hop. A second NoC is dedicated for read responses and a third NoC supports off-chip traffic, e.g., with a master processor and external shared memory. There is no documentation available on how the arbitration in the NoC routers is performed on a conflict. We explored the processor and measured considerable latency variations depending on the NoC load. Therefore, we cannot (yet) recommend it for applications with tight timing constraints.

We have implemented a distributed shared memory in the T-CREST multicore [29]. We use two instances of the S4NOC [36]: one is used to write to a remote SPM or transmit a read request, and the second is used to return the read result. The SPMs are mapped into different address ranges in the global address range, and the read or write address determines which SPM to access. As several remote read requests may arrive at one core in successive clock cycles, the read results (one per clock cycle) may queue up waiting for their slot to be sent on the read response NoC. In the worst case, this could be $n - 1$ words for an n core system. To minimize the length of this queue, the TDM schedule for the return NoC is optimized and aligned to the read request schedule. As S4NOC uses TDM arbitration and a static schedule, we can provide guarantees on latency bounds for reads and writes. As reads need to travel a NoC twice, their latency is double the latency of writes.

Operating system support to virtualize SPMs on a distributed shared on-chip memory is presented in the ShaVe-ICE project [41]. Similar to Epiphany and our solution, each core contains a local SPM and is connected via a NoC. The operating system support is to manage the changing demand of threads for local memory by allocating and deallocating memory on the local or a remote SPM. When allocating on a remote core, the hop distance is taken into account for the allocation policy.

3.6 Direct Links and Memory Between Cores

Another way to structure communication between cores is to have direct links between neighboring cores, organized in a mesh or folded torus. The main benefit of such an organization is that it is a local link and fully supports two types of parallel applications: (1) applications organized in a computing pipeline or (2) physical simulations, such as finite element simulation where access to the neighbor elements is needed.

The link can be as simple as a FIFO queue or more sophisticated, like a dual-port memory between cores. Isaac Liu uses dual-port memories for a multicore organization of a precision timed machine in the evaluation of his Ph.D. thesis [20]. He implemented a real-time computational fluid dynamics simulator on a multicore PRET [21]. The cores use so-called *privately shared* SPMs between cores to provide point-to-point communication channels.

Although less flexible than a fully blown NoC, direct links may be implemented very efficiently and being, therefore, a practical solution. This form of communication has not yet received much attention when discussing multicore communication.

3.7 One-Way Shared Memory

A quite exotic form of on-chip communication is the so-called *one-way shared memory* [33]. The one-way memory uses the TDM scheduled S4NOC for communication but uses a very simple NI. Each core contains a core local memory connected to the NI. The main idea is that the NoC continuously copies data blocks between the core-local memories. There is one communication channel between each pair of cores. The NoC reads from the senders' core-local memory and writes into the receiver's core-local memory. As this update is performed in one direction only, we call this architecture a *one-way memory*.

The routers have a fixed, pre-programmed schedule. For symmetric structures, such as the torus, all routers execute the same schedule [3]. One such schedule is one TDM round in which one word is transferred between each core. To transfer a memory block of n words, we need n TDM rounds.

The simplicity of the one-way memory paradigm results in very low resource usage. The resource consumption of the NoC and the NI, which implements the one-way memory, is lower than other NoC solutions. This simplicity, i.e., low logical element usage, can be translated either into lower power consumption or higher NoC bandwidth. Higher NoC bandwidth is achieved simply by duplicating the local core memory or using wider NoC router links.

3.8 Additional Hardware Support for Message Passing

The previous sections presented on-chip communication architectures that can be used for message passing. However, we can provide additional hardware to optimize the performance of message passing further.

To reduce the overhead of message passing, a tight integration of message passing instructions into the processor pipeline has been proposed [26]. A RISC-V processor has been extended with a send, receive, and source instructions to allow fast message passing of short messages over a NoC. Additionally, to optimize the checking for ready to send and receive messages available, four branch instructions have been added.

The NI of the Argo NoC [42] includes a local memory and a DMA machinery to transfer data from the local memory to the TDM based NoC. The DMA contains a table with entries of memory regions that shall be sent to different cores. Each virtual channel may have its entry in the table. A message is created in the local memory by the processor, an entry into the DMA table is programmed, and the DAM started. The message transfer happens in parallel to program execution on the processor core.

CSP uses messages not only for data transfer but also as synchronization points between tasks (called processes in CSP). The CSP rendezvous can be implemented by exchanging two messages. We extended a ring-based NoC on a multicore Java processor with explicit support for this synchronization [10]. As an optimization, the NoC supports a dedicated *Ack* command for the rendezvous.

4   Evaluation

We have built several of the proposed hardware solutions in the context of the T-CREST [34] multicore processor Patmos [38]. The hardware is described in Chisel [1] and available in open source at https://github.com/t-crest/patmos. As Patmos uses the open-core protocol to interface to IO devices and memory, all those multicore devices are implemented with this interface.

To enable wider adaption of our multicore hardware, we are currently in the process of extracting those devices into its own GitHub repository https://github.com/schoeberl/soc-comm. There we will use a simple interface definition and will provide bridges for the open-core protocol, Wishbone, and AXI.

4.1   Experimental Setup

We compare different solutions by evaluating them in an FPGA. The default configuration for T-CREST supports the Altera DE2-115 development board. The FPGA on this board, the Intel/Altera Cyclone IV EP4CE115 FPGA, is big enough to build a system with up to 9 cores. All experiments use the 9-core version of T-CREST. We have chosen the 9-core setup as this is a regular setup for a NoC (3×3 cores), and is the largest setup that fits in the FPGA used.

The Patmos cores are configured with a single-issue pipeline, an 8 KB method cache with 16 methods, a 4 KB write-through data cache, a 2 KB stack cache, a 1 KB instruction SPM and a 2 KB local SPM. External memory is 2 MB with an access time of 21 clock cycles for a burst of 4 32-bit words for a single core. For multicores, the main memory is TDM arbitrated, resulting in access time between 21 and $n \times 21$ clock cycles for n cores.

We use a shared SPM of 16 KB that is TDM arbitrated. The SPM with ownership is configured as a pool of 16 SPMs, each of 1 KB. We measured read access times to the SPM and the ownership SPM. For access to the TDM arbitrated SPM, we observe all possible access times, i.e., for the 9 core version between 3 and 10 clock cycles. We perform the same measurement with the SPM with ownership. As expected, we observe a constant access time of 1 clock cycle.

4.2 Benchmark

For the evaluation, we implement a producer and a consumer who exchange messages. As all presented solutions have no time interference from communication on other channels, it is enough to measure a single virtual channel. We measure throughput in clock cycles, to provide a measurement that is only dependent on the architecture and not on the achievable clock frequency in concrete technology. With a know maximum clock frequency, the maximum bandwidth in bytes per second can be easily computed.

For comparison with a NoC we use the S4NOC [36], configured for 9 cores. The resulting schedule length for the TDM scheduling of the NoC packets is 10 clock cycles for an all-to-all schedule. Therefore, the maximum bandwidth per virtual channel is 10 clock cycles per word. Note that this all-to-all configuration provides $8 \times 9 = 72$ channels, resulting in an overall bandwidth of 7.2 words per clock cycle.

The NIs for the S4NOC consist of FIFO buffers for the sender and receiver. The sender FIFO contains entries for 32-bit data and the send slot number as a representation of the destination address. The receive FIFO includes the read data and the receive slot number as a representation of the sending core. We use small FIFOs built out of registers.

4.3 Measured Throughput

Table 1 shows throughput in clock cycles per word of messages of different sizes on different communication devices. The long access time to shared main memory dominates the low throughput, showing the need for on-chip communication. For all memory-based devices the throughput increases with the message length, as the overhead of sending a message is less dominating. However, we observe an increase in the number of clock cycles between 16-word messages and 32-word messages. We explored the generated code and find that the compiler unrolls loops up to 16 iterations, explaining this anomaly. At 32 or more iterations, the compiler generates code for a standard loop. The throughput of the shared SPM is close to the limit of the access time of one word per 9 clock cycles. For the SPM with ownership, which has a guaranteed access latency of 1 clock cycle, the loop overhead of sending the data dominates.

For the NoC device, we performed two experiments. In the first experiment, we let the producer send as fast as possible without handshaking, assuming that the consumer is fast enough to cover the maximum throughput. As the TDM schedule of the 9 core NoC is 10 clock cycles per TDM round, the 10.1 clock cycles

Table 1. Measured throughput, in clock cycles per word for one channel.

Configuration	Message size (32-bit words)	Throughput (clock cycles per word)
Main memory	8	236.4
Main memory	16	212.9
Main memory	32	201.3
Main memory	64	195.7
Shared SPM	8	12.4
Shared SPM	16	11.1
Shared SPM	32	18.9
Shared SPM	64	18.6
SPM with ownership	8	5.7
SPM with ownership	16	4.9
SPM with ownership	32	9.9
SPM with ownership	64	9.5
S4NOC, unconstraint sender	-	10.1
S4NOC, with handshaking	-	12.0

per word are close to the NoC limit. In the second experiment, we used a double buffer of 2 times 4 words (in the NI FIFO) and handshaking so that every 4 words are acknowledged by the receiver. This small buffer and the handshaking ensures that the sender will never overrun the receiver, but introduces an overhead of just 20 % compared to the theoretical maximum throughput.

4.4   Resource Consumption

Table 2 shows the resource requirements of the three different multicore communication devices for 9 cores. The resources are given in logic cells (LC) that contain a 4-bit lookup table, registers (D flip-flops), and on-chip memory. The shared SPM is relatively cheap, as it needs logic only for a simple TDM arbiter for 9 cores. The SPM with ownership contains a pool of 16 SPMs that are multiplexed for 9 cores and therefore need a considerable amount of combinational logic (high LC count). The S4NOC is in the resource requirements between the single SPM and the SPM with ownership but needs no on-chip memory. The relative high register count comes from the small FIFOs built out of registers. We can change the FIFO to use on-chip memories; two per node, one for send and one for receive.

The three solutions scale differently with respect to the maximum clocking frequency. As a baseline, the Patmos processor can be clocked at 80 MHz within this FPGA. The NoC is a distributed design and therefore scales best. The 3×3 S4NOC can be clocked faster than 200 MHz, clearly not being the bottleneck in the system. The single shared SPM has a single merge point and limits the system

Table 2. Resource requirement of different communication devices.

Device	LCs	Registers	Memory
Shared SPM	654	490	16 KB
SPM with ownership	8694	77	16 KB
S4NOC	5517	4454	0 KB

frequency to about 70 MHz. We assume one pipeline stage, which increases read access latency by one clock cycle, should be enough to increase the maximum clocking frequency to be higher than the 80 MHz of the processor cores. However, moving to a 4 × 4 organization of the single SPM may reduce the clocking frequency further. The SPM with ownership has the worst clock frequency of just 50 MHz. Adding one pipeline stage should help, but this would double the access latency from 1 to 2 clock cycles.

4.5   Discussion

When we look at the performance, the resource requirement, and the clock frequency, there is no clear winner between the three solutions. The cheapest solution is the shared SPM, but the access time in clock cycles for a producer-consumer workload is higher than at the other two solutions. The SPM with ownership has the highest throughput in clock cycles, but also the highest hardware demand and the lowest clock frequency. This solution should probably be clustered with fewer cores or fewer SPMs in the pool. The NoC solution is probably the sweet spot having medium resource requirement, throughput between the single SPM and the SPM with ownership, and, perhaps most important, scales well with a higher core count.

In summary, a combination of a NoC for the global traffic combined with locally clustered shared SPMs may be the right solution. This combination of a NoC and shared SPMs is similar to the Kalray architecture, but we propose to have clusters that use a shared SPM overlap for a more flexible continuum for communication.

5   Conclusion

Multicore processors used in cyber-physical systems need to support time-predictable computation and communication. As communication via shared main memory supported by a cache coherence protocol is hardly time-predictable, we need other forms of core-to-core communication. In this paper, we explored different forms of hardware support for on-chip message passing between cores. Shared on-chip memories with a time-predictable arbitration, such as time-division multiplexing, provide an efficient solution for around a dozen cores. For more cores, a distributed communication architecture, such as a network-on-chip. is a better scaling solution. Also, hybrid solutions using shared memories in clusters, which are connected by a network-on-chip, are an option. The usage of multicore processors in safety-critical cyber-physical systems is not yet common. Future applications and experiments will tell which on-chip communication solution will be the most preferred one.

Acknowledgment. The work presented in this paper was partially funded by the Danish Council for Independent Research | Technology and Production Sciences under the project PREDICT (no. 4184-00127A). (http://predict.compute.dtu.dk/)

References

1. Bachrach, J., et al.: Chisel: constructing hardware in a scala embedded language. In: The 49th Annual Design Automation Conference (DAC 2012), pp. 1216–1225. ACM, San Francisco, June 2012
2. Becker, M., Dasari, D., Nicolic, B., Akesson, B., Nelis, V., Nolte, T.: Contention-free execution of automotive applications on a clustered many-core platform. In: 28th Euromicro Conference on Real-Time Systems (ECRTS), pp. 14–24, July 2016. https://doi.org/10.1109/ECRTS.2016.14
3. Brandner, F., Schoeberl, M.: Static routing in symmetric real-time network-on-chips. In: Proceedings of the 20th International Conference on Real-Time and Network Systems (RTNS 2012), Pont a Mousson, France, pp. 61–70, November 2012. https://doi.org/10.1145/2392987.2392995
4. Cruz, R.L.: A calculus for network delay. I. Network elements in isolation. IEEE Trans. Inf. Theory **37**(1), 114–131 (1991). https://doi.org/10.1109/18.61110
5. Cruz, R.L.: A calculus for network delay. II. Network analysis. IEEE Trans. Inf. Theory **37**(1), 132–141 (1991). https://doi.org/10.1109/18.61110
6. Dally, W.J., Towles, B.: Route packets, not wires: on-chip interconnection networks. In: DAC, pp. 684–689. ACM (2001)
7. Dupont de Dinechin, B., van Amstel, D., Poulhiès, M., Lager, G.: Time-critical computing on a single-chip massively parallel processor. In: Conference on Design, Automation and Test in Europe, DATE 2014, pp. 97:1–97:6. European Design and Automation Association, Leuven (2014)
8. Dupont de Dinechin, B., Durand, Y., van Amstel, D., Ghiti, A.: Guaranteed services of the NoC of a manycore processor. In: International Workshop on Network on Chip Architectures (NoCArc), pp. 11–16. ACM, New York, December 2014. https://doi.org/10.1145/2685342.2685344
9. Goossens, K., Hansson, A.: The AEthereal network on chip after ten years: goals, evolution, lessons, and future. In: Proceedings of the 47th ACM/IEEE Design Automation Conference (DAC 2010), pp. 306–311 (2010)
10. Gruian, F., Schoeberl, M.: Hardware support for CSP on a Java chip-multiprocessor. Microprocess. Microsyst. **37**(4–5), 472–481 (2013). https://doi.org/10.1016/j.micpro.2012.08.004
11. Hansson, A., Subburaman, M., Goossens, K.: aelite: a flit-synchronous network on chip with composable and predictable services. In: Proceedings of the Conference on Design, Automation and Test in Europe (DATE 2009), Leuven, Belgium, pp. 250–255 (2009)
12. Heckmann, R., Ferdinand, C.: Worst-case execution time prediction by static program analysis. Technical report, AbsInt Angewandte Informatik GmbH. Accessed Nov 2013

13. Hennessy, J., Patterson, D.: Computer Architecture: A Quantitative Approach, 4th edn. Morgan Kaufmann Publishers, Burlington (2006)
14. Hoare, C.A.R.: Monitors: an operating system structuring concept. Commun. ACM **17**(10), 549–557 (1974). https://doi.org/10.1145/355620.361161
15. Hoare, C.A.R.: Communicating sequential processes. Commun. ACM **21**(8), 666–677 (1978). https://doi.org/10.1145/359576.359585
16. Homewood, M., May, D., Shepherd, D., Shepherd, R.: The IMS T800 transputer. IEEE Micro **7**(5), 10–26 (1987). https://doi.org/10.1109/MM.1987.305012
17. Kasapaki, E., Schoeberl, M., Sørensen, R.B., Müller, C.T., Goossens, K., Sparsø, J.: Argo: a real-time network-on-chip architecture with an efficient GALS implementation. IEEE Trans. Very Large Scale Integr. (VLSI) Syst. **24**, 479–492 (2016). https://doi.org/10.1109/TVLSI.2015.2405614
18. Le Boudec, J.Y.: Application of network calculus to guaranteed service networks. IEEE Trans. Inf. Theory **44**(3), 1087–1096 (1998). https://doi.org/10.1109/18.669170
19. Lee, E.A., Messerschmitt, D.G.: Synchronous data flow. Proc. IEEE **75**(9), 1235–1245 (1987). https://doi.org/10.1109/PROC.1987.13876
20. Liu, I.: Precision Timed Machines. Ph.D. thesis, EECS Department, University of California, Berkeley, May 2012
21. Liu, I., Reineke, J., Broman, D., Zimmer, M., Lee, E.A.: A PRET microarchitecture implementation with repeatable timing and competitive performance. In: Proceedings of IEEE International Conference on Computer Design (ICCD 2012), October 2012
22. Lohstroh, M., et al.: Actors revisited for time-critical systems. In: Proceedings of the 56th Annual Design Automation Conference 2019, DAC 2019, pp. 152:1–152:4. ACM, New York (2019). https://doi.org/10.1145/3316781.3323469
23. May, D., Shepherd, R.: Occam and the transputer. In: Proceedings of the IFIP WG 10.3 Workshop on Concurrent Languages in Distributed Systems: Hardware Supported Implementation, pp. 19–33. Elsevier North-Holland Inc., New York (1985)
24. Metzlaff, S., Mische, J., Ungerer, T.: A real-time capable many-core model. In: Proceedings of 32nd IEEE Real-Time Systems Symposium: Work-in-Progress Session (2011)
25. Mische, J., Frieb, M., Stegmeier, A., Ungerer, T.: Reduced complexity many-core: timing predictability due to message-passing. In: Knoop, J., Karl, W., Schulz, M., Inoue, K., Pionteck, T. (eds.) ARCS 2017. LNCS, vol. 10172, pp. 139–151. Springer, Cham (2017). https://doi.org/10.1007/978-3-319-54999-6_11
26. Mische, J., Frieb, M., Stegmeier, A., Ungerer, T.: PIMP my many-core: pipeline-integrated message passing. In: Pnevmatikatos, D.N., Pelcat, M., Jung, M. (eds.) SAMOS 2019. LNCS, vol. 11733, pp. 199–211. Springer, Cham (2019). https://doi.org/10.1007/978-3-030-27562-4_14
27. Olofsson, A., Nordström, T., ul Abdin, Z.: Kickstarting high-performance energy-efficient manycore architectures with Epiphany. In: Matthews, M.B. (ed.) Proceedings of Asilomar Conference on Signals, Systems and Computers, pp. 1719–1726. IEEE (2014)
28. Paukovits, C., Kopetz, H.: Concepts of switching in the time-triggered network-on-chip. In: Proceedings of the 14th IEEE International Conference on Embedded and Real-Time Computing Systems and Applications (RTCSA 2008), pp. 120–129, August 2008. https://doi.org/10.1109/RTCSA.2008.18
29. Petersen, M.B., Riber, A.V., Andersen, S.T., Schoeberl, M.: Time-predictable distributed shared on-chip memory. Microprocess. Microsyst. (2019). https://doi.org/10.1016/j.micpro.2019.102896

30. Ptolemaeus, C. (ed.): System Design, Modeling, and Simulation using Ptolemy II. Ptolemy.org, Berkeley (2014)
31. Puffitsch, W., Sørensen, R.B., Schoeberl, M.: Time-division multiplexing vs network calculus: a comparison. In: Proceedings of the 23th International Conference on Real-Time and Network Systems (RTNS 2015), Lille, France, November 2015. https://doi.org/10.1145/2834848.2834868
32. Schoeberl, M.: Time-predictable computer architecture. EURASIP J. Embedded Syst. **2009**, 17 p. (2009). Article ID 758480. https://doi.org/10.1155/2009/758480
33. Schoeberl, M.: One-way shared memory. In: 2018 Design, Automation and Test in Europe Conference Exhibition (DATE), pp. 269–272, March 2018. https://doi.org/10.23919/DATE.2018.8342017
34. Schoeberl, M., et al.: T-CREST: time-predictable multi-core architecture for embedded systems. J. Syst. Architect. **61**(9), 449–471 (2015). https://doi.org/10.1016/j.sysarc.2015.04.002
35. Schoeberl, M., Chong, D.V., Puffitsch, W., Sparsø J.: A time-predictable memory network-on-chip. In: Proceedings of the 14th International Workshop on Worst-Case Execution Time Analysis (WCET 2014), Madrid, Spain, pp. 53–62, July 2014. https://doi.org/10.4230/OASIcs.WCET.2014.53
36. Schoeberl, M., Pezzarossa, L., Sparsø, J.: A minimal network interface for a simple network-on-chip. In: Schoeberl, M., Hochberger, C., Uhrig, S., Brehm, J., Pionteck, T. (eds.) ARCS 2019. LNCS, vol. 11479, pp. 295–307. Springer, Heidelberg (2019). https://doi.org/10.1007/978-3-030-18656-2_22
37. Schoeberl, M., Pezzarossa, L., Sparsø J.: S4noc: a minimalistic network-on-chip for real-time multicores. In: 12th International Workshop on Network on Chip Architectures (NoCArc 2019). ACM, October 2019. https://doi.org/10.1145/3356045.3360714
38. Schoeberl, M., Puffitsch, W., Hepp, S., Huber, B., Prokesch, D.: Patmos: a time-predictable microprocessor. Real-Time Syst. **54**(2), 389–423 (2018). https://doi.org/10.1007/s11241-018-9300-4
39. Schoeberl, M., Sørensen, R.B., Sparsø J.: Models of communication for multicore processors. In: Proceedings of the 11th Workshop on Software Technologies for Embedded and Ubiquitous Systems (SEUS 2015). pp. 44–51. IEEE, Auckland, April 2015. https://doi.org/10.1109/ISORCW.2015.57
40. Schoeberl, M., Strøm, T.B., Baris, O., Sparsø J.: Scratchpad memories with ownership. In: 2019 Design, Automation and Test in Europe Conference Exhibition (DATE) (2019)
41. Shoushtari, M., Donyanavard, B., Bathen, L.A.D., Dutt, N.: Shave-ice: sharing distributed virtualized SPMS in many-core embedded systems. ACM Trans. Embed. Comput. Syst. **17**(2), 47:1–47:25 (2018). https://doi.org/10.1145/3157667
42. Sparsø J., Kasapaki, E., Schoeberl, M.: An area-efficient network interface for a TDM-based network-on-chip. In: Proceedings of the Conference on Design, Automation and Test in Europe, DATE 2013, pp. 1044–1047. EDA Consortium, San Jose (2013)
43. Whitby-Strevens, C.: The transputer. SIGARCH Comput. Archit. News **13**(3), 292–300 (1985). https://doi.org/10.1145/327070.327269

Towards Creating a Deployable Grasp Type Probability Estimator for a Prosthetic Hand

Mehrshad Zandigohar$^{(\boxtimes)}$, Mo Han, Deniz Erdoğmuş, and Gunar Schirner

Northeastern University, Boston, MA 02115, USA
{zandi,han,erdogmus,schirner}@ece.neu.edu

Abstract. For lower arm amputees, prosthetic hands promise to restore most of physical interaction capabilities. This requires to accurately predict hand gestures capable of grabbing varying objects and execute them timely as intended by the user. Current approaches often rely on physiological signal inputs such as Electromyography (EMG) signal from residual limb muscles to infer the intended motion. However, limited signal quality, user diversity and high variability adversely affect the system robustness. Instead of solely relying on EMG signals, our work enables augmenting EMG intent inference with physical state probability through machine learning and computer vision method. To this end, we: (1) study state-of-the-art deep neural network architectures to select a performant source of knowledge transfer for the prosthetic hand, (2) use a dataset containing object images and probability distribution of grasp types as a new form of labeling where instead of using absolute values of zero and one as the conventional classification labels, our labels are a set of probabilities whose sum is 1. The proposed method generates probabilistic predictions which could be fused with EMG prediction of probabilities over grasps by using the visual information from the palm camera of a prosthetic hand. Our results demonstrate that InceptionV3 achieves highest accuracy with 0.95 angular similarity followed by 1.4 MobileNetV2 with 0.93 at ~20% the amount of operations.

Keywords: Learning from multimodal data · Neural networks and deep learning · Signal detection pattern recognition and classification

1 Introduction

Prosthetic hands aim to compensate part of the lost ability of lower arm amputees. In order to correctly enact the intent of the user, prosthetic hands consider individual finger motion control, grasp type selection, and open close commands. In this work we focus on grasp type selection.

State-of-the-art approaches try to classify the amputee's Electromyography (EMG) signals of the residual limb muscles into meaningful motions. This approach has drawbacks which adversely affect its robustness in real life situations

© Springer Nature Switzerland AG 2020
R. Chamberlain et al. (Eds.): CyPhy 2019/WESE 2019, LNCS 11971, pp. 44–58, 2020.
https://doi.org/10.1007/978-3-030-41131-2_3

[1,11]. For instance, they need calibration pretty often; the unexpected electrode shifting could distort the EMG signals; muscle fatigue and/or limb disposition adversely affect the EMG patterns; and some amputees may lack critical muscles which EMG classification rely on. These insufficiencies have led researchers to use more sources of information to understand human intent [12]. With the rise of Convolutional Neural Networks [5,14,19,23,25,27,28], studies on using visual information as a source of information for the prosthetic hand have been conducted [4,7–9,12,26], which focus on classifying images into a grasp type.

Figure 1 demonstrates the overview of our prosthetic hand design, where an EMG sensor is attached to user's arm and the collected EMG signals are used to infer the human intent while the grasp probability estimator provides physical state information using the images captured from the palm camera of the prosthetic hand. The resulting predictions from both EMG and vision are then combined in Fusion module to form a final decision. This work focuses on the grasp probability estimation to enable efficient and accurate fusion of the physical information.

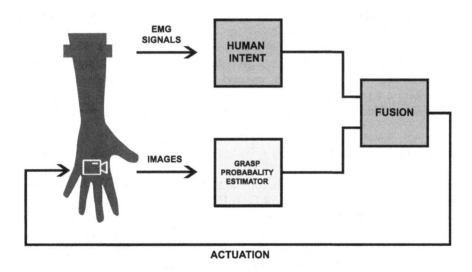

Fig. 1. System components and flow of information.

The conventional vision-based classifiers try to estimate the probable grasp type based on absolute values of one and zero assigned to each class as labels during training. However, in the context of grasp estimation, this approach has 2 drawbacks: (1) not every object is limited to a single gesture capable of grabbing that object, i.e. there might be more than a way to grab an object; (2) Each potential grasp type for a specific object might not have the same level of preference for different users. Therefore, the predicted value for each grasp type could be represented much more accurately as probabilities over grasps which sum up to 1. Therefore, to facilitate physical information from the camera with human intent provided by EMG, probability based estimation yields much more information over fusing the absolute predictions.

On the other hand, while having an accurate prediction helps with inferring the human intent for selecting a grasp type, given the real-time constraints of inference for prosthetic hands, the network should behave in a timely manner to meet real-time deadlines. In this work we:

1. Provide a probability distribution based neural network rather than training on absolute values of zero and one to capture the true nature of capable gestures for grabbing a specific object and provide more information of the possible grasp types when combined with EMG inference probabilities.
2. We also study performance of different networks based on the amount of computation each network has to select efficient architectures to transfer which enables embedded and real-time predictions considering their limited compute power.

Using the proposed method, InceptionV3 as our best probability estimator reaches 0.95 angular similarity followed by 1.4 MobileNetV2 with 0.02 loss while improving performance by 5.02X. As a result, fusion of visual data with EMG data is enabled considering performance limitations. Details on EMG and fusion modules are out of the scope of this paper.

The paper continues with Sect. 2 providing the overview of our prosthetic hand. Following that, Sect. 3 our method for selecting an efficient transfer source. Section 4 presents the details of training. Section 5 evaluates the proposed method and provides results, and finally Sect. 6 concludes this paper.

2   Prosthetic Hand

Figure 2 shows the actual prosthetic robotic hand produced by our collaborators. The hand is a 3-D printed model of OpenBionics hand [21] with a USB endoscopic camera attached on its side. The actuators are position controlled, and would stop actuation once the drawn current exceeds some threshold. All components use ROS Melodic Morenia [22] for communicating between themselves, i.e. EMG sensor, embedded camera, actuator and fusion units.

Figure 1 demonstrates high level system integration and flow of information in this work. To predict the intent of the amputee, a classifier on the EMG signal is used in the form of a probability distribution over five grasp types. Moreover, the system is augmented with a visual grasp type probability estimator fed with the images from an embedded camera in the hand to output another distribution over the same grasp types. This is merely based on the feedback from the environment to compensate EMG deficiencies. Given the information from human intent and visual characteristics, the fusion unit aggregates the two probability distributions into the most probable grasp type considering the confidence of each unit. To have a more reliable decision, this process is repeated and averaged over two seconds to make the final decision. This decision is further sent to the control unit in order to actuate the prosthetic robotic hand to execute the grasp.

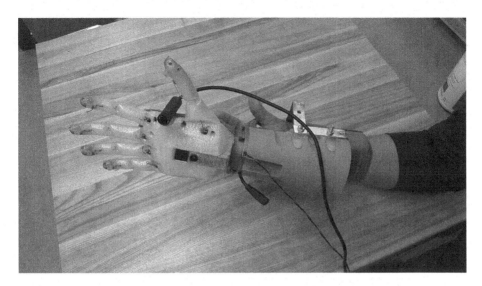

Fig. 2. Prosthetic hand with camera attached.

In order for the fusion unit to make the most timely decision, the visual grasp probability estimator should process as many frames as the camera generated per second to be real-time, which is 30 fps in our work. As we target mobile deployment of vision system, challenges arise due to low power constraints and limited compute performance. Therefore, smaller models with less number of computations are preferred to the more accurate but computationally intensive networks. While there are researches for deployment of DNNs to an embedded target, including optimizations such as pruning, quantization, tensor fusion, kernel auto-tuning, multi-stream execution, dynamic tensor memory and precision calibration, these are outside the scope of this paper and we try to provide a platform-independant approach for selecting efficient networks.

3   Selecting Efficient Transfer Architectures

While deep neural networks (DNNs) have shown promising results on many tasks, due to their tremendous number of parameters (i.e. over 25.6M parameters in ResNet50), fully training DNNs from scratch requires a large set of data. This challenge is well solved by transfer leaning. Transfer learning has shown impressive results on applications with similar domains where there is not enough data or computing resources to train a deep network from scratch [30]. In computer vision studies, ImageNet [5] has been the most widely used benchmark on problems including but not limited to transfer learning [6,24], object detection [16] and image segmentation [3,13]. Torralba and Efros [29] show that many datasets before Imagenet were biased and not general enough to be transferred to other domains.

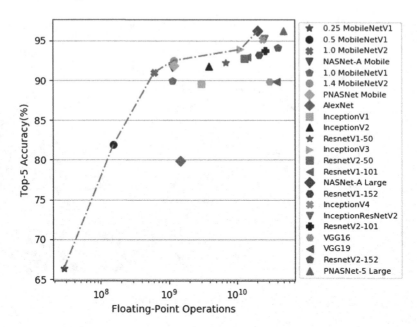

Fig. 3. Accuracy vs. number of floating point operations for several pretrained ImageNet models.

There are many networks trained on the large ImageNet dataset including AlexNet [20], VGG [25], MobileNet [15], ResNet [14], Inception [28], and NASNet [31] with different accuracies and architectural differences. To choose an architecture as the transfer source for the new task, one can choose the most accurate model as the base model. In [18], authors has shown that better ImageNet models provide better feature layers for transferring the learned knowledge from one domain to another. However, more accurate models generally consist of more parameters and demand more computation which results in poor inference performance.

As an initial platform-independent indicator of computation demand, this paper focuses on number of floating point operations. This allows for a high-level reasoning to compare different neural networks relatively with each other and explore the computation demand vs. accuracy trade-off. While suitable for this purpose, the number of floating point operations is not a substitute for estimating execution time on an actual deployment target. This would require taking into account significantly more implementation detail, such as: deployment target (CPU, GPU, neural-network accelerator), float vs. fixed point and quantization, various target-dependent optimizations. We consider as a second phase the target-dependent exploration. This work focuses on the first phase of network exploration and training.

To this end, we have studied 23 pretrained ImageNet models given our accuracy and performance objectives depicted in Fig. 3. The vertical axis provides the Top-5 accuracy of each model and the horizontal axis shows the number of floating point operations required to execute inference for that network in log scale. In general, we can observe that as the accuracy of a model improves, the number of floating point operations also increase.

To avoid training all models which takes tremendous effort and time, we exploit multi-objective selection also known as Pareto Efficiency [2] for selecting the efficient models. Given a system with function $f : R^n \to R^m$, feasible decisions X is related to feasible criterion vectors Y as follows:

$$Y = \{y \in R^m : y = f(x), x \in X\} \tag{1}$$

and therefore the Pareto Frontier is:

$$P(Y) = \{y' \in Y : \{y'' \succ y', y'' \neq y'\} = \emptyset\} \tag{2}$$

where the efficient models are those on the Pareto Frontier, $P(Y)$, demonstrated by the dash-dotted line in Fig. 3.

Using the aforementioned method, InceptionV3, 1.4 MobileNetV2, 1.0 MobileNetV2, 0.5 MobileNetV1, 0.25 MobileNetV1 and NASNet-A Large are selected as efficient models. The selected networks strictly dominate other models and are not dominated by any other, and hence lie on Pareto Frontier. The selected networks cover the most efficient yet effective architectures. NASNet-A Large is excluded here due to very large size of the network, making training impossible on the current infrastructure.

4   Transfer Learning

In this section, we provide details on the dataset, architectural specifications and methodology used for transferring the selected ImageNet models to the problem of grasp probability estimation.

4.1   Dataset

The data used in this work is based on [12]. The dataset consists of 4130 images, which were augmented from 413 hand-perspective images of 102 ordinary objects including office and daily supplies, utensils, and complex-shaped objects. In the process of learning, the environments and image backgrounds could differ from the practice, which may introduce interference and redundant information during the feature extraction. To focus the learning on the object shape instead of the mutative background, the objects were segmented from the raw images which makes the training independent and orthogonal from the random environment. In addition, to enlarge the dataset and add arbitrary background information to respond to the variable environments, the segmented objects were superposed on a series of Gaussian-noised background. The specific augmentation processes are as follows: first the objects were cut out of the raw images and randomly blurred; then, background of Gaussian noise with random variance was added to

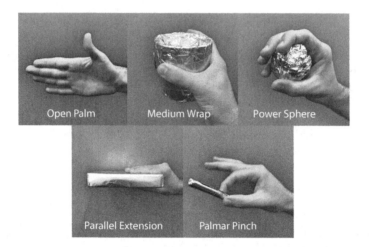

Fig. 4. The selected 5 grasp categories.

the bottom of the segmented object to increase the system robustness to different actual backgrounds; finally, the segmented and blurred object was placed in the Gaussian noise background at random location to form the final training image. In addition, the label set is limited within 5 gestures (Open Palm, Medium Wrap, Power Sphere, Parallel Extension and Palmar Pinch) based on their compliance with robotic implements and also their coverage ability for common objects of daily lives due to the similarity with the other grasp types. The Fig. 4 shows the 5 grasp types used.

Note that the inference problem to be solved is not a hard classification, which would predict a single category. Instead, the inference here needs to predict a probability distribution over grasp types which estimates the suitability of grasp types for a given object. This distribution has to match the distribution observed in the ground truth data. Ground truth data was collected by asking each labeler to rank the 5 grasp in decreasing order of preference to grab the object. These labels are obtained from 11 individuals. We used the most relevant grasp type among 5 grasp types for each object to create a probability distribution. The probability of grasp type i where it is chosen by n labelers from total of N labelers is:

$$p_i = n/N \tag{3}$$

Figure 5 demonstrates examples of the image data with their corresponding probability distribution over 5 possible labels.

4.2   Details on Transferring and Network Topology

To create networks suitable for the new domain and task, the features from the original pretrained model are extracted. This means the top layers, also known as the classifier part of the network, are excluded and not transferred. On top

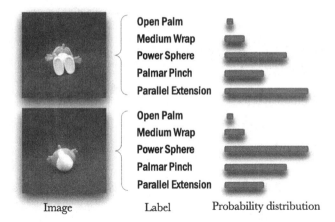

Image	Label	Probability distribution

Fig. 5. The images and corresponding labels. For each image, there exits a ground truth generated from 11 labelers, which is the probability distribution over 5 grasps. Same object from different views may lead to different distributions.

of the transferred features, a Global 2-D Average Pooling is added to reduce the spatial dimension followed by 3 Fully Connected layers with 256, 128 and 5 neurons respectively. The FC layers are stacked with ReLU activations except the last one wherein a Softmax is used as it transforms the prediction into a probability distribution.

Our methodology for training applied to all networks is two folded: (1) Firstly, we freeze all feature layers and replace the default top layers by our own customized top layers, and only train those top models added to the fixed features, as shown in Fig. 6. These layers are initialized with random wights using Xavier's method [10]. Then the optimizer with learning rate of 0.001 trains the network for 50 epochs. (2) After the top FC layers are trained on the target dataset, all other layers are unfreezed and the whole network is trained with a lower 0.0001 learning rate for another 50 epochs.

4.3   Training Setup

In both steps of training FC layers and fine-tuning the whole network afterwards, the models were trained using the batch size of 32 images using Adaptive Moment Estimation (Adam) optimizer [17]. As the format of labels and predictions are both probability distributions over grasp types, in order to minimize the difference between the current prediction and the ground truth we use the cross entropy (4) as the loss function, which measures the error between two distributions:

$$loss = -\frac{1}{n} \sum_{i=1}^{n} [y_i \log (p_i) + (1 - y_i)log(1 - p_i)] \tag{4}$$

Feature layers   Classification layers

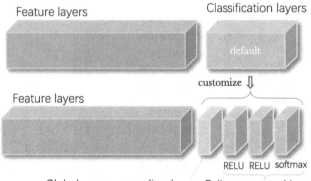

Global average pooling layer   Fully connected layers

Fig. 6. While training CNNs, we freeze all feature layers and replace the default top layers by our customized top layers, and only train those top models added to the fixed features.

where n is the number of categories; y_i and p_i are predicted and ground truth probabilities of grasp type i, respectively.

4.4 Evaluation Metric

The one-hot encoded labels used in conventional hard classifications problems fail to capture the true nature of grasp types since they can only encode one grasp type while gestures capable of grabbing a given object can be more than one. Moreover, absolute zero and one values used for labels in soft-classification would also fail to represent preference of one grasp type over the others. Each potential grasp type for a specific object might not have the same preference to the human over the others. To avoid this information loss, the value for each grasp type is represented as probabilities that sum up to 1. Therefore, there needs to be an evaluation metric that can calculate the error given the prediction and ground truth probability distributions. However, for our probability estimation problem, choosing an evaluation metric becomes challenging since it is not possible to clip probabilities to absolute values since it will result in significant information loss. In result, the evaluation metrics of conventional hard classification, such as Top-1 accuracy, cannot be applied.

To have a simple yet powerful metric, we propose angular similarity for evaluating the effectiveness of the model:

$$sim(u, v) = (1 - 2 \cdot arccos(\frac{u \cdot v}{\|u\|\|v\|})/\pi) \tag{5}$$

where u and v are vectors of probability distributions for prediction and the ground truth which are all positive and sum to 1. The angular similarity measures the angle between two given vectors which ranges from 0 to 1. A higher similarity indicates that the vectors are closer to each other, i.e. that the ground truth and the estimated distribution match more closely.

As an example to evaluate how probability values impact our proposed method, given ground truth probability $true = (1, 0, 0, 0, 0)$, $pred = (1, 0, 0, 0, 0)$ yields the highest value of 1. For $pred = (0.87, 0.13, 0, 0, 0)$ the evaluation metric yields good value of 0.9 and $pred = (0.76, 0.24, 0, 0, 0)$, $pred = (0.67; 0.34, 0, 0, 0)$, $pred = (0.58, 0.42, 0, 0, 0)$ and $pred = (0.5, 0.5, 0, 0, 0)$ result in angular similarity of 0.8, 0.7, 0.6 and 0.5 respectively. Note that $pred = (0, 1, 0, 0, 0)$ results in the lowest value of 0 which implies importance of the probability values order. It is also noteworthy to provide and example which examines both order and values of the predicted probabilities. Considering $pred = (0.2, 0.2, 0.2, 0.2, 0.2)$, will result in low performance of 0.3.

Moreover, comparing angular similarity to cosine similarity as an orientation based metric, it is a function of a proper distance when subtracted from 1, whereas in cosine similarity for small angles the resulting cosine values are very similar.

5   Results

We trained the proposed method using TenosrFlow on Pareto efficient models including InceptionV3, MobileNetV1 with 0.25 and 0.5 width multipliers (α) and MobileNetV2 with 1.0 and 1.4 width multipliers. Models were trained over 80% of dataset with batch size of 32 images for 50 epochs and validated on the 20% rest of the dataset. To monitor how well the training is performed for each model over iterations, the training and validation curves are depicted.

Figure 7a shows the fine-tuning cross entropy loss over the number of epochs for all models. The loss curves for all models converge as expected which demonstrate the model is well trained. However, the final cross entropy loss for 0.25 MobileNetV1 is higher than other networks due to significant reduction of number of learnable parameters.

To evaluate how precise each model is, the angular similarity comparison for the Pareto models are provided in Fig. 7b. The vertical axis is the validation angular similarity for each model over epochs, and we find that the ranking of the trained models with respect to their angular similarity is in total resemblance with the original pretrained models' accuracy on Imagenet.

Figure 8 compares the accuracy and performance of the selected models before and after transferring. On the left axis, the Top-5 accuracy of the pretrained model are provided. The right axis also depicts the angular similarity of the selected models after applying transfer learning. The number of floating point operations for each network in the source and target domains were calculated which is observable by the slight shift of the grasp probability estimation networks. This is due to the fact that the imageNet classification layers (fully connected) were replaced with the grasp estimation layers, which contain fewer neurons.

Moreover, since the number of operations related to the top layers of the pretrained models are much fewer than those of the extracted features, and the fact that the same amount of computation is required for the added top layers,

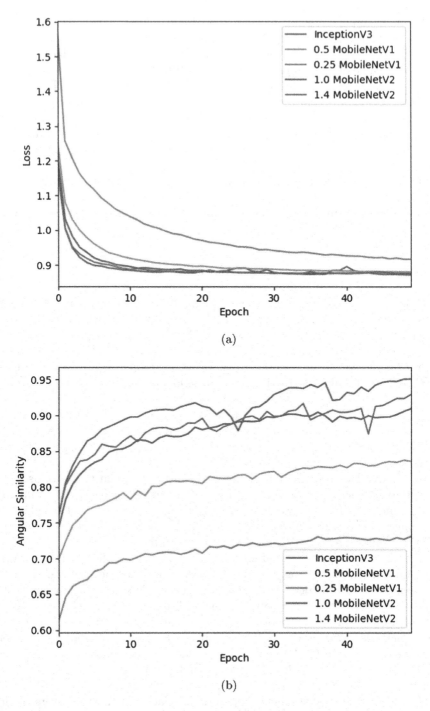

Fig. 7. (a) Fine-tuning loss of efficient models. (b) Validation angular similarity of the efficient models

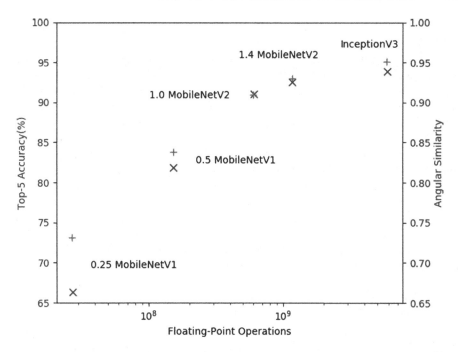

Fig. 8. Number of Floating point operations vs. accuracy evaluation of Pareto models before (blue crosses) and after (red pluses) training. Accuracy axis have the same range for a fair comparison. (Color figure online)

the total number of operations does not change significantly when transferring to the new dataset.

As depicted in Fig. 8, there is a trade-off between the computational demand and the accuracy of the Pareto models. In a computationally limited application with low intolerance for latency, networks with lower number of floating point operations such as 0.25 MobileNetV1 are preferred. However, as the models become less computationally intensive, they reach closer to the accuracy of a uniform random generator (0.5 angular similarity).

To compensate for EMG deficiencies, there needs to be an accurate yet efficient model for the visual classifier. While both InceptionV3 and 1.4 MobileNetV2 provide impressive angular similarity of 0.95 and 0.93 respectively, with 0.02 loss in angular similarity MobileNet has 19.88% (~1/5) of Inception's total number of floating-point operations, hence is expected to execute faster.

6   Conclusion

This work aims to restore the lost ability of lower arm amputees using robotic prosthetic hands via pre-defined grasp types. Our system aims to fuse probable grasp types based on visual information with human intent through EMG measurements. With the focus on the visual classifier, our approach utilizes transfer learning of ImageNet models to predict grasp type distributions given the objects visible from a camera integrated into the robotic hand.

To have an efficient yet accurate prediction, we studied several state-of-the-art models and excluded inefficient networks as a source of transferring knowledge. We also retrained the efficient networks on probabilistic labels instead of hard/soft ground truth labels to have an accurate representation of grasp types. This way, multiple grasp types with different preferences can be represented, suitable for grasp detection problem. To provide a suitable evaluation for the probability estimation, we proposed angular similarity as an intuitive evaluation metric. We also observed that the relative ordering of the selected models in terms of error/performance stays the same using the proposed metric after transferring. Using the proposed method, we selected the best neural network architecture for our prosthetic hand to enable efficient performance along with the EMG inference data. Using 1.4 MobileNetV2 provides 0.93 angular similarity with 20% of Inception's total number of floating-point operations, improving the performance by 5.02x with 0.02 loss in angular similarity.

Acknowledgement. This work is partially supported by NSF (CNS-1544895 at NEU; CNS-1544636 at WPI, CNS-1544815 at HMS).

References

1. Bitzer, S., Van Der Smagt, P.: Learning EMG control of a robotic hand: towards active prostheses. In: Proceedings 2006 IEEE International Conference on Robotics and Automation, ICRA 2006, pp. 2819–2823. IEEE (2006)
2. Breyer, F.: On the intergenerational pareto efficiency of pay-as-you-go financed pension systems. J. Inst. Theor. Econ. (JITE)/Zeitschrift für die gesamte Staatswissenschaft 643–658 (1989)
3. Chen, L.C., Papandreou, G., Kokkinos, I., Murphy, K., Yuille, A.L.: DeepLab: semantic image segmentation with deep convolutional nets, atrous convolution, and fully connected CRFs. IEEE Trans. Pattern Anal. Mach. Intell. **40**(4), 834–848 (2017)
4. DeGol, J., Akhtar, A., Manja, B., Bretl, T.: Automatic grasp selection using a camera in a hand prosthesis. In: 2016 IEEE 38th Annual International Conference of the Engineering in Medicine and Biology Society (EMBC), pp. 431–434. IEEE (2016)
5. Deng, J., Dong, W., Socher, R., Li, L.J., Li, K., Fei-Fei, L.: ImageNet: a large-scale hierarchical image database. In: IEEE Conference on Computer Vision and Pattern Recognition, CVPR 2009, pp. 248–255. IEEE (2009)
6. Donahue, J., et al.: DeCAF: a deep convolutional activation feature for generic visual recognition. In: International Conference on Machine Learning, pp. 647–655 (2014)
7. Ghazaei, G., Alameer, A., Degenaar, P., Morgan, G., Nazarpour, K.: An exploratory study on the use of convolutional neural networks for object grasp classification. In: 2nd IET International Conference on Intelligent Signal Processing 2015 (ISP), pp. 1–5, December 2015. https://doi.org/10.1049/cp.2015.1760

8. Ghazaei, G., Alameer, A., Degenaar, P., Morgan, G., Nazarpour, K.: Deep learning-based artificial vision for grasp classification in myoelectric hands. J. Neural Eng. **14**(3), 036025 (2017)
9. Gigli, A., Gregori, V., Cognolato, M., Atzori, M., Gijsberts, A.: Visual cues to improve myoelectric control of upper limb prostheses. In: 2018 7th IEEE International Conference on Biomedical Robotics and Biomechatronics (Biorob), pp. 783–788, August 2018. https://doi.org/10.1109/BIOROB.2018.8487923
10. Glorot, X., Bengio, Y.: Understanding the difficulty of training deep feedforward neural networks. In: Proceedings of the Thirteenth International Conference on Artificial Intelligence and Statistics, pp. 249–256 (2010)
11. Günay, S.Y., Quivira, F., Erdoğmuş, D.: Muscle synergy-based grasp classification for robotic hand prosthetics. In: Proceedings of the 10th International Conference on Pervasive Technologies Related to Assistive Environments, pp. 335–338. ACM (2017)
12. Han, M., et al.: From hand-perspective visual information to grasp type probabilities: deep learning via ranking labels. In: Proceedings of 12th ACM International Conference on Pervasive Technologies Related to Assistive Environments, pp. 256–263, June 2019. https://doi.org/10.1145/3316782.3316794
13. He, K., Gkioxari, G., Dollár, P., Girshick, R.: Mask R-CNN. In: Proceedings of the IEEE International Conference on Computer Vision, pp. 2961–2969 (2017)
14. He, K., Zhang, X., Ren, S., Sun, J.: Deep residual learning for image recognition. In: Proceedings of the IEEE Conference on Computer Vision and Pattern Recognition, pp. 770–778 (2016)
15. Howard, A.G., et al.: MobileNets: efficient convolutional neural networks for mobile vision applications. arXiv abs/1704.04861 (2017)
16. Huang, J., et al.: Speed/accuracy trade-offs for modern convolutional object detectors. In: Proceedings of the IEEE Conference on Computer Vision and Pattern Recognition, pp. 7310–7311 (2017)
17. Kingma, D., Ba, J.: Adam: a method for stochastic optimization. In: International Conference on Learning Representations, December 2014
18. Kornblith, S., Shlens, J., Le, Q.V.: Do better imagenet models transfer better? CoRR abs/1805.08974 (2018). http://arxiv.org/abs/1805.08974
19. Krizhevsky, A., Sutskever, I., Hinton, G.E.: ImageNet classification with deep convolutional neural networks. In: Advances in Neural Information Processing Systems, pp. 1097–1105 (2012)
20. Krizhevsky, A., Sutskever, I., Hinton, G.E.: ImageNet classification with deep convolutional neural networks. In: Pereira, F., Burges, C.J.C., Bottou, L., Weinberger, K.Q. (eds.) Advances in Neural Information Processing Systems 25, pp. 1097–1105. Curran Associates, Inc. (2012). http://papers.nips.cc/paper/4824-imagenet-classification-with-deep-convolutional-neural-networks.pdf
21. Liarokapis, M.V., Zisimatos, A.G., Mavrogiannis, C.I., Kyriakopoulos, K.J.: Open-Bionics: an open-source initiative for the creation of affordable, modular, lightweight, underactuated robot hands and prosthetic devices. In: 2nd ASU Rehabilitation Robotics Workshop (2014)
22. Quigley, M., et al.: ROS: an open-source robot operating system. In: ICRA Workshop on Open Source Software, vol. 3, p. 5. Kobe, Japan (2009)
23. Rezaei, B., et al.: Target-specific action classification for automated assessment of human motor behavior from video. Sensors **19**(19), 4266 (2019)
24. Sharif Razavian, A., Azizpour, H., Sullivan, J., Carlsson, S.: CNN features off-the-shelf: an astounding baseline for recognition. In: Proceedings of the IEEE Conference on Computer Vision and Pattern Recognition Workshops, pp. 806–813 (2014)

25. Simonyan, K., Zisserman, A.: Very deep convolutional networks for large-scale image recognition. arXiv 1409.1556, September 2014
26. Štrbac, M., Kočović, S., Marković, M., Popović, D.B.: Microsoft kinect-based artificial perception system for control of functional electrical stimulation assisted grasping. BioMed Res. Int. **2014** (2014)
27. Szegedy, C., et al.: Going deeper with convolutions. In: Proceedings of the IEEE Conference on Computer Vision and Pattern Recognition, pp. 1–9 (2015)
28. Szegedy, C., Vanhoucke, V., Ioffe, S., Shlens, J., Wojna, Z.: Rethinking the inception architecture for computer vision. In: Proceedings of the IEEE Conference on Computer Vision and Pattern Recognition, pp. 2818–2826 (2016)
29. Torralba, A., Efros, A.A., et al.: Unbiased look at dataset bias. In: CVPR, vol. 1, p. 7. Citeseer (2011)
30. Torrey, L., Shavlik, J.: Transfer learning. In: Handbook of Research on Machine Learning Applications and Trends: Algorithms, Methods, and Techniques, pp. 242–264. IGI Global (2010)
31. Zoph, B., Vasudevan, V., Shlens, J., Le, Q.V.: Learning transferable architectures for scalable image recognition. In: Proceedings of the IEEE Conference on Computer Vision and Pattern Recognition, pp. 8697–8710 (2018)

Reactors: A Deterministic Model for Composable Reactive Systems

Marten Lohstroh[1]([✉]), Íñigo Íncer Romeo[1], Andrés Goens[2], Patricia Derler[3], Jeronimo Castrillon[2], Edward A. Lee[1], and Alberto Sangiovanni-Vincentelli[1]

[1] Department of Electrical Engineering and Computer Sciences, UC Berkeley, Berkeley, USA
{marten,inigo,eal,alberto}@berkeley.edu
[2] Chair for Compiler Construction, TU Dresden, Dresden, Germany
{andres.goens,jeronimo.castrillon}@tu-dresden.de
[3] National Instruments, Austin, USA
patricia.derler@ni.com

Abstract. This paper describes a component-based concurrent model of computation for reactive systems. The components in this model, featuring ports and hierarchy, are called reactors. The model leverages a semantic notion of time, an event scheduler, and a synchronous-reactive style of communication to achieve determinism. Reactors enable a programming model that ensures determinism, unless explicitly abandoned by the programmer. We show how the coordination of reactors can safely and transparently exploit parallelism, both in shared-memory and distributed systems.

1 Introduction

In the mid-80s, David Harel and Amir Pnueli introduced the notion of *reactive* systems as those systems which maintain an ongoing interaction with their environments [28]. Arguing that a suitable decomposition mechanism for the development of complex reactive systems was lacking at the time, Harel proposed Statecharts [29], a formalism based on state machines. State machines, however, must keep track of a global state, a demand too stringent for programming today's distributed systems.

More recently, the term "reactive system" has been adopted by the reactive programming community, which is focused on building flexible, loosely-coupled, and scalable systems [34]. Central to the so-called reactive design patterns is the

The work in this paper was supported in part by the National Science Foundation (NSF), awards #CNS-1836601 (Reconciling Safety with the Internet) and #CNS-1739816 (Quantitative Contract-Based Synthesis and Verification for CPS Security) and the iCyPhy Research Center (Industrial Cyber-Physical Systems), supported by Camozzi Industries, Denso, Ford, Siemens, and Toyota. This work was also supported in part by the Center for Advancing Electronics Dresden (cfaed) and the German Academic Exchange Service (DAAD).

© Springer Nature Switzerland AG 2020
R. Chamberlain et al. (Eds.): CyPhy 2019/WESE 2019, LNCS 11971, pp. 59–85, 2020.
https://doi.org/10.1007/978-3-030-41131-2_4

idea of decomposing systems into non-blocking, asynchronous tasks that communicate via messages (or events). The ideas expressed in the Reactive Manifesto [10] can largely be seen as a revival of the concepts behind the Actor model by Hewitt and Agha [30]. While scalability, resilience, elasticity, and responsiveness—all tenets of the manifesto—are clearly important, the gains in these dimensions come at the loss of testability due to the admittance of nondeterminism. This is a rather high price to pay, because systematic testing is still the single most common technique for ensuring the correctness of software. We argue that the goals of reactive programming can also be achieved without adopting a nondeterministic programming model, with the advantage of maintaining the ability to reliably reproduce and debug potential problems.

In this paper we describe *reactors*, a model of computation that offers many desirable properties for designing and programming reactive systems. Our model is deterministic by construction while allowing for nondeterminism that is introduced explicitly. Unlike most reactive design patterns and programming models, timing is a fundamental element in the semantics of reactors. As such, reactors are also particularly suited for specifying real-time requirements in software. The carefully-coordinated relationship between logical and physical time during the execution of reactors allows for the detection and handling of timing violations. By the same token, safe-to-progress analysis (as it is known from Ptides [21,61] and Google Spanner [16]) can be leveraged to maintain a deterministic semantics between reactors distributed across networked nodes. Similar to reactive programming languages, the execution of reactors is governed by a dependency graph. More generally, this graph is a partial order which exposes parallelism that can be exploited at runtime. Finally, the interfaces of reactors readily expose dependencies, allowing their functionality to be treated as a black box, and opening up the possibility for a polyglot language design.

Reactors were first proposed in [46] and have been discussed in subsequent papers [44,45]. The main contribution of this paper is to provide a formal description of reactors as well as algorithmic descriptions of the key building blocks required for implementing a reactor runtime system.

1.1   The Case for Determinism

It may be argued that rapid recovery at run time to ensure correct behavior is preferable to statically asserting properties of software. After all, hardware failures, power outages, and other external influences can break the very assumptions in the programming model that imply determinism. While this is true, the dramatic success of software is squarely due to the high probability of hardware behaving deterministically, so the value of such a deterministic model is undeniable. Moreover, particularly in a cyber-physical system (CPS), the cost of recovery may be unacceptable, as the effects of unintended behavior could be irreversible–even disastrous. And even when recovery from unexpected errors is necessary, it is helpful to test those scenarios to assure that they are handled correctly.

We can look at Toyota's unintended acceleration case to underscore the impact of nondeterminism on testability. In the early 2000s, there were a number of serious car accidents involving Toyota vehicles that appeared to suffer from unintended acceleration. The US Department of Transportation contracted NASA to study Toyota software to determine whether software was capable of causing unintended acceleration. The study [52] was unable to find a "smoking gun," but concluded that the software was "untestable," making it impossible to rule out the possibility of unintended acceleration [33]. The software used a style of design that tolerates a seemingly innocuous form of nondeterminism. Specifically, state variables representing, for example, the most recent readings from a sensor, were accessed unguardedly by a multiplicity of threads. The spirit of this style of programming is to favor reactivity over consistency; the trade-off that is also central to the reactive programming paradigm. This programming style, however, renders software untestable, because, given any fixed set of inputs, the number of possible behaviors is vast.

A programming model can meaningfully limit the kinds of behaviors that a programmer can express. While weakening the constraints of a programming model can be useful for very specific optimization purposes, by far, most programmers will greatly benefit from a stricter rule set that facilitates the design of systems that will behave correctly and predictably [38]. Lightweight formal methods, such as type checking and static analysis, are well known to greatly reduce programming faults, for instance. The goal of reactors is to impose restrictions on the set of allowable behaviors without being *too* restrictive. For instance, the reactor model allows mutable shared state, but only across code segments that are guaranteed to execute sequentially to ensure mutual exclusion, and must execute in a predefined order to ensure determinism, making it much easier for the programmer to reason about side effects. Similarly, reactors are coordinated so that they automatically exploit opportunities for parallel execution, but only when possible without introducing nondeterminism. This relieves the programmer of the burdensome task of performing such coordination explicitly. In essence, the programming model prevents the formulation of programs that exhibit nondeterminism accidentally; nondeterminism is allowed, but it requires the express intent of the programmer.

1.2   Outline

The paper is organized as follows. We present the concept of reactors informally (Sect. 2) with a motivating example. We then proceed to formally define our model (Sect. 3) and show how our construction achieves a deterministic, synchronous-reactive model with a modular, hierarchical structure and an inherent notion of time. In Sect. 4, we explain how our model is amenable to distributed execution. We discuss related work in Sect. 5. Finally, we conclude and discuss avenues of future work in Sect. 6.

2   Reactors

In our model, a *reactor* is a collection of routines, called *reactions*, which share common *state*. The anatomy of a reactor is illustrated in Fig. 1. The quadrilateral in the top middle of the figure represents the reactor's state, with state variables s_i through s_n. Reactors can contain other reactors, connected in some topology, illustrated in the figure in the area below the reactor's state. A contained reactor has no access to its container's state, but it can be connected to its container's ports via reactions (annotated as n_p in Fig. 1, where p denotes the reaction's *priority*). The priorities assigned to reactions determine the order of execution of simultaneously triggered reactions. We distinguish between logical time t, which is the time of the model, represented as *tags* (as in the tagged signal model [39]), and physical time, as it would pass on a wall clock. In our model, simultaneity is a purely logical notion. Events in the reactor model are tagged; this orders them along a logical timeline. Two events (and therefore, the reactions they trigger) are simultaneous if and only if their tags are equal.

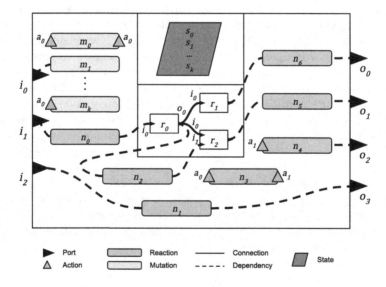

Fig. 1. Schematic representation of a reactor

The fundamental unit of execution is the reaction. Reactions are routines that may operate on the common state of the reactor and have access to a subset of the *input* and *output* ports of the reactor. Reactions may also communicate with other reactions through signals that are internal to a reactor; these are called *actions* and are depicted as the small triangles labeled a_i in Fig. 1. Ports and actions are named entities that can carry *values*. In an implementation, these would likely be typed, but for the sake of simplicity we omit types from our discussion. Reactions are opaque; they can modify the shared state of a reactor and have side effects, such as reading a sensor or driving an actuator, but these effects are not captured in the model.

The rounded boxes in the top-left corner of Fig. 1, annotated as m_p, where p denotes priority, are not reactions; we call them *mutations*. We make a distinction between reactions and mutations because, unlike a reaction, a mutation can modify the dependency graph of the reactor that contains it by adding connections to its topology, removing connections, and/or adding or removing its reactions. As a consequence, to preserve determinism, all mutations triggered at a given logical time t must be carried out prior to the execution of any contained reactions that are triggered at t. There are important advantages to limiting the scope of mutations to the internals of a reactor. For example, it allows mutations to be carried out without requiring any coordination with adjacent reactors. A mutation has to declare all the ports that it references. Hence, it can only establish new connections such that when this would introduce an algebraic loop, it would be detectable locally, considering only the elements contained by the reactor itself and without inspecting the broader connection topology the reactor is embedded in. In other words, hierarchy helps to contain the effects of run-time mutations.

The usage of *ports* (filled black triangles in the figure) establishes a clean separation between the functionality and composition of reactors; a reactor only references its own ports or ports of reactors it contains, not the ports of adjacent reactors. This is a key difference with Hewitt actors [31]—as featured in Akka [55], for instance—which address each other directly in a single shared address space. If, for a given tag, a reactor sets the value of an output port it has, this value will be propagated to the input ports of downstream reactors connected to it. Reactions are logically instantaneous. Logical time does not elapse during a reaction. Reactions have dependencies on input ports and antidependencies on output ports, shown as dashed edges in the figure. A reaction is not allowed to execute before all values associated with its dependencies are known (i.e., an upstream event with a tag t may not be emitted after a downstream reaction dependent on that event has already executed at t).

Just like in functional reactive programming languages, the dependency information of reactions is used to avoid so-called "glitches" (i.e., transient appearances of inconsistent data [15]) and ensure that execution unfolds in a predictable fashion. Rather than inferring dependencies from code, however, reactions must declare them, similar to how a function has to declare its arguments. This approach decouples the coordination problem from the implementation language, which led us to develop a meta language we call *Lingua Franca* (LF). This language serves the sole purpose of declaring and composing reactors, and superimposing a timing semantics on their execution. The program logic can then be written in the target language of choice. The specifics of the language and compiler toolchain are outside of the scope of this paper.

2.1   Runtime API

Reactions have access to a small set of primitives:

- LOGICALTIME: Returns the current *tag*;
- GET: Returns the value associated with given port/action at the current tag;
- SET: Binds given value to a given port at the current tag;
- PHYSICALTIME: Returns the last observed physical time; and
- SCHEDULE: Schedules given action with minimum delay of one *microstep*.

These primitives are the only means provided for reactors to interact with other reactors[1]. While GET and SET facilitate synchronous communication with reactions in other reactors, SCHEDULE is intended to trigger reactions within the *same* reactor, via an action. Actions can have a delay associated with them, which SCHEDULE uses to determine the tag of the resulting event. Moreover, an action must have a specified origin: *logical* or *physical*. When scheduled, an action with a logical origin (i.e., a logical action) will be scheduled relative to the last known logical time. Conversely, actions with a physical origin (i.e., physical actions) are scheduled relative to the last known physical time, a time value obtained from the platform. To avoid causality loops, logical actions are always scheduled with a minimum delay of one microstep. A microstep delay is an increment of the index in superdense time [3, 40, 47] with respect to the current logical time.

Like ports, actions can carry values. If more than once a particular action gets scheduled to occur at a particular time, the last set value persists. The same holds for ports. Multiple reactions could be triggered at the same logical time, and when two such reactions set the value of the same port, the earlier set value is overwritten. Because all triggered reactions within a reactor are executed in a predefined order, this semantics does not lead to nondeterminism, and it assures that each value is defined uniquely for each tag. Of course, this is only true if each port can have at most one incoming connection. This requirement has to be strictly enforced. Ports and actions that have not been set have the value *absent*. After all reactions for a given tag have been executed, the values of all ports are set to absent. In other words, ports and actions are, by default, not persistent.

The subtle interaction between logical and physical time in the reactor model establishes an interface between inherently asynchronous and nondeterministic concurrent tasks (e.g., a sensor that monitors a physical process) and deterministic computational tasks that benefit from testability and could require precise and predictable timing (e.g., to drive an actuator to influence said physical process). Rather than superimposing a deterministic world view on things that are inherently unpredictable, or, rejecting determinism entirely—thereby fundamentally compromising testability—reactors provide a model of computation that avoids this false dichotomy.

---

[1] Primitives used by a mutation to effect changes to its container's connection topology or its reactions are not discussed here due to space limitations.

While all reactors in a reactor program share the same logical and physical clock, reactor programs can interact with one another in a distributed setting, where each program has its own logical and physical clock. The preservation of a deterministic semantics in such a setting relies on assumptions about network delay and clock synchronization error. In this setting, reactions must have access to PHYSICALTIME to check for violations of these assumptions. This is explained in more detail in Sect. 4.

2.2 Example: Drive-by-Wire System

To illustrate how reactors behave, let us return to the Toyota example mentioned in the introduction and consider a power train implemented using reactors, illustrated using the diagram in Fig. 2. It features six reactors that jointly coordinate the control of the brakes and the engine. While this example is obviously oversimplified, it features enough complexity to allow us to highlight some of the most interesting aspects of our model. Following the "accessor" pattern from [12], each reactor in the figure (represented by a rectangular box) endows a complex subsystem of the car with a simple interface that allows it to be connected to other reactors. Connections are shown as solid lines in the diagram.

Consider the LP (left pedal) reactor, in Fig. 2, which is used to control the brakes. We assume that updates from the pedal are reported via an interrupt, which enables an interrupt service routine (ISR) that schedules an internal action. This internal action triggers a reaction that sets the value of the angle and on/off output ports. In order to avoid overwhelming the system, we assume that the interrupts have a minimum interarrival time. The values angle and on/off, if present, are propagated to BC (brake controller) and EC (engine controller), respectively. Notice that LP only has to set on/off at times that the pedal changes from being released to pressed and vice versa. This prevents the system from being burdened with handling insignificant events.

Let us now consider the EC reactor, which has three reactions. We interpret the number associated with each reaction as its execution priority; this way, we obtain an execution order in case both on/off and angle are present at the same logical time. The first reaction, EC.1, is triggered by on/off; it updates the state of the reactor to reflect that the brake pedal is currently pressed and sets the value of torque to zero. The second reaction is triggered by the angle input; it checks whether the brakes are applied, and if not, sets the torque output. The third and last reaction sets the value of check to trigger a reaction in the RP (right pedal) reactor, which represents the accelerator pedal. It only sets the value of check, however, if the brake pedal is known not to be pressed. This reaction is triggered by an action, which, in a naive implementation, could arrive at regularly spaced intervals. The frequency of these periodic actions, however, would have to match the maximum number of rotations per second of the crankshaft, which, under normal driving conditions, is rarely realized. Therefore, it would be more efficient to trigger the second reaction with variable intervals depending on the number of revolutions of the crank shaft.

The second reaction of RP is triggered by the check input and sets in motion some asynchronous activity that senses the angle of the accelerator pedal and writes it to the reactor's shared state. Before concluding the second reaction, an action is scheduled at the current time plus a *delay* of 2 ms, to give the ADC ample time to report its reading. The first reaction is triggered by this action and, in turn, triggers the second reaction in EC.

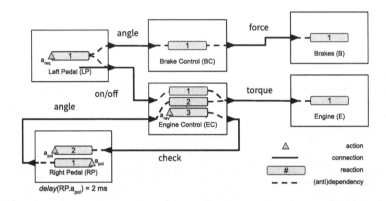

Fig. 2. Reactor that implements a simplified power train control module

The design assures that if the accelerator pedal is stuck or reports faulty readings, the car will still slow down in response to the break pedal being pressed; the engine is never allowed to apply torque when the brakes are applied. Note that this approach does not attempt to artificially eliminate nondeterminism that is intrinsic to the physical realization of the system; actions can occur sporadically, but the logic constituted by reactions *is* deterministic, and therefore, testable. The behavior of the system is relatively easy to reason about, and it is straightforward to formulate meaningful test cases to build confidence in the correctness of the implementation of the reactions.

Real-Time Constraints. In the example in Fig. 2, the first reaction of LP is triggered by an interaction with the environment; a process that reports a sensor value. The scheduling of physical action a_{req} effectively maps physical time to logical time. The event output by LP is timestamped with logical time t equal to physical time T. We can now impose a *deadline*[2] on the triggering of a reaction in downstream reactor B of, say, 5 ms. This means that the force input of the brakes must be observed before or when T reaches $t + 5$ ms. In other words, the deadline specifies a maximum end-to-end delay in physical time between the reaction that reports the braking and the reaction that applies the brakes. The execution engine can therefore, by comparing logical timestamps with physical time, check for deadline violations at run time. Moreover, the presence of the

---

[2] Deadlines are omitted from the formalization in Sect. 3 and are left as future work.

deadline enables Earliest Deadline First (EDF) scheduling. In combination with precision-timed hardware and Worst-Case Execution Time (WCET) analysis, static guarantees could be obtained with regard to timing of reactions [35,45].

3   Formalization

In this section we formalize the concept of reactors. Some of the central concepts we will introduce are described by lists of elements. In order to simplify notation, we will use the symbol for the element of a list to also denote a function that maps the list to the element corresponding to that symbol. For example, if x is defined as the list $x = (a, b)$, we reuse the symbols a and b to be functions that map x to its elements a and b, respectively. Thus, we will commonly use the notation $a(x)$, where x is a list, and a is the symbol of one of the elements in that list.

First, we need to introduce some notation. Let Σ be a set. We refer to the elements of Σ as *identifiers*. We will use identifiers to uniquely refer to various objects to be introduced. There is no need to further define the structure of identifiers.

Let $\mathfrak{V}$ be a set, which we refer to as the *set of values*. This set represents the data values exchanged between or within reactors. Similarly, we do not assume any structure in the values, i.e., reactors are untyped. We define one distinguished element in the value set: $\varepsilon \in \mathfrak{V}$ is called the *absent value*.

As motivated in Sect. 2, a reactor is a composite of various objects. Some of these objects have roles which are tightly intertwined with the model of computation in which reactors operate. This model of computation is the *discrete event* model. In discrete event systems, the execution of a program occurs at given *tags*. These tags belong to a denumerable and totally ordered set.

3.1   Notions of Time

Our model uses a superdense representation of time (see [40,47]). Each tag is denoted by a pair, of which the first element is a *time value*—an integer representation of time in some predefined unit (e.g., milliseconds or nanoseconds)—and the second element denotes a *microstep index*. Two events are logically simultaneous if and only if their tags are equal. Formally, the set of tags, $\mathbb{T}$ of the reactor execution model is $\mathbb{T} = \mathbb{N}^2$, where $\mathbb{N}$ is the set of natural numbers. We define a total order on $\mathbb{T}$ lexicographically: if $(a, b), (a', b') \in \mathbb{T}$, we say that $(a, b) < (a', b')$ if and only if $(a < a') \vee (a = a' \wedge b < b')$. $\mathbb{T}$ has an addition operation that operates element-wise. Using an integer representation for time ensures that addition is associative, which is not necessarily the case when using floating-point representations [17]. We define a function TIMEVAL on tags which extracts the time value: let $(a, b) \in \mathbb{T}$, then TIMEVAL $((a, b)) = a$.

Events are used to exchange messages between reactors.

Definition 1 (Event). *An event e is defined as a list $e = (\mathfrak{t}, \mathfrak{v}, \mathfrak{g})$, where $\mathfrak{t} \in \Sigma$ is called the **event trigger**, $\mathfrak{v} \in \mathfrak{V}$ the **trigger value**, and $\mathfrak{g} \in \mathbb{T}$ the **event tag**.*

Events inherit an order from their tags. If e and e' are events, we say that $e < e'$ if and only if $\mathfrak{g}(e) < \mathfrak{g}(e')$.

Definition 2 (Event queue). *We define the **event queue** $\mathcal{Q}_E$ as a set of events ordered by their tags.*

This model uses two distinct notions of time: *logical time* and *physical time*.

Definition 3 (Logical time). *Logical time is a monotonically increasing sequence of tags of the form (a, b), where a is referred to as the **time value** and to b as the **microstep index**.*

Definition 4 (Physical time). *Physical time refers to a time value that is obtained from a clock on the execution platform.*

Remark 1 (Time units). The time values of logical time and physical time must be given in some unit of measurement. In order to meaningfully relate two time values, their units must be the same. Whenever we omit units in expressions that relate time values, we simply assume the units match. Microstep indices, on the other hand, are unitless.

3.2   Reactors

We now proceed to define reactors. Note that reactors contain *reactions* and *mutations*. We first discuss reactors to clarify how the domain of constituents of a reaction or mutation is determined by the containing reactor.

Definition 5 (Priority set). *Let $\mathbb{Z}$ be the set of integer numbers, $\mathbb{Z}^+$ the set of integers larger than zero, $\mathbb{Z}^-$ the set of integers smaller than zero, and $*$ a symbol which is not an integer. The priority set, $\mathcal{P}$, is given by $\mathcal{P} = \mathbb{Z}^- \cup \mathbb{Z}^+ \cup \{*\}$. The set $\mathcal{P}$ has a partial order given by the order in $\mathbb{Z}$ extended with $* \leq *$ and $p < *$ for all $p \in \mathbb{Z}^-$.*

The use of $*$ is to allow particular reactions to be executed in parallel if they do not touch the reactor's state. For instance, reactions n_0, n_5, and n_6 in Fig. 1 would qualify as such if their only purpose is to relay values between ports.

Definition 6 (Action). *An action is a list $a = (x, d, \mathfrak{o})$, where $x \in \Sigma$ is the **action identifier**, $d \in \mathbb{N}$ is the **delay** of the action, and $\mathfrak{o} \in \mathfrak{O}$ is the **origin** of the action. We use the notation $d(x)$ to refer to the delay of a, and $\mathfrak{o}(x)$ to refer to its origin. As we will see, actions belong to exactly one reactor. If A is a set of actions, we will also let $x(A)$ denote the set of identifiers of each action in A.*

When a reaction or mutation schedules an event for an action, this event will have a tag that includes the action delay plus either the current logical time or the current physical time, depending on whether the action's origin is *logical* or *physical*, respectively. This is described in more detail in Algorithm 2 in Sect. 3.5.

Definition 7 (Reactor). *A reactor* r *is a list* $r = (I, O, A, S, \mathcal{N}, \mathcal{M}, \mathcal{R}, \mathcal{G},$ $P, \bullet, \diamond)$, *where*

1. $I \subseteq \Sigma$ *is a set of* ***inputs***,
2. $O \subseteq \Sigma$ *a set of* ***outputs***,
3. $A \subseteq \Sigma \times \mathbb{N} \times \mathfrak{O}$ *a set of* ***actions***,
4. $S \subseteq \Sigma$ *a set of* ***state variables***,
5. $\mathcal{N}$ *a set of* ***reactions***,
6. $\mathcal{M}$ *a set of* ***mutations***,
7. $\mathcal{R}$ *a set of* ***contained reactors***,
8. $\mathcal{G} \subseteq \left(\bigcup_{r \in \mathcal{R}} O(r) \right) \times \left(\bigcup_{r \in \mathcal{R}} I(r) \right)$ *a* ***topology graph***,
9. $P : \mathcal{N} \cup \mathcal{M} \to \mathcal{P}$ *the* ***priority function***, *and*
10. $\bullet, \diamond \in A(r)$ *actions called* ***initialization*** *and* ***termination***, *respectively*.

Given two reactors r *and* r', *the sets* $I(r)$, $O(r)$, $x(A(r))$, $S(r)$, $I(r')$, $O(r')$, $x(A(r'))$, *and* $S(r')$ *are all pairwise disjoint. Similarly, the sets* $\mathcal{R}(r)$ *and* $\mathcal{R}(r')$ *are disjoint, and so are the sets* $\mathcal{N}(r)$ *and* $\mathcal{N}(r')$ *and* $\mathcal{M}(r)$ *and* $\mathcal{M}(r')$.

Remark 2 (Hierarchy). We define an *atomic* reactor as above, with an empty contained reactor set and empty topology graph, and we call these degree-0 reactors. Then, for $n \geq 1$ we define a reactor of degree n as a reactor with a set $\mathcal{R}$ of reactors of degree at most $n - 1$ and a corresponding topology set. Moreover, the reactor set of a degree-n reactor contains at least one reactor of degree $n - 1$.

Reactors use their inputs and outputs to communicate with other reactors. Reactions and mutations can schedule events for actions in order to trigger the execution of other reactions or mutations contained in the same reactor.

Reactors can be built up hierarchically. As such, the reactor set lists the reactors contained by a reactor. The reaction and mutation sets list the reactions and mutations, respectively, contained by a reactor. The topology graph specifies how the reactors contained in a reactor are connected to each other. This graph consists of pairs (o, i), where o and i are the output and input of two reactors, respectively. If $(o, i), (o', i')$, are two different elements of $\mathcal{G}$, then $i \neq i'$; that is, inputs are connected to at most one output. The priority function plays a role in the concurrent execution of reactions and mutations and is discussed in Sect. 3.8. Initialization and termination actions are discussed in Sect. 3.7.

Let us consider the constituents of the reactor shown in Fig. 1: $I = \{i_i\}_{i=0}^2$, $O = \{o_i\}_{i=0}^3$, $A = \{a_i\}_{i=0}^1 \cup \{\bullet, \diamond\}$, $\mathcal{N} = \{n_i\}_{i=0}^6$, $\mathcal{M} = \{m_i\}_{i=0}^k$, and $\mathcal{R} = \{r_i\}_{i=0}^2$. The priorities of the reactions and mutations shown in the figure are equal to their respective subindices. The topology graph is the set of pairs which indicate connections from the outputs to the inputs of contained reactors. In the figure, these pairs are $(r_0.o_0, r_1.i_0)$ and $(r_0.o_0, r_2.i_0)$.

3.3   Reactions

We now discuss the elements that carry out computation in the reactor model. These are called reactions. First, we define a function to navigate the reactor hierarchy:

Definition 8 (Container function). *The container function C maps a reactor r to the reactor which contains it. The function returns $\top$ (pronounced "top") if no reactor contains r. Since the sets $\mathcal{R}(r), \mathcal{R}(r')$ are disjoint for $r \neq r'$, C is well-defined. Let r be a reactor. If $C(r) = \top$, we say that r is **top-level**. We also define the container function for reactions and mutations: let n be a reaction; then $C(n)$ yields the reactor r such that $n \in \mathcal{N}(r)$. The same applies to mutations. Finally, we define the container function for inputs, outputs, and action identifiers: let i, o, and a be an input, output, and action, respectively, of three reactors r, r', and r''. Then $C(i) = r$ if and only if $i \in I(r)$, $C(o) = r'$ if and only if $o \in O(r')$, and $C(x(a)) = r''$ if and only if $a \in A(r'')$. Similarly, the function C is well-defined here since all the relevant sets are pairwise disjoint for two distinct reactors.*

With this function in place, we state the definitions of reactions:

Definition 9 (Reaction). *A reaction n is defined as $n = (D, \mathcal{T}, B, D^\vee, H)$, where*

1. *$D \subseteq I(C(n)) \cup \bigcup_{r \in \mathcal{R}(C(n))} O(r)$ is a set of **dependencies**, identifiers on which the reaction depends in order to execute;*
2. *$\mathcal{T} \subseteq D \cup x(A(C(n)))$ is a set of **triggers**, identifiers whose events cause the execution of the reaction's body;*
3. *B is the **body** of the reaction (e.g., executable code);*
4. *$D^\vee \subseteq O(C(n)) \cup \bigcup_{r \in \mathcal{R}(C(n))} I(r)$ is the set of **antidependencies**, identifiers for which the reaction can produce events at the current logical time; and*
5. *$H \subseteq x(A(C(n)))$ is the set of **schedulable actions**, actions for which n can generate events.*

3.4 Mutations

Now we introduce the concept of a mutation. These are used to modify the internal structure of a reactor by connecting and disconnecting ports. Ports that a mutation declares as dependencies are the only sources that it can establish connections from. Ports that it declares as antidependencies are the only destinations that it can establish connections to. While mutations give reactors the ability to dynamically reconfigure their internal topology, the above constraints prevent a reactor from introducing dependencies between its ports of which its container is not already aware.

Definition 10 (Mutation). *A mutation m is defined as $m = (D, \mathcal{T}, B, D^\vee, H)$, where*

1. *$D \subseteq I(C(m))$ is a set of **dependencies**, identifiers on which the mutation depends in order to execute, and the only sources from which the mutation can establish connections;*
2. *$\mathcal{T} \subseteq D \cup x(A(C(m)))$ is a set of **triggers**, identifiers whose events cause the execution of the mutation's body;*

3. B is the **body** of the mutation (i.e., executable code);
4. $D^\vee \subseteq O(C(m)) \cup \bigcup_{r \in \mathcal{R}(C(m))} I(r)$ is the set of **antidependencies**, identifiers for which the mutation can produce events at the current logical time, and the only destinations to which the mutation can establish connections; and
5. $H \subseteq x(A(C(m))) \cup \bigcup_{r \in \mathcal{R}(C(m))} x(\{\bullet(r), \diamond(r)\})$ is the set of **schedulable actions**, actions for which m can generate events.

Reactions and mutations differ as follows:

- Mutations can modify the reactor topology; reactions cannot.
- A mutation can schedule initialization and termination actions for reactors that its container contains.
- The outputs of contained reactors are allowed in the dependencies of a reaction, but not in the dependencies of a mutation. This is important because, in contrast to reactions, mutations have the capability of scheduling initialization actions, which do not incur a microstep delay. Disallowing outputs of contained reactors rules out the introduction of undetectable causality loops.

Appendix A summarizes all definitions we introduce.

3.5 Event Generation

We will find it convenient to have available functions that return the reactions which depend on the given input, and which are antidependent on the given output. We find no reason to introduce new notation. Thus, we define the maps

$$\mathcal{N}(i) = \{n \in \mathcal{N}(C(i)) \mid i \in D(n)\} \text{ and}$$
$$\mathcal{N}(o) = \{n \in \mathcal{N}(C(o)) \mid o \in D^\vee(n)\}.$$

We define $\mathcal{M}(i)$ and $\mathcal{M}(o)$ for mutations in a similar manner. Moreover, given an identifier t, we will identify the reactions and mutations that are triggered by t. We define

$$\mathcal{T}(t) = \{k \in \mathcal{N}(C(t)) \cup \mathcal{M}(C(t)) \mid t \in \mathcal{T}(k)\}.$$

We now discuss how events are created. The body of a reaction is a container for application code in the reactor framework. Let n be a reaction. Then the body $B(n)$ of this reaction is allowed to run two functions that affect the execution environment: SCHEDULE and SET.

A reaction can only execute SET on its antidependencies. The execution of SET in the body of a reaction propagates the set value to downstream ports and adds triggered reactions to $\mathcal{Q}_R$, the set of reactions to be executed at the current logical time. SET is shown in Algorithm 1.

A reaction can only call SCHEDULE on its set of schedulable actions. The event created on a call to schedule is shown in Algorithm 2. The algorithm shows that reactions can add an additional delay to the delay of a schedulable action

Algorithm 1. Propagate values to downstream ports

1: **procedure** SET(port, value)
2:      WRITEVALUE(port, value)
3:      reactionsAndMutations ← $\mathcal{T}$(port)
4:      $r \leftarrow C(C(\text{port}))$
5:      topology ← $\mathcal{G}(r)$
6:      **for all** $(o, i) \in$ topology **do**
7:          **if** port $= o$ **then**
8:              WRITEVALUE(i, value)
9:              reactionsAndMutations ← reactionsAndMutations $\cup$ $\mathcal{T}(i)$
10:         **end if**
11:     **end for**
12:     $\mathcal{Q}_R \leftarrow \mathcal{Q}_R \cup$ reactionsAndMutations
13: **end procedure**

---

upon scheduling. Note also that SCHEDULE can be called synchronously, from a reaction, but also asynchronously, from another thread of execution. Mutual exclusion between concurrent calls to SCHEDULE is achieved via locking. The same mutex is also used in NEXT, the function that drives the execution of triggered reactions (see Sect. 3.8). The mutex protects the event queue $\mathcal{Q}_E$, as well as the variable t that holds the current logical time, from data races.

Algorithm 2. Schedule an action

1: **procedure** SCHEDULE(a, additionalDelay, value)
2:      interval ← $d(a)$ + additionalDelay
3:      LOCK(mutex)   ▷ Mutual exclusivity with concurrent SCHEDULE and NEXT
4:      **if** $\mathfrak{o}(a) =$ Physical **then**
5:          tag ← (PHYSICALTIME() + interval, 0)
6:      **else**
7:          **if** interval $= 0$ **and** $a \neq \bullet(C(x(a)))$ **then**
8:              tag ← LOGICALTIME() + (0, 1)   ▷ Add microstep delay
9:          **else**
10:             tag ← (TIMEVAL(LOGICALTIME()), 0) + (interval, 0)
11:         **end if**
12:     **end if**
13:     $e \leftarrow (x(a), \text{value}, \text{tag})$
14:     $\mathcal{Q}_E \leftarrow \mathcal{Q}_E \setminus \{e' \in \mathcal{Q}_E \mid \mathfrak{t}(e') = \mathfrak{t}(e) \wedge \mathfrak{g}(e') = \mathfrak{g}(e)\}$ ▷ Overwrite if already set
15:     $\mathcal{Q}_E \leftarrow \mathcal{Q}_E \cup \{e\}$
16:     UNLOCK(mutex)   ▷ Release mutex
17: **end procedure**

3.6   Dependencies

During the execution of a reactor, there may be multiple events scheduled at the same logical time. These events may trigger multiple reactions and mutations.

In what order can these reactions and mutations execute? We arrange reactions in a partial order based on their dependencies and priority with respect to other reactions within a reactor. Let k and k' be mutations or reactions. We say that $k \prec k'$ if k' has a dependency on an antidependency of k or if $C(k) = C(k') \wedge (P(k) < P(k'))$.

The analysis of dependencies excludes actions because actions (with exception of •) are always scheduled at least one microstep time unit into the future.

Example: The dependency graph obtained from our example in Fig. 2 is shown in Fig. 3. Notice that EC.1 ← EC.2 ← EC.3 and RP.1 ← RP.2 are due to reaction priority; the other edges in the graph are due to dependencies and antidependencies on ports and the connections between those ports.

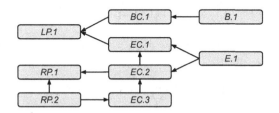

Fig. 3. Dependency graph implied by the reactor topology in Fig. 2

Definition 11 (Graph function). *Let r be a reactor. The graph function $\gamma(r)$ returns a graph whose vertices are all reactions and mutations contained in the hierarchy of r and whose directed edges denote dependencies between vertices. The graph function is computed according to Algorithm 3.*

These are the steps of the algorithm:

- L2. Make the vertices and edges of the dependency graphs of the constituent reactors of r part of the graph of r. We define the union of graphs to operate element-wise (i.e., on the vertex sets and edge sets).
- L3. Make the mutations and reactions of r vertices of the graph.
- L4. Use the topology to connect the reactions and mutations of contained reactors.
- L5–6. Connect the reactions of r to the reactions and mutations of the constituent reactors of r. Note that the functions $\mathcal{N}$ and $\mathcal{M}$, when applied to inputs and outputs, return the reactions and mutations which list that input as a dependency or the reactions and mutations that list that output as an antidependency.
- L7. For all reactions and mutations of this reactor, we add an edge to the graph between two reactions or mutations when the priority of one is smaller than the priority of the other.
- L8. Make all reactions and mutations of the contained reactors dependent on the mutations of the container reactor. This is necessary because mutations can change the operation of the container reactor and can schedule the initialization action of the contained reactors with zero delay.

After computing the dependency graph using Algorithm 3, the graph must be checked for directed cycles. Cyclic dependency graphs must be rejected, as they represent algebraic loops; we do not handle them.

Algorithm 3. Construct dependency graph

1: **procedure** $\gamma(r)$
2:     $(V, E) \leftarrow \bigcup_{r' \in \mathcal{R}(r)} \gamma(r')$
3:     $V \leftarrow V \cup \mathcal{N}(r) \cup \mathcal{M}(r)$
4:     $E \leftarrow E \cup \bigcup_{(o,i) \in \mathcal{G}(r)} (\mathcal{N}(i) \cup \mathcal{M}(i)) \times (\mathcal{N}(o) \cup \mathcal{M}(o))$
5:     $E \leftarrow E \cup \bigcup_{\substack{n \in \mathcal{N}(r) \\ i \in D^{\vee}(n) \backslash O(r)}} (\mathcal{N}(i) \cup \mathcal{M}(i)) \times \{n\}$
6:     $E \leftarrow E \cup \bigcup_{\substack{n \in \mathcal{N}(r) \\ o \in D(n) \backslash I(r)}} \{n\} \times (\mathcal{N}(o) \cup \mathcal{M}(o))$
7:     $E \leftarrow E \cup \bigcup_{k,k' \in \mathcal{N}(r) \cup \mathcal{M}(r)} \{(k, k') \mid P(k') < P(k)\}$
8:     $E \leftarrow E \cup \left(\bigcup_{r' \in \mathcal{R}(r)} \mathcal{N}(r') \cup \mathcal{M}(r') \right) \times \mathcal{M}(r)$
9:     **return** (V, E)
10: **end procedure**

3.7   Initialization and Termination

All reactors have a special initialization action •. At the start of executing a reactor program, the execution environment generates one event at tag $(T, 0)$ for the initialization action of the top-level reactor. Every reactor contains a mutation that is triggered by that reactor's initialization action; this mutation initializes that reactor and schedules an event with no microstep delay on the initialization actions of all reactors that its container reactor contains.

Reactors also have a special action ◇, called termination. Reactors have the ability to schedule • and ◇ actions of their contained reactors. Upon processing a termination action (which implies the need for the existence of a reaction or mutation which is triggered by the termination action), a reactor can forward that action to its contained reactors in order for the hierarchy to terminate safely. The ◇ action is scheduled *with* a microstep delay, to allow any ongoing reactions to conclude before termination is set into motion.

3.8   Execution

The execution of reactors is based on a discrete-event model of computation that guarantees determinacy, a property that can be proven by showing the existence of unique fixed points over generalized metric spaces given that the dependency graph that governs the execution (see Sect. 3.6) contains no directed cycles [43,

---

Algorithm 4. Process events for the next tag

1: **procedure** NEXT()
2:      LOCK(mutex)   ▷ Mutual exclusivity with concurrent SCHEDULE
3:      **if** $\mathcal{Q}_E = \emptyset$ **then return**
4:      **end if**
5:      **while** $True$ **do**
6:          $T \leftarrow$ PHYSICALTIME()
7:          $t_{\text{next}} \leftarrow \mathfrak{g}(\text{PEEK}(\mathcal{Q}_E))$ ▷ Obtain the tag of the first-in-line event
8:          **if** $T \geq t_{\text{next}}$ **then**
9:              **break**
10:         **else**   ▷ Wait until $\mathcal{Q}_E$ changes or physical time matches tag
11:             TIMEDWAITFOREVENTQUEUECHANGE(TIMEVAL(t_{next}))
12:         **end if**
13:     **end while**
14:     $t \leftarrow t_{\text{next}}$ ▷ Advance logical time
15:     CLEARALL()   ▷ Clear all inputs, outputs, actions
16:     $\mathcal{Q}_R, \text{doneSet}, \text{execSet} \leftarrow \emptyset, \emptyset, \emptyset$
17:     $\mathcal{E} \leftarrow \{e \in \mathcal{Q}_E \mid \mathfrak{g}(e) = t\}$ ▷ Gather events for current time t
18:     $\mathcal{Q}_E \leftarrow \mathcal{Q}_E \setminus \mathcal{E}$
19:     UNLOCK(mutex)   ▷ Release mutex
20:     **for all** $e \in \mathcal{E}$ **do**
21:         WRITEVALUE($\mathfrak{t}(e)$, $\mathfrak{v}(e)$)   ▷ Set the value associated with identifier $\mathfrak{t}(e)$
22:     **end for**
23:     $\mathcal{Q}_R \leftarrow \bigcup_{e \in \mathcal{E}} \mathcal{T}(\mathfrak{t}(e))$ ▷ Reactions and mutations triggered by events
24:     **repeat**
25:         **for all** $k \in \text{execSet}$ **do**
26:             **if** ISDONE(k) **then**   ▷ Check whether executing element is done
27:                 $\text{doneSet} \leftarrow \text{doneSet} \cup \{k\}$
28:                 $\text{execSet} \leftarrow \text{execSet} \setminus \{k\}$
29:             **end if**
30:         **end for**
31:         **if** $\mathcal{Q}_R \neq \emptyset$ **then**   ▷ Execute something, if possible
32:             **if** THREADISAVAILABLE() **then**
33:                 $P \leftarrow \mathcal{Q}_R \cup \text{execSet}$
34:                 $\text{readyForExec} \leftarrow \{p \in P \mid \nexists p' \in P.\ p' < p\}$
35:                 $\text{readyForExec} \leftarrow \text{readyForExec} \setminus \text{execSet}$
36:                 **if** $\text{readyForExec} \neq \emptyset$ **then**
37:                     $k \leftarrow$ SELECT(readyForExec)
38:                     $\text{execSet}, \mathcal{Q}_R \leftarrow \text{execSet} \cup \{k\}, \mathcal{Q}_R \setminus \{k\}$
39:                     RUNINTHREAD(k)
40:                 **else**
41:                     WAITUNTILNUMBEROFIDLETHREADSHASINCREASED()
42:                 **end if**
43:             **else**
44:                 WAITUNTILTHREADHASBECOMEAVAILABLE()
45:             **end if**
46:         **else**
47:             **if** $\text{execSet} \neq \emptyset$ **then**
48:                 WAITUNTILNUMBEROFIDLETHREADSHASINCREASED()
49:             **end if**
50:         **end if**
51:     **until** $\mathcal{Q}_R \cup \text{execSet} = \emptyset$
52: **end procedure**

48]. The execution environment keeps a notion of a global event queue $\mathcal{Q}_E$ that tracks events scheduled to occur in the future, and of a reaction queue $\mathcal{Q}_R$ that sorts reactions to be executed at the current logical time by dependency. While the event loop can be implemented in a single thread, the algorithms discussed in this section assume a multi-threaded implementation. A single mutex lock is used to guarantee thread-safe operation on the only two shared data structures: t and $\mathcal{Q}_E$. A major advantage of this design is that the use of a single lock ensures deadlock-freedom. At the beginning of execution, logical time starts at a value of $t = (T, 0)$, and it can only increase as execution progresses. Logical time increases when there are no further reactions to be executed and there are one or more events in $\mathcal{Q}_E$ with a tag greater that has a time value greater than or equal to the current physical time T.

Algorithm 4 shows how the code of reactions and mutations is executed. The algorithm proceeds as follows:

- L5–13. Determine what the next logical time should be, based on the event that is currently on top of $\mathcal{Q}_E$, and wait for physical time to match the time value of the tag. The procedure TIMEDWAITFOREVENTQUEUECHANGE blocks until either the event queue was modified or the specified physical time was reached, whichever comes first. TIMEDWAITFOREVENTQUEUECHANGE is expected to release the mutex and reacquire it after receiving a signal that an event has been added to $\mathcal{Q}_E$. This allows concurrent invocations of SCHEDULE to proceed while NEXT is waiting. In an implementation based on POSIX threads, `pthread_cond_timedwait` could be used for this.
- L14. Advance logical time to match the smallest tag currently in $\mathcal{Q}_E$.
- L15. Set the values of all ports and actions to ε.
- L17. Obtain events to process at the current logical time.
- L19. Release the mutex, allowing concurrent calls to SCHEDULE to proceed.
- L20–22. Set triggers according to the value of the event.
- L23. Obtain all reactions and mutations triggered by any of the events with a tag equal to the current logical time and insert them into $\mathcal{Q}_R$.
- L24–30. If a reaction or mutation that has been under execution is done, move that reaction or mutation to doneSet and remove it from execSet.
- L32–39. The routine THREADISAVAILABLE reports whether the runtime system has a thread available for executing the selected reaction of mutation. If this is the case, on L34–35, select one reaction or mutation from the set of minimal elements of items which are either under execution or pending, excepting, naturally, the set of executing reactions or mutations. It is ensured that no reaction or mutation ends up executing concurrently with (or after) any reaction or mutation that depends on it. Note that the computation of the minimal elements uses the order on reactions and mutations defined in Sect. 3.6.
- L41. If all pending tasks have dependencies on currently-executing tasks, wait until one of the currently-executing tasks concludes, freeing up a thread. With POSIX threads, WAITUNTILNUMBEROFIDLETHREADSHASINCREASED could be implemented using `pthread_cond_wait`.

- L44. If there are pending tasks, but the runtime system does not have resources to accept a new task, wait until it can accept a new task. Again, `pthread_cond_wait` could be used to implement the wait.
- L48. If there are no pending tasks, but there are tasks currently in execution, wait until at least one of the tasks under execution finishes.
- L51. We iterate the loop L24–51 until there remain no reactions or mutations to be executed, and there are none currently under execution.

4   Distributed Execution of Reactors

We will now describe how reactor programs are executed when distributed over multiple nodes communicating over network. Many of the concepts around distributed execution have been introduced in prior work on Ptides [62] and are applied to reactors here. We can use Ptides to preserve the deterministic semantics of reactors across distributed reactor programs, which requires us to make some assumptions about our system. Each node in the distributed system maintains its own event queue and contains a clock that monitors and keeps track of the passing of physical time. The clocks are synchronized across nodes with a known bound E on the clock synchronization error. Sending messages between distributed nodes takes time, but we assume a known upper bound on the network delay L between any two nodes in the network.

Let us consider the example in Fig. 2 and assume the reactors are distributed across multiple engine control units (ECUs). The reactor network is split up into multiple, distributed reactor networks. While automotive networks often do have provisions for deterministic communication, many networks do not guarantee in-order processing of messages, thus potentially causing the receipt of messages out of order. We can also envision an extension of this system with car-to-car communication to enable safe lane-switching, platooning, intersection management, or emergency slow down. Networks used for such communication are typically not giving any guarantees on the order of transfer of messages.

Similar to sensing and actuation wrapped in reactions, network communication is performed in the body of reactions. A network sending reaction must combine the event value together with the current logical time t and implement the network transmission. To ensure timely sending of network messages, a deadline on the network sending the reaction is required. Note that a deadline > 0 increases the delay on a path between sensors and actuators.

Just like a network sending a reaction, a reaction receiving a message from the network implements network communication in the body of the reaction. We assume an interrupt upon receipt of the network that triggers an action, which, in turn, triggers the network receiving reaction. This reaction unpacks the timestamp t_m in the message and uses it to determine when it is safe to process the message. A network receiver in this programming model must ensure that messages are forwarded to other reactors in logical timestamp order. A network receiver that receives a message m at physical time T with timestamp t_m cannot release the message until $t_m + E + L$ to ensure that no other messages are in the network with an earlier timestamp. When physical time matches or exceeds $t_m + E + L$, the message is safe to process. A network receiving reaction will therefore schedule an action a with `additionalDelay` $= t_m + E + L - t_c$, where t_c is the current logical time on the node. A reaction triggered by a will release the message into the local reactor program.

A violation of the assumptions of clock synchronization error E or network delay L is detected if a network receiver gets a message with timestamp t at physical time T with $T > t + E + L$ (see Fig. 4). Once such an error is detected, the mitigation is application dependent, ranging from ignoring such erroneous network messages to an immediate stop of the program. While we do not discuss strategies for dealing with such an error, we want to stress that the strength of this programming model is in the ability to detect such errors.

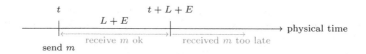

Fig. 4. Message exchange between distributed reactors

By relating physical time to logical time at sensors, actuators and network interfaces, deterministic behavior is implemented without the need for a central coordinator. The analysis of whether a distributed reactor program can be implemented on a given set of nodes is performed for each node individually, by treating network interfaces like sensors and actuators.

5   Related Work

The Actor model by Hewitt and Agha [1,31] can be considered the basis for reactors. In it, actors execute concurrently and communicate via asynchronously passed messages, with no guarantees on the order or timing of message arrival. Implementations can be found in several modern languages and software libraries, most notably Erlang [2] by Ericsson, Scala actors [27], Akka [11], and Ray [50]. The messaging is address-based, and an actor can send messages to any other actor just using its address, including actors it creates. This flexibility can be leveraged to make distributed systems more resilient. Dataflow models [9,19,36] and process networks [32,37] can be seen as subsets of actor models with deterministic semantics that allows for explicit nondeterminism. Stemming from the embedded systems community, fixed graph topologies in these models enable improved static analysis and optimization [53].

The reactive programming community is concerned with developing event-driven and interactive applications using a wide array of software technologies ranging from programming frameworks like ReactiveX [49], Akka [11,60], and Reactors.IO [54] to language-level constructs like event loops [58], futures [5], promises [23], and reactive extensions [49]. For a more comprehensive survey on reactive programming techniques, see [4]. Writing software for reactive systems is difficult when the control flow of a program is driven by external events not under the control of the programmer, since the conventional imperative programming paradigm cannot be used. A major goal of reactive programming approaches is providing abstractions to express programs as reactions to external events (the observer pattern) and abstracting away the flow of time. Reactors have the same goal, but instead make use of synchronized time to coordinate such that their reactions yield predictable results.

In many reactive programming frameworks, futures are used to promote an imperative, sequential programming style, which avoids an explicit continuation passing style (also known as "callback hell" [20]), but makes it even more confusing for the programmer when nondeterminism rears its head. Actor-based frameworks like Ray and Akka rely heavily on futures. All this programmatic support makes reactive systems especially difficult to debug [6,59]. Another significant problem with some of the frameworks, libraries or language primitives commonly used in reactive programming is that they invite programmers to break the semantics of the underlying model, mixing models and losing many of the advantages obtained from them [57].

A different class of very successful models that reactors draw from are discrete-event models. These models, common in hardware modeling and simulation, have time as a core element in their semantics. Discrete events are, by design, the model of computation underlying reactors. From a language level, our language proposition is very close to hardware description languages, like Verilog or VHDL. Noteworthy is the comparison with SystemC [25,42], and the related SpecC [24], of which reactors are particularly reminiscent.

On the software engineering side, reactors are probably closest to synchronous languages and Functional Reactive Programming (FRP). In fact, the discrete event model can be seen as a special case of the model behind synchronous languages [41]. Synchronous languages like Esterel [8], Lustre [26] and SIGNAL [7] make time an essential part of the language design. Here, discrete time ticks are purely logical and not being synchronized to real, wall clock time. This is reminiscent of the signals used in FRP languages, like Fran [22] or FrTime [15], or more modern languages like Elm [18]. Unlike reactors, FRP works with pure functions and does not deal with side effects like reading sensors or operating actuators, which are essential in cyber-physical systems. In addition, these systems typically require a central runtime, which makes a dynamic, distributed execution infeasible.

The reactive extensions [13] to AmbientTalk make this actor-based language for mobile application design into one that is very similar to reactors. In particular, it stores a topology graph and can execute distributedly, albeit without avoiding glitches [4]. Myter et al. [51] show how to avoid glitches in reactive distributed systems using distributed dependency graphs and logical   clocks to timestamp values propagated through the system. Timestamps are used to decouple distributed components thus voiding the need for central coordinators and, in effect, implementing a *Globally Asynchronous, Locally Synchronous* (GALS) [14] system. Myter *et al.* propose an execution runtime which guarantees that a distributed reactive system eventually reaches a consistent state. Our work shares several key ideas with this approach, such as the use of logical time and the construction of dependency graphs to circumvent the need for central coordination, although modeling and implementations choices differ considerably. In addition, our work is based on ideas presented in Ptides [62], where logical time is carefully linked to a notion of physical time that is assumed to be synchronized across nodes with a known error tolerance. This allows for an always (not just eventual) consistent state. In addition, we can now reason about end-to-end delays and timing violations, which can help detect errors in the assumptions about the system or the execution behavior of a system.

6   Conclusions

Reactors are software components that borrow concepts from actors, dataflow models, synchronous-reactive models, discrete event systems, object-oriented programming, and reactive programming. They promote modularity through the use of ports, use hierarchy to preserve locality of causality effects, and provide a clean interface between asynchronous tasks and reactive programs without compromising the ability to obtain deterministic reactions to sporadic inputs. This makes reactors particularly well suited as a programming model for implementing cyber-physical systems, and more broadly, reactive systems that are expected to deliver predictable, analyzable, and testable behavior.

We have shown how the reactor execution model takes advantage of concurrency that is naturally exposed in reactor programs; we leave performance benchmarks, as well as analyses of different scheduling policies and a more thorough discussion of deadlines and runtime mutations as future work. We are currently developing a compiler tool chain that takes reactor definitions and compositions written in the Lingua Franca meta-language and transforms them into executable target code. Among features we intend to develop for this language are declarative primitives for the orchestration of distributed reactor programs, runtime mutations based on state machines, and real-time scheduling analysis for precision-timed hardware platforms like Patmos [56] and FlexPRET [63].

Acknowledgement. The authors thank the anonymous reviewers for their perceptive feedback on an earlier version of this paper.

A   Summary of the Reactor model

Execution environment objects	
Set of identifiers	Σ (an abstract set)
Set of values	$\mathfrak{V}$ (an abstract set)
Absent value	$\varepsilon \in \mathfrak{V}$
Set of priorities	$\mathcal{P} = \mathbb{Z}^- \cup \mathbb{Z}^+ \cup \{*\}$
Event queue	$\mathcal{Q}_E$
Reaction queue	$\mathcal{Q}_R$
Logical time	t
Physical time	T
Set of tags	$\mathbb{T} = \mathbb{N}^2$
Set of origins	$\mathfrak{O} = \{\text{Logical}, \text{Physical}\}$
Reactors	
Reactor instance	$r = (I, O, A, S, \mathcal{N}, \mathcal{M}, \mathcal{R}, \mathcal{G}, P, \bullet, \diamond)$
Set of input ports for r	$I(r) \subseteq \Sigma$
Set of output ports for r	$O(r) \subseteq \Sigma$
Set of actions for r	$A(r) \subseteq \Sigma \times \mathbb{N} \times \mathfrak{O}$
Initialization action for r	$\bullet(r) \in A(r)$
Termination action for r	$\diamond(r) \in A(r)$
Set of state identifiers for r	$S(r) \subseteq \Sigma$
Set of reactions contained in r	$\mathcal{N}(r)$
Set of mutations contained in r	$\mathcal{M}(r)$
Set of contained reactors of r	$\mathcal{R}(r)$
Topology of reactors in $\mathcal{R}(r)$	$\mathcal{G}(r) \subseteq$
	$\left(\bigcup_{r' \in \mathcal{R}(r)} O(r') \right) \times \left(\bigcup_{r' \in \mathcal{R}(r)} I(r') \right)$
Priority function	$P : \mathcal{N} \cup \mathcal{M} \to \mathcal{P}$
Reactor containing reactor r	$C(r)$
Inputs and outputs	
Input, output instance	$i, o \in \Sigma$
Reactions dependent on $i \in I(r)$	$\mathcal{N}(i) = \{n \in \mathcal{N}(C(i)) \mid i \in D(n)\}$
Reactions antidependent on $o \in O(r)$	$\mathcal{N}(o) = \{n \in \mathcal{N}(C(o)) \mid o \in D^\vee(n)\}$
Actions	
Action instance	$a = (x, d, \mathfrak{o})$
Action identifier	$x \in \Sigma$
Action delay	$d \in \mathbb{T}$
Action origin	$\mathfrak{o} \in \mathfrak{O}$

Events	
Event instance	$e = (\mathfrak{t}, \mathfrak{v}, \mathfrak{g})$
Event trigger	$\mathfrak{t} \in \Sigma$
Event value	$\mathfrak{v} \in \mathfrak{V}$
Event tag	$\mathfrak{g} \in \mathbb{T}$
Set of reactions and mutations triggered by trigger $\mathfrak{t}$	$T(\mathfrak{t}) = \{k \in \mathcal{N}(C(\mathfrak{t})) \cup \mathcal{M}(C(\mathfrak{t})) \mid \mathfrak{t} \in T(k)\}$

Reactions	
Reaction instance	$n = (D, T, B, D^\vee, H)$
Set of reaction dependencies	$D(n) \subseteq I(C(n)) \cup \left(\bigcup_{r \in \mathcal{R}(C(n))} O(r) \right)$
Set of reaction triggers	$T(n) \subseteq D(n) \cup x(A(C(n)))$
Reaction body	$B(n)$
Set of reaction antidependencies	$D^\vee(n) \subseteq O(C(n)) \cup \left(\bigcup_{r \in \mathcal{R}(C(n))} I(r) \right)$
Set of schedulable actions	$H(n) \subseteq x(A(C(n)))$
Reactor containing reaction n	$C(n)$
Reaction priority	$P(n) \in \mathbb{Z}^+ \cup \{*\}$
Priority of unordered reactions	$\forall q \in \mathbb{Z}^- \; \forall p \in \mathbb{Z}^+.$ $(n < *) \wedge (p \not> *) \wedge (* \not> p) \wedge (* \leq *)$

Mutations	
Mutation instance	$m = (D, T, B, D^\vee, H)$
Set of mutation dependencies	$D(m) \subseteq I(C(m))$
Set of mutation triggers	$T(m) \subseteq D(m) \cup x(A(C(m)))$
Mutation body	$B(m)$
Set of mutation antidependencies	$D^\vee(m) \subseteq O(C(m)) \cup \left(\bigcup_{r \in \mathcal{R}(C(m))} I(r) \right)$
Set of schedulable actions	$H \subseteq x(A(C(m))) \cup \{x(a) \mid \forall r \in \mathcal{R}(C(x)). \, a \in \{\bullet(r), \diamond(r)\}\}$
Reactor containing mutation m	$C(m)$
Mutation priority	$P(m) \in \mathbb{Z}^-$

References

1. Agha, G.: ACTORS: A Model of Concurrent Computation in Distributed Systems. The MIT Press Series in Artificial Intelligence. MIT Press, Cambridge (1986)
2. Armstrong, J., Virding, R., Wikström, C., Williams, M.: Concurrent programming in Erlang, 2nd edn. Prentice Hall (1996)
3. Bai, Y.: Desynchronization: From macro-step to micro-step. In: 2018 16th ACM/IEEE International Conference on Formal Methods and Models for System Design (MEMOCODE), pp. 1–10, October 2018
4. Bainomugisha, E., Carreton, A.L., Cutsem, T.V., Mostinckx, S., Meuter, W.D.: A survey on reactive programming. ACM Comput. Surv. (CSUR) **45**(4), 52 (2013)
5. Baker Jr., H.C., Hewitt, C.: The incremental garbage collection of processes. ACM Sigplan Not. **12**(8), 55–59 (1977)
6. Banken, H., Meijer, E., Gousios, G.: Debugging data flows in reactive programs. In: 2018 IEEE/ACM 40th International Conference on Software Engineering (ICSE), pp. 752–763. IEEE (2018)

7. Benveniste, A., Le Guernic, P.: Hybrid dynamical systems theory and the SIGNAL language. IEEE Trans. Autom. Control **35**(5), 525–546 (1990)
8. Berry, G., Gonthier, G.: The Esterel synchronous programming language: design, semantics, implementation. Sci. Comput. Program. **19**(2), 87–152 (1992)
9. Bilsen, G., Engels, M., Lauwereins, R., Peperstraete, J.A.: Static scheduling of multi-rate and cyclo-static DSP applications. In: Workshop on VLSI Signal Processing. IEEE Press (1994)
10. Bonér, J., Farley, D., Kuhn, R., Thompson, M.: The reactive manifesto (2014). http://www.reactivemanifesto.org/
11. Bonér, J., Klang, V., Kuhn, R., et al.: Akka library (2011–2019). http://akka.io
12. Brooks, C., et al.: A component architecture for the Internet of Things. Proc. IEEE **106**(9), 1527–1542 (2018)
13. Lombide Carreton, A., Mostinckx, S., Van Cutsem, T., De Meuter, W.: Loosely-coupled distributed reactive programming in mobile ad hoc networks. In: Vitek, J. (ed.) TOOLS 2010. LNCS, vol. 6141. Springer, Heidelberg (2010). https://doi.org/10.1007/978-3-642-13953-6_3
14. Chapiro, D.M.: Globally-asynchronous locally-synchronous systems. Ph.D. thesis, Stanford University, October 1984
15. Cooper, G.H., Krishnamurthi, S.: Embedding dynamic dataflow in a call-by-value language. In: Sestoft, P. (ed.) ESOP 2006. LNCS, vol. 3924. Springer, Heidelberg (2006). https://doi.org/10.1007/11693024_20
16. Corbett, J.C., et al.: Spanner: Google's globally-distributed database. In: OSDI (2012)
17. Cremona, F., Lohstroh, M., Broman, D., Lee, E.A., Masin, M., Tripakis, S.: Hybrid co-simulation: it's about time. Softw. Syst. Model. **18**, 1622–1679 (2017)
18. Czaplicki, E., Chong, S.N.: Asynchronous functional reactive programming for GUIs. In: Proceedings of the 34th ACM SIGPLAN Conference on Programming Language Design and Implementation-PLDI 2013. ACM Press (2013)
19. Dennis, J.B.: First version data flow procedure language. Report MAC TM61, MIT Laboratory for Computer Science (1974)
20. Edwards, J.: Coherent reaction. In: Proceedings of the 24th ACM SIGPLAN Conference Companion on Object Oriented Programming Systems Languages and Applications, pp. 925–932. ACM (2009)
21. Eidson, J., Lee, E.A., Matic, S., Seshia, S.A., Zou, J.: Distributed real-time software for cyber-physical systems. Proc. IEEE (Spec. Issue CPS) **100**(1), 45–59 (2012)
22. Elliott, C., Hudak, P.: Functional reactive animation. In: ACM SIGPLAN Notices, vol. 32, pp. 263–273 (1997)
23. Friedman, D.P., Wise, D.S.: The impact of applicative programming on multiprocessing. Indiana University, Computer Science Department (1976)
24. Gajski, D.: SpecC: Specification Language and Methodology. Kluwer Academic Publishers, Norwell (2000)
25. S.C.S.W. Group, et al.: 1666–2011-IEEE standard for standard SystemC language reference manual (2012)
26. Halbwachs, N., Caspi, P., Raymond, P., Pilaud, D.: The synchronous data flow programming language LUSTRE. Proc. IEEE **79**(9), 1305–1319 (1991)
27. Haller, P., Odersky, M.: Scala actors: unifying thread-based and event-based programming. Theor. Comput. Sci. **410**(2–3), 202–220 (2009)
28. Harel, D., Pnueli, A.: On the development of reactive systems. In: Apt, K.R. (ed.) Logics and Models of Concurrent Systems, vol. 13, pp. 477–498. Springer, Heidelberg (1985). https://doi.org/10.1007/978-3-642-82453-1_17

29. Harel, D.: Statecharts: a visual formalism for complex systems. Sci. Comput. Program. **8**(3), 231–274 (1987)
30. Hewitt, C.: Viewing control structures as patterns of passing messages. J. Artif. Intell. **8**(3), 323–363 (1977)
31. Hewitt, C., Bishop, P.B., Steiger, R.: A universal modular ACTOR formalism for artificial intelligence. In: Proceedings of the 3rd International Joint Conference on Artificial Intelligence. Standford, CA, USA, 20–23 August 1973, pp. 235–245 (1973)
32. Kahn, G.: The semantics of a simple language for parallel programming. In: Proceedings of the IFIP Congress 74, pp. 471–475. North-Holland Publishing Co. (1974)
33. Koopman, P.: A case study of Toyota unintended acceleration and software safety (2014). http://betterembsw.blogspot.com/2014/09/a-case-study-of-toyota-unintended.html
34. Kuhn, R., Hanafee, B., Allen, J.: Reactive Design Patterns. Manning Publications Company (2017)
35. Lee, E., Reineke, J., Zimmer, M.: Abstract PRET machines. In: 2017 IEEE Real-Time Systems Symposium (RTSS), pp. 1–11, December 2017
36. Lee, E.A., Messerschmitt, D.G.: Synchronous data flow. Proc. IEEE **75**(9), 1235–1245 (1987)
37. Lee, E.A., Parks, T.M.: Dataflow process networks. Proc. IEEE **83**(5), 773–801 (1995)
38. Lee, E.A.: The problem with threads. Computer **39**(5), 33–42 (2006)
39. Lee, E.A., Sangiovanni-Vincentelli, A.: A framework for comparing models of computation. IEEE Trans. Comput.-Aided Des. Circuits Syst. **17**(12), 1217–1229 (1998)
40. Lee, E.A., Zheng, H.: Operational semantics of hybrid systems. In: Morari, M., Thiele, L. (eds.) HSCC 2005. LNCS, vol. 3414, pp. 25–53. Springer, Heidelberg (2005). https://doi.org/10.1007/978-3-540-31954-2_2
41. Lee, E.A., Zheng, H.: Leveraging synchronous language principles for heterogeneous modeling and design of embedded systems. In: EMSOFT, pp. 114–123. ACM (2007)
42. Liao, S., Tjiang, S., Gupta, R.: An efficient implementation of reactivity for modeling hardware in the Scenic design environment. In: Design Automation Conference. ACM (1997)
43. Liu, X., Matsikoudis, E., Lee, E.A.: Modeling timed concurrent systems. In: Baier, C., Hermanns, H. (eds.) CONCUR 2006. LNCS, vol. 4137, pp. 1–15. Springer, Heidelberg (2006). https://doi.org/10.1007/11817949_1
44. Lohstroh, M., Lee, E.A.: Deterministic actors. In: 2019 Forum for Specification and Design Languages (FDL), pp. 1–8, 2–4 September 2019
45. Lohstroh, M., Schoeberl, M., Jan, M., Wang, E., Lee, E.A.: Work-in-progress: programs with ironclad timing guarantees. In: 2019 International Conference on Embedded Software (EMSOFT), October 2019
46. Lohstroh, M., et al.: Actors revisited for time-critical systems. In: Proceedings of the 56th Annual Design Automation Conference 2019, DAC 2019, Las Vegas, NV, USA, 02–06 June 2019, pp. 152:1–152:4. ACM (2019)
47. Maler, O., Manna, Z., Pnueli, A.: Prom timed to hybrid systems. In: de Bakker, J.W., Huizing, C., de Roever, W.P., Rozenberg, G. (eds.) REX 1991. LNCS, vol. 600. Springer, Heidelberg (1992). https://doi.org/10.1007/BFb0032003

48. Matsikoudis, E., Lee, E.A.: The fixed-point theory of strictly causal functions. Technical report UCB/EECS-2013-122, EECS Department, University of California, Berkeley, 9 June 2013

49. Meijer, E.: Reactive extensions (Rx): curing your asynchronous programming blues. In: ACM SIGPLAN Commercial Users of Functional Programming, CUFP 2010, pp. 11:1–11:1. ACM, New York (2010)

50. Moritz, P., et al.: Ray: a distributed framework for emerging AI applications. simarXiv:1712.05889v2 [cs.DC] 30 Sept 2018 (2018)

51. Myter, F., Scholliers, C., De Meuter, W.: Distributed reactive programming for reactive distributed systems. arXiv preprint arXiv:1902.00524 (2019)

52. NASA Engineering and Safety Center: National highway traffic safety administration Toyota unintended acceleration investigation. Technical assessment report, NASA, 18 January 2011

53. Parks, T.M.: Bounded scheduling of process networks. Ph.D. thesis. Technical report UCB/ERL M95/105, UC Berkeley (1995)

54. Prokopec, A.: Pluggable scheduling for the reactor programming model. In: Ricci, A., Haller, P. (eds.) Programming with Actors. LNCS, vol. 10789. Springer, Cham (2018). https://doi.org/10.1007/978-3-030-00302-9_5

55. Roestenburg, R., Bakker, R., Williams, R.: Akka in Action. Manning Publications Co. (2016)

56. Schoeberl, M., Puffitsch, W., Hepp, S., Huber, B., Prokesch, D.: Patmos: a time-predictable microprocessor. Real-Time Syst. **54**(2), 389–423 (2018)

57. Tasharofi, S., Dinges, P., Johnson, R.E.: Why do scala developers mix the actor model with other concurrency models? In: Castagna, G. (ed.) ECOOP 2013. LNCS, vol. 7920. Springer, Heidelberg (2013). https://doi.org/10.1007/978-3-642-39038-8_13

58. Tilkov, S., Vinoski, S.: Node. js: using JavaScript to build high-performance network programs. IEEE Internet Comput. **14**(6), 80–83 (2010)

59. Torres Lopez, C., Gurdeep Singh, R., Marr, S., Gonzalez Boix, E., Scholliers, C.: Multiverse debugging: non-deterministic debugging for non-deterministic programs (2019)

60. Vernon, V.: Reactive Messaging Patterns with the Actor Model: Applications and Integration in Scala and Akka. Addison-Wesley Professional (2015)

61. Zhao, Y., Lee, E.A., Liu, J.: A programming model for time-synchronized distributed real-time systems. In: Real-Time and Embedded Technology and Applications Symposium (RTAS), pp. 259–268. IEEE (2007)

62. Zhao, Y., Liu, J., Lee, E.A.: A programming model for time-synchronized distributed real-time systems. In: 13th IEEE Real Time and Embedded Technology and Applications Symposium, RTAS 2007, pp. 259–268, April 2007

63. Zimmer, M., Broman, D., Shaver, C., Lee, E.A.: FlexPRET: a processor platform for mixed-criticality systems. In: Real-Time and Embedded Technology and Application Symposium (RTAS) (2014)

Simulation and Tools

Guaranteed Simulation of Dynamical Systems with Integral Constraints and Application on Delayed Dynamical Systems

Paul Rousse[1]([⊠]), Julien Alexandre dit Sandretto[2]([⊠]),
Alexandre Chapoutot[2]([⊠]), and Pierre-Loïc Garoche[1]([⊠])

[1] ONERA, 31400 Toulouse, France
{paul.rousse,pierre-loic.garoche}@onera.fr
[2] U2IS, ENSTA Paris, Institut Polytechnique de Paris, 91120 Palaiseau, France
{julien.alexandre-dit-sandretto,alexandre.chapoutot}@ensta-paristech.fr

Abstract. A reachable set computation method for dynamical systems with an integral constraint over the input set is proposed. These models are typical in robustness analysis when studying the impact of bounded energy noises over a system response and can also model a large family of complex systems. The reachable set is over-approximated using a guaranteed set-based integration method within the interval arithmetic framework.

A Runge-Kutta guaranteed integration scheme with pessimistic bounds over the input provides a first conservative bound over the reachable tube. Then, the integral constraint is used to define a contractor over the reachable tube. This contractor and a propagation step are successively applied on the over-approximation until a fixed point is reached. We evaluated our algorithm with DynIbex library to simulate a delayed system, *i.e.*, an infinite dimensional system that can be modeled as a linear time-invariant system subject to an integral quadratic constraint. Our approach is shown to be tractable and enables the use of interval arithmetic and guaranteed integration for a richer set of dynamical systems.

Keywords: Numerical integration · Dynamical systems with integral constraint · Interval arithmetic

1 Introduction

In this paper, we present a method to compute the flowpipe of a dynamical system with an integral inequality constraint between an unknown input disturbance and the state trajectory. The interval arithmetic and guaranteed simulation frameworks are used. With additional assumptions about the dynamic of the disturbance, the integral constraint gives bounds over the set of disturbances.

© Springer Nature Switzerland AG 2020
R. Chamberlain et al. (Eds.): CyPhy 2019/WESE 2019, LNCS 11971, pp. 89–107, 2020.
https://doi.org/10.1007/978-3-030-41131-2_5

A contractor over the set of reachable states is defined out of these bounds. This contractor is then used in a fixed point algorithm with a propagation step (as described in [1]). Our algorithm is implemented using DynIbex library [2] and applied to overapproximate the flowpipe of a dynamical system with an inner delay.

In dynamical system's analysis, two signal norms are frequently used: the ∞-norm (that corresponds to the maximum vector norm over the time domain) and the 2-norm (that corresponds to the signal's energy). A signal with a 2-norm bound can be equivalently defined with an integral constraint. Disturbances with ∞-norm bounds are naturally handled by guaranteed integration frameworks. Disturbances with 2-norm have been less studied by the community despite their modeling power. In control theory, many relationships between signals and systems are expressed in terms of 2-norm gains. In Hybrid systems analysis, 2-norm input-output gains have been derived (as in [21]) and can be used to compute overapproximation of the reachable set. [7] proposes the use of model reduction methods to verify large systems. No error bound is used during the verification of the approximated system. In fact, such bounds exist and can be expressed as a 2-norm gain relationship with the input signal. Many complex systems can be, as well, described by a linear time-invariant dynamical system disturbed by a 2-norm bounded signal [17].

Related Works. In the first paragraph, we motivate our choice of model with a challenging application: differential equation with inner delays. The next paragraphs review works in reachability analysis for dynamical systems with integral constraints.

Simulation of differential equations with inner delays is a notoriously complex problem [26,28]. In [8], the author propose to compute an inner and outer approximation of a delayed system's flowpipe. The solution to the differential delay equation is obtained by integrating ordinary differential equations (ODE) over small steps. The solutions over these time intervals are recursively used until the final time of integration is reached. The infinite dimensional state of the delay (i.e. the memory of the delay) is sampled in time. Taylor series and a classical integration method are used to solve the ODE. In [6], the simulation trace is obtained with a similar approach. Along the simulation trace, a bound over the numerical integration error is derived by solving an optimization problem. In [30], set-boundary based reachability analysis method initially developed for ODE is extended to delay differential equations. A sensitivity analysis is used get an inner and outer approximation of the reachable set. In [6,8,26,28,30], an outer approximation of past states is used to solve the delay differential equation, local properties (Taylor remainder, local contraction of the flowpipe and sensitivity analysis) are used to get guaranteed bound over the reachable state. In [25], the stability of linear systems with constant delays is studied. The state of the delay operator is expressed as a weighted sum of polynomials functions and a remaining noise signal. It can be shown that these weights are solution of a linear time-invariant system subject to a disturbance. The disturbance satisfies an energetic constraint. Delays modeled as an integral quadratic constraint have also been used for reachability analysis of delay systems in [20]. The reachable tube is overapproximated using a time-varying ellipsoidal set with time-dependent polynomial radius and center. The overapproximating relationship can be expressed as the positivity of a polynomial over the state and time space. An SDP solver is used to find a solution. The SDP solver provide a certificate of positivity for all positive polynomial and thus the overapproximation relationship can be guaranteed. In this work, the system with delay is as well modeled by an integral quadratic constraint to build a contractor. An initial reachable tube can be roughly overapproximated using guaranteed integration tools. Then, the contractor is used to reduce the pessimism of this reachable tube. To apply this contraction, we use forward propagation of the reachable set as in [22].

Computing the reachable set of dynamical systems with integral constraints can be expressed as an optimal control problem as in [10,16]. A state belongs to the reachable set if the maximum integral value satisfies the positivity constraint along its trajectory. Standard tools from optimal control can then be used. This optimization problem can be locally solved (see, e.g., with the Pontryagin Maximum Principle -PMP-, see [9,10,16,29]) leading to a local description of the reachable set boundary. It also can be solved globally (using Hamilton-Jacobi-Bellman -HJB- viscosity subsolutions, see [27]) leading to global constraints over the reachable set. These methods rely on numerical integration of (partial) differential equations and are often subject to numerical instabilities.

HJB and PMP based methods propagate the constraints along the flow of the dynamical system. Occupation measures and barrier certificates methods aim at finding constraints over the reachable tube of a dynamical system: [21] uses integral constraints for verification purposes using barrier certificates where the positivity of the integral is ensured by using a nonnegative constant multiplier: [11,14] use an occupation measure approach where the integral constraint can be incorporated as a constraint over the moment of the trajectories. A hierarchy of semi-definite conditions is derived for polynomial dynamics. Then, off-the-shelf semi-definite programming solvers are used to solve the feasibility problem. Optimization-based methods do not usually take advantage of the model structure as they consider a large class of systems (convex, Lipschitz or polynomial dynamics for example).

For linear system subject to Integral Quadratic Constraints (IQC), the reachability problem can be expressed as the classical Linear Quadratic Regulator problem [24]. Optimal trajectories belong to a time-varying parabolic surface, whose quadratic coefficients are the solution to a Riccati differential equation. [10,23] describes the reachable set of LTI systems with terminal IQC. [13] formalizes the problem with a game theory approach. Recent works showed that the ellipsoidal method developed in [15] can be extended to a so-called Paraboloid method [22] to get the exact characterization of the reachable set of such systems.

Contributions:

- we developed a framework to analyze systems with integral constraints between an unknown disturbance and the state. We make an additional

assumption about the disturbance dynamic. This assumption asserts that the variation of the disturbance is bounded. We then define a contractor over the set of trajectories. This contractor is used in a fixed point algorithm.
– we use models from robust control theory into guaranteed numerical integration.

Plan: In Sect. 2, we define the system of interest. Guaranteed numerical integration for unconstrained systems is presented in Sect. 3. The main contribution of this work is presented in Sect. 4. Since the integral constraint cannot be directly handled by guaranteed integration software such as DynIbex, we make further assumptions about the disturbance dynamic. These hypotheses are then used to define a narrowing operator out of the integral constraint. In Sect. 5, our approach is used to compute the reachable set of a dynamical system with inner delays. We compare this method to a set-based method.

Notations. $\mathbb{IR}$ is the set of intervals over $\mathbb{R}$, interval vectors are noted in bold letters. Let the norm of $[\mathbf{x}] \in \mathbb{IR}^n$ be $[\![\mathbf{x}]\!] = max_{x \in [\mathbf{x}]} \|x\|$. For an interval $[\mathbf{x}] \in \mathbb{IR}$, let $\overline{[\mathbf{x}]} = \sup_{x \in [\mathbf{x}]} x$. For $n \in \mathbb{N}$ and an interval I of $\mathbb{R}$, $\mathrm{L}^2_{loc}(\mathbb{R}^+; \mathbb{R}^n)$ is the set of locally square integrable functions from I to $\mathbb{R}^n$.

2   System with Integral Constraint over the State

Let the following system:

$$\begin{cases} \dot{x} = f(t, x, w) \\ x(0) \in \mathbf{x_0} \end{cases} \tag{1}$$

where w is an unknown disturbance in $\mathrm{L}^2_{loc}(\mathbb{R}^+; \mathbb{R}^m)$ that satisfies the integral constraint, for any $\tau \geq 0$:

$$\int_0^\tau \|w(s)\|^2 \, ds \leq \int_0^\tau g(s, x(s)) ds \tag{2}$$

where $g : \mathbb{R}^+ \times \mathbb{R}^n$ is a given function.

Many systems can be modeled in such way. The robust control community makes frequent use of this model where the integral constraint overapproximates the behavior of complex systems, *e.g.*, saturations, delays and bounded nonlinearities to cite few of them.

Remark 1. The integral constraint does not give any bounds on the disturbance as it can be easily understood from the unit energy disturbed system

$$\begin{cases} \dot{x} = -x + w \\ x(0) = 0 \\ 1 \geq \int_0^1 w^2(\tau) d\tau \end{cases} \tag{3}$$

Let w be defined for any $\epsilon > 0$ by

$$\begin{cases} w(\tau) = \dfrac{1}{\epsilon} & \text{when } \tau \in [0, \epsilon] \\ w(\tau) = 0 & \text{otherwise.} \end{cases}$$

Since $\int_0^1 w^2(\tau)d\tau = 1$, the inequality in Eq. (3) is verified for every $\epsilon > 0$, however no bounds can be determined for w since $w(0) \to \infty$ when $\epsilon \to 0$. Please note that the system defined in Eq. (3) has a bounded reachable set even if the disturbance cannot be bounded at any given time (see [4, Chap. 8.1.2]).

3 Interval Analysis and Guaranteed Numerical Integration

A presentation of the main mathematical tools is given in this section. First, the basics of *interval analysis* is provided in Sect. 3.1. Then, a short introduction of *validated numerical integration* is presented in Sect. 3.2.

3.1 Interval Analysis

The simplest and most common way to represent and manipulate sets of values is *interval arithmetic* (see [18]). An interval $[x_i] = [\underline{x_i}, \overline{x_i}]$ defines the set of reals x_i such that $\underline{x_i} \le x_i \le \overline{x_i}$. $\mathbb{IR}$ denotes the set of all intervals over reals. The size (or width) of $[x_i]$ is denoted by $w([x_i]) = \overline{x_i} - \underline{x_i}$.

Interval arithmetic extends to $\mathbb{IR}$ elementary functions over $\mathbb{R}$. For instance, the interval sum, *i.e.*, $[x_1] + [x_2] = [\underline{x_1} + \underline{x_2}, \overline{x_1} + \overline{x_2}]$, encloses the image of the sum function over its arguments.

An interval vector or a *box* $[\mathbf{x}] \in \mathbb{IR}^n$, is a Cartesian product of n intervals. The enclosing property basically defines what is called an *interval extension* or an *inclusion function*.

Definition 1 (Inclusion function). *Consider a function $f : \mathbb{R}^n \to \mathbb{R}^m$, then $[f]: \mathbb{IR}^n \to \mathbb{IR}^m$ is said to be an inclusion function of f to intervals if*

$$\forall [\mathbf{x}] \in \mathbb{IR}^n, \quad [f]([\mathbf{x}]) \supseteq \{f(\mathbf{x}), \mathbf{x} \in [\mathbf{x}]\} \ .$$

It is possible to define inclusion functions for all elementary functions such as $\times$, $\div$, sin, cos, exp, etc. The *natural* inclusion function is the simplest to obtain: all occurrences of the real variables are replaced by their interval counterpart and all arithmetic operations are evaluated using interval arithmetic. More sophisticated inclusion functions such as the centered form, or the Taylor inclusion function may also be used (see [12] for more details).

Example 1 (Interval arithmetic). A few examples of arithmetic operations between interval values are given

$$[-2, 5] + [-8, 12] = [-10, 17]$$
$$[-10, 17] - [-8, 12] = [-10, 17] + [-12, 8] = [-22, 25]$$
$$[-10, 17] - [-2, 5] = [-15, 19]$$
$$\frac{[-2, 5]}{[-8, 12]} = [-\infty, \infty]$$
$$\frac{[3, 5]}{[8, 12]} = \left[\frac{3}{12}, \frac{5}{8}\right]$$
$$\left[\frac{3}{12}, \frac{5}{8}\right] \times [8, 12] = \left[2, \frac{15}{2}\right]$$

In the first example of division, the result is the interval containing all the real numbers because denominator contains 0.

As an example of inclusion function, we consider a function p defined by

$$p(x, y) = xy + x \ .$$

The associated natural inclusion function is

$$[p]([x], [y]) = [x][y] + [x],$$

in which variables, constants and arithmetic operations have been replaced by its interval counterpart. And so $p([0, 1], [0, 1]) = [0, 2] \subseteq \{p(x, y) \mid x, y \in [0, 1]\} = [0, 2]$. ∎

In the constraint programming community, complex equality and inequality constraints can be handled using so-called *contractors*. A contractor is an operator that associates to a set one of its subset that contains all the points where the constraint is verified (see [5]).

Definition 2. *For a constraint f that maps $\mathbb{R}^n$ to a truth value, a contractor Ctc of f associates to a subset of $\mathbb{R}^n$ to a subset of $\mathbb{R}^n$. For any $[\mathbf{b}], [\mathbf{b}'] \in \mathbb{IR}^n$, Ctc must verifies the following properties:*

- *the contractance: $Ctc([\mathbf{b}]) \subseteq [\mathbf{b}]$,*
- *the conservativeness: $\forall x \in [\mathbf{b}] \backslash Ctc([\mathbf{b}])$, $f(x)$ is not satisfied,*
- *the monotonicity: $[\mathbf{b}'] \subseteq [\mathbf{b}] \Rightarrow Ctc([\mathbf{b}']) \subseteq Ctc([\mathbf{b}])$*

3.2   Validated Numerical Integration Methods

Mathematically, differential equations have no explicit solutions, except for few particular cases. Nevertheless, the solution can be numerically approximated with the help of integration schemes such as Taylor series [19] or Runge-Kutta methods [2,3].

In the following, we consider a *generic* parametric differential equation as an *interval initial value problem* (IIVP) defined by

$$\begin{cases} \dot{\mathbf{y}} = F(t, \mathbf{y}, \mathbf{x}, \mathbf{p}, \mathbf{u}) \\ 0 = G(t, \mathbf{y}, \mathbf{x}, \mathbf{p}, \mathbf{u}) \\ \mathbf{y}(0) \in \mathcal{Y}_0, \mathbf{x}(0) \in \mathcal{X}_0, \mathbf{p} \in \mathcal{P}, \mathbf{u} \in \mathcal{U}, t \in [0, t_{\text{end}}] \ , \end{cases} \tag{4}$$

with $F : \mathbb{R} \times \mathbb{R}^n \times \mathbb{R}^m \times \mathbb{R}^r \times \mathbb{R}^s \mapsto \mathbb{R}^n$ and $G : \mathbb{R} \times \mathbb{R}^n \times \mathbb{R}^m \times \mathbb{R}^r \times \mathbb{R}^s \mapsto \mathbb{R}^m$. The variable $\mathbf{y}$ of dimension n is the differential variable while the variable $\mathbf{x}$ is an algebraic variable of dimension m with an initial condition $\mathbf{y}(0) \in \mathcal{Y}_0 \subseteq \mathbb{R}^n$ and $\mathbf{x}(0) \in \mathcal{X}_0 \subseteq \mathbb{R}^m$. In other words, differential-algebraic equations (DAE) of index 1 are considered, and in the case of $m = 0$, this differential equation simplifies to an ordinary differential equation (ODE). Note that usually, the initial values of algebraic variable $\mathbf{x}$ are computed by numerical algorithms used to solve DAE but we consider it fixed here for simplicity. Variable $\mathbf{p} \in \mathcal{P} \subseteq \mathbb{R}^r$ stands for parameters of dimension r and variable $\mathbf{u} \in \mathcal{U} \subseteq \mathbb{R}^s$ stands for a control vector of dimension s. We assume standard hypotheses on F and G to guarantee the existence and uniqueness of the solution to such problem.

A validated simulation of a differential equation consists in a discretization of time, such that $t_0 \leqslant \cdots \leqslant t_{\text{end}}$, and a computation of enclosures of the set of states of the system $\mathbf{y}_0, \ldots, \mathbf{y}_{\text{end}}$, by the help of a guaranteed integration scheme. In details, a guaranteed integration scheme is made of

- an integration method $\Phi(F, G, \mathbf{y}_j, t_j, h)$, starting from an initial value $\mathbf{y}_j$ at time t_j and a finite time horizon h (the step-size), producing an approximation $\mathbf{y}_{j+1}$ at time $t_{j+1} = t_j + h$, of the exact solution $\mathbf{y}(t_{j+1}; \mathbf{y}_j)$, *i.e.*, $\mathbf{y}(t_{j+1}; \mathbf{y}_j) \approx \Phi(F, G, \mathbf{y}_j, t_j, h)$;
- a truncation error function $\text{lte}_\Phi(F, G, \mathbf{y}_j, t_j, h)$, such that

$$\mathbf{y}(t_{j+1}; \mathbf{y}_j) = \Phi(F, G, \mathbf{y}_j, t_j, h) + \text{lte}_\Phi(F, G, \mathbf{y}_j, t_j, h).$$

Basically, a validated numerical integration method is based on a numerical integration scheme such as Taylor series [19] or Runge-Kutta methods [2,3] which is extended with interval analysis tools to bound the *local truncation error*, *i.e.*, the distance between the exact and the numerical solutions. Mainly, such methods work in two stages at each integration step, starting from an enclosure $[\mathbf{y}_j] \ni \mathbf{y}(t_j; \mathbf{y}_0)$ at time t_j of the exact solution, we proceed by:

i. a computation of an *a priori* enclosure $[\tilde{\mathbf{y}}_{j+1}]$ of the solution $\mathbf{y}(t; \mathbf{y}_0)$ for all t in the time interval $[t_j, t_{j+1}]$. This stage allows one to prove the existence and the uniqueness of the solution.
ii. a computation of a tightening of state variable $[\mathbf{y}_{j+1}] \ni \mathbf{y}(t_{j+1}; \mathbf{y}_0)$ at time t_{j+1} using $[\tilde{\mathbf{y}}_{j+1}]$ to bound the local truncation error term $\text{lte}_\Phi(F, G, \mathbf{y}_j, t_j, h)$.

A validated simulation starts with the interval enclosures $[\mathbf{y}(0)]$, $[\mathbf{x}(0)]$, $[\mathbf{p}]$ and $[\mathbf{u}]$ of respectively, $\mathcal{Y}_0$, $\mathcal{X}_0$, $\mathcal{P}$, and $\mathcal{U}$. It produces two lists of boxes:

- the list of discretization time steps: $\{t_0, \ldots, t_{\mathrm{end}}\}$;
- the list of state enclosures at the discretization time steps: $\{[\mathbf{y}_0], \ldots, [\mathbf{y}_{\mathrm{end}}]\}$;
- the list of *a priori* enclosures: $\{[\widetilde{\mathbf{y}}_0], \ldots, [\widetilde{\mathbf{y}}_{\mathrm{end}}]\}$.

Figure 1 represents the enclosures $[\widetilde{\mathbf{y}}_i]$ and $[\mathbf{y}_i]$ and their membership properties with the trajectories of the dynamical system.

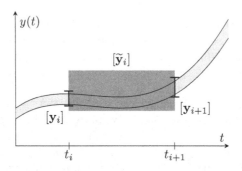

Fig. 1. The trajectories (in light gray) are overapproximated by $[\mathbf{y}_i]$ (thick line segment) at time step t_i. The *a priori* enclosure $[\widetilde{\mathbf{y}}_i]$ (in gray) contains the trajectories over the time interval $[t_i, t_{i+1}]$.

4   Dynamical Systems with Integral Constraints

This section presents the main contribution of our work. For system described by Eq. (1) subject to the integral constraint defined by Eq. (2), we compute an overapproximation of its flowpipe over the time domain $[0, T]$, where the time horizon $T > 0$ is given. A first overapproximation of the flowpipe is computed using pessimistic bounds over the disturbances. The integral constraint in Eq. (2) is used to derive contractor. This contractor and a propagation step are applied in a fixed point algorithm until a contraction factor is reached. We run the algorithm over a simple example.

4.1   Extended System

We extend the system's state with the integral value corresponding to the integral constraint in Eq. (2):

$$\begin{cases} \dot{z}(t) = g(t, x(t)) - \|w(t)\|^2 \\ z(0) = 0 \end{cases} \tag{5}$$

Then, Eq. (2) can be equivalently expressed for z:

$$\forall t \in \mathbb{R}^+, z(t) \geq 0. \tag{6}$$

As mentioned in Remark 1, no L_∞ bounds can be derived for L_2 bounded signals. To study such systems, we make further assumptions about the disturbance:

Assumption 1. *w is continuous, differentiable and of continuous derivative over $\mathbb{R}^+$.*

This assumption seems reasonable in the case of real systems modeling since disturbances modeled by integral constraints correspond to physical quantities. Since the continuity of a function over a closed interval implies its boundedness, Assumption 1 implies that the signal w is bounded and of bounded variation over $[0, T]$. Therefore, there exists $[\mathbf{w}] \in \mathbb{IR}^m$ and $[\mathbf{w}'] \in \mathbb{IR}^m$ such that for all $t \in [0, T]$:

$$\begin{cases} w(t) \in [\mathbf{w}] \\ \dot{w}(t) \in [\mathbf{w}'] \end{cases} \tag{7}$$

Using Assumption 1 and Eq. (5), the following system will be studied:

$$\mathcal{S} : \begin{cases} \dot{x}(t) = f(t, x(t), w(t)) \\ \dot{z}(t) = g(t, x(t), w(t)) - \|w(t)\|^2 \\ \dot{w}(t) \in [\mathbf{w}'] \\ x(0) \in [\mathbf{x_0}] \\ z(0) = 0 \\ 0 \leq z(t) \\ w(t) \in [\mathbf{w}] \end{cases} \tag{8}$$

where $[\mathbf{x_0}] \in \mathbb{IR}^n$ is the set of initial states. We use the following notation $(x, z, w) \in \mathcal{S}$ iff $(x, w) \in \mathbb{L}^2_{loc}([0, T]; \mathbb{R}^n) \times \mathbb{L}^2_{loc}([0, T]; \mathbb{R}) \times \mathbb{L}^2_{loc}([0, T]; \mathbb{R}^m)$ is a trajectory of $\mathcal{S}$.

Equation (7) gives prior bounds over the disturbance w. They can be used to propagate the trajectories using standard guaranteed integration frameworks. Thanks to this, we get a first a priori overapproximation of the reachable set. In the next section, we use this first overapproximation and a contractor (defined out of the integral inequality) in a fixed point algorithm in order to get a tighter overapproximation of the reachable set.

4.2 Bounds over w

In this section, Eq. (7) and the integral constraint in Eq. 6 are used to derive bounds over the disturbance w. These bounds are then used to define a contractor over the *a priori* enclosure of the trajectories.

We present a preliminary result to Property 2:

Property 1. For $[\mathbf{v}] \in \mathbb{IR}^p$, $p \in \mathbb{N}$ and $r > 0$, if $[\![\mathbf{v}]\!] \leq r$ then $[\mathbf{v}] \subset [-r, r]^p$.

Proof. In an Euclidean space, the norm 1 and norm 2 satisfies $\sqrt{v_1^2 + \cdots + v_p^2} \leq |v_1| + \cdots + |v_p|$ for any $(v_1, \ldots, v_p) \in \mathbb{R}^p$. ∎

When w satisfies Eq. (7) and a given integral constraint, hard bounds (meaning in ∞-norm) can be derived over w:

Property 2. For a $w \in \mathbf{L}^2_{loc}([0, h]; \mathbb{R}^m)$ defined over an interval of length $h > 0$. If w satisfies Eq. (7) (with given bounds $[\mathbf{w}], [\mathbf{w}'] \in \mathbb{IR}^m$), then for any $r > 0$:

$$\int_0^h \|w(\tau)\|^2 \, d\tau \le r \Rightarrow \forall \tau \in [0, h], w(\tau) \in [\mathbf{W_r}],$$

where $[\mathbf{W_r}] = [-k, k]^n$ with $k = \sqrt{\frac{r}{h}} + \frac{h}{2}[\![\mathbf{w}']\!]$ (where $[\![\mathbf{w}']\!]$ is the maximum Euclidean norm over the elements of $[\mathbf{w}']$).

Proof. By applying the Cauchy-Schwartz inequality between the signal w and $t \mapsto 1$ for the inner product of square integrable function, we have:

$$\left\| \int_0^h w(\tau) d\tau \right\|^2 \le h \int_0^h \|w(\tau)\|^2 \, d\tau \le hr.$$

By Eq. (7), $w(\tau) = w_0 + \int_0^\tau w_1(\kappa) d\kappa$ with $w_0 \in [\mathbf{w}]$ and $w_1(\cdot) \in [\mathbf{w}']$. Using the reverse triangular inequality, we have:

$$\left\| \int_0^h w_0 d\tau \right\| \le \sqrt{rh} + \left\| \int_0^h \int_0^\tau w_1(\kappa) d\kappa \right\|.$$

Then, we get:

$$\|h w_0\| \le \sqrt{hr} + \frac{h^2}{2}[\![\mathbf{w}']\!]. \tag{9}$$

This relationship is derived over $[0, h]$ but is also valid for any time interval $[t, t + h]$ of width h, $t > 0$. Therefore, by using Property 1 and Eq. (9), we have: $\forall \tau \in [0, h], w(\tau) \in [\mathbf{W_r}]$. ∎

We then use Property 2 to derive bounds in the specific case of Eq. (5). Let a system trajectory $(x, z, w) \in \mathcal{S}$, such that at a given $t \in [0, T]$ and $h > 0$ s.t. $t + h \in [0, T]$, and for all $\tau \in [t, t + h]$:

$$\begin{cases} (x(t), z(t), w(t)) \in [\mathbf{y_t}] \\ (x(\tau), z(\tau), w(\tau)) \in [\tilde{\mathbf{y}}_t] \end{cases} \quad \text{where} \quad \begin{cases} [\mathbf{y_t}] = [\mathbf{x_t}] \times [\mathbf{z_t}] \times [\mathbf{w_t}] \\ [\tilde{\mathbf{y}}_t] = [\tilde{\mathbf{x}}_t] \times [\tilde{\mathbf{z}}_t] \times [\tilde{\mathbf{w}}_t] \end{cases}. \tag{10}$$

The trajectories belong to $[\mathbf{y_t}]$ at t and are in $[\tilde{\mathbf{y}}_t]$ between $[t, t + h]$. At $t + h$, for a given $t \ge 0$ and a given $h \ge 0$, Eq. (8) implies that z satisfies:

$$z(t + h) = z(t) + \int_t^{t+h} g(t, x(t)) d\tau - \int_t^{t+h} \|w(\tau)\|^2 \, d\tau.$$

By applying Eq. 6 at $t + h$ implies that $z(t + h) \ge 0$, we have the following relationship:

$$\int_t^{t+h} \|w(\tau)\|^2 \, d\tau \le z(t) + \int_t^{t+h} g(\tau, x(\tau)) d\tau. \tag{11}$$

Let the function

$$q(z, x) = z + \int_t^{t+h} g(\tau, x(\tau)) d\tau. \tag{12}$$

By using an interval evaluation $[q]$ of q, the upperbound of $q(z, x)$ can be evaluated for $z \in [\mathbf{z_t}]$ and $x \in [\tilde{\mathbf{x}}_t]$. We denote by $\overline{[q]([\mathbf{z_t}], [\tilde{\mathbf{x}}_t])}$ this upperbound. For any $w \in \mathbb{L}^2_{loc}([t, t+h], [\tilde{\mathbf{w}}_t])$, Eq. 11 implies:

$$\int_t^{t+h} \|w(\tau)\|^2 \, d\tau \le \overline{[q]([\mathbf{z_t}], [\tilde{\mathbf{x}}_t])}.$$

Then, Property 2 can be used to derive bounds over the disturbance w:

Property 3. For a $w \in \mathbb{L}^2_{loc}([t, t+h]; \mathbb{R}^m)$ defined over an interval of length $h > 0$, $t > 0$. If w satisfies Eq. (7) (with given bounds $[\mathbf{w}], [\mathbf{w'}] \in \mathbb{IR}^m$), then for any $\tau \in [t, t+h]$:

$$w(\tau) \in [\mathbf{W_q}], \tag{13}$$

where $[\mathbf{W_q}]([\tilde{\mathbf{x}}_t], [\mathbf{z_t}]) = [-r, r]^m$ with $r = \sqrt{\frac{\overline{[q]([\mathbf{z_t}], [\tilde{\mathbf{x}}_t])}}{h}}$ and q defined in Eq. (12).

Proof. This is a direct application of Property 2. ■

We then define the operator over $[\mathbf{y_t}]$ and $[\tilde{\mathbf{y}}_t]$

$$\mathcal{C}([\mathbf{y_t}], [\tilde{\mathbf{y}}_t]) = ([\mathbf{y_t}] \cap [\mathbf{Y_g}]([\tilde{\mathbf{x}}_t], [\mathbf{z_t}]), [\tilde{\mathbf{y}}_t] \cap [\mathbf{Y_g}]([\tilde{\mathbf{x}}_t], [\mathbf{z_t}])) \tag{14}$$

where $[\mathbf{y_t}]$ and $[\tilde{\mathbf{y}}_t]$ are defined in Eq. (10),

$$[\mathbf{Y_g}] = [-\infty, \infty]^n \times [0, \infty] \times [\mathbf{W_q}],$$

with $[\mathbf{W_q}]$ defined in Property 3.

Proposition 1. $\mathcal{C}$ *defined in Eq.* (14) *is a contractor.*

Proof. By Property 3, we have, for $\tau \in [t, t+h]$,

$$w(\tau) \in [\mathbf{W_q}],$$

i.e., all the disturbance signals of $\mathcal{S}$ belongs to $[\mathbf{W_q}]$, so the contractor is conservative. Since the contractor is defined as an intersection with $[\mathbf{y}_t]$ and $[\tilde{\mathbf{y}}_t]$ respectively, we have

$$([\mathbf{y}_t], [\tilde{\mathbf{y}}_t]) \subseteq \mathcal{C}([\mathbf{y}_t], [\tilde{\mathbf{y}}_t]),$$

$\mathcal{C}$ is contractive. For any $([\mathbf{y}'_t], [\tilde{\mathbf{y}}'_t])$ such that $[\mathbf{y}'_t] \subseteq [\mathbf{y}_t]$ and $[\tilde{\mathbf{y}}'_t] \subseteq [\tilde{\mathbf{y}}_t]$,

$$\mathcal{C}([\mathbf{y}'_t], [\tilde{\mathbf{y}}'_t]) \subseteq \mathcal{C}([\mathbf{y}_t], [\tilde{\mathbf{y}}_t]),$$

i.e. $\mathcal{C}$ is monotone. ■

4.3   Integral Constraint Propagation

The contractor defined by Eq. (14) is used in a fixed point algorithm as in [1]. A priori enclosure of the trajectory is computed using bounds Eq. (7) over w. The integration algorithm gives

– the discretization time steps: $\{t_0, \ldots, t_{end}\}$;
– the state enclosure at the discretization time steps: $\mathcal{Y}^0 = \{[\mathbf{y}_0^0], \ldots, [\mathbf{y}_{end}^0]\}$;
– the *a priori* enclosures: $\widetilde{\mathcal{Y}}^0 = \{[\widetilde{\mathbf{y}}_0^0], \ldots, [\widetilde{\mathbf{y}}_{end}^0]\}$.

We then apply the contractor over each couple of discretized time-step boxes $[\mathbf{y}_i^0] \in \mathcal{Y}^0$ and their associated *a priori* enclosures $[\widetilde{\mathbf{y}}_i^0] \in \widetilde{\mathcal{Y}}^0$. These 2 steps are repeated in a fixed point algorithm until the contraction factor is lower than a given value. In this approach, time steps are computed at the first iteration of the algorithm and are not updated.

Example 2. We study the following linear time-invariant system disturbed by an unknown signal w constrained by a 2-norm inequality:

$$\begin{cases} \dot{x}(t) = -x(t) + w(t) \\ \int_0^t w(\tau)^2 d\tau \leq \int_0^t 0.01 x(\tau)^2 d\tau \\ x(0) \in [-1, 1] \end{cases} \qquad (15)$$

with $[\mathbf{w}] = [-1, 1]$ and $[\mathbf{w}'] = [-1, 1]$ in Eq. (7) for $t \in [0, 2.5]$. Figure 2 shows the reachable set of this dynamical system computed with the method described in this section.

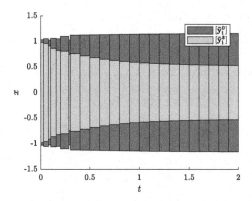

Fig. 2. Computation of the overapproximation of the reachable set of Example 2 using the algorithm presented in Sect. 4. Blue boxes corresponds to the *a priori* enclosures at the first iteration of the algorithm $\widetilde{\mathcal{Y}}^0$, green boxes are the *a priori* enclosure at the 3rd iteration $\widetilde{\mathcal{Y}}^3$ of the algorithm. (Color figure online)

5   Examples

In this part, we present applications of the method described in Sect. 4 for a tank system (Subsect. 5.1) and a delayed system (Subsect. 5.2). The results are discussed in the Subsect. 5.3.

5.1   Tank System

We consider a 2-tanks system (see Fig. 3) described by the following dynamical equation

$$\begin{cases} \dot{h}_1 = -r_1\sqrt{h_1} + w \\ \dot{h}_2 = -r_2\sqrt{h_2} + r_1\sqrt{h_1} \\ \int_0^\tau w(\tau)^2 d\tau \leq \int_0^t \left(r_2\sqrt{h_2(\tau)}\right)^2 d\tau \end{cases}, \tag{16}$$

with initial conditions:

$$\begin{cases} h_1(0) = 1 \\ h_2(0) = 0 \end{cases}.$$

$r_1 = 0.1$ and $r_2 = 0.001$ are given constants depending on the hole diameter, h_1 and h_2 are the respective level of water of tanks 1 and 2. The pump is operated externally and is considered as an unknown disturbance, we model it as the set of signals w that verify the integral constraint in Eq. (16).

The plot in Fig. 3 corresponds to the reachable set overapproximation computed using the algorithm described in Sect. 4. The overapproximation of the reachable set over h_1 is larger that over h_2. This is a consequence that the disturbance is directly added into the Tank 1 (to h_1) and is filtered by Tank 1 before influencing Tank 2. At $t = 0.6$, the reachable set over h_1 computed with the integral constraint is 9 times smaller than the reachable set computed with only the prior bound over the unknown disturbance w (see Figs. 3a and b).

5.2   Delayed System with Integral Quadratic Constraint

For $u, v \in \mathbb{L}^2_{loc}(\mathbb{R}^+; \mathbb{R})$, the delay operator D_h over an input signal u is defined by the following relationship:

$$v = D_h(u) \Leftrightarrow \begin{cases} v(t) = u(t - h) & \text{for all } t \geq h \\ v(t) = 0 & \text{otherwise.} \end{cases} \tag{17}$$

Guaranteed integration of differential equation with delays is challenging. Since they act as a memory of the past input signal over an interval of width h, the state of the delay belongs to $\mathbb{L}^2_{loc}([0, h], \mathbb{R})$. The dimension of the system state space is therefore non finite.

The stability of linear time-invariant (LTI) systems with internal delays is studied in [25]. The state of the delay is projected over finite Legendre polynomial basis. These projections are time-dependent values since the state of the

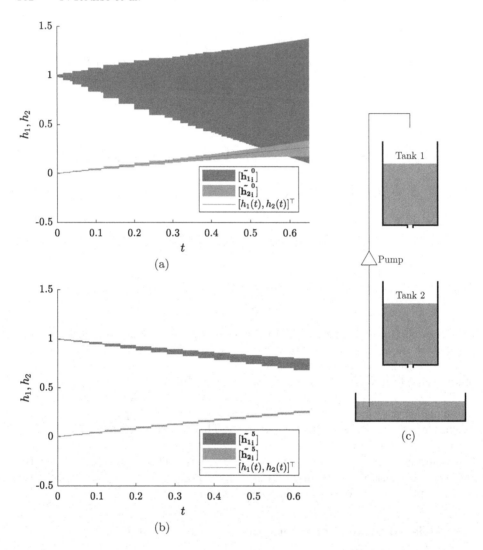

Fig. 3. The tank system described by Eq. (16) is represented in Fig. 3c. The algorithm presented in Sect. 4 is used to compute the overapproximation of h_1 (in blue) and h_2 (in orange). In Fig. 3a, the prior overapproximation of the reachable set $\widetilde{\mathcal{Y}}^0$ is shown. Figure 3b shows the *a priori* enclosures $\widetilde{\mathcal{Y}}^5$ at the 5th iteration of the algorithm. (Color figure online)

delay is also time-varying. The time derivative of these projections only depends on the input of the delay operator. Then the norm of the state is overapproximated using a Bessel inequality. By integrating this inequality, we get an Integral Quadratic Constraint (IQC) between the output of the delay operator, its input, the derivative of its inputs, the projections over the truncated basis of Legendre polynomial and an error signal. The IQC models the energy of the Legendre expansion's remainder (i.e. the error signal). In [25], the stability of the delayed LTI system is assessed for all possible error signal which verifies the derived IQC. We use this IQC to overapproximate the reachable set of such system.

In what follows, we use the first order of the IQC relationship described in [25, Theorem 5]. The state ξ corresponds to the average value of the delay's state. The remaining energy of the state is bounded by an integral quadratic constraint.

$$\begin{cases} \dot{\xi}(t) = -15\xi(t) + 1.5v(t) - w(t) \quad \text{with} \quad \xi(0) = 0 \\ \text{under the IQC} \int_0^t w(s)^2 ds \leq \int_0^t \left[0.0025\dot{v}(s)^2 - 0.75\left(v(s) - \xi(s)\right)^2 \right] ds \end{cases}$$

$$(18)$$

The IQC system Eq. (18) is used to overapproximate the delay in the following system:

$$\begin{cases} \dot{x} = -x - k_c D_h(x) \\ x(0) = 0 \end{cases} \tag{19}$$

where $k_c = 4$ and $h = 0.01$. Equations (17, 18 and 19) are then combined in a unique linear time-invariant system with an integral quadratic constraint.

$$\begin{cases} \dot{X}(t) = AX + B_w w(t) + B_u u(t) \\ X(0) = \begin{bmatrix} 0 \\ 0 \end{bmatrix} \\ \int_0^t w(\tau)^2 d\tau \leq \int_0^t \begin{bmatrix} X(\tau) \\ u(\tau) \end{bmatrix}^\top M \begin{bmatrix} X(\tau) \\ u(\tau) \end{bmatrix} \end{cases} \tag{20}$$

where the matrices are defined by

$$A = \begin{bmatrix} 1.0417 & 15.6250 \\ -6.0417 & -15.6250 \end{bmatrix}, B_w = \begin{bmatrix} 1.0000 \\ -1.0000 \end{bmatrix}, B_u = \begin{bmatrix} 1.0417 \\ -0.0417 \end{bmatrix}$$

and

$$M = \begin{bmatrix} -12.4566 & -30.5990 & 0.0434 \\ -30.5990 & -68.3594 & 0.6510 \\ 0.0434 & 0.6510 & 0.0434 \end{bmatrix}.$$

The bounds in Eq. (13) are $[\mathbf{w}] = [-10, 10]$ and $[\mathbf{w'}] = [-1, 1]$. The initial noise set is defined such that $[\mathbf{w_0}] = [\mathbf{w}]$.

Figure 4 corresponds to the flowpipe of the delayed system modeled with the integral quadratic constraint. Y_{IQC} is the reachable tube of the corresponding system.

5.3   Discussion

The main motivation of this work is to use Integral quadratic constraint (IQC) models in a guaranteed integration framework. IQC models are widely used in

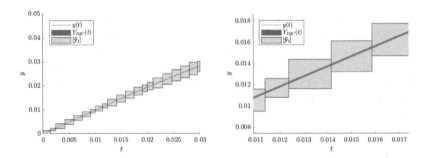

Fig. 4. Computation of the flowpipe of the system Eq. (20) using guaranteed numerical integration framework described in Sect. 3 and the contractor $\mathcal{C}$ introduced in Sect. 4. y (the blue line) corresponds to the response of the delayed system. Y_{IQC} is the exact flowpipe of system computed using the paraboloid method presented in [22]. (Color figure online)

the robust control community for stability analysis of dynamical systems. When the IQC system is stable, there exists an invariant over the set of states (x, z) and the maximal reachable z value (i.e. the maximal integral value reachable) is bounded for any trajectory.

In our approach, such an invariant does not exists. The overapproximation of the maximal reachable z is constantly increasing. Consequently, bounds provided by the fixed point algorithm are also strictly increasing. When these bounds reach the prior bounds given by Eq. (7) over the disturbance, the reachable set tends to the reachable set computed without the integral constraint. Figure 5 corresponds to the reachable set of Example 2 for a larger horizon of integration. The integral constraints provide bounds over w. However, when the energy level is too high, these bounds are strictly included in bounds given by Eq. (7). At $t = 15$ s, the reachable set converges to the reachable set of the system with no integral constraint between the disturbance and the state.

The bounds of the noise input depends on the result of the used guaranteed set integration method. Therefore, if the later are too pessimistic, the proposed contraction method will only rely on the bounds $[\mathbf{w}]$ and $[\mathbf{w}']$ of Eq. (7).

In our approach, a larger class of systems is considered compared to the linear case treated in [22]. Contrary to IQC models, only the dependence in the disturbance needs to be quadratic for the integral constraint.

In term of scalability, our approach needs the state of the original dynamical system to be extended from n variables to $p = n+m+1$ variables (m states for w, 1 state for z). Since the noise signal span in a subspace of R^n, m is always smaller than n. Since m is often close to 1 (the delay modeled as an integral quadratic constraint introduce a 1 dimensional noise signal), p is close to n (or $2n$ in the worst case). However only the integration part can suffer from the dimension of the system. Based on the advantage of our approach, a less expansive integration method can be used for large systems for a similar result.

We presented 2 examples. A non-linear system in Sect. 5.1 and a linear system with delay in Sect. 5.2. A similar approach could be applied to non-linear system with delay since the integration method can handle non-linear differential equations.

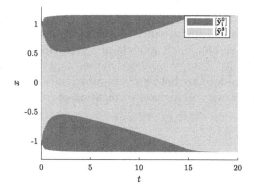

Fig. 5. Computation of the flowpipe of the system Eq. (3) in Example 2 over $[0, 20]$ using guaranteed numerical integration framework described in Sect. 3 and the contractor $\mathcal{C}$ introduced in Sect. 4. In blue, the reachable set when only Eq. (7) is used (*i.e.*, when the integral constraint is not used). In green, the reachable set of the system when the integral constraint is taken into account. (Color figure online)

6 Conclusion

We presented a method to compute an overapproximation of the reachable tube for dynamical systems with integral constraints over the input set. The integral constraint is expressed as a contractor over the set of trajectories and used in a fixed point algorithm together with a propagation process.

The method developed in this work is guaranteed (we compute an overapproximation of the reachable tube). However, our overapproximations tend to constantly grow in size, even when the reachable set is known to be bounded. At each time instant, the integral term of the integral constraint is overapproximated by an interval, its upper bound is used to compute bounds over disturbances. For a trajectory, the worst case disturbance consumes all the integral constraint and the best case disturbance consumes none of it. So the integral level is always growing and at the same time, the reachable set is overapproximated with the worst case disturbance level. In future works, a template based scheme will be used to overapproximate the maximum reachable integral value of the constraint.

Models with integral constraints are a classical tool from the robust control community. In this field, they represent energy gains between signals of the system and a disturbance signal. Many complex systems can be analyzed in this way. In future works, more applications will be discussed. More specifically, error bounds over reduced models can be expressed as a 2-norm constraints with the input signal of the system. Simplification of models is very appealing for guaranteed integration since the computational time is mainly dependent on the system dimension. Being able to reduce the order of the system and to bound the error with a 2-norm gain would lead to more efficient algorithm.

Our method provides ways to verify physical systems where the sensors are subject to energy bounded disturbances. Currently, most of these noise models are bounds over the signal. Such models are problematic when they disturb an integrating dynamic. Energy bounded noises might lead to more realistic noise models and therefore to better overapproximation of dynamical system reachable set. Future work will include verification of robotic systems subject to sensor noises.

References

1. Alexandre dit Sandretto, J., Chapoutot, A.: Contraction, propagation and bisection on a validated simulation of ODE. In: Summer Workshop on Interval Methods (2016)
2. Alexandre dit Sandretto, J., Chapoutot, A.: Validated explicit and implicit Runge-Kutta methods. Reliab. Comput. **22**, 79–103 (2016)
3. Alexandre dit Sandretto, J., Chapoutot, A.: Validated simulation of differential algebraic equations with Runge-Kutta methods. Reliab. Comput. **22** (2016)
4. Boyd, S., El Ghaoui, L., Feron, E., Balakrishnan, V.: Linear Matrix Inequalities in System and Control Theory, vol. 15. SIAM, Philadelphia (1994)
5. Chabert, G., Jaulin, L.: Contractor programming. Artif. Intell. **173**, 1079–1100 (2009)
6. Chen, M., Fränzle, M., Li, Y., Mosaad, P.N., Zhan, N.: Validated simulation-based verification of delayed differential dynamics. In: Fitzgerald, J., Heitmeyer, C., Gnesi, S., Philippou, A. (eds.) FM 2016. LNCS, vol. 9995, pp. 137–154. Springer, Cham (2016). https://doi.org/10.1007/978-3-319-48989-6_9
7. Chou, Y., Chen, X., Sankaranarayanan, S.: A study of model-order reduction techniques for verification. In: Abate, A., Boldo, S. (eds.) NSV 2017. LNCS, vol. 10381, pp. 98–113. Springer, Cham (2017). https://doi.org/10.1007/978-3-319-63501-9_8
8. Goubault, E., Putot, S., Sahlmann, L.: Inner and outer approximating flowpipes for delay differential equations. In: Chockler, H., Weissenbacher, G. (eds.) CAV 2018. LNCS, vol. 10982, pp. 523–541. Springer, Cham (2018). https://doi.org/10.1007/978-3-319-96142-2_31
9. Graettinger, T.J., Krogh, B.H.: Hyperplane method for reachable state estimation for linear time-invariant systems. J. Optim. Theory Appl. **69**(3), 555–588 (1991)
10. Gusev, M.I., Zykov, I.V.: On extremal properties of boundary points of reachable sets for a system with integrally constrained control. In: Proceedings of 20th World Congress International Federation of Automatic Control, vol. 50, pp. 4082–4087. Elsevier (2017)
11. Henrion, D., Korda, M.: Convex computation of the region of attraction of polynomial control systems. IEEE Trans. Autom. Control **59**(2), 297–312 (2014)
12. Jaulin, L., Kieffer, M., Didrit, O., Walter, É.: Applied Interval Analysis. Springer, London (2001). https://doi.org/10.1007/978-1-4471-0249-6

13. Jönsson, U.: Robustness of trajectories with finite time extent. Automatica **38**(9), 1485–1497 (2002)
14. Korda, M.: Moment-sum-of-squares hierarchies for set approximation and optimal control. Ph.D. thesis, EPFL, Switzerland (2016)
15. Kurzhanski, A.B., Varaiya, P.: On ellipsoidal techniques for reachability analysis. Part I: external approximations. Optim. Methods Softw. **17**(2), 177–206 (2002)
16. Lee, E.B., Markus, L.: Foundations of Optimal Control Theory. Wiley, New York (1976)
17. Megretski, A., Rantzer, A.: System analysis via integral quadratic constraints. IEEE Trans. Autom. Control **42**(6), 819–830 (1997)
18. Moore, R.E.: Interval Analysis. Prentice Hall, Upper Saddle River (1966)
19. Nedialkov, N.S., Jackson, K., Corliss, G.: Validated solutions of initial value problems for ordinary differential equations. Appl. Math. Comput. **105**(1), 21–68 (1999)
20. Pfifer, H., Seiler, P.: Integral quadratic constraints for delayed nonlinear and parameter-varying systems. Automatica **56**, 36–43 (2015)
21. Prajna, S., Jadbabaie, A.: Safety verification of hybrid systems using barrier certificates. In: Alur, R., Pappas, G.J. (eds.) HSCC 2004. LNCS, vol. 2993, pp. 477–492. Springer, Heidelberg (2004). https://doi.org/10.1007/978-3-540-24743-2_32
22. Rousse, P., Garoche, P.-L., Henrion, D.: Parabolic set simulation for reachability analysis of linear time invariant systems with integral quadratic constraint. In: Proceedings of European Control Conference, Naples (2019)
23. Savkin, A.V., Petersen, I.R.: Recursive state estimation for uncertain systems with an integral quadratic constraint. IEEE Trans. Autom. Control **40**(6), 1080–1083 (1995)
24. Scherer, C.W., Veenman, J.: Stability analysis by dynamic dissipation inequalities: on merging frequency-domain techniques with time-domain conditions. Syst. Control Lett. **121**, 7–15 (2018)
25. Seuret, A., Gouaisbaut, F.: Hierarchy of LMI conditions for the stability analysis of time-delay systems. Syst. Control Lett. **81**, 1–7 (2015)
26. Shampine, L.F., Thompson, S.: Numerical solution of delay differential equations. In: Gilsinn, D.E., Kalmár-Nagy, T., Balachandran, B. (eds.) Delay Differential Equations, pp. 1–27. Springer, Boston (2009). https://doi.org/10.1007/978-0-387-85595-0_9
27. Soravia, P.: Viscosity solutions and optimal control problems with integral constraints. Syst. Control Lett. **40**(5), 325–335 (2000)
28. Szczelina, R.: Rigorous integration of delay differential equations. Ph.D. thesis (2015)
29. Varaiya, P.: Reach set computation using optimal control. In: Inan, M.K., Kurshan, R.P. (eds.) Verification of Digital and Hybrid Systems. NATO ASI Series, vol. 170, pp. 323–331. Springer, Heidelberg (2000). https://doi.org/10.1007/978-3-642-59615-5_15
30. Xue, B., Mosaad, P.N., Fränzle, M., Chen, M., Li, Y., Zhan, N.: Safe over- and under-approximation of reachable sets for delay differential equations. In: Abate, A., Geeraerts, G. (eds.) FORMATS 2017. LNCS, vol. 10419, pp. 281–299. Springer, Cham (2017). https://doi.org/10.1007/978-3-319-65765-3_16

Advanced Hazard Analysis and Risk Assessment in the ISO 26262 Functional Safety Standard Using Rigorous Simulation

Adam Duracz[3], Ayman Aljarbouh[1](✉), Ferenc A. Bartha[3],
Jawad Masood[3], Roland Philippsen[2], Henrik Eriksson[4], Jan Duracz[2],
Fei Xu[2], Yingfu Zeng[3], and Christian Grante[5]

[1] GIPSA-lab, Grenoble INP, University of Grenoble Alpes, Grenoble, France
`ayman.aljarbouh@univ-grenoble-alpes.fr`
[2] School of Information Technology, Halmstad University, Halmstad, Sweden
`{roland.philippsen,jan.duracz,fei.xu}@hh.se`
[3] Department of Computer Science, Rice University, Houston, TX, USA
`{adam.duracz,ferenc.a.bartha,yingfu.zeng}@rice.edu`
[4] Dependable Systems, SP Technical Research Institute of Sweden, Boras, Sweden
[5] AB Volvo Group Trucks Technology, Gothenburg, Sweden

Abstract. With the increasing level of automation in road vehicles, the traditional workhorse of safety assessment, namely, physical testing, is no longer adequate as the sole means of ensuring safety. A standard safety assessment benchmark is to evaluate the behavior of a new design in the context of a risk-exposing test scenario. Manual or computerized analysis of the behavior of such systems is challenging because of the presence of non-linear physical dynamics, computational components, and impacts. In this paper, we study the utility of a new technology called rigorous simulation for addressing this problem. Rigorous simulation aims to combine some of the benefits of traditional simulation methods with those of traditional analytical methods such as symbolic algebra. We develop and analyze in detail a case study involving an Intersection Collision Avoidance (ICA) test scenario using the hazard analysis techniques prescribed in the ISO 26262 functional safety standard. We show that it is possible to formally model and rigorously simulate the test scenario to produce informative results about the severity of collisions. The work presented in this paper demonstrates that rigorous simulation can handle models of non-trivial complexity. The work also highlights the practical challenges encountered in using it.

Keywords: Rigorous simulation · Model verification and validation · Domain specific languages · ISO 26262 hazard analysis · Validated numerics · Interval arithmetic · Safety testing · Model-based testing

© Springer Nature Switzerland AG 2020
R. Chamberlain et al. (Eds.): CyPhy 2019/WESE 2019, LNCS 11971, pp. 108–126, 2020.
https://doi.org/10.1007/978-3-030-41131-2_6

1   Introduction

Over the last five years, the automotive industry has demonstrated increasing willingness to commercialize highly advanced driving functions, such as autonomous driving, platooning, lane departure warning systems, self-parking, etc. These advances promise to improve safety, comfort, economy, and sustainability. However, due to the computationally intensive nature of advanced driving functions, traditional physical testing is no longer sufficient. To complement physical testing, analytic and computational methods and tools including design, modeling, synthesis, simulation [24,34], and symbolic algebra [35] are needed. In this work, we focus on simulation.

Rigorous simulation [26] was introduced to combine the ease of use and scalability of simulation with the rigor of symbolic methods. The idea is to achieve ease of use by having the same user interface as traditional simulation (model in, simulation traces out), to achieve scalability by using refined but-still-essentially-the-same numerical algorithms, and to achieve rigor by ensuring that the numerical algorithms only produce provably correct *enclosures* for all outputs. The field of *validated numerics* [34] provides exactly that. Validated numerics algorithms keep track of all possible errors in the computation of all results. Enclosures are representations of sets that consist of an estimated result and a guaranteed upper bound on the error of this estimate. This makes rigorous simulation a promising tool for analyzing safety-critical systems, where all types of error, from uncertainty or computational methods, are considered.

The Next Generation Test Methods for Active Safety Functions (NG-Test) research project is an industry/academia collaboration aimed at investigating ways to mitigate the difficulties with the use of physical testing for safety evaluation. In this project, we extended ACUMEN modeling language [1,33] with support for rigorous simulation. ACUMEN facilitates modeling of complex systems through its support of a simple syntactic language with compositional constructs.

In this paper, we extend results presented in [14,22]. We show how rigorous simulation can be used to support safety analysis for realistic models of road vehicles. For industrial relevance, we focus on Hazard Analysis and Risk Assessment (HARA) as prescribed by the ISO 26262 functional safety standard [19]. We present a rigorous simulation -based severity analysis with a more realistic and significantly improved Intersection Collision Avoidance (ICA) model, including a combination of multiple braking criteria based on recommendations from the automotive industry, a more precise model of the sensor range (trapezoid), and support for simulating scenarios in different terrain. The main contribution of this paper is to demonstrate how rigorous simulation is a useful tool in providing rigorous bounds on Automotive Safety Integrity Level (ASIL), which can not be obtained by using traditional simulation, as traditional simulation can miss collision events (e.g. see Scenario 11.2 in Sect. 5.1 and Fig. 4).

The paper is organized as follows: Sect. 2 introduces Hazard Analysis and Risk Assessment (HARA) in the ISO 26262 functional safety standard. As an example of how the standard is applied, Sect. 3 describes a realistic case study that analyzes an Intersection Collision Avoidance (ICA) scenario. Section 4 introduces the vehicle and collision models in detail, and describes a key challenge in modeling and rigorously simulating the test scenario, especially the model dynamics, events, impacts, and the ICA algorithm. Section 5 discusses the results of the rigorous simulation and demonstrates its advantage in providing acceptable bounds on the severity class for different initial conditions and parameters of the test scenario. Finally, we discuss the related work and summarize the contribution and the future work in Sects. 6 and 7, respectively.

2   Hazard Analysis and Risk Assessment (HARA) in the ISO 26262 Standard

In 2011, International Organization for Standardization (ISO) released a standard for functional safety of electrical and/or electronic systems installed in road vehicles [19]. The standard recognizes three stages of the safety life cycle: concept development, product development, and after start-of-production. The ISO 26262 standard prescribes that the concept development phase should include a Hazard Analysis and Risk Assessment (HARA). A hazard is a *possible* source of harm caused by the malfunctioning behavior of an item. A risk is the *probability* of a harm. To manage risk, auxiliary quantitative measures of severity, exposure, and likelihood are introduced. Risk is taken as the product of these three quantities. Severity is a measure of potential injury that follows from a given hazard. Exposure is the expected frequency of the hazard. Likelihood is the probability that an accident will occur.

A risk classification scheme called Automotive Safety Integrity Level (ASIL) breaks down risks intro three dimensions: severity (S), exposure (E) and controllability (C). Compared to simple likelihood, controllability is the likelihood that the driver can act to prevent an injury. The ASIL can be used to signal to the system developers the level of attention or investment that is needed to mitigate the risk associated with a particular hazard.

A four-level classification is used for severity and controllability, with 0 for lowest level and 3 for the highest. Exposure is represented by a number between 0 and 4. As part of HARA, every hazard is given a classification in terms of each of these three dimensions. If there is doubt, a conservative (upper bound) classification is made. The lowest severity level, S0, is dedicated to consequences having only material damages, and in that case no ASIL assignment is required. The lowest exposure level, E0, is dedicated to extremely unusual or incredible situations and requires no ASIL assignment. Between each exposure class, there is one order of magnitude in probability. Controllability is not exclusive to the driver of the item-equipped vehicle but, rather, all people at risk are considered. Between each controllability class there is one order of magnitude in probability.

3   An Intersection Collision Avoidance (ICA) Scenario

We will consider a test scenario for an advanced emergency braking system (AEBS) for commercial vehicles. The scenario was used as a common milestone

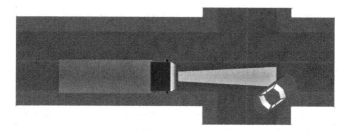

Fig. 1. Overview of the test scenario. (Color figure online)

for the parties participating in the NG-TEST project, as a step beyond an initial one-dimensional rear-end collision avoidance scenario. It is based on an EU regulation [16] that describes requirements and a type-approval test procedure. In the test procedure, path plans are given for two adjacent vehicles coming together at a four-way intersection as illustrated in Fig. 1. In the path plans illustrated by this figure, the distance between the test and target vehicles is at least 120 m when testing begins. The truck's mass is 55 t and it travels at 80 ± 2 km/h, while the car has a mass of 1.5 t and travels at 12 ± 2 km/h. We model the collision between the two vehicles as a set of vehicle configurations on their paths, that is, the collision is prevented by only controlling the acceleration of each vehicle along its path, never controlling vehicle steering. The first vehicle is a truck (gray/blue in Fig. 1) and the second vehicle is a car (red in Fig. 1).

While making a turn, the car enters the path of truck by making a right turn in the intersection. The car, then, is detected by the truck. Detection occurs when the rectangle that bounds the car intersects the yellow trapezoid that models the sensor area of the truck. Thus, the truck's AEBS sensor can detect the car already during the turn. The truck is equipped with an idealized sensor with a field-of-view modeled by a symmetric trapezoid (with length = 50 m, near-width = 1 m, far-width = 2 m). We assume that the AEBS sensor of the truck measures the position and speed of the car, and transmits this information to the truck on-board controller. The truck has to use this information to avoid a collision. To reduce the uncertainty in the behavior of the truck, we consider a human driving model in each vehicle with three modes: acceleration A, cruising C, and braking B (Sect. 4.3). The system can start in any of these modes and the car can switch from acceleration, to cruising, to braking, to model its approach to the intersection. The control approach for collision avoidance is entirely based upon the construction of a set C parametrized by values for Time-To-Collision (TTC), Critical Warning Distance (CWD) and Critical Braking Distance (CBD) indicating a future collision. Together with TTC, the distance CWD, respectively CBD, is used to determine when the truck should activate its Pre-Braking mode, respectively Braking mode. If the boundary of the set C is reached, then control applies instantaneously. Otherwise, no control is needed.

In the following sections, equations for the controller are introduced, with excerpts of Acumen code used to generate the results presented in Sect. 5.

3.1 Critical Warning Distance and Critical Breaking Distance

The critical warning distance (CWD) is a distance used as a threshold to give a warning to the driver when the vehicle spacing d is less than this distance. The critical braking distance (CBD) can be defined similarly the system applies full braking when d is less than the critical braking distance. Many CWD and CBD algorithms have been proposed by automotive companies [36]. In our test scenario, we consider Mazda CBD and Honda CWD algorithms.

Mazda's CBD Algorithm. Mazda's algorithm uses the following function for defining CBD

$$d_b = \frac{1}{2} \cdot \left(\frac{v_1^2}{\alpha_1} - \frac{v_2^2}{\alpha_2} \right) + v_1 \cdot \zeta_1 + v_{\mathrm{rel}} \cdot \zeta_2 + \eta_0, \tag{1}$$

where v_1 is the velocity of the following vehicle, $v_{\mathrm{rel}} = v_1 - v_2$ is the relative velocity between the two vehicles, α_1 and α_2 are the maximum deceleration of the leading and the following vehicle, respectively. η_0 is a headway offset, and ζ_1 and ζ_2 account for the system and the driver delays, respectively. In our implementation, the variables ζ_1, ζ_2, and η_0 are neglected.

Honda's CWD Algorithm. Honda's algorithm uses the following approximation for defining CBD

$$d_w = 2.2 v_{\mathrm{rel}} + 6.2. \tag{2}$$

The following Acumen code calculates the CBD and CWD:

```
db = 0.5*(y1'*y1'/(9.81*fri0)-(y1'-yvdiff)*(y1'-yvdiff)/(9.81*fri0)),
dw = (2.2 * abs(yvdiff)) + 6.2.
```

3.2 Time-to-Collision (TTC)

The Time-To-Collision (TTC) is defined as the time (in seconds) needed for two vehicles to collide. The mechanism for calculating TTC depends on the configuration of the directional dynamics of the engaged vehicles (Sect. 4.2).

The following Acumen code demonstrates the use of TTC in collision detection when the truck is sensing the car.

```
match TestProcedureLevel with
[ "A"->if -ydiff < ttcpb*yvdiff || distance < dw then
state1+ = "2-Pre-Brake" noelse
| "B"->if -ydiff < ttcpb*yvdiff then state1+ = "2-Pre-Brake" noelse
| "C"->if distance < dw then state1+ = "2-Pre-Brake" noelse ]
```

Setting the mode `state1` of the truck to `Pre-Brake` signals that the truck started pre-braking. A match statement is used to select a condition for switching the mode. The (instantaneous) transition is expressed as a *discrete assignment* (+ =) and switching conditions are expressed as if statements (conditionals). Analogous code handles switching from pre-braking to braking. In that case, instead of the critical warning distance `dw`, the critical braking distance `db` is used in the conditionals. We implemented three levels of test procedure reflecting the reliability of the ICA collision detection (Sect. 4.3). Level A represents the most reliable test procedure, where the estimated TTC, CWD, and CBD are all used in the collision detection. In Level B only TTC is relevant in the collision detection, while in Level C only CWD and CBD are considered. Each test procedure level corresponds to a case of the match statement.

4   Vehicle and Collision Models

In the following, we introduce the vehicle and collision models in detail. We use control theoretic methods used in intelligent transportation [9,10].

4.1   Definition of Vehicle Dynamics (Pre-Collision)

By representing each vehicle as a standard control-theoretic input-output system, the state of vehicle $i \in \{1,2\}$ along its path is given as a tuple $S_i = \{X_i, O_i, U_i, f_i, h_i\}$, where $X_i = P_i \times V_i \subset \mathbb{R}^2$ is the state space describing all the admissible continuous states (p_i, v_i), where $p_i \in P_i$ and $v_i \in V_i$ are the longitudinal displacement and the tangential velocity of the center of mass of vehicle i, respectively. Therefore, the state vector of the entire system is given as $(p, v) = (p_1, p_2, v_1, v_2)$. The output space is $O_i \subset \mathbb{R}^m$, and $h_i : O_i \times X_i$ is the set-valued output map that associates outputs with elements of the state space X_i. $U_i = [u_{iL}, u_{iH}]$ is the control input space representing the scalar combination of all possible pedal and brake torque inputs (positive when the vehicle accelerates and negative when the vehicle brakes), where u_{iL} represents the maximum brake torque command, and u_{iH} represents the maximum throttle torque command. The constraints on the control input is to ensure that the resulting control action is within the admissible actuator range. The function $f_i : X_i \times U_i \to X_i$ is a vector field modeling the dynamics of the vehicle i as $f_i = (\frac{dp_i}{dt}, \frac{dv_i}{dt}) = (v_i, w_i)$, where $w_i = 0$ if $(v_i = 0 \wedge \alpha_i < 0) \vee (v_i = v^{\max} \wedge \alpha_i > 0)$ or α_i otherwise, with $\alpha_i = a \cdot u_i + b - c \cdot v_i^2$, where $a > 0$ is the acceleration coefficient, $b < 0$ represents the static friction term, and $c > 0$ with the $c \cdot v_1^2$ term modeling air drag. For sake of simplicity, the static friction and air drag can be neglected.

Having `state2 = Post-Turn` models the cruising dynamics of the car after the turn. `ydiff` and `yvdiff` gives the differences between the vehicles' position and speed, respectively (i.e. the relative position and velocity). The threshold on the TTC for pre-braking is `ttcpb`.

The ICA system (Sect. 4.3) will issue a throttle command to the car modeled by entering the mode `Act`, while issuing a brake command to the truck when a future collision is detected. These commands are issued in a manner that does not cause the violation of predefined speed limits (either traffic laws or comfort levels). This implies that the automatic control commands do not create hazardous driving conditions for other vehicles not directly involved.

```
| "2-Post-Turn" -> rot2' = 0, x2' = 0, y2'' = 0,
if abs(yvdiff) > 0 then match TestProcedureLevel with
[ "A" ->  if -ydiff < ttcpb*yvdiff || distance < dw then
state2+ = "3-Act" noelse
| "B" -> if -ydiff < ttcpb*yvdiff then state2+ = "3-Act" noelse
| "C" -> if distance < dw then state2+ = "3-Act" noelse ] noelse.
```

Detecting that we have reached the time-to-collision threshold for activating pre-braking is done by evaluating the expression -ydiff < ttcpb*yvdiff. This check is basically equivalent to the condition (y1-y2)/(y1'-y2') >= ttcpb. The difference is that it avoids using division because it is a partial function that would result in a simulation error when the two vehicles reach the same speed. As discussed in Sect. 5.2, taking such errors into account is important in modeling for rigorous simulation.

The braking mode of the truck is active when state1 is equal to Brake. It is braking until collision or until its speed y1' reaches zero. In the latter case it stops, and this is modeled by entering the state Stopped. The acceleration rate for the truck 1 in the model is a1. Its control input for pre-braking is given by u1pb and for full braking by u1fb. The value mu represents the surface friction.

```
| "3-Brake" -> if y1' > 0 then x1' = 0, y1'' = a1 * u1fb * mu
else state1+ = "4-Stopped".
```

4.2 Calculating Time-to-Collision

A key element in detecting a collision is the calculation of a future collision point $p_+ = (p_{x+}, p_{y+})$, and the Time-To-Collision TTC for each vehicle to reach this point. A pair-wise collision detection algorithm is used to compute the points of collision, and then the time TTC. In this algorithm, a future collision point (p_{x+}, p_{y+}) is calculated using the coordinates and angles of the pair of vehicles,

$$p_{x+} = \frac{(p_{2y} - p_{1y}) - (p_{2x} \tan \theta_2 - p_{1x} \tan \theta_1)}{\tan \theta_1 - \tan \theta_2}, \tag{3}$$

$$p_{y+} = \frac{(p_{2x} - p_{1x}) - (p_{2y} \cos \theta_2 - p_{1y} \cos \theta_1)}{\cos \theta_1 - \cos \theta_2}, \tag{4}$$

where p_{ix} and p_{iy} are the x and y coordinates representing the location of the vehicle i, and the θ represents the angle between the line drawn from the same orientation or point of reference used by both vehicles and the path plan of the vehicle. After a collision point is found, TTC is then calculated by

$$TTC_i = \frac{|\vec{r}_+ - \vec{r}_i|}{\vec{v}_i} \cdot sign((\vec{r}_+ - \vec{r}_i) \cdot \vec{v}_i), \tag{5}$$

where for $i \in \{1, 2\}$, $\vec{v}_i$ is velocity of vehicle i, $\vec{r}_+$ is the future collision coordinate vector (p_{x+}, p_{y+}), and $\vec{r}_i$ is the coordinate vector (p_x, p_y). A future collision is detected if $\text{TTC}_1 = \text{TTC}_2$.

However, for some collision scenarios, future collision points cannot be computed by this formula.

We summarize these special scenarios in the following two cases:

1. **Collision on the intersection:** When the vehicle orientation lines are perpendicular, that is, $|\theta_i - \theta_j| = 90°$, then (3) and (4) become

$$p_{x+} = p_{2x}, \quad p_{y+} = p_{1y}. \tag{6}$$

2. **Front/Rear side Collision:** When the vehicle orientation lines are parallel, as for example, $\theta_{ij} = 0°$ (Rear-side collision) or $\theta_{ij} = 180°$ (Front-side collision), where $\theta_{ij} = |\theta_i - \theta_j|$, then the collision point is estimated by using the dynamic equations of the vehicles motion. A collision occurs when

$$\sqrt{(p_{1x} - p_{2x})^2 + (p_{1y} - p_{2y})^2} = 0. \tag{7}$$

If there is no valid solution for (7), the two vehicles are not at risk to collide.

4.3   The ICA System

The Intersection Collision Avoidance (ICA) system can be viewed as a parallel composition of hybrid automata with explicit modes [2–7,18], with one automaton per vehicle. The continuous state of either vehicle can be either A (accelerating), B (braking), or C (cruising). Each mode corresponds to a combination of such dynamics, and represents the continuous behaviour that is possible in that mode. The modes are $q_1 = \{A, B, C\}$, $q_2 = \{C, B\}$, $q_3 = \{A\}$, $q_4 = \{B\}$. The hybrid automata representing the ICA system is shown in Appendix A.

In the test procedure, a haptic warning (pre-brake $= 2\,\text{m/s}^2$) is issued when the TTC is less than 3.5 s. At TTC $= 2.5$ s, full braking ($5\,\text{m/s}^2$) is performed.

Figure 2 shows a hierarchical hybrid automaton that illustrates the continuous dynamics and key state variables that comprise the model. For space reasons, guard conditions and reset maps have been left out. In the "No Collision" mode, the dynamics of each vehicle are controlled by a separate automaton. Initial parameters passed to the Scenario sub-model determine the initial positions and velocities for the two vehicles, as well as the braking/acceleration applied when the car enters its "Accelerating" mode. The modes of the truck automaton correspond to different levels of engagement of the truck's sensor and AEBS. The car automaton controls the car's behaviour through and after the turn. How the car 2 turns is determined by two parameters, ρ (rotation) and τ (turning radius). Two key events can occur in the model. The first event is detecting when the car enters the truck's sensor area. This is represented by the switching from "Cruising" to "Sensing", where the finite state machine of the truck still operates in mode $q_1 = \{A, B, C\}$ during these two phases. Note that, a transition from the mode q_1 to the mode q_2 is not possible unless the truck state enters the "Sensing" subset of q_1 (see Fig. 2). The second event is when the car collides with the truck. This is represented by the switch from "No Collision" to "A Collision Happened". The conditions for both events are similar, in that they are triggered by conditions that correspond to the intersection between two polygons. Computing the coordinates of rectangle corners based on the position and orientation of each vehicle requires using non-linear (trigonometric) functions. As mentioned earlier, the expected TTC, CWD, and CBD are used to trigger transitions between the "Sensing/Pre-Braking" and "Pre-Braking/Full Braking" modes of the Truck automaton, as well as to trigger the transition "Cruising/Accelerating" modes of the car automaton.

5   Simulation Results and Discussion

Modeling and simulation were done in the ACUMEN integrated modeling and simulation environment [1]. Integrated in this tool are a code editor, both traditional and rigorous simulators, and a plotter; data table and 3D visualisation facilities. We now present and analyze the results of simulating the model presented in the previous section. This is followed by a summary of practical issues that arose during the process of modeling and rigorous simulation of this system.

5.1   Computing the Severity Class Using Simulation

Figure 3 summarizes five scenarios that were used in the case study. Associated with each scenario is a set of initial conditions and parameters, that influence the results of the simulation. They include whether or not the car will make a turn in the intersection (state2, rot2), whether the car will accelerate after making the turn (u2a), and whether there will be a collision (related to ttcpb, ttcfb, u1pb, u1fb). Scenarios 2–4 were constructed to exhibit collisions with three different severity classes. Scenario 11 was constructed to bring the vehicles close to each other without a collision. Scenario 11.2 is a variant of Scenario 11 with additional uncertainty in its parameters. It is constructed to produce a conservative rigorous simulation result that includes the possibility of a collision.

It is worth noting that standard model verification tools can be used for HARA and ASIL classification. However, these tools simply answer yes or no to the question of whether a severity class is possible or not for a given test scenario. While our method answers the same question, it also provides bounds on all modeled quantities, including those that are needed for ASIL classification, that is, the pre-collision and post-collision velocities that are necessary to compute severity classes.

Figure 4 includes the simulated values of $\Delta yv2$ (change in velocity of the car due to collision) at the end time for a given pair of traditional and rigorous

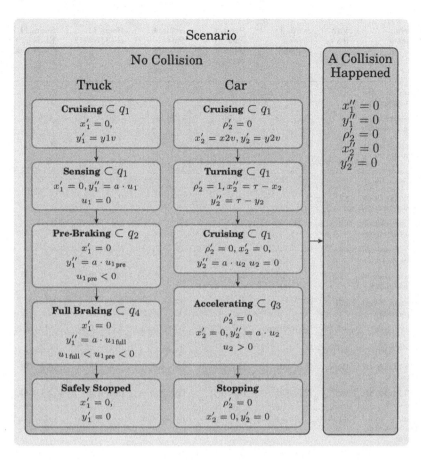

Fig. 2. A hierarchical hybrid automaton representation of the system.

simulations of the same scenario. The traditional simulations were executed on the extreme values (those that contribute to increasing $\Delta yv2$) of the parameter bounds used for the rigorous simulation. In Scenarios 2, 3, 4 and 11 the results are consistent, with the caveat that the outcome of the rigorous simulator includes the lower severity classes corresponding to its over-approximation of $\Delta yv2$. In Scenario 11.2 the rigorous simulation result is also conservative. In this case, the traditional simulation (of the extreme values of the parameters used in the scenario) yields no collision, while the enclosure produced by the rigorous simulation yields the possibility of a collision with severity class 1 or 2. The results show that rigorous simulation is able to produce useful bounds on the severity class and that, in different cases, the rigorously computed severity classification can be conservative and have different levels of precision. The enclosure for the car velocity change from the collision produced, when simulating the first three scenarios in, is shown in Fig. 5.

Scenario parameter[†]	Var. name	Scen. 2 Slow collision	Scen. 3 Fast collision Sense in-turn	Scen. 4 Fast collision Sense post-turn	Scen. 11 EU347/2012	Scen. 11.2 EU347/2012 Full truck velocity range
V1 initial position in x dimension (m)	x1	0	0	0	0	0
V1 initial position in y dimension (m)	y1	-75	-135	-170	-120	-120
V1 initial speed in x dimension (m/s)	x1v	0	0	0	0	0
V1 initial speed in y dimension (m/s)	y1v	19.55	30	40.2	[22.5, 22.8]	[21.6, 22.8]
V1 initial position in x dimension (m)	x2	9	9	9	0	0
V2 initial position in y dimension (m)	y2	0	0	0	0	0
V2 initial speed in x dimension (m/s)	x2v	-3	-3	-3	0	0
V2 initial speed in y dimension (m/s)	y2v	0	0	0	[2.7, 2.8]	[2.7, 2.8]
V2 control input for acceleration	u2a	0	1	0.75	0	0
V2 initial mode	state2	0-Pre-Turn	0-Pre-Turn	0-Pre-Turn	2-Post-Turn	2-Post-Turn
V2 rotation (ρ)	rot2	0	0	0	$\pi/2$	$\pi/2$
V1 pre-brake ttc threshold (s)	ttcpb	[3.5, 4.0]	[2.0, 2.5]	[3.5, 4.0]	[3.4, 3.5]	[3.4, 3.5]
V1 full-brake ttc threshold (s)	ttcfb	[2.5, 3.0]	[0.7, 1.0]	[2.5, 3.0]	[2.4, 2.5]	[2.4, 2.5]
V1 control input for pre-brake deceleration	u1pb	[-1.35, -1.25]	[-1, -0.9]	[-0.75, -0.5]	[-1.4, -1.35]	[-1.4, -1.35]
V1 control input for full-brake deceleration	u1fb	[-2.25, -2.15]	[-2, -1.8]	[-1.6, -1.2]	[-2.3, -2.25]	[-2.3, -2.25]

Fig. 3. Summary of parameters for collision scenarios. † The truck and the car are abbreviated as V1 and V2 respectively.

Figure 6 demonstrates how the simulated values of $\Delta yv2$ (change in velocity of the car due to collision) is used in the severity class classification for Scenario 2.

In these examples, the full brake deceleration is less than it should be. The figure shows the effect of the resulting collisions (Fig. 4) on the velocity of the car. The collisions happen around time 5, 6 and 4 for Scenarios 2, 3 and 4, respectively. The dotted horizontal lines indicate the upper bounds for the severity classes S1 (6 m/s, lower dotted line) and S2 (11 m/s upper dotted line). The plot for Scenario 2 shows that severity does not go beyond level S1, while the plot for Scenario 3 shows that severity does not go beyond level S2.

Simulation result/parameter	Scen. 2	Scen. 3	Scen. 4	Scen. 11	Scen. 11.2
Change in velocity of Vehicle 2 (car) due to collision					
Rigorous	[-5.9, 5.6]	[-12.4, 9.8]	[-11, 52]	0	[-8.3, 7.2]
Traditional	4.5	6.7	42.5	0	0
Severity class corresponding to change in velocity					
Rigorous	1	{1,2}	{1,2,3}	None	{1,2}
Traditional	1	2	3	None	None
Runtime (seconds)					
Rigorous	2,468	244	1,616	1,562	5,527
Traditional	6	10	10	10	11
Maximum time step	2^{-8}	2^{-1}	2^{-1}	2^{-9}	2^{-9}
Minimum time step	2^{-8}	2^{-9}	2^{-9}	2^{-9}	2^{-9}
Taylor approx. order	2	3	2	3	3

Fig. 4. Summary of results for simulation scenarios.

Comparing with the results from traditional simulation, in rigorous simulation, the bounds corresponding severity classes in Fig. 4 are guaranteed to take two important types of error into account: that which is expressed in the model as an uncertain parameter, and that which arises from numerical approximations during simulation. Thus, compared to traditional simulation, rigorous simulation lifts some of the burden in inferring the ASIL of a hazardous event away from the modeler and on to the simulation tool. In Fig. 4, each Scenario was executed using uncertain model parameters, specified as intervals in the model. Interval-valued parameters can be used to reflect variability of components such as sensors or brakes (corresponding respectively to the Time-To-Collision, Pre-Brake and Full-Brake thresholds ttcpb/ttcfb and the control inputs u1pb/u1fb).

5.2 Remarks About Our Developing the Model Using Acumen

ACUMEN allows the user to run the same model using traditional and rigorous simulation. The traditional simulation is faster, and in the case of an error in the model, it produces simpler error messages. We found it convenient to use non-rigorous simulation to develop the model, before switching to rigorous simulation. In the following, we mention the challenges that we encountered when switching between the traditional and rigorous simulators during our work on the model.

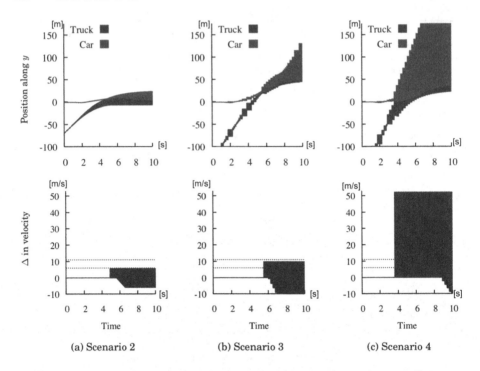

Fig. 5. Enclosures for vehicle positions and change in velocity due to collision.

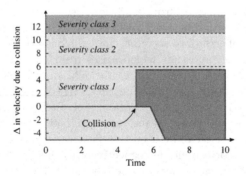

Fig. 6. Summary of results Scenario 2.

1. **Avoiding missed events.** The relatively complex geometry of the sensor field-of-view made us implement sensing using general intersection computations. As the shapes involved are convex polygons, we opted to check for intersections between the edges. This is one of the benefits of using rigorous simulation. Namely, during the first edge intersection in front/rear collisions, the respective segments become collinear. In traditional simulation, the user needs to implement additional, superfluous conditionals in the model.

Rigorous simulation never misses any intersections, making the modeling task more intuitive, and the resulting simulations more robust.

2. **Avoiding undefined operations.** A pervasive problem when working with rigorous numerical computation is that over-approximation is inevitable. The main underlying cause is that standard interval arithmetic ignores dependencies between variables. This dependence problem shows itself when evaluating an expression that contains the same variable more than once. For example, evaluating $x - x$ with $x = [0,1]$ using interval arithmetic gives $x - x = [0,1] - [0,1] = [-1,1] \neq 0$. Mitigating the dependence problem is a major concern in validated numerics. Common approaches rely on state representations that keep track of dependencies between values [12,15,21] and on algorithms that avoid evaluating expressions with wide intervals [25].

Over-approximation can give rise to operations being evaluated outside their domain. An example we encountered with this model is division by zero. In standard interval arithmetic, division is only defined when the denominator interval does not contain zero. Occasionally, over-approximation can be avoided by increasing the precision of the simulation. This may be achieved by subdivision that is simultaneously subdividing in space and decreasing the time step used. The improved precision (small resulting interval) can eliminate the problem of getting an interval that contains zero. However, this approach may lead to longer simulation times and can simply fail to solve the problem when the result is an open interval adjacent to (but not including) zero. In such cases it is important to consider whether the model can be reformulated to avoid the use of a partial operation. A practical example that arose in this model is a condition $a < b/c$, which was replaced with $a * c < b$ to avoid the problem under the assumption that c is positive, and $a * c > b$ when it is non-positive. The most obvious lesson that can be drawn from this experience is that it is better to avoid the use of partial functions when total functions would suffice. A deeper insight is that rigorous simulation tools *nudge the user* in the direction of such better modeling practices sooner than traditional tools.

3. **Selecting the simulation time step.** In traditional numerical simulation, reducing simulation time steps generally leads to longer simulations, but yields more precise results (until we get to very small time steps). The situation is considerably more involved with rigorous simulations. First, decreasing the time step might lead to a loss of precision known as the *wrapping effect* [25]. Second, both increasing and decreasing simulation steps can increase computational cost. Depending on the dynamics of a model, choosing a smaller step may help us obtain a conclusive outcome from a simulation. For example, one of the scenarios (described in Sect. 3) supported by the model has the vehicles come close to collision but still averts it. As shown in Fig. 7, selecting a step that is too large (2^{-5}, light colors) yields enclosures that include paths corresponding to a collision, which is insufficient to rule out the possibility of a collision. Decreasing the step by a factor of three (to 2^{-8}, dark colors) shows conclusively that the collision does not occur. However, this does increase computational cost. Increasing simulation time

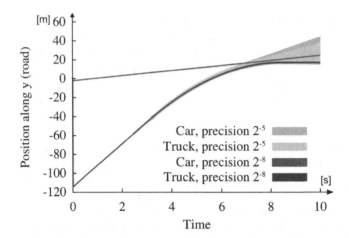

Fig. 7. Enclosures computed with two different step sizes.

steps can also increase runtime. This happens because it can lead to greater uncertainty in the values of variables, which in turn can lead to more branching. Branching can happen when multiple time steps are needed to determine conclusively that an enclosure does cross an event guard. It is possible that this problem is compounded if, before the branches can be recombined, they lead to more branching. In such situations, decreasing the step can lead to a faster simulation, by reducing the time spent on crossing event boundaries.

6   Related Work

Commercial tools exist that specifically support ISO 26262 HARA, for example: RiskCAT [29], medini analyze [23], SOX2 [32] and Polarium ALM [8]. These tools automatically determine ASILs based on the selected S, E, and C values for each hazardous event. However, they do not explicitly support design decisions and analyses of severity and exposure classes through modeling, and simulation.

There are also tools for formal analysis of models. Two such examples are Simulink Design Verifier [31] and SCADE Suite Design Verifier [30]. Both tools use the Prover Plug-In [27] for model and/or equivalence checking. However, this is limited to discrete-time control systems and does not handle hybrid systems.

Several reachability analysis tools for hybrid automata [2,4–7,18] can be used for problems related to the automotive domain. Tools like SpaceEx [17], Flow* [11,28], C2E2 [13] can produce reach set-based over-approximations. However, for scalability, reachability tools are limited to specific classes of problems.

Theorem proving has also been successfully used to verify the safety of a protocol for distributed cruise control on multi-lane roads [20]. Compared to our work, the work in [20] focuses on the analysis of systems with dynamically varying number of vehicles in a set of connected lanes. Rather than modeling the position of a vehicle in two-dimensional space, lane-change is modeled by gradual destruction and creation of state variables in the parallel, one-dimensional systems that represent each lane. The model in [20] does not include the collision dynamics, and thus does not provide information to derive its severity class. Furthermore, current implementations theorem provers tools rely on symbolic algebra and techniques that require the existence of analytical tools, which may limit their applicability compared to tools based on validated numerics.

7   Conclusions and Future Work

This paper demonstrates how rigorous simulation can be used to assist in ensuring the safety of advanced driving functions. In particular, we focus on its use to study the severity of collisions in a safety testing scenario based on the guidelines of the ISO 26262 standard. We present a detailed account of the model developed for the case study along with the results of rigorous simulation of this model with different parameters, and report on practical challenges that we encountered along with suggested workarounds.

In the future, we would like to focus on better understanding and on improving the performance of the current implementation of rigorous simulation in ACUMEN. In particular, we plan to explore better ways to reduce and control branching. For example, we suspect that the current implementation generates significant branching computations that can be avoided with relatively small changes to key algorithm parameters around an event. More precise simulations of models with uncertain initial state can be achieved by splitting the uncertainties and running a separate simulation for each combination of parts. We plan to add support for automating this kind of batch simulation into ACUMEN. The proposed collision scenarios were treated as a case studies in this paper. In the future, we plan to consider more general approach, that is, a general collision scenario with multiple vehicles (more than a truck and a car) present in the scene.

Acknowledgments. This work is supported by US National Science Foundation award CPS-1136099, Swedish Knowledge Foundation, Center for Research on Embedded Systems (CERES), VINNOVA (Dnr. 2011-01819), the European University of Brittany, and the Regional Council of Brittany.

Appendix A

Figure 8 demonstrates the finite state machine of the ICA's system with all possible transitions between modes.

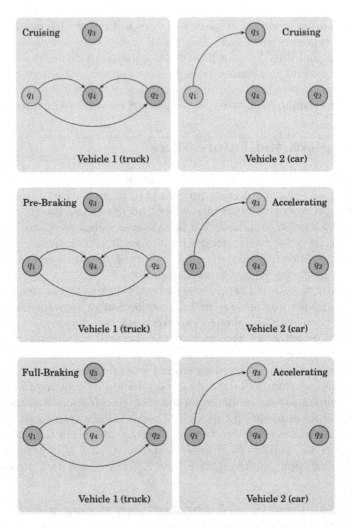

Fig. 8. The finite state machine of the ICA's system with all possible transitions between modes.

References

1. Acumen (2016). http://acumen-language.org

2. Aljarbouh, A.: Accelerated simulation of hybrid systems: method combining static analysis and run-time execution analysis (Simulation Accélérée des Systèmes Hybrides: méthode combinant analyse statique et analyse à l'exécution). Ph.D. thesis, University of Rennes 1, France (2017). https://tel.archives-ouvertes.fr/tel-01614081
3. Aljarbouh, A.: Non-standard zeno-free simulation semantics for hybrid dynamical systems. In: Ganty, P., Kaâniche, M. (eds.) VECoS 2019. LNCS, vol. 11847, pp. 16–31. Springer, Cham (2019). https://doi.org/10.1007/978-3-030-35092-5_2
4. Aljarbouh, A., Caillaud, B.: On the regularization of chattering executions in real time simulation of hybrid systems. In: 11th Baltic Young Scientists Conference, Tallinn, Estonia, p. 49, July 2015. https://hal.archives-ouvertes.fr/hal-01246853
5. Aljarbouh, A., Caillaud, B.: Robust simulation for hybrid systems: chattering path avoidance. In: Proceedings of the 56th Conference on Simulation and Modelling (SIMS 56), Linköping University, Sweden, 7–9 October 2015, pp. 175–185, No. 119. Linköping University Electronic Press, Linköpings universitet (2015)
6. Aljarbouh, A., Caillaud, B.: Chattering-free simulation of hybrid dynamical systems with the function mock-up interface 2.0. In: Proceedings of the First Japanese Modelica Conferences, Tokyo, Japan, 23–24 May 2016. Linköping University Electronic Press, Linköpings universitet (2016)
7. Aljarbouh, A., Zeng, Y., Duracz, A., Caillaud, B., Taha, W.: Chattering-free simulation for hybrid dynamical systems semantics and prototype implementation. In: 2016 IEEE International Conference on Computational Science and Engineering, CSE 2016, and IEEE International Conference on Embedded and Ubiquitous Computing, EUC 2016, and 15th International Symposium on Distributed Computing and Applications for Business Engineering, DCABES 2016, Paris, France, 24–26 August 2016, pp. 412–422 (2016). https://doi.org/10.1109/CSE-EUC-DCABES.2016.217
8. ALM-PLM (2015). http://polarion.com
9. Baskar, L.D., De Schutter, B., Hellendoorn, J., Papp, Z.: Traffic control and intelligent vehicle highway systems: a survey. IET Intel. Transp. Syst. 5(1), 38–52 (2011)
10. Basma, F., Tachwali, Y., Refai, H.H.: Intersection collision avoidance system using infrastructure communication. In: 2011 14th International IEEE Conference on Intelligent Transportation Systems (ITSC), pp. 422–427. IEEE, Washington, DC (2011)
11. Chen, X., Ábrahám, E., Sankaranarayanan, S.: Flow*: an analyzer for non-linear hybrid systems. In: Sharygina, N., Veith, H. (eds.) CAV 2013. LNCS, vol. 8044, pp. 258–263. Springer, Heidelberg (2013). https://doi.org/10.1007/978-3-642-39799-8_18
12. De Figueiredo, L.H., Stolfi, J.: Affine arithmetic: concepts and applications. Numer. Algorithms 37(1–4), 147–158 (2004)
13. Duggirala, P.S., Mitra, S., Viswanathan, M., Potok, M.: C2E2: a verification tool for stateflow models. In: Baier, C., Tinelli, C. (eds.) TACAS 2015. LNCS, vol. 9035, pp. 68–82. Springer, Heidelberg (2015). https://doi.org/10.1007/978-3-662-46681-0_5
14. Duracz, A., Eriksson, H., Bartha, F.Á., Zeng, Y., Xu, F., Taha, W.: Using rigorous simulation to support ISO 26262 hazard analysis and risk assessment. In: 2015 IEEE 12th International Conference on Embedded Software and Systems (ICESS), pp. 1093–1096. IEEE, August 2015
15. Duracz, J., Farjudian, A., Konečný, M., Taha, W.: Function interval arithmetic. In: Hong, H., Yap, C. (eds.) ICMS 2014. LNCS, vol. 8592, pp. 677–684. Springer, Heidelberg (2014). https://doi.org/10.1007/978-3-662-44199-2_101

16. EU Regulation No. 347/2012: Type-approval requirements for certain categories of motor vehicles with regard to advanced emergency braking systems (2012)
17. Frehse, G., et al.: SpaceEx: scalable verification of hybrid systems. In: Gopalakrishnan, G., Qadeer, S. (eds.) CAV 2011. LNCS, vol. 6806, pp. 379–395. Springer, Heidelberg (2011). https://doi.org/10.1007/978-3-642-22110-1_30
18. Henzinger, T.A.: The theory of hybrid automata. In: Logic in Computer Science, pp. 278–292. IEEE Computer Society, New Brunswick (1996)
19. ISO26262: Road vehicles - functional safety (2011)
20. Loos, S.M., Platzer, A., Nistor, L.: Adaptive cruise control: hybrid, distributed, and now formally verified. In: Butler, M., Schulte, W. (eds.) FM 2011. LNCS, vol. 6664, pp. 42–56. Springer, Heidelberg (2011). https://doi.org/10.1007/978-3-642-21437-0_6
21. Makino, K., Berz, M.: Taylor models and other validated functional inclusion methods. Int. J. Pure Appl. Math. 4, 4 (2003)
22. Masood, J., Philippsen, R., Duracz, J., Taha, W., Eriksson, H., Grante, C.: Domain analysis for standardised functional safety: a case study on design-time verification of automatic emergency braking. In: International Federation of Automotive Engineering Societies 2014 World Automotive Congress, Maastricht, The Netherlands, 2–6 June 2014. FISITA (2014)
23. Medini analyze (2015). http://ikv.de
24. Mosterman, P.J.: An overview of hybrid simulation phenomena and their support by simulation packages. In: Vaandrager, F.W., van Schuppen, J.H. (eds.) HSCC 1999. LNCS, vol. 1569, pp. 165–177. Springer, Heidelberg (1999). https://doi.org/10.1007/3-540-48983-5_17
25. Nedialkov, N.S., Jackson, K.R., Corliss, G.F.: Validated solutions of initial value problems for ordinary differential equations. Appl. Math. Comput. 105(1), 21–68 (1999)
26. Nedialkov, N.S., Von Mohrenschildt, M.: Rigorous simulation of hybrid dynamic systems with symbolic and interval methods. In: 2002 Proceedings of the American Control Conference, vol. 1, pp. 140–147. IEEE (2002)
27. Prover (2015). http://prover.com
28. Ramdani, N., Nedialkov, N.S.: Computing reachable sets for uncertain nonlinear hybrid systems using interval constraint-propagation techniques. Nonlinear Anal. Hybrid Syst. 5(2), 149–162 (2011)
29. RiskCAT (2015). http://cats-tools.de
30. SCADE design verifier (2015). http://esterel-technologies.com
31. Simulink design verifier (2015). http://mathworks.com
32. SOX2 (2015). http://enco-software.com
33. Taha, W.: Acumen: an open-source testbed for cyber-physical systems research. In: Mandler, B., et al. (eds.) IoT360 2015. LNICST, vol. 169, pp. 118–130. Springer, Cham (2016). https://doi.org/10.1007/978-3-319-47063-4_11
34. Tucker, W.: Validated Numerics: A Short Introduction to Rigorous Computations (2011)
35. Ueda, K., Matsumoto, S.: Hyrose: a symbolic simulator of the hybrid constraint language HydLa. In: Computer Software, vol. 30. Citeseer (2013)
36. Zhang, Y., Antonsson, E.K., Grote, K.: A new threat assessment measure for collision avoidance systems. In: 2006 IEEE Intelligent Transportation Systems Conference, ITSC 2006, pp. 968–975. IEEE, September 2006. https://doi.org/10.1109/ITSC.2006.1706870

Practical Multicore Extension of Functionally and Temporally Correct Real-Time Simulation for Automotive Systems

Wonseok Lee[1], Jaehwan Jeong[2], Seonghyeon Park[2], and Chang-Gun Lee[2(✉)]

[1] Hyundai R&D Center, Hwaseong-Si, Gyeonggi-Do 18280, Korea
won.seok.django@gmail.com
[2] Seoul National University, Gwanak-ro 1, Gwanak-gu, Seoul 08826, Korea
{jhjeong,seonghyeonpark}@rubis.snu.ac.kr, cglee@snu.ac.kr,
https://rubis.snu.ac.kr/

Abstract. Existing simulation methods cannot provide functionally and temporally correct simulations for the cyber-side of automotive systems since they do not correctly model temporal behaviours such as varying execution times and task preemptions. To address such limitations, our previous work proposes a novel simulation technique that guarantees the functional and temporal simulation correctness. However, the simulation technique is designed assuming a single core simulator. In this work, we extend the single core simulator targeting a multicore simulator to enhance the simulation capacity. In this multicore extension, a major challenge is the inter-core interferences in a multicore environment, which causes unpredictability of simulated job execution times, which in turn makes it hard to model the timings of the real cyber-side of an automotive system. To overcome the challenge, this paper empirically analyzes the inter-core interferences for typical automotive workloads and proposes a practical multicore extension approach, which can still provide a functionally and temporally correct simulation, without using complex inter-core isolation mechanisms. Our experimental study shows that the proposed multicore extension approach can significantly improve the simulation capacity over the previous single core simulator while still preserving simulation correctness.

Keywords: Real-time simulation · Multicore simulator · Automotive systems

1 Introduction

Simulating an automotive system based on an accurate simulation model is essential to correctly predict its final performance at the design phase. Incorrect prediction due to imprecise simulation model causes painful repetition of design changes and re-implementations.

© Springer Nature Switzerland AG 2020
R. Chamberlain et al. (Eds.): CyPhy 2019/WESE 2019, LNCS 11971, pp. 127–152, 2020.
https://doi.org/10.1007/978-3-030-41131-2_7

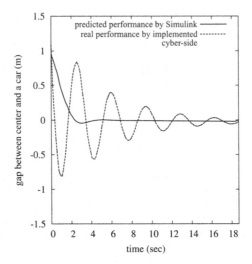

Fig. 1. Predicted performance and real performance of LKAS [8]

Figure 1 shows significant gap between the predicted performance of LKAS (Lane Keeping Assistance System) by Simulink [15]—most widely used simulator in the automotive industry and the real performance. The reason why the real performance is not observed on existing simulation tools is that they only focus on functional behaviours of the system and do not carefully consider the temporal behaviours caused by varying execution times and task preemptions on ECU (Electronic Control Unit) environments.

For both functionally and temporally correct simulation of the cyber-side of an automotive system while guaranteeing real-time interaction with its physical-side, our previous work [18] transforms the real-time simulation problem into a real-time job scheduling problem on a single core simulator PC and shows a significant improvement on the real-time simulation capacity compare to the other pre-existing simulation methods.

However, the limitation for the single core simulator is that it cannot simulate a entire car system which consists of 70–80 ECUs [9]. Our previous single core method uses the property that simulation PC has more powerful performance than ECU. e.g. Core i7-9700K [7] in PC vs. TC275 [5] in ECU. However, it is impossible to simulate around 70–80 ECUs by only one single core(See Fig. 7 in [18]). In this paper, in order to overcome the lack of simulation capacity for a entire car system, we aim at extending the single core simulator to the multi-core simulator to increase the real-time simulation capacity. Our previous single core simulator keeps the functional and temporal simulation correctness relying on the "execution time mapping property" from the PC execution time to the ECU execution time, which is essential for the simulator PC to correctly model jobs' start/finish times on the ECU from their execution times on the simulator PC. However, such execution time mapping property is not easily preserved on multicore simulator PC due to interferences on inter-core shared memory resources such as LLC (last-level cache), memory bus, and main memory, etc. That is, even for the same job, its execution time on a core of the simulator PC largely varies depending on the amount of interferences from other cores executing other jobs. Thus, the execution time of a job measured on the simulator PC cannot be directly mapped to its ECU execution time. Due to this reason, the simple minded extension of our previous single-core based simulation method to multicore would not work.

To overcome the challenge, this paper proposes a practical approach. First, we conduct intensive empirical study on the actual amount of inter-core interference focusing on real automotive workload. From such study, we find that the execution time mapping property can be preserved even on the multicore simulator PC by a static partitioning of simulation target tasks onto multiple cores satisfying the local cache size constraint to avoid severe inter-core interferences without using complicated isolation mechanisms such as shared cache partitioning [12], memory bandwidth partitioning [21] and DRAM bank partitioning [20]. Second, we propose a heuristic task partitioning method that effectively considers precedence relations among tasks for their maximally concurrent executions on multicore under the local cache size constraint. Our extensive experiments say that the proposed heuristic can effectively increase the capacity of functionally and temporally correct simulation.

This paper is organized as follows. In Sect. 2, we survey related works. Then, Sect. 3 explains the idea of functionally and temporally correct simulation on single core simulator which we want to extend to the multicore. In Sect. 4, we empirically analyzes the inter-core interferences and derive a practical approach for multicore extension. In Sect. 5, we propose our heuristic approach for multicore simulator. In Sect. 6, we evaluate our approach. Finally, Sect. 7 concludes the paper.

2 Related Works

To predict the final performance of the cyber-side of an automotive system at the design phase, simulation tools such as Simulink [15] are widely used in industry. However, they mimic only functional behaviours of the system and do not consider temporal behaviours which will occur once the system is implemented on the ECUs. The simulated tasks on Simulink are ideally executed while ignoring the temporal differences caused by ECU environments. Moreover, Simulink is focusing on offline simulations which do not interact with the real-time physical-side.

To simulate the system while interacting with the real-time physical-side, real-time simulation on AutoBox [3] is commonly used. However, AutoBox provides only rapid prototyping of the system and does not consider the timings of the real target ECUs. The temporal behaviours of the simulated tasks are determined only by the performance of AutoBox hardware, and users do not have any control knob to model the real target ECUs' performance which determines the actual temporal behaviours and the final performance.

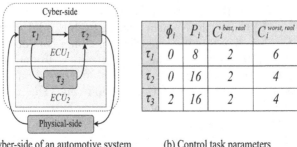

	ϕ_i	P_i	$C_i^{best,\,real}$	$C_i^{worst,\,real}$
τ_1	0	8	2	6
τ_2	0	16	2	4
τ_3	2	16	2	4

(a) Cyber-side of an automotive system   (b) Control task parameters

Fig. 2. Example automotive system

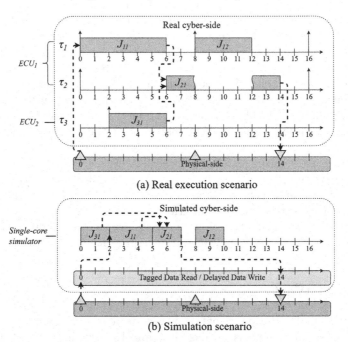

(a) Real execution scenario

(b) Simulation scenario

Fig. 3. Execution scenario and simulation scenario of example automotive system

To accurately model the temporal behaviors on the real target ECUs, we can think of cycle-accurate instruction set simulators [2,13,19]. However, they are too slow to provide the real-time simulation interacting with the real-time physical side.

To achieve the two goals at the same time, i.e., (1) the real-time interaction with the physical side and (2) the functionally and temporally correct simulation, our previous work [18] proposes a novel simulation method. However, the proposed method uses only a single core of the simulator PC and hence its simulation capacity is limited.

To increase the simulation capacity, a brief idea of using multiple cores of the simulation PC based on G-EDF (Global-Earliest Deadline First) is proposed [17]. However, it does not consider the invalidation of execution time mapping property due to inter-core interferences and job migrations from core to core. Thus, it cannot guarantee the functional and temporal correctness of the simulation.

3   Overview of Single Core Simulation

For the functionally and temporally correct simulation, the simulated cyber system should interact with the physical system at the same time with the same value as the real cyber system. However, the physical interaction times and values are not deterministic due to non-deterministic task execution times. To address such non-determinism, our previous single-core simulation method [18] makes a precedence graph among simulated jobs including all possible non-determinism. From the precedence graph, it executes jobs one by one while resolving the non-determinism once a job's execution time on the simulation PC is known and hence its mapped ECU execution time is known.

Since it is the baseline for extending to the multicore simulation PC, our previous method is briefly explained in this section using a simple example of Fig. 2. In the figure, the cyber-side of an automotive system to be simulated consists of three control tasks τ_1, τ_2, and τ_3. The data producer/consumer relations among the tasks or physical-side are denoted by directed edges as in Fig. 2(a). τ_1 and τ_2 are mapped to ECU_1 and τ_3 is mapped to ECU_2. The communication channel between ECUs, e.g., CAN or FlexRay, is not shown here and the communication time between tasks in different ECUs is assumed to be zero for the simplicity of explanation. A detailed description of TDMA bus delay(i.e. communication time between ECUs) is already addressed in our previous work, at Appendix B [18].

Each task, τ_i, is realized on its mapped ECU as a periodic task and can be represented as a five-tuple.

$$\tau_i = (F_i, \Phi_i, P_i, C_i^{best,real}, C_i^{worst,real})$$

where F_i is the function that τ_i executes, Φ_i is the task offset, P_i is the period of τ_i. $C_i^{best,real}$ and $C_i^{worst,real}$ represent the best case and the worst case execution times on its mapped ECU, respectively. The parameters of the three tasks are given in Fig. 2(b). The j-th job of τ_i that is released at $\Phi_i + (j-1)P_i$ is denoted by J_{ij}.

If the RM (Rate Monotonic) scheduling policy is used on ECU_1 and ECU_2, we can expect one of their possible execution scenarios as Fig. 3(a) shows[1]. The time points where the cyber and physical-side interact each other are marked as triangles, and one of the data paths from the physical read to the physical write is denoted by dashed directed arrows considering the real automotive tasks' properties, i.e., **Most recent data use** and **Entry read/Exit write**. In the

---

[1] There can be many different execution scenarios on the real cyber system since every job J_{ij} can have any execution time within $[C_i^{best,real}, C_i^{worst,real}]$.

Fig. 3(a), J_{11} reads the most recent data from the physical-side at time 0, i.e., entry read, and produces output at time 6, i.e., exit write. J_{21} that is also released at time 0 has a lower priority than J_{11} on ECU_1. Thus, it starts executing at time 6. At that time, its another predecessor J_{31} has been already completed on ECU_2. Thus, J_{21} reads the data from J_{11} and J_{31}. After that, it is preempted by J_{12} at time 8 and resumes at time 12. Then, it finishes its execution at time 14 and produces its output to the physical side.

For such a real execution scenario, the simulated cyber-side should interact with the physical side at the same time with the same value as the real cyber system. For this, our previous single-core simulation method leverages the following properties of the simulation PC:

- **Faster execution than ECU:** Since PC has more powerful performance than ECU, the execution times of F_is are much faster on the simulator than that of on the ECU. e.g., Core i7-9700K [7] in PC vs. TC275 [5] in ECU.
- **Tagged/Delayed Data Read/Write:** The simulator can log all of physical read/write data with time-tags. The simulator can execute the F_is with any specific tagged physical read data. Similarly, the simulator can write the delayed output data to the physical-side at any specific time point.
- **Execution time mapping functions:** For every F_i, there exist execution time mappings between the simulator and the ECU. That is, when J_{ij} is executed on the simulator for the time of e_{ij}^{sim}, we can estimate its execution time on the ECU, $e_{ij}^{real} = M_i(e_{ij}^{sim})$ where M_i represents the execution time mapping function.

Leveraging those properties, our simulator can execute the simulated jobs as in Fig. 3(b) such that its effect to the physical side is the same as the real cyber system, i.e., functionally and temporally correct simulation. In Fig. 3(b), we assume that $e_{ij}^{real} = 2 * e_{ij}^{sim}$ for all F_is. At time 0, the single-core simulator logs the physical-side data with its time-tag 0. The data logging time is assumed negligibly small. Then, it executes J_{31}. When J_{31}'s execution finishes, the simulator knows that J_{31}'s PC execution time is 2 as shown in Fig. 3(b) and its ECU mapped execution time is 4. Thus, the simulator knows that J_{31}'s finish time on the real cyber system is 6 as shown in Fig. 3(a). Then, the simulator starts executing J_{11} with the time-0 tagged physical data. After J_{11}'s execution finishes, J_{21} starts its execution. At this moment, the simulator already finished J_{11} and J_{31} and hence knows that their real finish time is 6 using the execution time mapping function. Thus, the simulator knows that the most recent data that J_{21} read in the real cyber system are the ones from J_{11} and J_{31}. This way, the previously non-deterministic precedence relations among jobs are now deterministically resolved. Thus, the simulator can start J_{21}'s execution with the correct data. Similarly, after the simulator finishes J_{21} and J_{12}, using their PC execution times and their mapped ECU execution times, the simulator can predict the real finish time of J_{21} is time 14 as shown in Fig. 3(a). Thus, the simulator holds J_{21}'s output and delay its physical write until 14 as shown in Fig. 3(b). This is an example that shows how the non-deterministic physical write time is resolved as deterministic by progressive executions of simulated jobs.

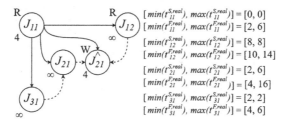

$$[min(t_{11}^{S,real}), max(t_{11}^{S,real})] = [0, 0]$$
$$[min(t_{11}^{F,real}), max(t_{11}^{F,real})] = [2, 6]$$
$$[min(t_{12}^{S,real}), max(t_{12}^{S,real})] = [8, 8]$$
$$[min(t_{12}^{F,real}), max(t_{12}^{F,real})] = [10, 14]$$
$$[min(t_{21}^{S,real}), max(t_{21}^{S,real})] = [2, 6]$$
$$[min(t_{21}^{F,real}), max(t_{21}^{F,real})] = [4, 16]$$
$$[min(t_{31}^{S,real}), max(t_{31}^{S,real})] = [2, 2]$$
$$[min(t_{31}^{F,real}), max(t_{31}^{F,real})] = [4, 6]$$

Fig. 4. Job-level precedence graph of the example automotive system

More formally, we can say that the simulation is functionally and temporally correct if all the simulated jobs can be scheduled while satisfying:

- **Physical-read constraint:** For any job J_{ij} who reads physical-side data, the simulator should schedule it later than its actual start time on the real cyber-side. i.e.,

$$t_{ij}^{S,sim} \geq t_{ij}^{S,real} \tag{1}$$

where $t_{ij}^{S,sim}$ and $t_{ij}^{S,real}$ represent the start time of J_{ij} on the simulator and the real cyber-side, respectively.

- **Physical-write constraint:** For any job J_{ij} who writes its produced data to the physical-side, the simulator should finish it before its actual finish time on the real cyber-side, i.e.,

$$t_{ij}^{F,sim} \leq t_{ij}^{F,real} \tag{2}$$

where $t_{ij}^{F,sim}$ and $t_{ij}^{F,real}$ represent the finish time of J_{ij} on the simulator and the real cyber-side, respectively.

- **Producer/consumer constraint:** For any pair of jobs, $J_{i'j'}$ and J_{ij}, if $J_{i'j'}$ is a producer job of J_{ij} on the real cyber-side, the simulator should finish $J_{i'j'}$ before starting J_{ij}, i.e.,

$$t_{i'j'}^{F,sim} \leq t_{ij}^{S,sim} \tag{3}$$

To schedule the simulated jobs while meeting all of the above constraints, the simulator has to know $t_{ij}^{S,real}$ and $t_{ij}^{F,real}$ which are non-deterministic in the beginning due to the varying execution times of the jobs. To tackle this challenge, the previously proposed simulation method with a single-core [18] transforms the simulation problem to a real-time job scheduling problem with job-level precedence requirements and progressively resolves the non-determinism by executing simulated jobs one-by-one. Here, we briefly review the method using the example automotive system in the Fig. 2. The simulation problem for the cyber-side of an automotive system in the Fig. 2 can be transformed to a job-level precedence graph scheduling problem as shown in Fig. 4. At the left-side of the Fig. 4, each vertex represents the job to be simulated. The tags, 'R' or 'W', at the upper-left corner of the jobs show the physical read/write constraints that the

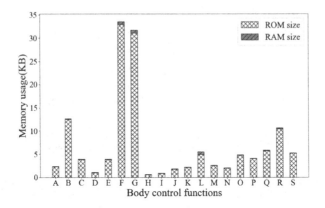

Fig. 5. Memory size of functions for body control module implemented by Renault [16]

tagged jobs have. Each edge shows the pre-execution condition between the jobs where hat-job ($\hat{J}_{21}$) is virtually added job which has zero-execution time and is needed only for deriving pre-execution conditions. The solid edge $(J_{i'j'}, J_{ij})$ represents the deterministic edge which means $J_{i'j'}$ should be finished before J_{ij} starts. The dashed edge $(J_{i'j'}, J_{ij})$ represents the non-deterministic edge which means it is not known yet whether $J_{i'j'}$ should be finished before J_{ij} or not. The closed-intervals at the right-side of the Fig. 4 represent the expected $t_{ij}^{S,real}$, $t_{ij}^{F,real}$ ranges which are varied by the execution times of the jobs. The numbers at the lower-left corner of the jobs show the deadlines which are calculated based on the deterministic edges and the $t_{ij}^{S,real}$, $t_{ij}^{F,real}$ ranges.

To schedule the jobs in the job-level precedence graph, the simulator first finds a job which does not have any unfinished deterministic predecessor. If the found job does not have the physical read constraint, it adds this job to the ready queue of the simulator. If the found job has the physical read constraint, it adds the found job only when Eq. (1) holds, i.e., current time is later than its start time on the real cyber-side. Out of the jobs in the ready queue, one of them is scheduled based on EDF (Earliest-Deadline-First) scheduling policy according to their assigned deadlines. Whenever a job in the ready queue is finished, its execution time on the simulator, e_{ij}^{sim}, becomes known, so its execution time on the real cyber-side, $e_{ij}^{real} = M_i(e_{ij}^{sim})$, is also known. Using the e_{ij}^{real}, the simulator progressively narrows the $t_{ij}^{S,real}$, $t_{ij}^{F,real}$ ranges. At this step, the non-deterministic edges are either determined as deterministic edges or removed based on the narrowed $t_{ij}^{S,real}$, $t_{ij}^{F,real}$ ranges, which results in an updated job-level precedence graph. Lastly, the simulator re-assigns the deadline of each job using the updated job-level precedence graph. By iterating the above processes, the proposed simulation method continues executing the simulated jobs using a single core of the simulation PC until the end of the required simulation interval or until a deadline is violated, which is a failure of real-time simulation.

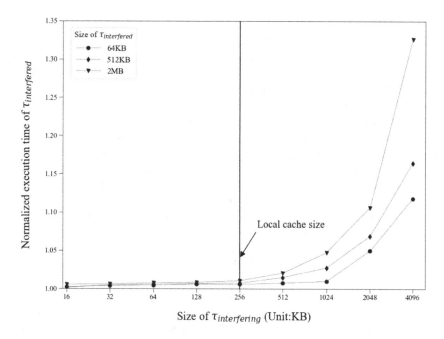

Fig. 6. Experimental result for inter-core interferences

Note that the previous single-core simulation method relies on the execution time mapping function to correctly resolve the non-determinism of the job-level precedence graph. The existence of the execution time mapping function in a single-core simulation PC is well justified in [18]. However, in the multicore environment of the simulation PC, it is reported that the inter-core interferences at the shared memory such as the shared last-level cache and DRAM cause the delay spike of the executed job as high as 600% of its normal execution time [14]. It means that e_{ij}^{sim} observed by the simulator not only depends on the actual computation amount but also heavily depends on the memory interferences from other cores. Thus, it is hard to estimate e_{ij}^{real} from e_{ij}^{sim} observed by the simulator.

This is the key challenge we encounter when we extend the previous single-core simulator to the multicore simulator.

4 Empirical Analysis for Deriving a Practical Approach for Multicore Simulator

To minimize the inter-core interferences at the shared memory of multicore systems, the isolation techniques such as shared cache partitioning [12], memory bandwidth partitioning [21] and DRAM bank partitioning [20]. However, implementing those techniques on the PC is very complex requiring OS kernel modifications and even hardware changes.

Instead, focusing on automotive system tasks, we aim at finding a practical approach that can be easily implemented on the PC to prevent unpredictable inter-core interferences at the shared memory and hence make the existence of the execution time mapping functions valid even in the multicore environment. Since the automotive system tasks run on ECU which has limited memory resource, they are normally implemented to access the small memory section. For example, Fig. 5 shows the such small memory usages ranging from 1 KB to 35 KB of the automotive functions composing the body control module of Renault (Due to the confidentiality reasons, the specific information of each function is not given). If they are compiled on the simulation PC, we can expect the similar amount of memory footprint although the ISAs (Instruction Set Architectures) of PC and ECU are different. Thus, if a set of such small memory footprint tasks can reside within the per-core local cache which has 256 KB size in most modern general-purpose PC, after the cold starts at their initial executions, their accessed memory blocks will be copied to the local cache of each core and rarely evicted. Thus, they rarely access the shared memory and hence their execution times may not be severely affected by shared memory accesses from other cores.

In order to justify this conjecture, we make a synthetic task denoted by τ that accesses to an integer array in sequential order and calculate the sum of element-wide power. We use such a synthetic task τ since we can freely control its memory footprint size and its computation amount by controlling the array size. As a multicore simulation PC, we use a i7-3610QM [6] 4 core equipped Intel CPU which has a 256 KB local cache for each core and a 6 MB shared LLC. To obtain the base execution time of τ denoted by e^{sim}, we run it 5000 times exclusively on a single core keeping all other cores idle. Our experiments say that from the second to the 5000th execution times except the cold start execution, that is, the first one, are almost the same. Thus, we use their average as e^{sim}.

In order to investigate how much τ's execution time is affected by the inter-core interferences, we now concurrently run one τ denoted by $\tau_{interfered}$ on core-1 and the other τs denoted by $\tau_{interfering}$ on core-2 and core-3 as changing their array sizes. In this experiment, the measured execution time of $\tau_{interfered}$ is denoted by $e^{sim}_{interfered}$. Figure 6 plots the normalized execution time of $\tau_{interfered}$, i.e., $\frac{e^{sim}_{interfered}}{e^{sim}}$. As increasing the size of $\tau_{interfering}$, the normalized execution time of $\tau_{interfered}$ tends to increase. Such increase becomes sharper when $\tau_{interfered}$ is larger. This is because the size increase of $\tau_{interfered}$ makes a number of shared memory accesses larger that can be delayed by the shared memory accesses from $\tau_{interfering}$ concurrently running on two cores. Nevertheless, when the sizes of $\tau_{interfered}$ and $\tau_{interfering}$ is smaller than 256 KB, the normalized execution time of $\tau_{interfered}$ is very close to 1.0, that is negligible execution time increase due to inter-core interferences, regardless of the size of $\tau_{interfering}$. This is because $\tau_{interfered}$'s memory access is mostly contained within the local cache and hence its execution time is rarely delayed by shared memory accesses of $\tau_{interfering}$ on core-2 and core-3.

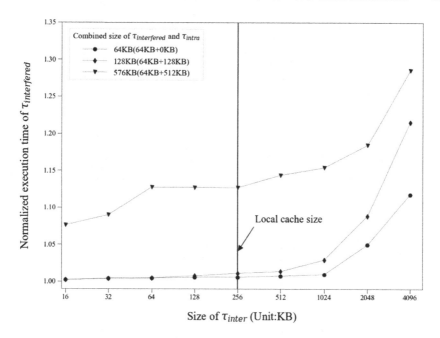

Fig. 7. Experimental result for inter-core interferences with intra-core interferences

In order to investigate both intra-core and inter-core interferences all together, in Fig. 7, we concurrently run multiple tasks. More specifically, on core-1, one τ denoted by $\tau_{interfered}$ fixing its size as 64 KB and another τ denoted by τ_{intra} as changing its array size to 0 KB, 128 KB and 512 KB. On core-2 and core-3, one τ each denoted by τ_{inter} as increasing its size from 16 KB to 4 MB. The y-axis of the Fig. 7 is the normalized execution time of $\tau_{interfered}$ while the x-axis is the size of τ_{inter}. Conclusionally, even though $\tau_{interfered}$ execution is affected both by other task τ_{intra} on core-1, i.e., intra-core interferences, and by the other tasks τ_{inter}s on core-2 and core-3, i.e., inter-core interferences, when each (1) the total size of $\tau_{interfered}$ and τ_{intra}, and (2) size of τ_{inter} is kept smaller than 256 KB, their combined effect is still minor, that is, the normalized execution time is very close to 1.0.

Practical Finding 1: This empirical study says that if we map tasks to a core such that their total memory usage is contained within a local cache, we can avoid severe inter-core interferences.

Next, in order to investigate the task migration effect from one core to another, we migrate τ over core-1 and core-2 back and forth. When we run τ on 2 cores, we first run τ once on core-1 to avoid the cold start effect. Then, for the second run of τ, to model m migrations, we divide its access loop count by $m + 1$ and run each divided piece migrating over core-1 and core-2 back and forth. The total execution time of τ which migrates over core-1 and core-2 is denoted by $e^{sim}_{migration}$. Its normalized execution time relative to e^{sim} is plotted in

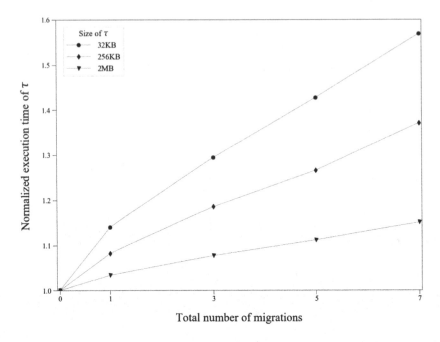

Fig. 8. Experimental result for migration effect

Fig. 8. From the Fig. 8, we can observe that τ's execution time is largely affected by task migrations. Also, the migration effect is more severe when the task size is smaller. Because the small size τ with 32 KB mostly hits on L1 cache on one core, but if it is migrated to another core, a relatively large reload cost should be added to its execution time.

This severe migration effect on the task execution time prevents a global scheduling method like a G-EDF from being a practical job scheduling method for our multicore simulator.

Practical Finding 2: This empirical study says that we have to use a partitioned multicore scheduling method to avoid the non-negligible execution time variations due to task migrations.

Combining the above two practical findings, we derive the following:

Practical Finding 3: For the existence of the execution time mapping functions even in the multicore simulation PC, a practical approach to avoid the execution time variations due to inter-core interferences and migrations, without using the complex isolation methods, is to use a partitioned scheduling approach subject to the following local cache constraint:

$\forall c_i \in \mathbb{C}$,

$$\sum_{\forall \tau_j \ mapped \ to \ c_i} (MEM_{\tau_j}) \leq Local \ cache \ size \ of \ c_i \qquad (4)$$

where $\mathbb{C} = \{c_1, c_2, ...\}$ represents the set of cores on the multicore simulator and MEM_{τ_j} represents the memory footprint size of task τ_j.

5   Proposed Heuristic for Task Partitioning

The analysis in Sect. 4 tells us that the existence of the execution time mapping function is valid even in the multicore simulation PC environment, if we use a partitioned multicore scheduling subject to the local cache constraint in Eq. (4). Thus, our practical approach to extending our previous simulated job scheduling algorithm from the single core PC to the multicore PC is as follows:

- First, we find a partitioning of the given task set, e.g, Fig. 2, into the given number of cores satisfying the local cache constraint for each core. The tasks in each partition are statically mapped to a core meaning that jobs from those tasks can only be executed on the mapped core.
- Second, we dynamically manage the job-level precedence graph and progressively execute the simulated jobs in the same way of the single core simulation PC [18]. Only difference in the multicore simulation PC is that, among jobs whose all deterministic predecessors have already finished, we choose up to m earliest deadline jobs not just one, where m denotes the number of cores in multicore simulation PC. Those m jobs are executed on their statically mapped cores.

This way, we can keep the validity of the execution time mapping functions of all the tasks in the multicore simulation PC as well. Thus, the proof for the functionally and temporally correct real-time simulation in the single core PC [18] still works in the multicore simulation PC.

Now, our remaining problem is to find a good task partitioning solution satisfying the local cache constraint. The problem is reducible to bin packing decision problem which is known as NP-Complete [4]. When we consider exhaustive search of the whole possible partitioning cases, the size of solution space equals to $S(|\mathbb{T}|, |\mathbb{C}|)$ where S represents the second kind of Stirling number which exponentially increases according to the number of tasks and cores. e.g., $S(9, 4) = 7770, S(10, 4) = 34105$. Since there is no polynomial time algorithm and the whole solution space is too large to exhaustively search, the heuristic approaches such as Best-fit-first, Worst-fit-first can be considered to practically find the partitioning [11]. However, those heuristics are not likely to give good task partitioning solution since they only focus on the packing of item(task) without considering the job-level precedence graph of the given task set. A good task partitioning solution is one that can maximize the concurrent executions of simulated jobs using multicore respecting all the precedence constraints of the job-level precedence graph, in order to maximize the chance of finishing all of them before their deadlines in the simulation duration. To this end, we propose Smallest-blocking-first heuristic which partitions the given tasks considering potential parallelism in the job-level precedence graph.

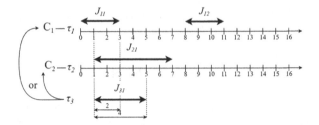

Fig. 9. Intuition of Smallest-blocking-first heuristic

We first give the intuition of Smallest-blocking-first heuristic using Fig. 9. Let's assume that the tasks τ_1 and τ_2 are already mapped to c_1 and c_2, respectively, as shown in the figure. Thus, jobs of τ_1, e.g., J_{11} and J_{12}, will be executed on c_1 and jobs of τ_2, e.g., J_{21}, will be executed on c_2. Each bidirectional arrow represents the job of each task where its left-end means $EEST_{ij}$ (Expected Earliest Start Time) of J_{ij} at the simulator, and its right-end means $ELFT_{ij}$ (Expected Latest Finish Time) of J_{ij} at the simulator. The duration $[EEST_{ij}, ELFT_{ij}]$ is a *conservative active interval* during which J_{ij} may be using its mapped core. Thus, when we determining which core τ_3 should be mapped to, we consider how much of J_{31}'s conservative active interval overlaps with those of τ_1 jobs and τ_2 jobs. If the τ_3 is mapped to c_1, the length of overlapped interval of is 2 as Fig. 9 shows. Since the only one job can be executed on a core at a time, one of the J_{11} and J_{31} will be blocked for up to 2 time units. On the other hand, if τ_3 is mapped to c_2, the overlapped interval is 4, which means one of J_{21} and J_{31} will be blocked for up to 4 time units. Thus, the overlapped interval of the conservative active intervals of a pair of two tasks can be interpreted as a potential pairwise blocking factor, i.e., inverse of the potential pairwise parallelism, when they are mapped to the same core. Thus, the proposed Smallest-blocking-first heuristic always choose the smallest blocking core at every decision to maximize the potential parallelism. In the example of Fig. 9, Smallest-blocking-first maps the τ_3 to the c_1 which has lower blocking value.

Now, the rest of this section explains how to find $EEST_{ij}$ and $ELFT_{ij}$ from the job-level precedence graph and how to use them to compute the pairwise blocking for the Smallest-blocking-first heuristic.

5.1   Finding the Expected Earliest Start Time at the Simulator

The more predecessors a job has in the job-level precedence graph, the later its possible start time will be, since it can start only after all of its predecessors finish. Therefore, to conservatively expect the $EEST_{ij}$s as early as possible one, we need to consider as few as possible precedence relations in the job-level precedence graph. To this end, we eliminate all the non-deterministic edges, which are not sure to be deterministic or removed during the simulation, from the job-level precedence graph. Figure 10(a) shows the original job-level precedence graph with non-deterministic edges for the example of Fig. 4. For the job-level

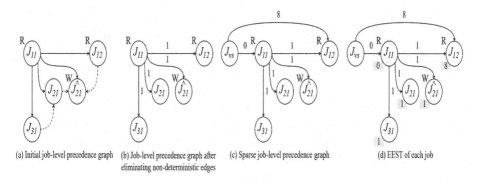

(a) Initial job-level precedence graph   (b) Job-level precedence graph after eliminating non-deterministic edges   (c) Sparse job-level precedence graph   (d) EEST of each job

Fig. 10. Construction of sparse graph and $EEST_{ij}$ of each job for the example job-level precedence graph

precedence graph, Fig. 10(b) shows the job-level precedence graph after eliminating all the non-deterministic edges.

After eliminating the non-deterministic edges from the job-level precedence graph, we assign the edge weights to the remaining edges following:

$$w(J_{ij}, J_{kl}) = C_i^{best,sim} \tag{5}$$

where $C_i^{best,sim}$ represents the best case execution time of τ_i on the simulator. Figure 10(b) also shows such assigned weights.

Since we assign the edge weights as the best case execution time of the predecessor job, the length of the longest path from the initially scheduled job to the J_{ij} equals to the $EEST_{ij}$ when we assume the infinite number of simulator cores which provides ideally parallelized execution. The job-level precedence graph after eliminating non-deterministic edges forms a DAG (Directed Acyclic Graph) as it is already proven that the job-level precedence graph with only deterministic edges cannot contain a cycle [18]. Since there exists a polynomial time algorithm to find the longest path on the DAG, we can find the $EEST_{ij}$ of each job in polynomial time [1].

However, unlike the normal DAG, our job-level precedence graph has a constraint about the start time of each job as the Eq. (1) shows. It means that the start time of the J_{ij} who has physical read constraint is affected by not only its predecessor jobs but also its actual start time on the real cyber-side. In other words, although the physical read job does not have any unfinished deterministic predecessor, it cannot be added to the ready queue of the simulator until its actual start time on the real cyber-side.

To consider such constraint, we add a virtual start job J_{vs} to the job-level precedence graph and connect it to the jobs who have physical read constraint as in Fig. 10(c). In addition, we also connect the J_{vs} to all the jobs who do not have any predecessor with zero-weight. These edges allow us to regard the J_{vs} as a single start job of the job-level precedence graph by collecting all the jobs who might could be initially scheduled. In summary, the weights of newly connected edges are assigned following:

$$w(J_{vs}, J_{ij}) = \begin{cases} min(t_{ij}^{S,real}), & \text{when } J_{ij} \text{ has} \\ & \text{phy. read constraint} \\ 0, & \text{otherwise} \end{cases} \quad (6)$$

As we mentioned at the Sect. 3, the start time interval $[min(t_{ij}^{S,real}), max(t_{ij}^{S,real})]$ is progressively narrowed during the simulation. i.e., the value of $min(t_{ij}^{S,real})$ keeps increasing. By assigning the least narrowed $min(t_{ij}^{S,real})$ value as the weight of edge from the J_{vs} to the J_{ij} who has physical read constraint, we can force the length of the longest path from the J_{vs} to the J_{ij} to be larger than the earliest start time of J_{ij} on the real cyber-side.

After adding the virtual start job and assigning the corresponding edge weights, we find the lengths of the longest path from the J_{vs} to each job as Fig. 10(d) shows. The shaded box at the lower-left corner of each job J_{ij} represents the length of the longest path which equals to $EEST_{ij}$.

5.2   Finding the Expected Latest Finish Time at the Simulator

Similar with the start time, the more predecessors a job has in the job-level precedence graph, the later its finish time will be. Therefore, to conservatively expect the $ELFT_{ij}$s as late as possible one, we need to consider as many as possible precedence relations in the job-level precedence graph. To this end, in this time, we regard the non-deterministic edges as the deterministic edges. However, when we consider both of deterministic and non-deterministic edges, the job-level precedence graph may contain cycles which makes it impossible to define the longest path from the job to the another job. Therefore, we first resolve the cycle by eliminating the one of the non-deterministic edges composing a cycle.

Whenever a job in the job-level precedence graph finishes, the simulator checks below inequality using the narrowed $t_{ij}^{S,real}$, $t_{ij}^{F,real}$ ranges for all of the remaining non-deterministic edges (J_{kl}, J_{ij})s:

$$max(t_{kl}^{S,real}) < min(t_{ij}^{S,real}) \quad (7)$$

If the above inequality holds, the non-deterministic edge (J_{kl}, J_{ij}) becomes deterministic [18]. During the simulation, the value of $max(t_{kl}^{S,real})$ keeps decreasing and $min(t_{ij}^{S,real})$ keeps increasing according to the narrowed $t_{ij}^{S,real}$, $t_{ij}^{F,real}$ ranges. Therefore, it intuitively implies that a smaller difference between $max(t_{kl}^{S,real})$ and $min(t_{ij}^{S,real})$ likely makes the non-deterministic edge deterministic at the end. On the other hand, a larger value of $max(t_{kl}^{S,real}) - min(t_{ij}^{S,real})$ likely makes the non-deterministic edge deleted at the end. From this speculation, we delete the non-deterministic edge who has the largest $max(t_{kl}^{S,real}) - min(t_{ij}^{S,real})$ value among the non-deterministic edges composing the cycle. Since

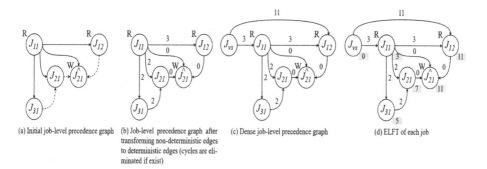

(a) Initial job-level precedence graph (b) Job-level precedence graph after transforming non-deterministic edges to deterministic edges (cycles are eliminated if exist) (c) Dense job-level precedence graph (d) ELFT of each job

Fig. 11. Construction of dense graph and $ELFT_{ij}$ of each job for the example job-level precedence graph

there exist plenty of polynomial time cycle detection algorithms [10], we can resolve the cycles in polynomial time by repeating the deletion of such non-deterministic edge until no more cycle is detected. Figure 11(b) shows the job-level precedence graph transformed from the original one in Fig. 11(a) by transforming non-deterministic edges to deterministic and eliminating cycles if any.

After resolving the cycles, we assign the edge weights to the remaining edges following:

$$w(J_{ij}, J_{kl}) = C_k^{worst,sim} \tag{8}$$

where $C_k^{worst,sim}$ represents the worst case execution time of τ_k on the simulator. Figure 11(b) also shows such assigned weights.

Then, we add the virtual start job and its corresponding edges from the J_{vs} to the jobs who have physical read constraint or do not have any predecessor as in Fig. 11(c). The weights of edges from J_{vs} are assigned following:

$$w(J_{vs}, J_{ij}) = \begin{cases} max(t_{ij}^{S,real}) \\ \quad + C_i^{worst,sim}, & \text{when } J_{ij} \text{ has} \\ & \text{phy. read constraint} \\ C_i^{worst,sim}, & \text{otherwise} \end{cases} \tag{9}$$

Unlike the $EEST$ case, we assign the edge weights using the worst case execution time of the successor job such that the finish time will be as late as possible. Such weights also make the virtual start job force the physical read jobs to start and finish as late as possible. i.e., they start at the latest start time on the real cyber-side, $max(t_{ij}^{S,real})$, and are executed for the worst case execution time, $C_i^{worst,sim}$.

This weight assignment allows us to regard the length of the longest path from the J_{vs} to the J_{ij} as the latest finish time $ELFT_{ij}$ of the J_{ij} on the cycle-eliminated job-level precedence graph if we assume the ideally parallelized execution, i.e., infinite number of cores. In Fig. 11(d), such computed $ELFT_{ij}$ for each job is denoted as the shaded box at the lower-right corner of each job.

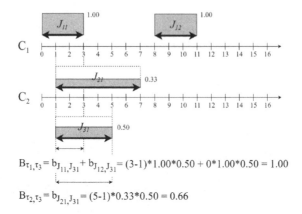

$$B_{\tau_1,\tau_3} = b_{J_{11},J_{31}} + b_{J_{12},J_{31}} = (3-1)*1.00*0.50 + 0*1.00*0.50 = 1.00$$

$$B_{\tau_2,\tau_3} = b_{J_{21},J_{31}} = (5-1)*0.33*0.50 = 0.66$$

Fig. 12. Weighted intervals and task-wise blocking values for the example job-level precedence graph

Note that unlike the $EEST_{ij}$, we cannot guarantee $ELFT_{ij}$ is always later than the actual finish time of the simulated job J_{ij} since we speculatively eliminate cycles and assume the infinite number of cores. Nevertheless, we can still use $ELFT_{ij}$ as a good end delimiter for the active interval of J_{ij} to approximately compute the potential blocking factor among tasks.

5.3 Weighting the $[EEST_{ij}, ELFT_{ij}]$ Intervals

Our conservative approach to find $[EEST_{ij}, ELFT_{ij}]$ intervals may leads us to expect too wide intervals which cannot precisely predict the pairwise blocking among tasks. Since the job J_{ij} can be executed only up to for $C_i^{worst,sim}$ within the interval $[EEST_{ij}, ELFT_{ij}]$, we weight the each interval as follow:

$$w([EEST_{ij}, ELFT_{ij}]) = \frac{C_i^{worst,sim}}{ELFT_{ij} - EEST_{ij}} \tag{10}$$

Figure 12 shows the resulting weighted intervals and pairwise blocking values for the example job-level precedence graph in the Fig. 4. The figure represents the situation where τ_1 and τ_2 are already mapped to c_1, c_2, respectively, and we are determining which core τ_3 should be mapped to. The pairwise blocking between τ_i and τ_j, B_{τ_i,τ_j}, is defined as the sum of their job-wise blocking, $b_{J_{ik},J_{jl}}$:

$$B_{\tau_i,\tau_j} = \sum_{\forall J_{ik} \in \tau_i} \sum_{\forall J_{jl} \in \tau_j} b_{J_{ik},J_{jl}} \tag{11}$$

Algorithm 1. Proposed task partitioning algorithm

1: $\mathbb{T} \leftarrow \{\tau_1...\tau_n\}$ // *set of tasks*
2: $\mathbb{C} \leftarrow \{c_1...c_m\}$ // *set of cores*
3: $\mathbb{U} \leftarrow \{U_1 = 0...U_m = 0\}$ // *mem. usage of each core*
4: $\mathbb{P} \leftarrow \{P_1 = \emptyset...P_m = \emptyset\}$ // *task partition of each core*
5: **for** $\tau_i \in \mathbb{T}$ **do**
6:    $core_{min} \leftarrow -1$
7:    $block_{min} \leftarrow \infty$
8:    **for** $P_j \in \mathbb{P}$ **do**
9:       **if** $U_j + MEM_{\tau_i} > local\ cache\ size\ of\ c_j$ **then**
10:          continue
11:       **end if**
12:       $block \leftarrow 0$
13:       **for** $\tau_k \in P_j$ **do**
14:          $block = block + B_{\tau_i,\tau_k}$
15:       **end for**
16:       **if** $block < block_{min}$ **then**
17:          $block_{min} \leftarrow block$
18:          $core_{min} \leftarrow j$
19:       **end if**
20:    **end for**
21:    **if** $core_{min} = -1$ **then**
22:       Task partitioning failed!
23:    **else**
24:       $U_{core_{min}} = U_{core_{min}} + MEM_{\tau_i}$
25:       $P_{core_{min}} = P_{core_{min}} \cup \{\tau_i\}$
26:    **end if**
27: **end for**

The job-wise blocking $b_{J_{ik},J_{jl}}$ between J_{ik} and J_{jl} is defined as the weighted product of overlapped length:

$$b_{J_{ik},J_{jl}} = the\ length\ of\ overlapped\ interval$$
$$* w([EEST_{ik}, ELFT_{ik}])$$
$$* w([EEST_{jl}, ELFT_{jl}])$$

$$(12)$$

For example, the pairwise blocking between τ_1 and τ_3, B_{τ_1,τ_3}, is defined as the sum of their job-wise blockings $b_{J_{11},J_{31}}$ and $b_{J_{12},J_{31}}$ as in Fig. 12. When we consider $b_{J_{11},J_{31}}$, the overlapped interval is $[1, 3]$ and weights of each interval are 1.00 and 0.50 respectively. Thus, $b_{J_{11},J_{31}}$ is 2 * 1.00 * 0.50 = 1.00. On the other hand, since $[EEST_{12}, ELFT_{12}]$ and $[EEST_{31}, ELFT_{31}]$ do not overlap each other, $b_{J_{12},J_{31}}$ is zero. Thus, the pairwise blocking between τ_1 and τ_3 is $B_{\tau_1,\tau_3} = 1.00$.

5.4   Task Partitioning Heuristic Using Pairwise Blocking

Using the above way of computing the pairwise blocking between two tasks, our proposed heuristic task partitioning can be formally described as Algorithm 1.

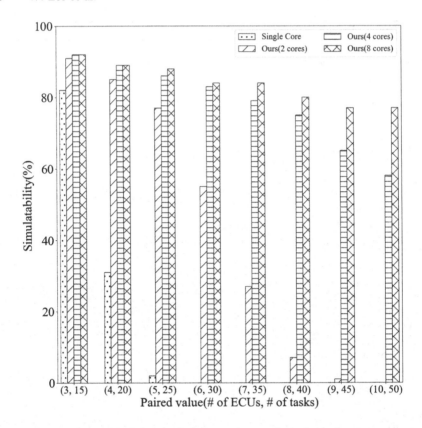

Fig. 13. Simulatability according to the number of simulator cores

For each task τ_i, the for loop from Line 8 to Line 20 checks each partition P_j mapped to each core c_j.

- to see if the local cache constraint is violated if τ_i is added to P_j (from Line 9 to Line 11),
- to accumulate the pairwise blocking between the newly added task τ_i and the already mapped tasks (from Line 12 to Line 15), and
- to see if the accumulated pairwise blocking for the current partition P_j is the minimum (from Line 16 to Line 19)

After the for loop, the algorithm maps τ to the core with minimum accumulated blocking among the cores satisfying the local cache constraint.

6   Evaluation

To evaluate our proposed approach, we measure the "simulatability" of our simulation method using randomly synthesized cyber-sides of an automotive system.

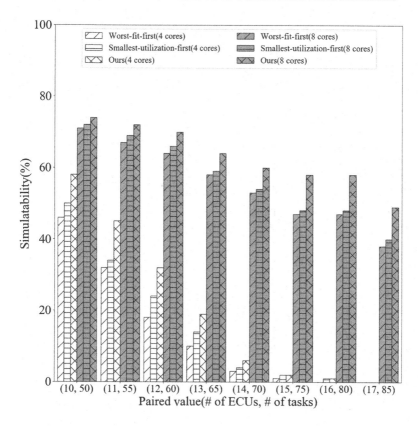

Fig. 14. Simulatability compared to the other task partitioning heuristics

i.e., how many of them can guarantee functionally and temporally correct real-time simulation [18]. In the rest of this paper, by "cyber-side", we mean the cyber-side of an automotive system which is similarly given as the Fig. 2.

At first, in Fig. 13, we conduct a experiment to see how much simulatability can be improved by our proposed multicore extension (named **Ours**(m) where m is the number of cores) over the previous single core simulator (named **Single core**). For this, we synthesize 9,000 random cyber-sides. Each cyber-side is synthesized as follows. The number of ECUs is determined from $uniform[3, 10]$. The number of tasks on each ECU is fixed as 5. Out of all the tasks in each cyber-side, 20% of them read data from the physical-side. Similarly, another 20% of them write data to the physical-side. The data producer/consumer relations among the tasks are randomly configured, but the total number of producer/consumer relations does not exceed the number of tasks in each cyber-side. For each task τ_i, its task parameters are randomly generated as follows. Its task period P_i is randomly selected from $\{5\,\mathrm{ms}, 10\,\mathrm{ms}, 20\,\mathrm{ms}, 25\,\mathrm{ms}, 50\,\mathrm{ms}, 100\,\mathrm{ms}\}$ while the offset Φ_i is assumed as zero. The worst case execution time $C_i^{worst,real}$ is determined from $uniform(0, 20]\%$ of the P_i. The best case execution time $C_i^{best,real}$ is determined

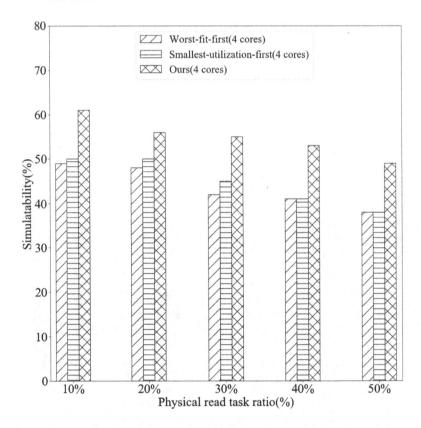

Fig. 15. Simulatability as changing the physical read task ratio

from $uniform(0, 100]\%$ of the $C_i^{worst,real}$. For all the tasks in each cyber-side, we assume the following simple execution time mapping function:

$$e_{ij}^{real} = \frac{e_{ij}^{sim}}{3} \tag{13}$$

For each of such synthesized cyber-sides, we run the simulation during the ten hyper periods and count it simulatable if no deadline violation is observed. In order to focus on precedence relations among tasks rather than tasks' memory sizes, we assume that the memory usage of each task is extremely small, so even all of them can be fit into a local cache of a core.

For such conducted experiment, Fig. 13 compares the simulatability by **Single core** and by **Ours(2 cores)**, **Ours(4 cores)**, **Ours(8 cores)** for the different pairs of no. of ECUs and no. of tasks. Note that larger numbers of ECUs and tasks imply more complex cyber-sides. From the figure, we can observe that the simulatability of **Single core**, the baseline, drops down to 0% when the number of ECUs and tasks pair is (6, 30). On the other hand, our proposed approach using 8 cores, **Ours(8 cores)**, still has 84% simulatability for the same

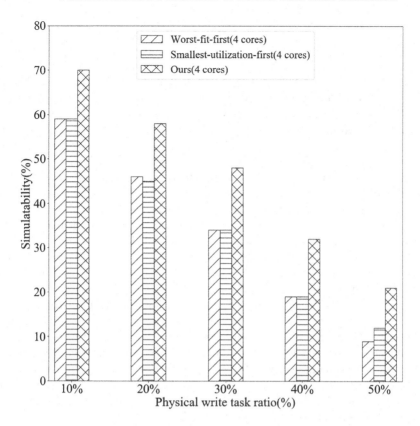

Fig. 16. Simulatability as changing the physical write task ratio

number of ECUs and tasks pair, i.e., (6, 30). Furthermore, by comparing **Ours(2 cores)**, **Ours(4 cores)**, and **Ours(8 cores)**, we can also see that our proposed approach scalably schedules the more ECUs and tasks in line with the increasing number of simulator cores.

Secondly, in Fig. 14, we conduct another experiment to compare our proposed approach with other task partitioning heuristics. For this, we synthesize another 9,000 random cyber-sides in the same way as in Fig. 13 except that the number of ECUs is determined from $uniform[10, 17]$ for focusing on more complex cyber-sides. In the figure, we compare our task partitioning algorithm with the following commonly used heuristics:

- **Worst-fit-first:** It considers only memory constraint. It places the new task in a core where it fits loosest. i.e., a core who has the largest remaining local cache size after placing MEM_{τ_i}
- **Smallest-utilization-first:** It considers only utilization of each core. It places the new task in a core which has the smallest utilization where the utilization of a core c_i, $Util_{c_i}$, is defined as below:

$$Util_{c_i} = \sum_{\forall\ \tau_j\ mapped\ to\ c_i} \frac{C_j^{worst,real}}{P_j} \tag{14}$$

Figure 14 shows that **Ours** always has better simulatability than **Worst-fit-first** and **Smallest-utilization-first** in both cases of using **4 cores** and **8 cores**. The simulatability improvement by **Ours** over **Worst-fit-first** and **Smallest-utilization-first**, confirms that our Smallest-blocking-first heuristic can effectively consider the job-level precedence graph while other heuristics cannot.

In order to more deeply investigate how the physical interactions of the given cyber-side affect the simulatability, we conduct another experiments in Figs. 15 and 16. For this, we additionally synthesize another 9,000 cyber-sides in the same way as the previous experiments except that we vary the physical read/write task ratios while fixing the number of ECUs as 10. Figure 15 shows the simulatability as increasing the physical read task ratio from 10% to 50% while keeping the physical write task ratio as 20%. From the figure, we can observe that the simulatability tends to decrease as increasing the physical read task ratio, for all of **Ours**, **Worst-fit-first**, and **Smallest-utilization-first**. This is because the more physical read tasks imply the more physical read constraint in Eq. (1), which forces more jobs to wait until their actual start times on the real cyber-side although they do not have any unfinished deterministic predecessors. Nevertheless, the simulatability of **Ours** decreases less than **Worst-fit-first** and **Smallest-utilization-first** making more significant improvement, since **Ours** employing Smallest-blocking-first well considers the $[EEST_{ij}, ELFT_{ij}]$ intervals which reflect the actual start time on the real cyber-side.

Similarly, Fig. 16 shows the simulatability as increasing the physical write task ratio from 10% to 50% while keeping the physical read task ratio as 20%. Since the more physical write tasks in the cyber-side imply the more physical write constraint in Eq. (2), the higher physical write task ratio gives more harsh deadline requirements that the simulator should meet. We can see this tendency through the decreasing simulatability of **Ours**, **Worst-fit-first**, and **Smallest-utilization-first** according to the increasing physical write task ratio. We can also validate that our consideration about the $[EEST_{ij}, ELFT_{ij}]$ efficiently handles the physical write tasks by the increasing simulatability gap between **Ours** and other heuristics.

7   Conclusion

This paper proposes the multicore extension of previously proposed functionally and temporally correct single core simulator. For this, we first empirically analyze the actual inter-core interferences and derive that a practical multicore extension without using complex inter-core isolation mechanisms is a partitioned multicore scheduling subject to per-core local cache constraint. We also show that the local cache constraint is not too strict to satisfy, if we focus on the practical usecases of the real automotive system tasks. Then, we propose a heuristic task partitioning algorithm that aims to maximize concurrent job executions on multicore simulation PC respecting all job-level precedence relations necessary for the functionally and temporally correct real-time simulation. Our experimental study shows significant improvement of simulatability, i.e., simulation capacity, by our proposed multicore extension of the previous single core simulator.

In our future work, we plan to extend our coverage of the simulation to more complex automotive systems such as self-driving cars which normally have immense memory usage and super-large computation amount. We also plan to investigate the simulation behavior of safety-relevant automotive tasks, e.g. ISO-26262-related monitoring function, whose operational nature is totally different from the normal control tasks. By investigating such tasks and bring those tasks into the simulator, we believe our simulator would be more beneficial in terms of evaluating the overall safety of an automotive system. In the long term, we plan to make our functionally and temporally correct simulation approach as a general simulator applicable for a broader spectrum of CPSs.

Acknowledgement. This research was supported by the MSIT (Ministry of Science and ICT), Korea, under the SW Starlab (IITP-2015-0-00209) supervised by IITP (Institute for Information & Communications Technology Promotion). The authors would like to thank Hyundai-Kia Motor Company, Korea, for the cooperation and financial support in this research project.

References

1. Ando, E., Nakata, T., Yamashita, M.: Approximating the longest path length of a stochastic dag by a normal distribution in linear time. J. Discret. Algorithms **7**(4), 420–438 (2009)
2. Binkert, N., et al.: The gem5 simulator. ACM SIGARCH Comput. Architect. News **39**(2), 1–7 (2011)
3. dSPACE: version 8.4.0.150421 (R2014b). dSPACE GmbH., Wixom, Michigan (2018)
4. Garey, M.R., Johnson, D.S.: Computers and Intractability: A Guide to the Theory of NP-completeness (Series of Books in the Mathematical Sciences), ed. Computers and Intractability, vol. 340 (1979)
5. Infineon: Tricore 27x (2018). https://www.infineon.com/cms/en/product/microcontroller/32-bit-tricore-microcontroller/aurix-safety-joins-performance/aurix-family-tc27xt/. Accessed 1 Nov 2018
6. Intel: Core i7–3610qm (2012). https://ark.intel.com/products/64899/Intel-Core-i7-3610QM-Processor-6M-Cache-up-to-3-30-GHz-. Accessed 8 Nov 2018
7. Intel: Core i7–9700k (2018). https://www.intel.com/content/www/us/en/products/processors/core/i7-processors/i7-9700k.html (2018). Accessed 1 Nov 2018
8. Joo, H., We, K.S., Kim, S., Lee, C.G.: An end-to-end tool for developing CPSs from design to implementation (2016)
9. Navet, N., Song, Y., Simonot-Lion, F., Wilwert, C.: Trends in automotive communication systems. Proc. IEEE **93**(6), 1204–1223 (2005)
10. Nivasch, G.: Cycle detection using a stack. Inf. Process. Lett. **90**(3), 135–140 (2004)

11. Ong, H.L., Magazine, M.J., Wee, T.: Probabilistic analysis of bin packing heuristics. Oper. Res. **32**(5), 983–998 (1984)
12. Qureshi, M.K., Patt, Y.N.: Utility-based cache partitioning: a low-overhead, high-performance, runtime mechanism to partition shared caches. In: 39th Annual IEEE/ACM International Symposium on Microarchitecture, MICRO-39, pp. 423–432. IEEE (2006)
13. Sanchez, D., Kozyrakis, C.: ZSim: fast and accurate microarchitectural simulation of thousand-core systems. In: ACM SIGARCH Computer Architecture News, vol. 41, pp. 475–486. ACM (2013)
14. Sha, L., et al.: Single core equivalent virtual machines for hard real–time computing on multicore processors. Technical report (2014)
15. Simulink: version 8.4.0.150421 (R2014b). MathWorks Inc., Natick, Massachusetts (2014)
16. Stern, S., Gencel, C.: Embedded software memory size estimation using cosmic: a case study. In: International Workshop on Software Measurement (IWSM), vol. 39 (2010)
17. We, K.S.: Functionally and temporally correct simulation for cyber-physical systems. Ph.D. thesis, Seoul National University (2017)
18. We, K.S., Kim, S., Lee, W., Lee, C.G.: Functionally and temporally correct simulation of cyber-systems for automotive systems. In: 2017 IEEE Real-Time Systems Symposium (RTSS), pp. 68–79. IEEE (2017)
19. Yourst, M.T.: PTLsim: a cycle accurate full system x86–64 microarchitectural simulator. In: 2007 IEEE International Symposium on Performance Analysis of Systems & Software, pp. 23–34. IEEE (2007)
20. Yun, H., Mancuso, R., Wu, Z.P., Pellizzoni, R.: PALLOC: DRAM bank-aware memory allocator for performance isolation on multicore platforms. In: 2014 IEEE 20th Real-Time and Embedded Technology and Applications Symposium (RTAS), pp. 155–166. IEEE (2014)
21. Yun, H., Yao, G., Pellizzoni, R., Caccamo, M., Sha, L.: MemGuard: memory bandwidth reservation system for efficient performance isolation in multi-core platforms. In: 2013 IEEE 19th Real-Time and Embedded Technology and Applications Symposium (RTAS), pp. 55–64. IEEE (2013)

Constraint-Based Modeling and Symbolic Simulation of Hybrid Systems with HydLa and HyLaGI

Yunosuke Yamada$^{(\boxtimes)}$, Masashi Sato, and Kazunori Ueda

Department of Computer Science and Engineering, Waseda University,
3-4-1, Okubo, Shinjuku-ku, Tokyo 169-8555, Japan
{yunosuke,masashi,ueda}@ueda.info.waseda.ac.jp

Abstract. Hybrid systems are dynamical systems that include both continuous and discrete changes. Modeling and simulation of hybrid systems can be challenging due to various kinds of subtleties of their behavior. The declarative modeling language HydLa aims at concise description of hybrid systems by means of constraints and constraint hierarchies. HyLaGI, a publicly available symbolic simulator of HydLa, featured error-free computation with symbolic parameters. Based on symbolic computation, HyLaGI provides various functionalities including nondeterministic execution, handling of infinitesimal quantities, and construction of hybrid automata. Nondeterministic execution in the framework of constraint programming enables us to solve inverse problems by automatic parameter search. This paper introduces these features by means of example programs. This paper also discusses our experiences with HydLa programming, which is unique in that its data and control structures are both based on constraint technologies. We discuss its expressive power and our experiences with modeling using constraint hierarchies.

Keywords: Hybrid systems · Constraints · Symbolic simulation

1 Introduction

Hybrid systems [12] are dynamical systems which include both continuous and discrete changes. To put it differently, hybrid systems are dynamical systems whose description involves case analysis. Because of the case analysis, simulation of hybrid systems can easily go qualitatively wrong, and techniques for rigorous simulation are very important.

Modeling of hybrid systems, as opposed to continuous systems or discrete systems, is itself a challenge. The best-known modeling technique is hybrid automata [9] with an explicit notion of states, but designing fundamental language constructs, especially those for *declarative* (as opposed to procedural) modeling seems to be an open problem. Although there have been a number of proposals of modeling languages (see [5] for a comprehensive survey), most high-level languages aim for the modeling of complex hybrid systems [1,16], leaving the quest for fundamental modeling constructs rather unexplored.

© Springer Nature Switzerland AG 2020
R. Chamberlain et al. (Eds.): CyPhy 2019/WESE 2019, LNCS 11971, pp. 153–178, 2020.
https://doi.org/10.1007/978-3-030-41131-2_8

We take a *constraint-based* approach to the above two questions, i.e., rigorous simulation and modeling constructs. Constraints are a *necessary* ingredient in any modeling technique of hybrid systems in that they all handle differential equations. However, virtually all high-level modeling languages come with other language constructs to provide the language with control structures. For instance, Modelica [16] appears to be close to our goal in that its main feature is *non-causal*, constraint-based modeling, but Modelica also supports imperative constructs to simulate models for which explicit sequencing of events is necessary. Another high-level language, Zélus [4], builds on the framework of synchronous programming into which ordinary differential equations (ODEs) were integrated. Accordingly, the research question we are going to address is:

> *"Are constraints and constraint solving adequate, by themselves, for the concise modeling and rigorous simulation of hybrid systems?"*

The modeling language HydLa [20, 21] and its implementation HyLaGI [13, 14] were built as an attempt to answer that question.

Constraint programming for hybrid systems is not new; for example, Hybrid CC [8] was born as an extension of concurrent constraint programming. While Hybrid CC retained the flavor of process calculi, HydLa, inspired by Hybrid CC, adopted *constraint hierarchy* [3] for concise modeling of hybrid systems, as will be exemplified soon.

The constraint-based approach has another advantage—the ability to express *partial information* and handle it with *rigorous symbolic computation* based on consistency checking. Constraints include the notion of intervals such as $x \in [1.0, 3.5]$. As an important application, they also allow natural handling of *parametric* hybrid systems, i.e., hybrid systems with symbolic parameters, which is useful for the understanding, analysis and design of hybrid systems. Some verification tools such as KeYmaera X [7] and dReach [10] also took a rigorous, symbolic approach. Unlike these and like Acumen [18], HyLaGI was designed as a simulation tool whose primary goal was to help understanding of hybrid systems (as opposed to the solving of decision problems). There are other tools for rigorous simulation. For instance, Acumen [18] and Flow* [6] adopt (numerical) interval enclosure techniques while we take a symbolic approach to handle parametric systems. Another symbolic simulator was reported in [17], but unlike it our algorithm provides exhaustive search.

1.1 HydLa by Example

Let us introduce HydLa by a simple example.

Figure 1 shows a HydLa model of a bouncing particle. In HydLa, each variable is treated as a function of time; for example, a variable y is an abbreviation of a function y(t) ($t \geq 0$) and represents the height of the particle, while y' and y'' stand for its speed and acceleration, both being functions of time.

The first three lines are the definitions of named constraints (called *constraint modules* or simply *modules*) represented using differential equations and logical

```
1 INIT    <=> 7 < y < 12 & y' = 0.
2 FALL    <=> [](y'' = -10).
3 BOUNCE  <=> [](y- = 0 => y' = -4/5 * y'-).
4
5 INIT, (FALL << BOUNCE).
6 //#hylagi -p10
```

Fig. 1. A bouncing particle model in HydLa with an uncertain initial state.

connectives. `INIT` stands for a constraint defining the (uncertain) initial position and the speed of the particle. `FALL` represents free fall, while `BOUNCE` represents bouncing. The temporal logic operator `[]`, called "always", indicates that a constraint holds and keeps holding after it is generated. The postfix operator `-` indicates the left limit of the value of the variable; for example, $y\text{-}(t)$ stands for $\lim_{t' \to t-0} y(t')$. The connective `=>` is logical implication. Line 5 declares how the three modules are composed. We can declare relative strength of modules: in our case, `FALL` is declared to be weaker than `BOUNCE` and is ignored when it is inconsistent with `BOUNCE`. Line 6 is a comment line showing default options given to HyLaGI (Sect. 3). Further details of HydLa will be described in Sect. 2.

1.2 HyLaGI and WebHydLa

We are developing an implementation HyLaGI to simulate HydLa programs. HyLaGI, available from GitHub[1], is implemented in C++ and uses the Boost library. We currently use Mathematica as a constraint solver and perform simulations by symbolic computation. This opens up various applications including the simulation and reasoning about models with symbolic parameters, handling of infinitesimal quantities, and checking of the inclusion properties of the sets of trajectories. Symbolic simulation assumes the existence of closed-form solutions of ODEs, which might sound like a rather strong restriction, but ODEs without closed-form solutions could be rigorously approximated using a family of ODEs with symbolic parameters (to enclose approximation errors) that have closed-form solutions, which is among our future work.

Figure 2 shows the output of HyLaGI from the program of Fig. 1. HyLaGI simulates a program in phases, which are an alternating sequence of point phases (PPs) and interval phases (IPs). A point phase represents discrete change, and an interval phase represents continuous change. HyLaGI represents the uncertain initial condition of `y` by generating a symbolic parameter `p[y,0,1]`, meaning a parameter representing the 0th derivative of `y` of the first phase. HyLaGI performs case analysis for uncertain models, but for this example it returns only one case with 10 phases. Information for a point phase includes the time and the values of variables, while that of an interval phase includes the time interval and trajectories (as functions of time) over that interval. In addition, it provides

---

[1] https://github.com/HydLa/.

```
 1 ------ Result of Simulation ------
 2 ---------parameter condition(global)---------
 3 p[y, 0, 1] : (7, 12)
 4 ---------Case 1---------
 5 ---------1---------
 6 ---------PP 1---------
 7 unadopted modules: {}
 8 positive  :
 9 negative  :
10 t : 0
11 y : p[y, 0, 1]
12 y' : 0
13 y'' : -10
14 ---------IP 2---------
15 unadopted modules: {}
16 positive  :
17 negative  :
18 t : 0->5^(-1/2)*p[y, 0, 1]^(1/2)
19 y : t^2*(-5)+p[y, 0, 1]
20 y' : t*(-10)
21 y'' : -10
22 ---------2---------
23 ---------PP 3---------
24 unadopted modules: {FALL}
25 unsat modules : {BOUNCE, FALL}
26 unsat constraints : {y''=-10, y'=-4/5*y'-}
27 positive  : y-=0=>y'=-4/5*y'-
28 negative  :
29 t : 5^(-1/2)*p[y, 0, 1]^(1/2)
30 y : 0
31 y' : 5^(-1/2)*8*p[y, 0, 1]^(1/2)
32 ---------IP 4---------
33 unadopted modules: {}
34 positive  :
35 negative  : y-=0=>y'=-4/5*y'-
36 t : 5^(-1/2)*p[y, 0, 1]^(1/2)->5^(-1/2)*p[y, 0, 1]^(1/2)*13/5
37 y : t^2*(-5)+18*5^(-1/2)*t*p[y, 0, 1]^(1/2)+p[y, 0, 1]*(-13)/5
38 y' : t*(-10)+18*5^(-1/2)*p[y, 0, 1]^(1/2)
39 y'' : -10
40
41 ... (omitted up to PP 9) ...
42
43 ---------IP 10---------
44 unadopted modules: {}
45 positive  :
46 negative  : y-=0=>y'=-4/5*y'-
47 t : 5^(-1/2)*p[y, 0, 1]^(1/2)*613/125->5^(-1/2)*p[y, 0, 1]^(1/2)
       *3577/625
48 y : t^2*(-5)+5^(-1/2)*t*p[y, 0, 1]^(1/2)*6642/125+p[y, 0,
       1]*(-2192701)/78125
49 y' : t*(-10)+5^(-1/2)*p[y, 0, 1]^(1/2)*6642/125
50 y'' : -10
51 ---------parameter condition(Case1)---------
52 p[y, 0, 1] : (7, 12)
53 # number of phases reached limit
```

Fig. 2. Simulation results of the bouncing particle up to 10 phases.

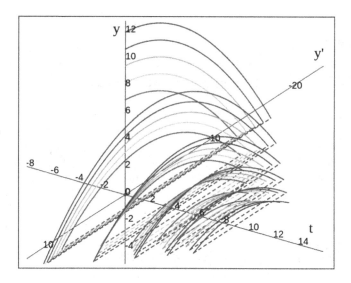

Fig. 3. Output of webHydLa for the bouncing particle model. Note that simulation was executed only once, after which the family of trajectories were rendered by the visualizer.

information about the constraints that determined these values or trajectories, which turned out to be extremely useful in debugging and construction of hybrid automata, as discussed in Sects. 3 and 4.

The output of Fig. 2 suggests that a visualization tool for the understanding of results is highly desirable. We have developed webHydLa[2] as an IDE for HydLa that can visualize simulation results in 2D and 3D. For example, the simulation result of the program in Fig. 1 is visualized as in Fig. 3.

1.3   Purpose and Outline of the Paper

HydLa and HyLaGI has been available for quite some time, but except for the language definition [20] and implementation techniques [13,14], the consequences and implications of the design and functionalities of HydLa and HyLaGI in the light of the modeling of various hybrid systems have not been reported. Reports on various ideas that went into our system were scattered over rather short papers (some of which in Japanese). Thus the purpose of the present paper is to report our constraint-based approach in a comprehensive way with a number of examples, discussing important details and findings not addressed by previous papers.

The rest of the paper is organized as follows. Section 2 briefly introduces the constructs of HydLa. Section 3 introduces functionalities of HyLaGI by various examples. Section 4 describes our experiences with constraint-based modeling

---

[2] http://webhydla.ueda.info.waseda.ac.jp/.

with HydLa. Section 5 introduces further examples involving parameter search. Section 6 concludes the paper.

2   The Constraint-Based Language HydLa

We briefly overview the modeling language HydLa. Please refer to [20] for further details of basic constructs and [13] for extended features implemented in HyLaGI and some subtle points.

As exemplified by the bouncing particle model of Fig. 1, a typical HydLa program consists of the definitions of constraints followed by the declaration of constraint hierarchy formed by the defined modules. Constraint hierarchy refers to a partially ordered set whose elements are combinations of modules allowed by the declaration and whose order is a set inclusion relation. Constraint hierarchy allows us to represent *ordinary or default* behavior and *special or exceptional* behavior in a concise manner. Constraints in the module INIT are defined without the [] operator and hold only at time 0. A constraint with => expresses a conditional constraint (also called a *guarded* constraint) whose consequent is enabled only when the antecedent (called a *guard*) holds. The constraint hierarchy declared in Line 5 indicates that BOUNCE is stronger than FALL and also that BOUNCE and INIT have the highest priority. At each point of time, HydLa adopts a maximal consistent set (MCS) of modules that respects constraint hierarchy. In this example, while the particle is floating, the set {INIT, FALL, BOUNCE} is adopted (note that INIT is vacuously satisfied after time 0, and BOUNCE is vacuously satisfied because of the false guard) and that when it collides with the floor, the MCS changes to {INIT, BOUNCE}. Note that a module which is not weaker than any other module in the constraint hierarchy is called a *required* module and is always enabled.

2.1   Syntax

The syntax of HydLa is shown in Fig. 4, where *dname, cname, vname* are symbolic names representing definitions, constraints and variables, respectively.

Here we describe language features not covered by Fig. 1. The definition *Def* says that we can define named declarations (that may include constraint hierarchies) as well as named constraints. It also says that definitions may have formal parameters $\vec{X}$. The syntax of a constraint C allows an *always* ($\square$) constraint to occur in the consequent of a guarded constraint. Examples of its use will be shown in Sect. 5. Note that, in the declaration *Decl*, the operator "$\ll$" binds tighter than the operator "," that imposes no relative priority. For example, $A \ll B, C$ is equal to $(A \ll B), C$.

Table 1 shows the correspondence between the abstract syntax of Fig. 4 and the concrete syntax used in example programs.

(HydLa program) P	$::=$	$(Def \mid Decl)^*$
(definition) Def	$::=$	$dname(\vec{X})\{Decl\} \mid cname(\vec{X}) \Leftrightarrow C$
(constraint) C	$::=$	$A \mid C \wedge C \mid G \Rightarrow C \mid \exists vname.C \mid \Box C \mid cname(\vec{E})$
(guard) G	$::=$	$A \mid G \wedge G \mid G \vee G \mid \neg G$
(atomic constraint) A	$::=$	$E\ Rop\ E$
(relational operator) Rop	$::=$	$= \mid \neq \mid > \mid \geq \mid < \mid \leq$
(expression) E	$::=$	$E\ Aop\ E \mid Prev \mid constant$
(arithmetic operator) Aop	$::=$	$+ \mid - \mid \times \mid \div \mid \ \hat{}$
(previous) $Prev$	$::=$	$D \mid D-$
(derivative) D	$::=$	$vname \mid D'$
(declaration) $Decl$	$::=$	$M \mid Decl, Decl \mid Decl \ll Decl$
(module) M	$::=$	$C \mid dname(\vec{E})$

Fig. 4. Syntax of HydLa.

Table 1. Correspondence between abstract and concrete syntax.

Abstract	Concrete	Abstract	Concrete	Abstract	Concrete	Abstract	Concrete
$\ll$	<<	$\leq$	<=	$\vee$	\/ or |	$\exists$	\
$\Leftrightarrow$	<=>	$\neq$	!=	$\wedge$	/\ or &		
$\geq$	>=	$\neg$	!	$\Box$	[]		

List Expressions. We often need to generate multiple objects (such as balls and cars) with the same property in the modeling of hybrid systems. As an extension of the syntax in Fig. 4, HydLa provides a list notation to simplify the description of such models. Here we explain their use by examples, leaving the full syntax with list expressions to the Appendix.

We introduce two types of list notation. The first type is the list of arithmetic expressions, which can be written extensionally or in a list comprehension notation. Range expressions of the form $\{l..h\}$ are also allowed. Range expressions have two applications; one is to express a list of consecutive values (such as $\{2*3+1..10\}$) and the other is to express a list of variables whose names end with consecutive digits. For instance, $\{x0..x4\}$ stands for the list of variables $\{x0, x1, x2, x3, x4\}$. The second type of list notation is to declare multiple instances of constraints. A list of priority declarations can also be written extensionally or in a list comprehension notation as in the example below.

For example, consider a road congestion model with five cars, of which the cars except the first one accelerates and deaccelerates depending on the distance from the car in front (Fig. 5). Figure 6 shows its HydLa model. Line 1 defines X to be the list of cars for which the notation $X[i]$ is available to access its ith element. Lines 3–6 define named constraints describing the properties of the cars. Lines 8–12 declare constraints imposed by the five cars, where $|X|$ represents

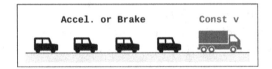

Fig. 5. A road congestion model.

```
 1  X := {x1..x5}.
 2
 3  INIT(x,x0,v0) <=> x = x0 & x' = v0.
 4  CONST(x)      <=> [](x'' = 0).
 5  BRAKE(x,xf)   <=> [](x'- >  0 & xf- - x- < 30 => x'' = -5).
 6  ACC(x, xf)    <=> [](x'- < 15 & xf- - x- > 50 => x'' =  3).
 7
 8  { INIT(X[i],100*i+i,4) | i in {1..|X|-1} }.
 9  INIT(X[|X|],100*|X|,8).
10  { CONST(X[i]) << (ACC(X[i],X[i+1]), BRAKE(X[i],X[i+1]))
11                                     | i in {1..|X|-1} }.
12  CONST(X[|X|]).
13  //#hylagi -p40
```

Fig. 6. A road congestion model in HydLa.

the cardinality of the list X. When we run this program, the distance between two cars is kept neither too close nor too distant as shown in Fig. 7.

Existential Quantifier. HydLa features *existential quantifiers* to generate variables dynamically.

Constraints with existential quantifiers are typically written in the consequents of guarded constraints and generate new trajectories when the guards hold. Quantified variables are given fresh names when the constraints containing those variables are expanded. In the modeling of HydLa, dynamic variables are often used as temporary variables that propagate constraints.

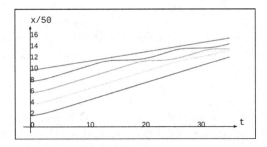

Fig. 7. Simulation result of the road congestion model in HydLa.

```
 1 INIT        <=> p = 65 & mode = 0.
 2 OFF         <=> [](mode = 0 => p' = -2).
 3 ON          <=> [](mode = 1 => p' = 1).
 4 MODE(l,r,m) <=> \x.(l < x < r & [](x' = -1)
 5                     & [](x- = 0 => mode = m)).
 6 SWITCHOFF <=> [](p- = 68 & mode = 1 => MODE(0.2,0.5,0)).
 7 SWITCHON  <=> [](p- = 62 & mode = 0 => MODE(0.2,0.5,1)).
 8
 9 INIT, [](mode' = 0) << (SWITCHON, SWITCHOFF).
10 OFF, ON.
```

Fig. 8. A thermostat model with delay in HydLa.

```
 1 FACTORIAL(n, ans)
 2          <=> (n = 0 => ans = 1)
 3          & (n > 0 => \x.(ans = n * x & FACTORIAL(n-1, x))).
 4 CALC_F <=> [](timer- = 1 => FACTORIAL(5, ans)).
 5 TIMER  <=> timer = 0 & [](timer' = 1).
 6
 7 TIMER, CALC_F.
```

Fig. 9. A model to calculate the factorial of 5.

Figure 8 is an thermostat model using an existential quantifier. The variable p represents the temperature. SWITCHON and SWITCHOFF are fired when the temperature reaches 62 or 68°, respectively, to switch the mode that decides the differential equation of p. The existentially quantified variables, written with \ instead of $\exists$, are used in the consequents as local timers to express the delay of mode change. Whenever p reaches 62 or 68°, a new instance of x is generated, is initialized to $[0.2, 0.5]$, decreases linearly, and changes the mode when it reaches 0.

A recursive constraint is another important use of existential quantifiers. Figure 9 is a somewhat contrived example to calculate the factorial of 5 at time 1. The module FACTORIAL consists of two guarded constraints, the base case and the recursive case. When the guard of CALC_F holds, FACTORIAL is expanded and its second guarded constraint is enabled. Then FACTORIAL is expanded recursively until the second argument reaches 0. Each time FACTORIAL is expanded, a fresh intermediate variable is created, and a network of constraints is constructed to propagate the calculation result. In this way, existential quantifiers for dynamic variable creation provide us with an alternative technique to superdense time for the modeling of multi-step instantaneous computation.

2.2   Semantics: Overview

In constraint-based languages, the natural plan for the study of the semantics would be to consider what a program represents (declarative semantics) first and then its computational aspects.

Declarative Semantics. The declarative semantics of a HydLa model is the set of trajectories allowed by the constraints given in the model, where HydLa takes maximal consistent sets of modules at each point of time, as stated in the beginning of Sect. 2 with an example. Here we describe some important aspects of the semantics.

Firstly, HydLa naturally allows models with uncertainties. This comes from the fact that (i) a set of constraints may have multiple solutions, most typically due to initial values given as intervals, and that (ii) a maximal consistent set of modules may not be uniquely determined. It is important to note that, in hybrid systems, quantitative uncertainties may result in qualitative uncertainties. For example, when a particle bounces on a floor with a hole, whether or not the particle eventually enters the hole and how many times it bounces before it enters the hole depend on the initial position and velocity of the ball. HyLaGI described in Sect. 3 is able to compute all possible solutions by case splitting.

Multiple solutions may occur even without parametric uncertainties. For instance, Fig. 10 is a program with a nondeterministic switch that may take the value 0 or 1 every time the value of `timer` reaches 1. Note that ON and STAY are given the second-to-highest priority because modules with the highest priority are *required* modules.

```
1  INIT   <=> switch = 0 & timer = 0.
2  CONST  <=> [](switch' = 0).
3  TIMER  <=> [](timer' = 1).
4  ON     <=> [](timer- = 1 => switch = 1 & timer = 0).
5  STAY   <=> [](timer- = 1 => switch = 0 & timer = 0).
6  TRUE   <=> [](1 = 1).
7
8  INIT, (CONST, TIMER) << (ON, STAY) << TRUE.
9  //#hylagi --fnd -p6
```

Fig. 10. A model with a nondeterministic switch.

Secondly, the constraints explicitly given in programs are usually not enough to determine solution trajectories. For instance, in the bouncing particle model of Fig. 1, we are implicitly assuming a *frame axiom* that the position of the ball is continuous except when discontinuity is deduced from explicitly given constraints; otherwise we cannot conclude that the particle starts to move from the floor after bouncing. We call it the *principle of implicit continuity*, and refer the readers to [13] for the details of how it is built into HydLa's constraint framework.

Expressive Power and Computable Trajectories. The syntax of HydLa allows a model `[](x + y = 0)`, which might make sense as a specification but not as an "executable" program. Indeed, no hybrid automaton corresponding to this model is likely to exist. It is therefore meaningful to consider what HydLa models (or programs) are executable. We propose that an *executable* program is a program whose set of trajectories can be represented in *explicit* form defined as follows, where we assume that t stands for the current time:

Definition 1. A trajectory of variables $x_1, \ldots, x_n$ is in *explicit* form if it is piecewisely represented as a (finite or infinite) set of equations $x_1 = E_{i1}, \ldots, x_n = E_{in}$ associated with a time interval T_i ($i = 1, 2, \ldots$) during which the above set of equations is effective. Each E_{ij} is a continuous function of t on the interval T_i. E_{ij} may also contain symbolic parameters $p_1, \ldots, p_m (m \geq 0)$ but not $x_1, \ldots, x_n$. The ends of each time interval T_i are also given using expressions that may contain $p_1, \ldots, p_m$. The set of allowed values of the parameters $p_1, \ldots, p_m$ are given as constraints (including equations and inequations), but these constraints must not contain t. The T_i's must be mutually disjoint, and $\bigcup_i T_i$ must be a single interval starting from time 0.

The purpose of simulation is to convert the constraints imposed by a HydLa program into this explicit form, whose example can be found in the simulation result of Fig. 2.

3   HyLaGI: A Symbolic Implementation of HydLa

HyLaGI is an implementation of HydLa that features rigorous simulation of possibly uncertain hybrid systems. The central technique to achieve this is symbolic constraint satisfaction. HyLaGI also employs interval computation internally in order to compute the time of the earliest possible discrete changes efficiently.

The nondeterministic simulation algorithm of HyLaGI repeats point phases (PPs) and interval phases (IPs) alternately until a termination condition (time limit or the number of phases) is satisfied. Calculation of IPs involves (i) solution of possibly parameterized ODEs and (ii) calculation of the time of the next discrete change as a minimization problem. Uncertainties represented by symbolic parameters may result in qualitative difference of trajectories as discussed in Sect. 2.2. In that event, HyLaGI automatically performs case analysis, narrowing the range of parameter values into each qualitatively different case. This symbolic case analysis is supported by quantifier elimination of the constraint solver. The readers are referred to [13] for the detailed simulation algorithm of HyLaGI.

The rest of this section will explain three key functionalities of HyLaGI enabled by the symbolic approach.

3.1   Assertion

HyLaGI provides an `ASSERT` construct using constraints, which can be used for bounded model checking of reachability properties. A property can be stated by

ASSERT(G), where G stands for a guard. The declarative meaning of ASSERT(G) is []G or [](!G => false), but we provide ASSERT as a separate construct to be able to distinguish verification conditions from model descriptions. ASSERT(G) stops simulation of the current branch of nondeterministic simulation if G becomes false. Assertion can be used not only for verification but also for solving inverse problems, as will be described in Sect. 5.

3.2   Epsilon Mode

The simulation of hybrid systems, say those modeling physical phenomena, may fall into a situation not considered by textbook laws of physics. For example,

1. a ball bouncing inside a box hits the wall and the floor at the same time,
2. a ball in contact with another ball is hit by the third ball, and
3. force is continually applied to an object in contact with another object to move both.

As for the first example, even if the simultaneity may happen with zero probability in reality, a *family* of trajectories of uncertain hybrid systems may well include it. One way of handling that situation is to consider the limit of situations where the ball hits the wall or the floor slightly earlier. The second and the third examples could also be considered as the limit of the situations where the two objects are slightly apart. HyLaGI is able to simulate such models by taking the limit of 'normal' situations, and it is called the *epsilon mode* [22].

In the epsilon mode (specified by the option "-en"), we can use a variable eps as an infinitesimal parameter as shown in Fig. 12. Here, n specifies the highest-order terms to be retained for eps, for which 1 is enough except when higher-order effects of eps need to be considered. In the epsilon mode, after the maximal consistent set of constraints and the current values of variables are computed in each phase, higher-order terms of eps are deleted (after performing Taylor expansion when necessary). When the simulation of all phases are completed, HyLaGI takes the limit (w.r.t. eps) of the expressions representing the trajectories of all phases.

For the example of three-body collision, HyLaGI will report "unsatisfiable constraints" (Sect. 4) at the time of collision because the law of two-body collision is not prepared for this situation. However, simulation can be performed if the two touching balls are slightly parted. For example, three-body collision shown in

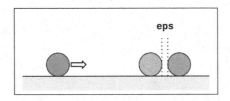

Fig. 11. Collision of three bodies.

```
1 INIT <=> x1 = 0 & x2 = 5 & x3 = 6+eps
2          & x1' = 1 & x2' = 0 & x3' = 0.
3 EPS  <=> 0 < eps < 0.1 & [](eps' = 0).
4 CONST(x) <=> [](x'' = 0).
5 COLLISION(xa, xb) <=>
6    [](xa- = xb- - 1 => xa' = xb'- & xb' = xa'-).
7
8 INIT, EPS.
9 (CONST(x1),CONST(x2),CONST(x3))
10    << (COLLISION(x1,x2), COLLISION(x2,x3)).
11 //#hylagi --fnd -p6 -e1
```

Fig. 12. HydLa model of three-body collision.

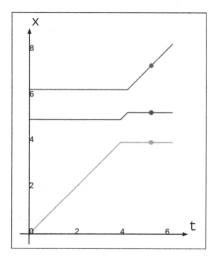

Fig. 13. Simulation result of Fig. 12.

Fig. 11 can be described as a HydLa program in Fig. 12. Three balls of diameter 1 are aligned in a straight line, where x2 and x3 are apart by eps, and x1 moves towards x2 at speed 1. The simulation result of the program of Fig. 12, which still retains eps, is shown in Fig. 13, where the horizontal axis represents time and the vertical axis represents the position x. When the value of eps is not too small, we can see from Fig. 13 that there are two collisions. The text output of the same simulation tells us that x2 will not move in the limit.

Lee et al. discussed the same model in detail in [11] (Fig. 8, p. 806) as a motivating example of their constructive modeling. Their (non-symbolic) approach introduces superdense time to handle simultaneous collisions, while we adopt functions of standard, real-valued time to represent trajectories and handle simultaneity by symbolic perturbation.

There are various variations of the three-body collision. Consider another three-ball model in which the central ball is hit from both sides simultaneously,

```
 1 | INIT <=> x1 = 0 & x2 = 5 & x3 = 10+eps
 2 |          & x1' = 1 & x2' = 0 & x3' = -1.
 3 | EPS  <=> -0.1 < eps < 0.1 & [](eps' = 0).
 4 | MASS <=> [](m1 = 0.2 & m2 = 1 & m3 = 5).
 5 | CONST(x) <=> [](x'' = 0).
 6 | COLLISION(xa,ma,xb,mb) <=>
 7 |     [](xa- = xb- - 1 =>
 8 |        xa' = (xa'-*(ma-mb) + 2*mb*xb'-)/(ma+mb)
 9 |      & xb' = (xb'-*(mb-ma) + 2*ma*xa'-)/(ma+mb)).
10 |
11 | INIT. EPS. MASS.
12 | (CONST(x1),CONST(x2),CONST(x3))
13 |    << (COLLISION(x1,m1,x2,m2), COLLISION(x2,m2,x3,m3)).
14 | //#hylagi --fnd -p12 -e1
```

Fig. 14. Collision of three bodies with different masses.

a problem discussed also by Lee et al. in [11] (Fig. 11, p. 807). Suppose the balls have mass as shown in Line 4 of Fig. 14. For this problem, the result differs depending on whether the value of eps is positive or negative, as shown in Fig. 15 (look at the trajectory of the central ball). Actually, the right-hand limit and left-hand limit do not coincide, and HyLaGI's automatic case analysis generates three cases depending on the sign of eps including the case of eps = 0 that gets stuck.

The Dirac delta function can also be represented using the epsilon mode. The (shifted) delta function can be considered as the limit $\lim_{\varepsilon \to +0}$ of a function whose value is 1/eps in a certain interval of width eps and 0 elsewhere as shown in Fig. 16. The function was used successfully for the simulation of impulse force in mechanics and impulse response of electrical circuits.

Another application of infinitesimal parameters is the simulation of analysis of hybrid systems that cause numerous discrete changes in a finite period of time. Although not integrated into the main branch of HyLaGI due to its experimental nature, the work reported in [2] analyzed the symbolic output of HyLaGI to recognize chattering behavior, including a physical model in [11] (p. 808), by the analysis of loop invariants.

Finally, we note that future applications of the epsilon mode is expected to include the handling of robustness and sensitivity at a symbolic level.

3.3   Hybrid Automaton Mode

HyLaGI performs symbolic simulation for a given number of phases or a given period of simulation time. However, we often see cases where different point phases or different interval phases are 'similar' to each other (as in the bouncing particle example) in the sense that they differ only in the values or trajectories of variables. Given that HyLaGI maintains the values of variables as constraints, we can check if the system's state of some phase is subsumed by the system's

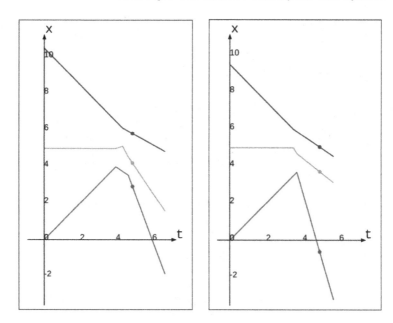

Fig. 15. Simulation result of Fig. 14.

```
1  TIMER <=> timer = 0 & [](timer' = 1).
2  EPS   <=> 0 < eps < 0.1 & [](eps' = 0).
3  OFF   <=> [](v = 0).
4  ON    <=> []((1 < timer < 1+eps) => v = 1/eps).
5
6  TIMER, EPS, (OFF << ON).
7  //#hylagi -e1
```

Fig. 16. HydLa model of an impulse function.

state of one of the previous phases, where a *state* can be defined to consist of (i) the values (or trajectories in the case of interval phases) of variables and (ii) the set of adopted modules. These two also determine (iii) whether each guard of the adopted guarded constraints holds or not. The checking of state subsumption can be done by constraint entailment checking, which can be translated into inconsistency checking by the relation $(P \Rightarrow Q) \equiv \neg(P \wedge \neg Q)$, and we can construct a possibly finite phase transition diagram representing infinite phase transitions. This feature has been implemented in HyLaGI as an optional *hybrid automaton mode*, an experimental mode for future work towards optimized simulation and unbounded model checking. We can see that the items displayed in each phase of HyLaGI's simulation result (Fig. 2) are sufficient to represent the current state of the model. An initial report on detailed algorithms for constructing hybrid automata can be found in [19], which discusses various subtleties in the construction. Note that we must properly parameterize the initial values of

```
1  INIT    <=> y > 0.
2  FALL    <=> [](y'' = -10).
3  BOUNCE <=> [](y- = 0 => y' = -4/5 * y'-).
4
5  INIT, FALL << BOUNCE.
6  //#hylagi --fha
```

Fig. 17. A bouncing particle model with parameterized initial height.

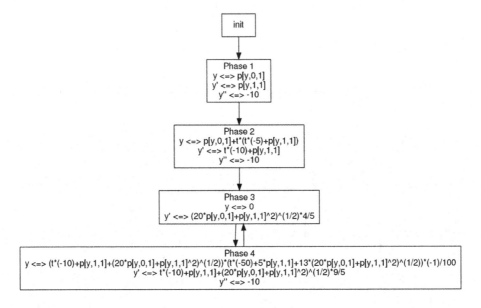

Fig. 18. State transition graph induced by HyLaGI from a HydLa model.

the variables in order to construct hybrid automata. For example, for a bouncing particle on the floor, we fully parameterize the initial height as shown in Fig. 17. In the hybrid automaton mode, the results can be obtained in the Graphviz format. Figure 18 shows the state transition graph obtained from the program in Fig. 17, where the odd-numbered phases represent discrete changes and the even-numbered phases represent continuous evolution.

4   Experiences with Constraint-Based Modeling

4.1   Discrete Asks and Continuous Asks

Guarded constraints in HydLa are one of the two main constructs that provides the language with control structure (the other construct being constraint hierarchy), corresponding to conditionals in other languages. From our experience with HydLa programming, we have learned that guarded constraints used to describe

```
1 INIT    <=> p = 65 & [](k1 = 1) & [](k2 = 2) & on = 0.
2 CONST <=> [](on' = 0).
3 ON      <=> [](on = 1 => p' =  k1).
4 OFF     <=> [](on = 0 => p' = -k2).
5 SWITCHON  <=> [](p- = 62 & on- = 0 => on = 1).
6 SWITCHOFF <=> [](p- = 68 & on- = 1 => on = 0).
7
8 INIT, ON, OFF, CONST << (SWITCHON, SWITCHOFF).
9 //#hylagi -p10
```

Fig. 19. A thermostat model in HydLa.

practical hybrid systems are categorized into two patterns. We call them *discrete ask* and *continuous ask*, after the terminology in concurrent constraint programming. *Discrete ask* is a guarded constraint which is enabled at isolated time points and triggers discrete changes. An example is BOUNCE in Fig. 1. Since discrete ask cancels a differential constraint at certain time points, it is usually given a higher priority than differential constraints. Continuous ask is a constraint whose guard continues to hold for a certain period of time during which the model makes continuous change according to the enabled consequent of the constraint. A thermostat model in Fig. 19 contains an example of continuous ask. The variable on represents the state of the thermostat whose value is discretely changed when the temperature p is about to exceed a certain threshold. The modules ON and OFF represent continuous asks; they refer to the variable on and have differential equations on the temperature in the consequents. The value of on is changed by SWITCHON and SWITCHOFF which are discrete asks. This example shows a design pattern in which a variable, called a state variable, can be used to represent the discrete state of a system and is referred to from the guards of continuous ask. In our experience, it is a good practice to write HydLa programs keeping the different roles of discrete ask and continuous ask in mind.

Note that HyLaGI does not allow existential quantifiers in the consequent of a continuous ask because such a consequent would generate an infinite number of variables and constraints. HyLaGI does not handle such cases and stops simulation.

4.2   Common Mistakes in Modeling

The design principle of HydLa is to take a constraint-centric approach to allow declarative and concise description of hybrid systems. In particular, constraint hierarchies are expected to autonomously impose the 'right amount' of constraints on variables so that the set of enabled constraints does not become over- or under-constrained. Still, we have seen many programs which do not compute trajectories or which compute unintended trajectories. In these cases, the debugging of declarative programs turned to be highly nontrivial to novice programmers.

```
1 INIT    <=> (x = 0 & y = 10 & y' = 0).
2 FALL    <=> [](x' = 1 & y'' = -10).
3 BOUNCE <=> [](y- = 0 => y' = -y'-).
4
5 INIT, (FALL << BOUNCE).
6 //#hylagi -p10
```

Fig. 20. A model with an unconstrained variable (1).

This motivated us to record a service log of webHydLa and analyze program errors, where each record contained (i) the HydLa program, (ii) the contents of **stdout** and **stderr**, and (iii) the 'hydat' file for visualization.

We analyzed 1017 HydLa programs after recording their standard output, error output and 766 hydat files passed to the webHydLa visualizer. The simulation results were divided into three categories:

1. normally terminated simulation (regardless of whether the result is intended or not),
2. simulation aborted by unsatisfiable constraints (in which the set of active constraints became inconsistent and none of them could be disabled), and
3. simulation in which some variable became totally unconstrained (which is semantically allowed but regarded as unintended).

We focus on the second and the third categories because they are specific to constraint programming.

Completely Unconstrained. 'Completely unconstrained' means that the constraints on the value of some variable become totally lost. HyLaGI does not stop execution for this event but generates a warning. The following are considered as possible causes of unconstrainedness.

1. a module that is defined but not declared (i.e., used),
2. lack of initial value constraints,
3. lack of 'always' ([]) constraints.

Since this is a warning not found in ordinary languages, we explain these causes using an example.

The first cause means that one simply forgot to use the defined constraint. On the other hand, the second and the third causes indicate insufficiency of constraints. For example, in the program of Fig. 20, x will become completely unconstrained after the second PP because the constraint on x is totally lost when the consequent of **BOUNCE** is enabled and **FALL** becomes unadopted temporarily. To fix the problem, we must either add a constraint x' = 1 to the consequent of **BOUNCE** or move x' = 1 from **FALL** to a new module.

Since this 'completely unconstrained' problem occurred much more frequently than expected, it was considered important to provide an *explanation*

```
1  INIT   <=> (y = 10 & y' = 0).
2  FALL   <=> [](y'' = -10).
3  BOUNCE <=> [](y- = 0 => y' = -y'-).
4
5  INIT, FALL, BOUNCE.
```

Fig. 21. A model causing inconsistency (1).

```
1  INIT  <=> (a = 0 & b = 0).
2  CONST <=> [](a' = 0).
3  CLOCK <=> [](b' = 1).
4  JUMP  <=> [](b = 3 => a = a + 1 & b = 0).
5
6  INIT, (CONST, CLOCK) << JUMP.
```

Fig. 22. A model causing inconsistency (2).

of the reason of unconstrainedness. We improved HyLaGI to infer and report whether the initial value constraint was insufficient or the *always* constraint was insufficient based on when the unconstrainedness occurred. If the first PP leaves any variable unconstrained, some initial value constraint is missing. If a variable becomes completely unconstrained after the first phase, we find, for each such variable, the module that caused the unconstrainedness. When the cause is the weakest module, HyLaGI displays a message "WARNING: x is completely unconstrained in a default module" because the module is supposed to represent default behavior. Otherwise, HyLaGI displays a message "WARNING: x is completely unconstrained in a non-default module".

Unsatisfiable Constraints. 'Unsatisfiable constraints' means that HyLaGI could not find a consistent set of constraint modules that respects constraint hierarchy. The following causes can be considered.

1. forgetting to define appropriate constraint hierarchy,
2. some of the required constraint modules, i.e., ones at the top of the constraint hierarchy, are mutually inconsistent or self-inconsistent.

For example, in Fig. 21, FALL and BOUNCE conflict with each other when the ball collides with the floor, but because there is no constraint hierarchy and all

```
1  Possible causes...
2  * {a} in {JUMP}
3  * {b} in {JUMP}
```

Fig. 23. Execution result of Fig. 22.

top-level modules are handled as required constraints (Sect. 2), FALL cannot be rejected and computation stops. In this case, the error can be easily resolved by declaring a hierarchy FALL << BOUNCE.

Consider another example in Fig. 22. When b becomes 3, a is incremented and b is reset to 0 by JUMP, so a looks like a counter and b looks like a clock. However, JUMP becomes inconsistent when (and only when) b = 3 because all variables of HydLa are immutable functions of time. As suggested by previous examples, an equation for discrete changes should mention the left limit values of variables, that is, JUMP should be written as [](b- = 3 => a = a- + 1 & b = 0).

When simulation generated unsatisfiable constraints, the reason of inconsistency is not easy to figure out in many cases. We thus let HyLaGI show which variables are in conflict within which modules. For example, given the program of Fig. 22, a message like Fig. 23 will be displayed in addition to the standard error message. The analysis is done as follows. The unsat modules line of the output (such as Fig. 2) tells the names of mutually inconsistent modules, and the corresponding unsat constraints line contains information about mutually inconsistent constraints. HyLaGI extracts variables from each of unsat constraints and collects corresponding modules from unsat modules. In this way, for each set of variables, a set of modules that make those variables over-constrained is derived as shown in Fig. 23.

5   Solving Inverse Problems

Inverse problems are to obtain initial conditions that yield given final goals. Inverse problems of hybrid systems are more intriguing than those of continuous systems in that initial and final states may be related by qualitatively different trajectories, e.g., trajectories of balls with different numbers of bounces. HyLaGI can solve inverse problems of hybrid systems by combining assertions and symbolic constraint solving with automatic case analysis of parameters. Note that our approach is based on forward symbolic simulation rather than reverse simulation from the goal state.

5.1   A Simple Example

Let us consider how to shoot a golf ball to make a hole-in-one (Fig. 24). A program is shown in Fig. 25. We parameterize the x component of the initial velocity, while the y component is defined so that the initial speed (norm of the velocity) is constant. The ball moves at a constant speed in the x direction, while it behaves like a bouncing ball in the y direction.

We use ASSERT to find the range of parameters for hole-in-one, Assume that the cup is 9.5 to 10 meters ahead. The constraint to be ASSERTed is the negation of the desired goal, i.e., !(y = 0 & 9.5 <= x <= 10), so that HyLaGI may find counterexamples.

Table 2 shows the behavior of the ball and the corresponding parameter ranges obtained from the program of Fig. 25, where *bounce* means that the ball bounces and *cup-in* means that the ball enters the cup.

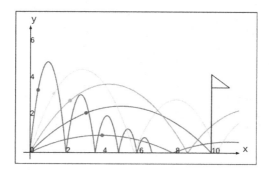

Fig. 24. A hole-in-one problem.

```
1 INIT    <=> x = 0 & y = 0 & 1 < x' < 9 & y' = (100 - x'^2)^0.5.
2 AXCONST <=> [](x'' = 0).
3 FALL    <=> [](y'' = -10).
4 BOUNCE  <=> [](y- = 0 => y' = -0.8*y'-).
5
6 ASSERT(!(y = 0 & 9.5 <= x <= 10)).
7 INIT, AXCONST, FALL << BOUNCE.
8 //#hylagi --fnd -p10
```

Fig. 25. Finding parameters for hole-in-one.

Table 2. Execution result of Fig. 25.

Behavior	Parameter range
Cup-in	$\left[\sqrt{\dfrac{5(20 - \sqrt{39})}{2}}, \sqrt{\dfrac{5(20 + \sqrt{39})}{2}}\right]$
Bounce, cup-in	$\left[5\sqrt{\dfrac{\frac{36 - \sqrt{935}}{2}}{3}}, \dfrac{5\sqrt{14} - 10}{3}\right]$
Bounce, bounce, cup-in	$\left[5\sqrt{\dfrac{244 - \sqrt{50511}}{122}}, 5\sqrt{\dfrac{2(61 - 6\sqrt{86})}{61}}\right]$
Bounce, bounce, bounce, cup-in	$\left[5\sqrt{\dfrac{\frac{1476 - \sqrt{1952951}}{82}}{3}}, 5\sqrt{\dfrac{\frac{2(369 - 2\sqrt{30134})}{41}}{3}}\right]$
Bounce, bounce, bounce, bounce	Others

5.2   Examples with Persistent Consequents

HydLa's syntax allows an *always* constraint $\Box C$ to appear in the consequent of an implication. Such a constraint is called a *persistent consequent*. A persistent

```
1 INIT    <=> 5 < y < 10 & y' = 0 & d = 0.
2 FALL    <=> [](y'' = -10).
3 CONST   <=> [](d' = 0).
4 BOUNCE  <=> [](y- = 0 => y' = -4/5 * y'- & d = d- + y'-^2 / 100).
5 BREAK   <=> [](d >= 4 => [](y'' = -10 & d' = 0)).
6
7 INIT, (FALL, CONST) << BOUNCE << BREAK.
8 ASSERT(y >= 0).
9 //#hylagi -p12 --fnd
```

Fig. 26. A bouncing ball damaging the floor.

Table 3. Execution result of Fig. 26.

Behavior	Parameter range
Bounce, bounce, bounce, bounce, bounce	(5, 7812500/968561)
Bounce, bounce, bounce, bounce, break	[7812500/968561, 312500/36121)
Bounce, bounce, bounce, break, through	[312500/36121, 12500/1281)
Bounce, bounce, break, through	[12500/1281, 10)

consequent $\Box(G \Rightarrow \Box C)$ is different from normal guarded constraints in that once the antecedent G holds, the consequent C continues to hold. The constraint $\Box C$ with the same priority as the original constraint is expanded in the constraint hierarchy. Since constraints once expanded are not removed, persistent consequents can represent irreversible effects or changes of the system.

Figure 26 is a model in which the floor of a bouncing ball accumulates damage from the ball and is eventually broken. In BOUNCE of Line 4, damage proportional to the square of the velocity at each collision is accumulated on the floor. If the accumulated damage exceeds a certain threshold, the ball keeps falling, meaning that the floor is broken. To figure out in which conditions the floor breaks, we assert the constraint that the height of the ball is non-negative. Table 3 shows the system behavior and corresponding parameter ranges computed by HyLaGI from the program in Fig. 26. Here, *bounce* means that the ball bounces on the floor, *break* means that the ball bounces and the floor breaks, and *through* means that the ball passes through the broken floor.

Finally, we show an example with constraint hierarchy with three strengths. Figure 27 is a model that searches for a winning strategy of a chicken race: we want to stop the car exactly at the goal position by keeping acceleration to a certain point and then braking. The braking position is parameterized. We have two persistent consequents, BRAKE and STAY, where STAY is given higher priority so that the car will not move backwards after stop. The ASSERTed constraint specifies the negation of the winning condition, and HyLaGI finds that the assertion fails when the parameter value is 625/2, from which we can see that the winning strategy is to start braking at 312.5 m from the starting point.

```
1 INIT  <=> x = 0 & x' = 0 & 0 < brkpt < 500 & [](brkpt' = 0).
2 ACC   <=> [](x'' = 3).
3 BRAKE <=> [](x- = brkpt- => [](x'' = -5)).
4 STAY  <=> [](x'- = 0      => [](x'' = 0)).
5
6 INIT, ACC << BRAKE << STAY.
7 ASSERT(!(x = 500 & x' = 0)).
8 //#hylagi --fnd
```

Fig. 27. Chicken race program.

6   Conclusion

In this paper, we first discussed our constraint-based approach to hybrid systems embodied as a modeling language HydLa and introduced various functionalities of HyLaGI, a symbolic simulator of hybrid systems expressed in HydLa. These functionalities, including nondeterministic execution, handling of infinitesimal quantities, and construction of hybrid automata, are realized since HyLaGI adopts symbolic computation. Then, we discussed several findings and experiences in the constraint-based modeling of hybrid systems including two different uses of guarded constraints and modeling errors mostly resulting from improper use of constraint hierarchy. Finally, we showed that HyLaGI could solve some inverse problems of hybrid systems and that persistent consequents are useful for modeling inverse problems.

Although HydLa has many unique features as described above, hybrid models that can be handled by the current version of HyLaGI are limited to relatively simple ones due to various limitations. In our experience, computation of the time of the next discrete change is the most difficult part for the constraint engine, due to which many models with closed-form solutions of ODEs could not be fully simulated to the end. To address this problem, Matsumoto et al. [15] reports how we can integrate symbolic versions of Affine arithmetic and the interval Newton method into our framework. Also, in order to reduce the complexity of constraints submitted to the constraint engine to improve the power of constraint solving, we have incorporated a number of optimization techniques into HyLaGI.

There are many other issues including the handling of models with many parameters and models with complicated differential equations such as DAEs and nonlinear ODEs. Still, we feel that the usefulness of our constraint-based framework is being established. Our future goal is to extend our framework by introducing useful results in the field of constraint programming and hybrid systems.

Acknowledgments. We would like to thank Shota Matsumoto for leading the development of the core part of HyLaGI. Early versions of HyLaGI are due to previous colleagues including Ken-ichi Hirose. Of the developers of many experimental features, Akira Takeguchi and Yoshiaki Wakatsuki were initial designers and implementors of the features mentioned in this paper. We thank all members of the project, including the above members, for discussions, development, and debugging. Thanks go also to anonymous reviewers for their detailed and constructive comments. The work is partially supported by Grant-in-Aid for Scientific Research (B) JP18H03223, JSPS, Japan.

A   Appendix

Figure 28 shows the syntax of HydLa with the list notation. As a key extension from Fig. 4, we newly introduce PL (priority list), EL (expression list), LC (list condition) and a list binding notation ":=". Both PL and EL consist of extensional and list comprehension notations. In the list comprehension notation, one can enumerate elements that satisfy conditions specified by LC. We can generate variables with successive serial numbers using range expressions (RE in Fig. 28) and bind them to upper-case variables using ":=". We can generate a list of module declarations in a similar manner. $MPname$, $ELname$, $PLname$, and $Iname$ stand for names for module priority definitions, expression lists, priority lists, and elements from iterators, respectively.

$$
\begin{array}{rl}
\text{(HydLa program) } P & ::= (Def \mid Decl)^* \\
\text{(definition) } Def & ::= MPname(\vec{X})\{MP\} \mid cname(\vec{X}) \Leftrightarrow C \\
 & \mid ELname := EL \mid PLname := PL \\
\text{(constraint) } C & ::= A \mid C \wedge C \mid G \Rightarrow C \mid \exists vname.\,C \mid \Box C \mid cname(\vec{E}) \\
\text{(list condition) } LC & ::= MPname \in PL \mid Iname \in EL \mid E \neq E \\
\text{(priority list) } PL & ::= \{MP(,MP)^*\} \mid \{MP \mid LC(,LC)^*\} \mid PLname \\
\text{(module priority) } MP & ::= C \mid MPname(\vec{E}) \mid MP, MP \mid MP \ll MP \\
\text{(guard) } G & ::= A \mid G \wedge G \mid G \vee G \mid \neg G \\
\text{(atomic constraint) } A & ::= E \, Rop \, E \\
\text{(relational operator) } Rop & ::= = \mid \neq \mid > \mid \geq \mid < \mid \leq \\
\text{(expression) } E & ::= E \, Aop \, E \mid Prev \mid constant \mid EL[E] \\
\text{(expression list) } EL & ::= \{E(,E)^*\} \mid \{E \mid LC(,LC)^*\} \mid ELname \mid RE..RE \\
\text{(arithmetic operator) } Aop & ::= + \mid - \mid \times \mid \div \mid \char`\^ \\
\text{(previous) } Prev & ::= D \mid D- \\
\text{(derivative) } D & ::= vname \mid D' \\
\text{(declaration) } Decl & ::= M \mid Decl, Decl \mid Decl \ll Decl \\
\text{(module) } M & ::= C \mid dname(\vec{E}) \mid PL \mid PL[E]
\end{array}
$$

Fig. 28. Syntax of HydLa with list notation.

References

1. Alur, R., et al.: Hierarchical hybrid modeling of embedded systems. In: Henzinger, T.A., Kirsch, C.M. (eds.) EMSOFT 2001. LNCS, vol. 2211, pp. 14–31. Springer, Heidelberg (2001). https://doi.org/10.1007/3-540-45449-7_2
2. Betsuno, K., Matsumoto, S., Ueda, K.: Symbolic analysis of hybrid systems involving numerous discrete changes using loop detection. In: Berger, C., Mousavi, M.R., Wisniewski, R. (eds.) CyPhy 2016. LNCS, vol. 10107, pp. 17–30. Springer, Cham (2017). https://doi.org/10.1007/978-3-319-51738-4_2
3. Borning, A., Freeman-Benson, B., Wilson, M.: Constraint hierarchies. LISP Symb. Comput. **5**(3), 233–270 (1992)
4. Bourke, T., Pouzet, M.: Zélus: a synchronous language with ODEs. In: HSCC 2013, pp. 113–118. ACM (2013)
5. Carloni, L.P., Passerone, R., Pinto, A., Sangiovanni-Vincentelli, A.L.: Languages and tools for hybrid systems design. Found. Trends Electron. Des. Autom. **1**(1/2), 1–193 (2006)
6. Chen, X., Ábrahám, E., Sankaranarayanan, S.: Flow*: an analyzer for non-linear hybrid systems. In: Sharygina, N., Veith, H. (eds.) CAV 2013. LNCS, vol. 8044, pp. 258–263. Springer, Heidelberg (2013). https://doi.org/10.1007/978-3-642-39799-8_18
7. Fulton, N., Mitsch, S., Quesel, J.-D., Völp, M., Platzer, A.: KeYmaera X: an axiomatic tactical theorem prover for hybrid systems. In: Felty, A.P., Middeldorp, A. (eds.) CADE 2015. LNCS (LNAI), vol. 9195, pp. 527–538. Springer, Cham (2015). https://doi.org/10.1007/978-3-319-21401-6_36
8. Gupta, V., Jagadeesan, R., Saraswat, V., Bobrow, D.G.: Programming in hybrid constraint languages. In: Antsaklis, P., Kohn, W., Nerode, A., Sastry, S. (eds.) HS 1994. LNCS, vol. 999, pp. 226–251. Springer, Heidelberg (1995). https://doi.org/10.1007/3-540-60472-3_12
9. Henzinger, T.A.: The theory of hybrid automata. In: LICS 1996, pp. 278–292. IEEE Computer Society (1996)
10. Kong, S., Gao, S., Chen, W., Clarke, E.: dReach: δ-reachability analysis for hybrid systems. In: Baier, C., Tinelli, C. (eds.) TACAS 2015. LNCS, vol. 9035, pp. 200–205. Springer, Heidelberg (2015). https://doi.org/10.1007/978-3-662-46681-0_15
11. Lee, E.A.: Constructive models of discrete and continuous physical phenomena. IEEE Access **2**, 797–821 (2014)
12. Lunze, J.: Handbook of Hybrid Systems Control: Theory, Tools, Applications. Cambridge University Press, Cambridge (2009)
13. Matsumoto, S.: Validated simulation of parametric hybrid systems based on constraints. Ph.D. thesis, Waseda University (2017)
14. Matsumoto, S., Kono, F., Kobayashi, T., Ueda, K.: HyLaGI: symbolic implementation of a hybrid constraint language HydLa. Electron. Notes Theor. Comput. Sci. **317**, 109–115 (2015)
15. Matsumoto, S., Ueda, K.: Symbolic simulation of parametrized hybrid systems with affine arithmetic. In: TIME 2016, pp. 4–11. IEEE Computer Society (2016)
16. Modelica Association: Modelica - Unified Object-Oriented Language for Systems Modeling: Language Specification (Version 3.4) (2007). https://modelica.org/documents/ModelicaSpec34.pdf
17. Ñañez, P., Risso, N., Sanfelice, R.G.: A symbolic simulator for hybrid equations. In: Proceedings of SummerSim 2014, pp. 18:1–18:8 (2014)

18. Taha, W., et al.: Acumen: an open-source testbed for cyber-physical systems research. In: Mandler, B., et al. (eds.) IoT360 2015. LNICST, vol. 169, pp. 118–130. Springer, Cham (2016). https://doi.org/10.1007/978-3-319-47063-4_11

19. Takeguchi, A., Wada, R., Matsumoto, S., Hosobe, H., Ueda, K.: An algorithm for converting hybrid constraint programs to hybrid automata. In: The 29nd JSSST Annual Conference, 2A-3 (2012). https://www.ueda.info.waseda.ac.jp/~ueda/pub/takeguchi_jssst_PPL2012.pdf. (in Japanese)

20. Ueda, K., Hosobe, H., Ishii, D.: Declarative semantics of the hybrid constraint language HydLa. Comput. Softw. **28**(1), 306–311 (2011). English translation: http://arxiv.org/abs/1910.12272

21. Ueda, K., Matsumoto, S., Takeguchi, A., Hosobe, H., Ishii, D.: HydLa: a high-level language for hybrid systems. In: 2nd Workshop on Logics for System Analysis (LfSA 2012, affiliated with CAV 2012), pp. 3–17 (2012)

22. Wakatsuki, Y., Matsumoto, S., Ito, T., Wada, T., Ueda, K.: Model analysis by using micro errors in hybrid constraint processing system HyLaGI. In: The 32nd JSSST Annual Conference (2015). http://jssst.or.jp/files/user/taikai/2015/GENERAL/general6-4.pdf. (in Japanese)

Formal Methods

Guaranteed Optimal Reachability Control of Reaction-Diffusion Equations Using One-Sided Lipschitz Constants and Model Reduction

Adrien Le Coënt[1]([✉]) and Laurent Fribourg[2]

[1] Department of Computer Science, Aalborg University,
Selma Largerløfs Vej 300, 9220 Aalborg, Denmark
`adrien.le-coent@ens-cachan.fr`
[2] LSV, ENS Paris-Saclay, CNRS, Université Paris Saclay,
91 Avenue du Président Wilson, 94235 Cachan Cedex, France
`fribourg@lsv.fr`

Abstract. We show that, for any spatially discretized system of reaction-diffusion, the approximate solution given by the explicit Euler time-discretization scheme converges to the exact time-continuous solution, provided that diffusion coefficient be sufficiently large. By "sufficiently large", we mean that the diffusion coefficient value makes the *one-sided Lipschitz constant* of the reaction-diffusion system negative. We apply this result to solve a finite horizon control problem for a 1D reaction-diffusion example. We also explain how to perform *model reduction* in order to improve the efficiency of the method.

1 Introduction

1.1 Guaranteed Reachability Analysis

Given a system of Ordinary Differential equations (ODEs) of dimension n satisfying standard conditions of existence and uniqueness of the solution, the area of *Numerical Analysis* makes use of numerical tools in order to compute the approximate value of the solution, starting at an initial point of $\mathbb{R}^n$, with high accuracy: 1st order methods (explicit/implicit Euler method, trapezoid rule), higher-order Runge-Kutta methods, etc. In contrast, the area of *Guaranteed (or Symbolic) Analysis* is devoted to the construction of an overapproximation of the set of solutions that start, not at a single point of $\mathbb{R}^n$, but from a dense compact set of initial points. Guaranteed analysis, in its modern form, has been initiated in the 60's by R.E. Moore and his creation of *Interval Arithmetic* [40]: the set of solutions (or trajectories) are overapproximated by a sequence of "rectangular sets", i.e., cross-product of intervals of $\mathbb{R}$. A set of arithmetic and differential calculus has been created for manipulating such sets. An overapproximation of the set of trajectories is computed using a Taylor development up to some order and an overestimation of the "Lagrange remainder". The method has been

© Springer Nature Switzerland AG 2020
R. Chamberlain et al. (Eds.): CyPhy 2019/WESE 2019, LNCS 11971, pp. 181–202, 2020.
https://doi.org/10.1007/978-3-030-41131-2_9

considerably refined in the 90's [11,12,35,43,44]. These recent techniques make use of different convex data structures such as parallelepipeds [35] or zonotopes [21,29] instead of rectangular sets in order to enclose the flow of ODEs.

Such methods are typically applied to the formal *proof* of correctness of ODE integration, and more generally, to guarantee that the solutions of the ODEs satisfy some desired properties. Guaranteed reachability analysis generally treats *linear* systems. Extensions to nonlinear systems have been proposed, e.g., in [4], using local linearizations (see also [38,39]).

1.2   Guaranteed Optimal Control

In presence of inputs, we can use guaranteed analysis to describe a law that allows the system to satisfy a desired property. This corresponds to the topic of *guaranteed (or correct-by-design) control synthesis*. Several works have recently applied guaranteed analysis to *optimal* control synthesis. Thus, in [49,50], the authors focus on a (finite time-horizon) optimal control procedure with a formal guarantee of safety constraint satisfaction, using zonotopes as state set representations. In [16], the authors focus on (periodically) sampled systems, and perform reachability analysis using convex polytopes as state set representations. In [19,27,37,46,47], the authors construct an over-approximation of the set of trajectories using a growth bound (bounding the distance of neighboring trajectories) exploiting the notion of *one-sided Lipschitz constant* (also called "logarithmic norm" or "matrix norm"). The notion of "one-sided Lipschitz (OSL) constant" has been introduced independently by Dahlquist [17] and Lozinskii [36] in order to derive error bounds in initial value problems (see survey in [51]). We used ourselves OSL constants in the context of symbolic optimal control in [14]. The main difference with previous work [19,27,37,46,47] is that our method makes use of explicit Euler's algorithm for ODE integration (cf. [32,33]) instead of sophisticated algorithms such as Lohner's algorithm [27] or interval Taylor series methods [44]. This leads us to a simple implementation of just a few hundred lines of Octave (see [31]).

As explained in [48], using the Dynamic Programming (DP) [10] one can approximate the "value" of the solution of Hamilton-Jacobi-Bellman (HJB) equations. In [18,48], the authors thus show how to use finite difference schemes, Euler time integration and DP for solving finite horizon control problems. Furthermore, they give *a priori* errors estimates which are first-order in the size Δt of the time discretization step; however, the error involves a constant $C(T)$ which depends *exponentially* on the length T of the finite horizon[1]. We solve here finite horizon control problems along the same lines (using finite difference, explicit Euler and DP) but, under the hypothesis of OSL *negativity* (see Sect. 1.3), we obtain an error upper bound that is *linear* in T (see Sect. 2.4, Theorem 2).

---

[1] $C(T) = O(e^{L_f T})$ where L_f is the Lipschitz constant associated with vector field f.

1.3 Reaction-Diffusion Equations

It is natural to adapt the optimal control methods of ODEs to the control of Partial Differential Equations (PDEs). This can be done by transforming the PDE into (a vast system of) ODEs, using space discretization techniques such as finite difference or finite element methods. In the present work, we focus on a particular class of *non-linear* PDEs called "reaction-diffusion" equations. Reaction-diffusion equations cover a variety of particular cases with important applications in mathematical physics, and in biological models such as the Schlögl model or the FitzHugh-Nagumo system [13]. The problem of optimal control of reaction-diffusion equations has been recently the topic of many works of (classical) numerical analysis: see, e.g., [9, 15, 20, 22, 41, 42].

The notion OSL constant can be naturally extended to PDEs and reaction-diffusion equations in particular, as shown in [5–8]. In these works, the authors focus on the case where the OSL constant associated with the reaction-diffusion equation is *negative*. In this case, the system has a *contractivity* (or "incremental stability") property which expresses the fact that all solutions converge exponentially to each other (see [52]).

In this work, we also study reaction-diffusion equations with negative OSL constants, but the equations are equipped with *control inputs*, and the problem of controlling these inputs in an optimal way is here considered.

1.4 Model Reduction

In order to reduce the large dimension of ODE systems originating from the PDE space discretization, Model Order Reduction (MOR) techniques are often used in conjunction with the analysis of ODE systems. The idea is to first infer the optimal control at a *reduced level*, then apply it at the original level. In the field of guaranteed analysis, the MOR technique of "balanced truncation" was used to treat *linear* systems (e.g., [3, 23, 24, 34]). In [25], a MOR technique based on spectral element method was coupled to an HJB approach for application to advection-reaction-diffusion systems (cf. [26] for application to semilinear parabolic PDEs). The MOR technique of "Proper Orthogonal Decomposition (POD)" was coupled to an HJB approach in [1, 2, 30]. Here, we couple our HJB-based method to a simple *ad hoc* reduction method (see Sect. 2.5).

The plan of the paper is as follows: We explain how to convert the reaction-diffusion equation into a system of ODEs by domain discretization in Sect. 2.1, and how to approximate the solution of the latter system using the explicit Euler scheme of time integration in Sect. 2.2. Our procedure for solving finite horizon control problems is explained in Sect. 2.3. In Sect. 2.4, we give an upper bound to the error between the approximate value thus computed and the exact optimal value. In Sect. 2.5, we explain how to perform MOR in order to treat systems of larger dimension. We conclude in Sect. 3.

2   Optimal Reachability Control of Reaction-Diffusion Equations

Let us consider the special class of PDEs called "reaction-diffusion" equations. For the sake of notation simplicity, we focus on 1D reaction-diffusion equations with Dirichlet boundary conditions (the domain Ω is of the form $[0, L] \subset \mathbb{R}$), but the method applies to 2D or 3D reaction-diffusion equations with other boundary conditions. A 1D *reaction-diffusion* system with Dirichlet boundary conditions is of the form:

$$\frac{\partial \mathbf{y}(t, x)}{\partial t} = \sigma \frac{\partial^2 \mathbf{y}(t, x)}{\partial x^2} + f(\mathbf{y}(t, x)), \quad t \in [0, T], \ x \in \Omega \equiv [0, L].$$

$$\mathbf{y}(t, 0) = u_0(t), \quad \mathbf{y}(t, L) = u_L(t), \quad t \in [0, T],$$

$$\mathbf{y}(0, x) = \mathbf{y}_0(x), \quad x \in \Omega \equiv [0, L].$$

Here, $\mathbf{y} = \mathbf{y}(t, x)$ is an $\mathbb{R}$-valued unknown function, Ω is a bounded domain in $\mathbb{R}$ with boundary $\partial\Omega := \{0, L\}$, and f is a function from $[0, T] \times \Omega$ to $[0, 1]$. Also $\mathbf{y}_0(x)$ is a given function called "initial condition", and σ a positive constant, called "diffusion constant".

The boundary control $u(\cdot) := (u_0(\cdot), u_L(\cdot))$ that we consider here, is a *piecewise constant* (or "staircase") function from $[0, T]$ to a *finite* set $U \subset [0, 1] \times [0, 1]$. The control $u(t)$ changes its value *periodically* at $t = \tau, 2\tau, \ldots$. We assume that $T = k\tau$ for some positive integer k. The constant τ is called the "switching (or sampling) period".

Given an initial condition $\mathbf{y}_0(\cdot)$ such that $\mathbf{y}_0(x) \in [0, 1]$ for all $x \in [0, L]$, we assume that, for any boundary control $u(\cdot)$, the solution $\mathbf{y}(\cdot, \cdot)$ of the system exists, is unique, and $\mathbf{y}(t, x) \in [0, 1]$ for all $(t, x) \in [0, T] \times [0, L]$.

2.1   Domain Discretization

A well-known approach in numerical analysis of PDEs (see, e.g., [28]) is to discretize in space by finite difference or finite element methods in order to transform the PDE into a system of ODEs.

Let M be a positive integer, $h = L/(M+1)$, and let Ω_h be a uniform grid with nodes $x_j = jh$, $j = 1, \ldots, M$. By replacing the 2nd order spatial derivative with the second order centered difference, we obtain a space-discrete approximation:

$$\frac{dy}{dt} = \sigma \mathcal{L}_h y + \sigma \varphi_h(t, u) + f(t, y),$$

with $y(t) = [y^1(t), \ldots, y^M(t)]^T$, $y^j(t) \approx \mathbf{y}(t, x_j)$, and

$$\mathcal{L}_h = \frac{1}{h^2} \begin{bmatrix} -2 & 1 & 0 & \cdots & 0 \\ 1 & -2 & 1 & \cdots & 0 \\ 0 & 1 & -2 & \cdots & 0 \\ & & \cdots & & \\ 0 & 0 & \cdots & 1 & -2 \end{bmatrix}$$

$$\varphi_h(t, u) = \frac{1}{h^2} [u_0(t), 0, \dots, 0, u_L(t)]^\top.$$

The point $y(t)$, often abbreviated as y, is thus an element of $S = [0, 1]^M$.

2.2   Explicit Euler Time Integration

Let us abbreviate the equation

$$\frac{dy}{dt} = \sigma \mathcal{L}_h y + \sigma \varphi_h(t, u) + f(t, y)$$

by:

$$\frac{dy}{dt} = f_u(t, y).$$

We denote by Y_{t,y_0}^u, the solution y of the system at time $t \in [0, \tau)$ controlled by mode $u \in U$, for initial condition y_0. Given a sequence of modes (or "pattern") $\pi := u_k \cdots u_1 \in U^k$, we denote by Y_{t,y_0}^π the solution of the system for mode u_k on $t \in [0, \tau)$ with initial condition y_0, extended continuously with the solution of the system for mode u_{k-1} on $t \in [\tau, 2\tau)$, and so on iteratively until mode u_1 on $t \in [(k-1)\tau, k\tau]$.

Let us now approximate the solution of the system by performing time integration with the *explicit Euler* scheme. This yields:

$$y_{n+1} = y_n + \tau f_u(t_n, y_n),$$

Here y_n is an approximate value of $y(t_n)$. Given a starting point $z \in \mathcal{X}$ and a mode $u \in U$, we denote by $\tilde{Y}_{t,z}^u$ the Euler-based image of z at time t via u for $t \in [0, \tau)$. We have: $\tilde{Y}_{t,z}^u := z + t \ f_u(z)$. We denote similarly by $\tilde{Y}_{t,z}^\pi$ the Euler-based image of z via pattern $\pi \in U^k$ at time $t \in [0, k\tau]$.

2.3   Finite Horizon Control Problems

Let us now explain the principle of the method of optimal control of ODEs used in [14], in the present context. We consider the *cost function*: $J_k : [0, 1]^M \times U^k \to \mathbb{R}_{\geq 0}$ defined by:

$$J_k(y, \pi) = \|Y_{k\tau,y}^\pi - y_f\|,$$

where $\| \cdot \|$ denotes the Euclidean norm in $\mathbb{R}^M$, and $y_f \in [0, 1]^M$ is a given "target" state.

We consider the *value function* $\mathbf{v}_k : [0, 1]^M \to \mathbb{R}_{\geq 0}$ defined by:

$$\mathbf{v}_k(y) := \min_{\pi \in U^k} \{J_k(y, \pi)\} \equiv \min_{\pi \in U^k} \{\|Y_{k\tau,y}^\pi - y_f\|\}.$$

Given $k \in \mathbb{N}$ and $\tau \in \mathbb{R}_{>0}$, we consider the following *finite time horizon optimal control problem*: Find for each $y \in [0, 1]^M$

– the *value* $\mathbf{v}_k(y)$, i.e.

$$\min_{\pi \in U^k} \{\|Y^\pi_{k\tau,y} - y_f\|\},$$

– and an *optimal pattern*:

$$\pi_k(y) := arg \min_{\pi \in U^k} \{\|Y^\pi_{k\tau,y} - y_f\|\}.$$

In order to solve such optimal control problems, a classical "direct" method consists in *spatially discretizing* the state space $S = [0,1]^M$ (i.e., the space of values of y). We consider here a uniform partition of S into a finite number N of cells of equal size: in our case , this means that interval $[0,1]$ is divided into K subintervals of equal size, and $N = K^M$. A cell thus corresponds to a M-tuple of subintervals. The center of a cell corresponds to the M-tuple of the subinterval midpoints. The associated grid $\mathcal{X}$ is the set of centers of the cells of S. The center $z \in \mathcal{X}$ of a cell C is considered as the *ε-representative* of all the points of C. We suppose that the cell size is such that $\|y - z\| \leqslant \varepsilon$, for all $y \in C$ (i.e. $K \geqslant \sqrt{M}/2\varepsilon$). In this context, the direct method proceeds as follows (cf. [14]): we consider the points of $\mathcal{X}$ as the vertices of a finite oriented graph; there is a connection from $z \in \mathcal{X}$ to $z' \in \mathcal{X}$ if z' is the ε-representative of the Euler-based image $(z + \tau f_u(z))$ of z, for some $u \in U$. We then compute using dynamic programming the "path of length k with minimal cost" starting at z: such a path is a sequence of $k+1$ connected points $z\ z_k\ z_{k-1}\ \cdots\ z_1$ of $\mathcal{X}$ which minimizes the distance $\|z_1 - y_f\|$. This procedure allows us to compute a pattern $\pi^\varepsilon_k(z)$ of length k, which approximates the optimal pattern $\pi_k(y)$.

Definition 1. *The function $next^u : \mathcal{X} \to \mathcal{X}$ is defined by:*

– $next^u(z) = z'$, *where z' is the ε-representative of $\tilde{Y}^u_{\tau,z}$.*

Definition 2. *For all point $x \in \mathcal{X}$, the* spatially discrete value function $\mathbf{v}^\varepsilon_k$: $\mathcal{X} \to \mathbb{R}_{\geqslant 0}$ *is defined by:*

– *for $k = 0$, $\mathbf{v}^\varepsilon_k(z) = \|z - y_f\|$,*
– *for $k \geqslant 1$, $\mathbf{v}^\varepsilon_k(z) = \min_{u \in U}\{\mathbf{v}^\varepsilon_{k-1}(next^u(z))\}$.*

Definition 3. *The approximate optimal pattern of length k associated to $z \in \mathcal{X}$, denoted by $\pi^\varepsilon_k(z) \in U^k$, is defined by:*

– *if $k = 0$, $\pi^\varepsilon_k(z) = nil$,*
– *if $k \geqslant 1$, $\pi^\varepsilon_k(z) = \mathbf{u}_k(z) \cdot \pi'$ where*

$$\mathbf{u}_k(z) = arg \min_{u \in U}\{\mathbf{v}^\varepsilon_{k-1}(next^u(z))\}$$

and $\pi' = \pi^\varepsilon_{k-1}(z')$ with $z' = next^{\mathbf{u}_k(z)}(z)$.

It is easy to construct a procedure $PROC^\varepsilon_k$ which takes a point $z \in \mathcal{X}$ as input, and returns an approximate optimal pattern $\pi^\varepsilon_k \in U^k$.

Remark 1. The complexity of $PROC^\varepsilon_k$ is $O(m \times k \times N)$ where m is the number of modes ($|U| = m$), k the time-horizon length ($T = k\tau$) and N the number of cells of $\mathcal{X}$ ($N = K^M$ with $K = \sqrt{M}/2\varepsilon$).

2.4   Error Upper Bound

Given a point $y \in S$ of ε-representative $z \in \mathcal{X}$, and a pattern π_k^ε returned by $PROC_k^\varepsilon(z)$, we are now going to show that the distance $\|\tilde{Y}_{k\tau,z}^{\pi_k^\varepsilon} - y_f\|$ converges to $\mathbf{v}_k(y)$ as $\varepsilon \to 0$. We first consider the ODE: $\frac{dy}{dt} = f_u(y)$, and give an upper bound to the error between the exact solution of the ODE and its Euler approximation (see [33]).

Definition 4. *Let μ be a given positive constant. Let us define, for all $u \in U$ and $t \in [0, \tau]$, $\delta_{t,\mu}^u$ as follows:*

$$ \text{if } \lambda_u < 0: \quad \delta_{t,\mu}^u = \left(\mu^2 e^{\lambda_u t} + \frac{C_u^2}{\lambda_u^2} \left(t^2 + \frac{2t}{\lambda_u} + \frac{2}{\lambda_u^2} \left(1 - e^{\lambda_u t} \right) \right) \right)^{\frac{1}{2}} $$

$$ \text{if } \lambda_u = 0: \quad \delta_{t,\mu}^u = \left(\mu^2 e^t + C_u^2 (-t^2 - 2t + 2(e^t - 1)) \right)^{\frac{1}{2}} $$

$$ \text{if } \lambda_u > 0: \quad \delta_{t,\mu}^u = \left(\mu^2 e^{3\lambda_u t} + \frac{C_u^2}{3\lambda_u^2} \left(-t^2 - \frac{2t}{3\lambda_u} + \frac{2}{9\lambda_u^2} \left(e^{3\lambda_u t} - 1 \right) \right) \right)^{\frac{1}{2}} $$

where C_u and λ_u are real constants specific to function f_u, defined as follows:

$$ C_u = \sup_{y \in S} L_u \| f_u(y) \|, $$

where L_u denotes the Lipschitz constant for f_u, and λ_u is the OSL constant associated to f_u, i.e., the minimal constant such that, for all $y_1, y_2 \in S$:

$$ \langle f_u(y_1) - f_u(y_2), y_1 - y_2 \rangle \leqslant \lambda_u \| y_1 - y_2 \|^2, $$

where $\langle \cdot, \cdot \rangle$ denotes the scalar product of two vectors of S.

Proposition 1 [33]. *Consider the solution Y_{t,y_0}^u of $\frac{dy}{dt} = f_u(y)$ with initial condition y_0 of ε-representative z_0 (hence such that $\|y_0 - z_0\| \leqslant \varepsilon$), and the approximate solution $\tilde{Y}_{t,z_0}^u$ given by the explicit Euler scheme. For all $t \in [0, \tau]$, we have:*

$$ \| Y_{t,y_0}^u - \tilde{Y}_{t,z_0}^u \| \leqslant \delta_{t,\varepsilon}^u. $$

Proposition 2. *Consider the system $\frac{dy}{dt} = f_u(y)$ with $f_u(y) := \sigma \mathcal{L}_h y + \sigma \varphi_h(t, u) + f(y)$. For a diffusion coefficient $\sigma > 0$ sufficiently large, the OSL constant λ_u associated to f_u is such that: $\lambda_u < 0$.*

Proof. Consider the ODE: $\frac{dy}{dt} = f_u(y) = \sigma \mathcal{L}_h y + \sigma \varphi_h(t, u) + f(y)$. For all $y_1, y_2 \in S$, we have: $\langle f(y_2) - f(y_1), y_2 - y_1 \rangle \leqslant \lambda_f \| y_2 - y_1 \|^2$, where λ_f is the OSL constant of f. Hence:

$$ \langle f_u(y_2) - f_u(y_1), y_2 - y_1 \rangle = \langle \sigma \mathcal{L}_h(y_2 - y_1) + f(y_2) - f(y_1), y_2 - y_1 \rangle $$
$$ \leqslant (y_2 - y_1)^\top (\sigma \mathcal{L}_h + \lambda_f)(y_2 - y_1). $$

Since $y^\top \mathcal{L}_h y < 0$ for all $y \in S$ (negativity of the quadratic form associated to $\mathcal{L}_h$), we have:

$$\lambda_u \|y_1 - y_2\|^2 \leqslant (y_2 - y_1)^T (\sigma \mathcal{L}_h + \lambda_f)(y_2 - y_1) < 0,$$

for $\sigma > 0$ sufficiently large. Hence $\lambda_u < 0$.   □

Lemma 1. *Consider the system $\frac{dy}{dt} = f_u(y)$ where the OSL constant λ_u associated to f_u is negative, and initial error $e_0 := \|y_0 - z_0\| > 0$. Let $G_u := \frac{\sqrt{3}e_0|\lambda_u|}{C_u}$. Consider the (smallest) positive root*

$$\alpha_u := 1 + |\lambda_u| G_u/4 - \sqrt{1 + (\lambda_u G_u/4)^2}$$

of equation: $-\frac{1}{2}|\lambda_u| G_u + (2 + \frac{1}{2}|\lambda_u| G_u)\alpha - \alpha^2 = 0$.
Suppose: $\frac{|\lambda_u| G_u}{4} < 1$. Then we have $0 < \alpha_u < 1$, and, for all $t \in [0, \tau]$ with $\tau \leqslant G_u(1 - \alpha_u)$:

$$\delta^u_{e_0}(t) \leqslant e_0.$$

Proof. See Appendix 1.

Remark 2. In practical case studies $|\lambda_u|$ is often small, and the term $(\lambda_u G_u/4)^2$ can be neglected, leading to $\alpha_u \approx |\lambda_u| G_u/4$ and $G_u(1 - \alpha_u) \approx G_u(1 - \frac{|\lambda_u| G_u}{4}) \approx G_u$.

Remark 3. It follows that, for $\tau \leqslant G_u(1 - \alpha_u)$, the Euler explicit scheme is *stable*, in the sense that initial errors are damped out.

Remark 4. If $\tau > G_u(1 - \alpha_u)$, we can make use of *subsampling*, i.e., decompose τ into a sequence of elementary time steps Δt with $\Delta t \leqslant G_u(1 - \alpha_u)$ in order to be still able to apply Lemma 1 (see Example 1). Let us point out that Lemma 1 (and the use of subsampling) allows to ensure set-based reachability with the use of procedure $PROC^\varepsilon_k$. Indeed, in this setting, the explicit Euler scheme leads to decreasing errors, and thus, point based computations performed with the center of a cell can be applied to the entire cell.

We suppose henceforth that the system $\frac{dy}{dt} = f_u(y)$ satisfies:

$$(H): \quad \lambda_u < 0, \quad \frac{|\lambda_u| G_u}{4} < 1 \quad \text{and} \quad \tau \leqslant G_u(1 - \alpha_u), \quad \text{for all } u \in U.$$

From Proposition 1 and Lemma 1, it easily follows:

Theorem 1. *Consider a system $\frac{dy}{dt} = f_u(y)$ satisfying (H), and a point $y \in S$ of ε-representative $z \in \mathcal{X}$. We have:*

$$\|Y^\pi_{t,y} - \tilde{Y}^\pi_{t,z}\| \leqslant \varepsilon, \quad \text{for all } \pi \in U^k \text{ and } t \in [0, k\tau].$$

Proposition 3. *Let $z \in \mathcal{X}$ and π^ε_k be the pattern of U^k returned by $PROC^\varepsilon_k(z)$. For all $\pi \in U^k$, we have:*

$$\|\tilde{Y}^{\pi^\varepsilon_k}_{k\tau,z} - y_f\| \leqslant \|\tilde{Y}^\pi_{k\tau,z} - y_f\| + 2k\varepsilon.$$

Proof. W.l.o.g., let us suppose that y_f is the origin O. Let us prove by induction on k:

$$\|\tilde{Y}^{\pi_k^\varepsilon}_{k\tau,z}\| \leqslant \|\tilde{Y}^{\pi}_{k\tau,z}\| + 2k\varepsilon.$$

Let $\pi_k^\varepsilon := u_k \cdots u_1$. The base case $k = 1$ is easy. For $k \geqslant 2$, we have:

$$\|\tilde{Y}^{\pi_k^\varepsilon}_{k\tau,z}\| = \|\tilde{Y}^{u_{k-1}\cdots u_1}_{(k-1)\tau,z_k}\| \text{ with } z_k = \tilde{Y}^{u_k}_{\tau,z} \text{ with } u_k = argmin_{u \in U}\{\mathbf{v}^\varepsilon_{k-1}(next^u(z))\}$$

$$\leqslant \|\tilde{Y}^{u_{k-1}\cdots u_1}_{(k-1)\tau,next^{u_k}(z_k)}\| + \varepsilon$$

$$\leqslant \|\tilde{Y}^{\pi'}_{(k-1)\tau,next^{u_k}(z_k)}\| + (2k-1)\varepsilon \text{ for all } \pi' \in U^{k-1} \text{ by induction hypothesis,}$$

$$\leqslant \|\tilde{Y}^{\pi'}_{(k-1)\tau,z'}\| + 2k\varepsilon \text{ for all } \pi' \in U^{k-1} \text{ and all } z' \in \{next^u(z) \,|\, u \in U\}$$

$$\leqslant \|\tilde{Y}^{\pi}_{\tau,z}\| + 2k\varepsilon \text{ for all } \pi \in U^k.$$

$\square$

Theorem 2. *Let* $y \in S$ *be a point of* ε-*representative* $z \in \mathcal{X}$. *Let* π_k^ε *be the pattern returned by* $PROC_k^\varepsilon(z)$, *and* $\pi^* := argmin_{\pi \in U_k}\|Y^\pi_{k\tau,y} - y_f\|$. *The discretization error* $E_\varepsilon(T) := |\|\tilde{Y}^{\pi_k^\varepsilon}_{k\tau,z} - y_f\| - \mathbf{v}_k(y)|$, *with* $\mathbf{v}_k(y) := \|Y^{\pi^*}_{k\tau,y} - y_f\|$ *and* $T = k\tau$, *satisfies:*

$$E_\varepsilon(T) \leqslant (2k+1)\varepsilon.$$

It follows that $\|\tilde{Y}^{\pi_k^\varepsilon}_{k\tau,z} - y_f\|$ *converges to* $\mathbf{v}_k(y)$ *as* $\varepsilon \to 0$.

Proof. W.l.o.g., let us suppose that y_f is the origin O. For all $\pi \in U^k$, we have by Proposition 3 and Theorem 1:

$$\|\tilde{Y}^{\pi_k^\varepsilon}_{k\tau,z}\| \leqslant \|\tilde{Y}^{\pi}_{k\tau,z}\| + 2k\varepsilon \leqslant \|Y^{\pi}_{k\tau,y}\| + (2k+1)\varepsilon.$$

Hence

$$\|\tilde{Y}^{\pi_k^\varepsilon}_{k\tau,z}\| \leqslant \min_{\pi \in U^k} \|Y^{\pi}_{k\tau,y}\| + (2k+1)\varepsilon = \|Y^{\pi^*}_{k\tau,y}\| + (2k+1)\varepsilon.$$

On the other hand, for all $\pi \in U^k$, it follows from Theorem 1:

$$\|Y^{\pi^*}_{k\tau,y}\| \leqslant \|Y^{\pi}_{k\tau,y}\| \leqslant \|\tilde{Y}^{\pi}_{k\tau,z}\| + \varepsilon.$$

Hence:

$$\|Y^{\pi^*}_{k\tau,y}\| \leqslant \|\tilde{Y}^{\pi_k^\varepsilon}_{k\tau,z}\| + \varepsilon.$$

Therefore we have: $|\|\tilde{Y}^{\pi_k^\varepsilon}_{k\tau,z}\| - \|Y^{\pi^*}_{k\tau,y}\|| \leqslant (2k+1)\varepsilon.$ $\square$

Remark 5. The error bound $E_\varepsilon(T)$ is thus *linear* in $k = T/\tau$. In order to decrease k, one can apply consecutively $p \geqslant 2$ modes *in a row* (without intermediate ε-approximation); this is equivalent to divide k by p, at the price of considering m^p "extended" modes instead of just m modes. (see Example 1, Fig. 2). An alternative for decreasing k is to increase τ (which may require in turn to decrease Δt for preserving assumption $\Delta t \leqslant G_u(1 - \alpha_u)$, see Remark 4).

Example 1. Consider the 1D reaction-diffusion system with Dirichlet boundary condition (see [45], bistable case):

$$\frac{\partial y(t,x)}{\partial t} = \sigma \frac{\partial^2 y(t,x)}{\partial x^2} + f(y(t,x)), \quad t \in [0,T], \ x \in [0,L]$$
$$y(t,0) = u_0, \quad y(t,L) = u_L,$$
$$y(0,x) = y_0(x), \quad x \in [0,L]$$

with $\sigma = 1, L = 4$ and $f(y) = y(1-y)(y-\theta)$ with $\theta = 0.3$. The control switching period is $\tau = 0.1$. The values of the boundary control $u = (u_0, u_L)$ are in[2]

$$U = \{(0,0), (0.2, 0.2), (0.4, 0.4), (0.6, 0.6), (0.8.0.8), (1,1)\}.$$

We discretize the domain $\Omega = [0,L]$ of the system with $M_1 = 5$ discrete points, using a finite difference scheme. Our program returns an OSL constant $\lambda_u = -0.322$ for all $u \in U$. Constant C_u varies between 10.33 and 11.85 depending on the values of u.

We then discretize each interval component of the space $S = [0,1]^{M_1}$ of values of y into 15 points with spacing $\eta = 1/15 \approx 0.066$. The grid $\mathcal{X}$ is of the form $\{0, \eta, 2\eta, \ldots, 15\eta\}^{M_1}$, and the initial error e_0 equal to $\varepsilon = \sqrt{M_1}\eta/2$. This leads to G_u varying between 0.00155 and 0.00178 depending on the value of $u \in U$. One checks: $\frac{|\lambda_u|G_u}{4} < 1$ for all $u \in U$. The time step upper bound required by Theorem 1 for ensuring numeric stability is 0.00155. Since the switching period is $\tau = 0.1$, we perform *subsampling* (see, e.g., [33]) by decomposing every time step $[i\tau, (i+1)\tau]$ $(1 \leqslant i \leqslant k-1)$ into a sequence of elementary Euler steps of length $\Delta t = \tau/100 < 0.00155$. This ensures that the system satisfies (H), hence, by Theorem 1, the explicit Euler scheme is stable and error $\|Y_{t,y_0}^\tau - \check{Y}_{t,z_0}^\tau\|$ never exceeds ε.

For objective with $y_f = (0.3, 0.3, 0.3, 0.3, 0.3)$ and horizon time $T = k\tau = 2$ (i.e., $k = 20$), our program[3] returns an approximate optimal controller in 2 minutes. Let z_0 be the ε-representative of $y_0 = 0.8x/L + 0.1(1 - x/L)$. Let π_k^ε be the pattern output by $PROC_k^\varepsilon(z_0)$. A simulation of $z(t) := \check{Y}_{t,z_0}^{\pi_k^\varepsilon}$ is given in Fig. 1 with $T = 2, \tau = 0.1$ $(k = 20)$, $\Delta t = \frac{\tau}{100}$. We have $\|z(T) - y_f\| \approx 0.276$. The simulation presents some similarity with simulations displayed in [45] (see, e.g., lower part of Fig. 6), with a phase control $u_0 = u_L > \theta$ (here, $u_0 = u_L = 0.4$) alternating with a phase control $u_0 = u_L < \theta$ (here, $u_0 = u_L = 0.2$). The discretization error $E_\varepsilon(T)$ is smaller than $(2k+1)\varepsilon = 41\sqrt{5}/30 < 3.1$.

Let us now proceed with extended modes of length $p = 2$ and $p = 4$, as explained in Remark 5. For $p = 2$ (i.e., $k = 10$), the control is synthesized in

---

[2] Note that, in [45], the values of the boundary control are in the full interval $[0,1]$, not in a finite set U as here. In [45], they focus, not on the bounding of computation errors during integration as here, but on a formal proof that the objective state $y_f = \theta$ $(0 < \theta < 1)$ is reachable in finite time iff $L < L^*$ for some threshold value L^*.

[3] The program, called "OSLator" [31], is implemented in Octave. It is composed of 10 functions and a main script totalling 600 lines of code. The computations are realised in a virtual machine running Ubuntu 18.06 LTS, having access to one core of a 2.3GHz Intel Core i5, associated to 3.5 GB of RAM memory.

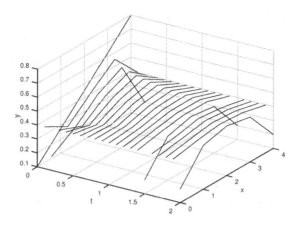

Fig. 1. Simulation of the system of Example 1 discretized with $M_1 = 5$ points, for initial condition $y_0 = 0.8x/L + 0.1(1 - x/L)$, objective $y_f = 0.3$ and horizon time $T = 2$ ($\tau = 0.1$, $\Delta t = \frac{\tau}{100}$).

7 mn of CPU time. The controller simulation is given in the left part of Fig. 2; we have: $\|z(T) - y_f\| \approx 0.445$ with $E_\varepsilon(T) < 1.57$. For $p = 4$ (i.e., $k = 5$), the computation of the control requires 8 h of CPU time. The corresponding simulation is given in the right part of Fig. 2; we now have: $\|z(T) - y_f\| \approx 0.164$ with $E_\varepsilon(T) < 0.82$.

2.5   Model Reduction

Let us consider the system $\mathcal{S}_2$ on space $S_{h_2} = [0, 1]^{M_2}$ (with M_2 even). The differential equation can be written under the form:

$$\frac{dy_2}{dt} = \sigma \mathcal{L}_{h_2} y_2 + \varphi_{h_2}(u) + f(y_2).$$

where $\mathcal{L}_{h_2}$ corresponds to the $(M_2 \times M_2)$ Laplacian matrix, and $h_2 = \frac{L}{M_2+1}$.

Let us consider the "reduced" system $\mathcal{S}_1$ defined on $S_{h_1} = [0, 1]^{M_1}$ with $M_1 = M_2/2$, defined by:

$$\frac{dy_1}{dt} = \sigma \mathcal{L}_{h_1} y_1 + \varphi_{h_1}(u) + f(y_1),$$

where $\mathcal{L}_{h_1}$ is the $(M_1 \times M_1)$ Laplacian matrix and $h_1 = \frac{L}{M_1+1}$.

With $M_1 = M_2/2$, we have $h_2 = \frac{L}{2M_1+1}$ $\left(= \frac{h_1(M_1+1)}{2M_1+1}\right)$. Let us consider the $(M_1 \times M_2)$ *reduction matrix*:

$$\Pi := \frac{1}{\sqrt{2}} \begin{bmatrix} 1 & 1 & 0 & \cdots & 0 & 0 \\ 0 & 0 & 1 & 1 & \cdots & 0 \\ & & \cdots & & & \\ 0 & 0 & \cdots & 0 & 1 & 1 \end{bmatrix}$$

Note that $\Pi\Pi^\top = \mathcal{I}_M$. Let us consider a point $w_0 \in S_{h_2}$, and let $z_0 = \Pi w_0 \in S_{h_1}$.

Theorem 3. *Consider the system $\mathcal{S}_2$ and a point $w_0 \in S_{h_2}$, and let $z_0 = \Pi w_0 \in S_{h_1}$. Let $Y_{w_0}^{h_2}$ and $Y_{z_0}^{h_1}$ be the solutions of $\mathcal{S}_2$ and $\mathcal{S}_1$ with initial conditions $w_0 \in S_{h_2}$ and $z_0 \in S_{h_1}$ respectively. We have:*

$$\forall t \geqslant 0 \quad \|\Pi Y_{w_0}^{h_2}(t) - Y_{z_0}^{h_1}(t)\| \leqslant \frac{K_2\sigma}{|\lambda_{h_1}|},$$

where

$$K_2 := \sup_{w \in S_{h_2}} \|(\Pi\mathcal{L}_{h_2} - \mathcal{L}_{h_1}\Pi)w\|,$$

and $\mathcal{L}_{h_2}$ (resp. $\mathcal{L}_{h_1}$) is the Laplacian matrix of size $M_2 \times M_2$ (resp. $M_1 \times M_1$).

Proof. Let us consider the system $\mathcal{S}_2$:

$$\frac{dy_2}{dt} = \sigma\mathcal{L}_{h_2}y_2 + \varphi_{h_2}(u) + f(y_2).$$

By application of the projection matrix Π, we get:

$$\frac{d\Pi y_2}{dt} = \sigma\Pi\mathcal{L}_{h_2}y_2 + \varphi_{h_1}(u) + f(\Pi y_2).$$

By subtracting pairwise with the sides of $\mathcal{S}_1$, we have:

$$\frac{d\Pi y_2}{dt} - \frac{dy_1}{dt} = \sigma(\Pi\mathcal{L}_{h_2}y_2 - \mathcal{L}_{h_1}y_1) + f(\Pi y_2) - f(y_1)$$

$$= F_{h_1}(\Pi y_2) - F_{h_1}(y_1) + \sigma(\Pi\mathcal{L}_{h_2} - \mathcal{L}_{h_1}\Pi)y_2,$$

where $F_{h_1}(y) = \sigma\mathcal{L}_{h_1}(y) + f(y)$ for $y \in S_{h_1}$. On the other hand, we have:

$$\frac{1}{2}\frac{d}{dt}(\|\Pi y_2 - y_1\|^2) = \langle\frac{d}{dt}(\Pi y_2 - y_1), \Pi y_2 - y_1\rangle$$
$$= \langle F_{h_1}(\Pi y_2) - F_{h_1}(y_1) + \sigma(\Pi\mathcal{L}_{h_2} - \mathcal{L}_{h_1}\Pi)y_2, \Pi y_2 - y_1\rangle$$
$$= \langle F_{h_1}(\Pi y_2) - F_{h_1}(y_1), \Pi y_2 - y_1\rangle$$
$$\quad + \sigma\langle(\Pi\mathcal{L}_{h_2} - \mathcal{L}_{h_1}\Pi)y_2, \Pi y_2 - y_1\rangle$$
$$\leqslant \lambda_{h_1}\|\Pi y_2 - y_1\|^2 + \sigma\langle(\Pi\mathcal{L}_{h_2} - \mathcal{L}_{h_1}\Pi)y_2, \Pi y_2 - y_1\rangle$$
$$\leqslant \lambda_{h_1}\|\Pi y_2 - y_1\|^2 + K_2\sigma\|\Pi y_2 - y_1\|$$

$$\text{with} \quad K_2 := \sup_{w \in S_{h_2}} \|(\Pi\mathcal{L}_{h_2} - \mathcal{L}_{h_1}\Pi)w\|$$

$$\leqslant \lambda_{h_1}\|\Pi y_2 - y_1\|^2 + K_2\sigma\frac{1}{2}(\alpha\|\Pi y_2 - y_1\|^2 + \frac{1}{\alpha}),$$

for all $\alpha > 0$. Choosing $\alpha > 0$ such that $K_2\sigma\alpha = -\lambda_{h_1}$, i.e.: $\alpha = -\frac{\lambda_{h_1}}{K_2\sigma}$, we have:

$$\frac{1}{2}\frac{d}{dt}(\|\Pi y_2 - y_1\|^2) \leqslant \frac{\lambda_{h_1}}{2}\|\Pi y_2 - y_1\|^2 - \frac{(K_2\sigma)^2}{2\lambda_{h_1}}.$$

Since $y_2(0) = w_0$ and $y_1(0) = z_0$, we get by integration:

$$\|\Pi y_2(t) - y_1(t)\|^2 \leqslant \frac{(K_2\sigma)^2}{\lambda_{h_1}^2}(1 - e^{\lambda_{h_1}t}) \leqslant \frac{(K_2\sigma)^2}{\lambda_{h_1}^2}.$$

Hence: $\|\Pi Y_{w_0}^{h_2}(t) - Y_{z_0}^{h_1}(t)\| \leqslant \frac{K_2\sigma}{|\lambda_{h_1}|}$ for all $t \geqslant 0$. $\qquad\square$

This proposition expresses that the reduction error is bounded by constant $\frac{K_2\sigma}{|\lambda_{h_1}|}$ when the same control modes are applied to both systems.[4]

Let $y_2^0 \in S_2$ and $y_2^f \in S_2$ be an initial and objective point respectively. Let $y_1^0 := \Pi y_2^0 \in S_1$ and $y_1^f := \Pi y_2^f \in S_1$ denote their projections. Suppose that π^ε is the pattern returned by $PROC_k^\varepsilon(y_1^0)$ for the reduced system S_1. Then, from Theorem 3, it follows that, when the *same* control π^ε is applied to the original system S_2 with $y_2(0) = y_2^0 \in S_2$, it makes the projection $\Pi y_2^{\pi^\varepsilon}(t) \in S_1$ reach a *neighborhood* of y_1^f at time $t = T$. Formally, we have:

$$\|Py_2^{\pi^\varepsilon}(T) - y_1^f\| \leqslant \|y_1^{\pi^\varepsilon}(T) - y_1^f\| + \frac{K_2\sigma}{|\lambda_{h_1}|}.$$

Example 2. Let us take the system defined in Example 1 as reduced system S_1 ($M_1 = 5$), and let us take as "full-size" system S_2 the system corresponding to $M_2 = 10$. Since the size of the grid $\mathcal{X}_2$ associated to S_2 is exponential in M_2, the size $\mathcal{X}_2$ is multiplied by $(1/\eta)^{M_2 - M_1} = 15^5 \approx 7.6 \cdot 10^5$ w.r.t. the size of the grid $\mathcal{X}_1$ associated to S_1. The complexity for synthesizing directly the optimal control of S_2 thus becomes intractable. On the other hand, if we apply to S_2 the optimal strategy $\pi^\varepsilon \in U^k$ found for S_1 in Example 1, we obtain a simulation depicted in Fig. 3 for extended mode of length 1, which is the counterpart of Fig. 1 with $M_2 = 10$ (instead of $M_1 = 5$), and has a very similar form. Likewise, if we apply to S_2 the optimal strategy $\pi^\varepsilon \in U^k$ found for S_1 in Example 1, we obtain a simulation depicted in Fig. 4 for extended modes of length 2 and 4, which is the counterpart of Fig. 2, and very similar to it. As seen above, we have:

$$\|\Pi y_2^{\pi^\varepsilon}(T) - y_1^f\| \leqslant \|y_1^{\pi^\varepsilon}(T) - y_1^f\| + \frac{K_2\sigma}{|\lambda_{h_1}|},$$

where $y_1^f = (0.3, 0.3, 0.3, 0.3, 0.3)$, and the reduction error is bounded by $\frac{K_2\sigma}{|\lambda_{h_1}|} = 17.9\,\sigma$.

The subexpression $\|y_1^{\pi^\varepsilon}(T) - y_1^f\|$ can be computed *a posteriori* by simulation: see Table 1 of Appendix 2, with $\sigma = 1$, $\sigma = 0.5$. The value of $\|y_2^{\pi^\varepsilon}(T) - y_2^f\|$ for S_2 is also given in Table 1 for comparison.

The upper bound $\|y_1^{\pi^\varepsilon}(T) - y_1^f\| + \frac{K_2\sigma}{|\lambda_{h_1}|}$ of the distance $\|Py_2^{\pi^\varepsilon}(T) - y_1^f\|$ is very conservative, due to *a priori* error bound $\frac{K_2\sigma}{|\lambda_{h_1}|}$. On can obtain *a posteriori* a much sharper estimate of $\|Py_2^{\pi^\varepsilon}(T) - y_1^f\|$ by simulation: see Table 2, Appendix 2.

3   Final Remarks

Using the notion of OSL constant, we have shown how to use the finite difference and explicit Euler methods in order to solve finite horizon control problems for

---

[4] By comparison, in [2], the error term originating from the POD model reduction is *exponential* in T (see $C_1(T, |x|)$ in the proof of Theorem 5.1).

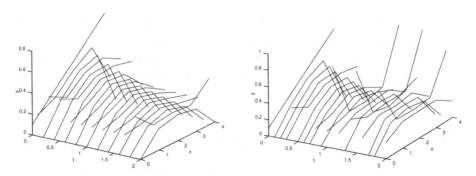

Fig. 2. Simulation of the system of Example 1 discretized with $M_1 = 5$ points, with extended modes of length 2 (left) and extended modes of length 4 (right).

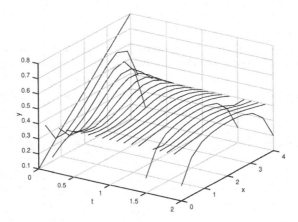

Fig. 3. Simulation of the system of Example 1, discretized with $M_2 = 10$ points, with extended mode of length 1.

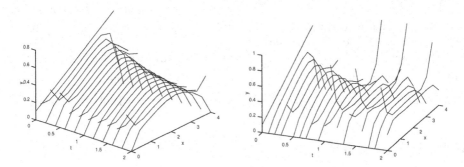

Fig. 4. Simulation of the system of Example 1, discretized with $M_2 = 10$ points, with extended modes of length 2 (left) and extended modes of length 4 (right).

reaction-diffusion equations. Furthermore, we have quantified the deviation of this control with the optimal strategy, and proved that the error upper bound is *linear* in the horizon length. We have applied the method to a 1D bi-stable reaction-diffusion equation, and have found experimental results similar to those of [45]. We have also given a simple and specific model reduction method which allows to apply the method to equations of larger size. In future work, we plan to apply the method to 2D reaction-diffusion equations (e.g., Test 1 of [2]).

Appendix 1: Proof of Lemma 1

Proof. It is easy to check that $0 < \alpha_u < 1$ when $\frac{|\lambda_u|G_u}{4} < 1$.

Let $t^* := G_u(1 - \alpha_u)$. Let us first prove $\delta_{e_0}(t) \leqslant e_0$ for $t = t^*$. We have:

$$-\frac{1}{2}|\lambda_u|G_u + (2 + \frac{1}{2}|\lambda_u|G_u)\alpha_u - \alpha_u^2 = 0.$$

Hence:

$$\frac{1}{2G_u(1 - \alpha_u)}\lambda_u G_u^2(1 - \alpha_u)^2 + 2\alpha_u - \alpha_u^2 = 0,$$

i.e.

$$\frac{1}{2t^*}\lambda_u(t^*)^2 + 2\alpha_u - \alpha_u^2 = 0.$$

We have: $-\frac{1}{4G_u^2 t^*}\lambda_u(t^*)^4 e^{\lambda_u t^*} \geqslant 0$. It follows:

$$\frac{1}{2t^*}\lambda_u(t^*)^2 + 2\alpha_u - \alpha_u^2 - \frac{1}{4G_u^2 t^*}\lambda_u(t^*)^4 e^{\lambda_u t^*} \geqslant 0.$$

Hence:

$$1 + \frac{1}{2t^*}\lambda_u(t^*)^2 - \frac{1}{G_u^2}((t^*)^2 + \frac{1}{4t^*}\lambda_u(t^*)^4 e^{\lambda_u t^*}) \geqslant 0.$$

By multiplying by t^*:

$$(t^* + \frac{1}{2}\lambda_u(t^*)^2) - \frac{1}{G_u^2}((t^*)^3 + \frac{1}{4}\lambda_u(t^*)^4 e^{\lambda_u t^*}) \geqslant 0.$$

Since $G = \sqrt{3}|\lambda_u|e_0/C_u$:

$$e_0^2(t^* + \frac{1}{2}\lambda_u(t^*)^2) + \frac{C_u^2}{\lambda_u^2}(-\frac{1}{3}(t^*)^3 - \frac{1}{12}\lambda_u(t^*)^4 e^{\lambda_u t^*}) \geqslant 0.$$

By multiplying by λ_u:

$$e_0^2(\lambda_u t^* + \frac{1}{2}\lambda_u^2(t^*)^2) + \frac{C_u^2}{\lambda_u^2}(-\frac{1}{3}\lambda_u(t^*)^3 - \frac{1}{12}\lambda_u^2(t^*)^4 e^{\lambda_u t^*}) \leqslant 0.$$

Note that, in the above formula, the subexpression $\lambda_u t^* + \frac{1}{2}\lambda_u^2(t^*)^2$ is such that:

$$\lambda_u t^* + \frac{1}{2}\lambda_u^2(t^*)^2 \geqslant e^{\lambda_u t^*} - 1$$

since $e^{\lambda_u t^*} - 1 = \lambda_u t^* + \frac{1}{2}\lambda_u^2(t^*)^2 e^{\lambda\theta} \leqslant \lambda_u t^* + \frac{1}{2}\lambda_u^2(t^*)^2$.

On the other hand, the subexpression $-\frac{1}{3}\lambda_u(t^*)^3 - \frac{1}{12}\lambda_u^2(t^*)^4 e^{\lambda_u t^*}$ is such that:

$$-\frac{1}{3}\lambda_u(t^*)^3 - \frac{1}{12}\lambda_u^2(t^*)^4 e^{\lambda_u t^*} \geqslant \frac{2t^*}{\lambda_u} + (t^*)^2 + \frac{2}{\lambda_u^2}(1 - e^{\lambda_u t^*})$$

since

$\frac{2t^*}{\lambda_u} + (t^*)^2 + \frac{2}{\lambda_u^2}(1 - e^{\lambda_u t^*})$

$= \frac{2t^*}{\lambda_u} + (t^*)^2 + \frac{2}{\lambda_u^2}(-\lambda_u t^* - \frac{1}{2}\lambda_u^2(t^*)^2 - \frac{1}{6}\lambda_u^3(t^*)^3 - \frac{1}{24}\lambda_u^4(t^*)^4 e^{\lambda_u\theta})$

$= \frac{2}{\lambda_u^2}(-\frac{1}{6}\lambda_u^3(t^*)^3 - \frac{1}{24}\lambda_u^4(t^*)^4 e^{\lambda_u\theta})$ for some $0 \leqslant \theta \leqslant t^*$

$= -\frac{1}{3}\lambda_u(t^*)^3 - \frac{1}{12}\lambda_u^2(t^*)^4 e^{\lambda_u\theta}$

$\leqslant -\frac{1}{3}\lambda_u(t^*)^3 - \frac{1}{12}\lambda_u^2(t^*)^4 e^{\lambda_u t^*}$.

It follows:

$$e_0^2(e^{\lambda_u t^*} - 1) + \frac{C_u^2}{\lambda_u^2}(\frac{2t^*}{\lambda_u} + (t^*)^2 + \frac{2}{\lambda_u^2}(1 - e^{\lambda_u t^*})) \leqslant 0.$$

$$e_0^2 e^{\lambda_u t^*} + \frac{C_u^2}{\lambda_u^2}(\frac{2t^*}{\lambda_u} + (t^*)^2 + \frac{2}{\lambda_u^2}(1 - e^{\lambda_u t^*})) \leqslant e_0^2.$$

i.e.

$$(\delta_{e_0}^u(t^*))^2 \leqslant e_0^2.$$

Hence: $\delta_{e_0}^u(t^*) \leqslant e_0$. It remains to show: $\delta_{e_0}^u(t) \leqslant e_0$ for $t \in [0, t^*]$.
Consider the 1rst and 2nd derivative $\delta'(\cdot)$ and $\delta''(\cdot)$ of $\delta(\cdot)$. We have:

$\delta'(t) = \lambda_u e_0^2 e^{\lambda_u t} + \frac{C_u^2}{\lambda_u^2}(2t + \frac{2}{\lambda_u} - \frac{2}{\lambda_u}e^{\lambda_u t})$

$\delta''(t) = \lambda_u^2 e_0^2 e^{\lambda_u t} + \frac{C_u^2}{\lambda_u^2}(2 - 2e^{\lambda_u t})$.

Hence $\delta''(t) > 0$ for all $t \geqslant 0$. On the other hand, for $t = 0$, $\delta'(t) = \lambda_u e_0^2 < 0$, and for t sufficiently large, $\delta'(t) > 0$. Hence, $\delta'(\cdot)$ is strictly increasing and has a unique root. It follows that the equation $\delta(t) = e_0$ has a unique solution t^{**} for $t > 0$. Besides, $\delta(t) \leqslant e_0$ for $t \in [0, t^{**}]$, and $\delta(t) \geqslant e_0$ for $t \in [t^{**}, +\infty)$. Since we have shown: $\delta(t^*) \leqslant e_0$, it follows $t^* \leqslant t^{**}$ and $\delta(t) \leqslant e_0$ for $t \in [0, t^*]$.   □

Appendix 2: Numerical Results

See Fig. 5.

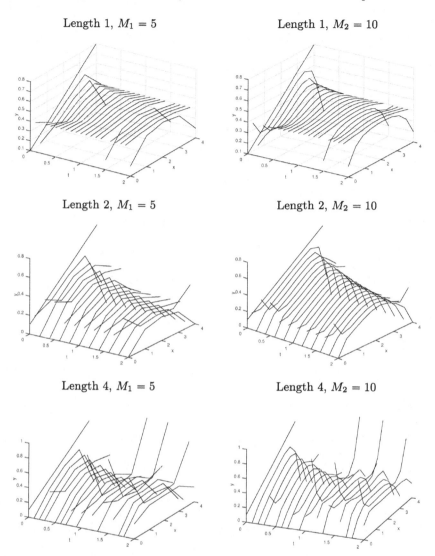

Fig. 5. Simulation of the controllers for $\sigma = 1$.

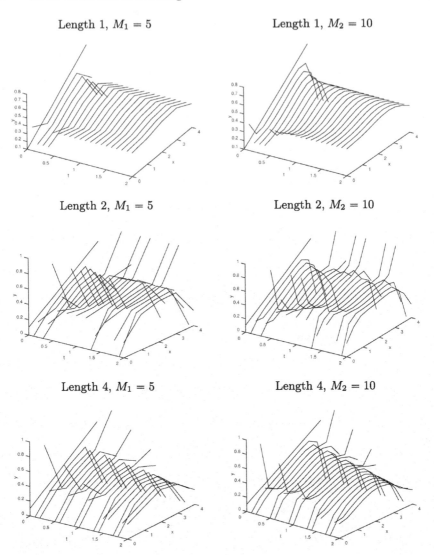

Fig. 6. Simulation of the controllers for $\sigma = 0.5$.

Table 1. Value $\|y_i^{\pi^{\varepsilon}}(T) - y_i^f\|$ for $\sigma = 1$ and $\sigma = 0.5$ ($T = 2$, $i = 1, 2$).

Dimension	Extended mode length	$\|y_i^{\pi^{\varepsilon}}(T) - y_i^f\|$ for $\sigma = 1$	$\|y_i^{\pi^{\varepsilon}}(T) - y_i^f\|$ for $\sigma = 0.5$
$i = 1$ ($M_i = 5$)	1	0.27642	0.33869
	2	0.44496	0.39068
	4	0.15294	0.22024
$i = 2$ ($M_i = 10$)	1	0.39904	0.50251
	2	0.50092	0.58500
	4	0.16738	0.31440

Table 2. Projection value $\|Py_2^{\pi^{\varepsilon}}(T) - y_1^f\|$ for $\sigma = 1$, $\sigma = 0.5$ ($T = 2$).

Extended mode length	$\|Py_2^{\pi^{\varepsilon}}(T) - y_1^f\|$ for $\sigma = 1$	$\|Py_2^{\pi^{\varepsilon}}(T) - y_1^f\|$ for $\sigma = 0.5$
1	0.67429	0.77322
2	0.27501	0.72322
4	0.31385	0.21481

References

1. Alla, A., Falcone, M., Volkwein, S.: Error analysis for POD approximations of infinite horizon problems via the dynamic programming approach. SIAM J. Control Optim. **55**(5), 3091–3115 (2017)
2. Alla, A., Saluzzi, L.: A HJB-POD approach for the control of nonlinear PDEs on a tree structure. CoRR, abs/1905.03395 (2019)
3. Althoff, M.: Reachability analysis of large linear systems with uncertain inputs in the Krylov subspace. CoRR, abs/1712.00369 (2017)
4. Althoff, M., Stursberg, O., Buss, M.: Reachability analysis of nonlinear systems with uncertain parameters using conservative linearization. In: Proceedings of the 47th IEEE Conference on Decision and Control, CDC 2008, 9–11 December 2008, Cancún, Mexico, pp. 4042–4048. IEEE (2008)
5. Aminzare, Z., Shafi, Y., Arcak, M., Sontag, E.D.: Guaranteeing spatial uniformity in reaction-diffusion systems using weighted L^2 norm contractions. In: Kulkarni, V.V., Stan, G.-B., Raman, K. (eds.) A Systems Theoretic Approach to Systems and Synthetic Biology I: Models and System Characterizations, pp. 73–101. Springer, Dordrecht (2014). https://doi.org/10.1007/978-94-017-9041-3_3
6. Aminzare, Z., Sontag, E.D.: Logarithmic Lipschitz norms and diffusion-induced instability. Nonlinear Anal. Theory Methods Appl. **83**, 31–49 (2013)
7. Aminzare, Z., Sontag, E.D.: Some remarks on spatial uniformity of solutions of reaction-diffusion PDEs. Nonlinear Anal. Theory Methods Appl. **147**, 125–144 (2016)
8. Arcak, M.: Certifying spatially uniform behavior in reaction-diffusion PDE and compartmental ODE systems. Automatica **47**(6), 1219–1229 (2011)
9. Barthel, W., John, C., Tröltzsch, F.: Optimal boundary control of a system of reaction diffusion equations. ZAMM J. Appl. Math. Mech./Zeitschrift für Angewandte Mathematik und Mechanik **90**(12), 966–982 (2010)

10. Bellman, R.: Dynamic Programming, 1st edn. Princeton University Press, Princeton (1957)
11. Berz, M., Hoffstätter, G.: Computation and application of Taylor polynomials with interval remainder bounds. Reliab. Comput. **4**(1), 83–97 (1998)
12. Berz, M., Makino, K.: Verified integration of ODEs and flows using differential algebraic methods on high-order Taylor models. Reliab. Comput. **4**(4), 361–369 (1998)
13. Casas, E., Ryll, C., Tröltzsch, F.: Optimal control of a class of reaction-diffusion systems. Comput. Optim. Appl. **70**(3), 677–707 (2018)
14. Le Coënt, A., Fribourg, L.: Guaranteed control of sampled switched systems using semi-Lagrangian schemes and one-sided Lipschitz constants. In: 58th IEEE Conference on Decision and Control, CDC 2019, Nice, France, 11–13 December 2019 (2019)
15. Court, S., Kunisch, K., Pfeiffer, L.: Hybrid optimal control problems for a class of semilinear parabolic equations. Discret. Contin. Dyn. Syst. **11**, 1031–1060 (2018)
16. da Silva, J.E., Sousa, J.T., Pereira, F.L.: Synthesis of safe controllers for nonlinear systems using dynamic programming techniques. In: 8th International Conference on Physics and Control (PhysCon 2017). IPACS Electronic Library (2017)
17. Dahlquist, G.: Stability and error bounds in the numerical integration of ordinary differential equations. Ph.D. thesis, Almqvist & Wiksell (1958)
18. Falcone, M., Giorgi, T.: An approximation scheme for evolutive Hamilton-Jacobi equations. In: McEneaney, W.M., Yin, G.G., Zhang, Q. (eds.) Stochastic Analysis, Control, Optimization and Applications. Systems & Control: Foundations & Applications. Springer, Boston (1999). https://doi.org/10.1007/978-1-4612-1784-8_17
19. Fan, C., Kapinski, J., Jin, X., Mitra, S.: Simulation-driven reachability using matrix measures. ACM Trans. Embedded Comput. Syst. (TECS) **17**(1), 21 (2018)
20. Finotti, H., Lenhart, S., Van Phan, T.: Optimal control of advective direction in reaction-diffusion population models. Evol. Equ. Control Theory **1**, 81–107 (2012)
21. Girard, A.: Reachability of uncertain linear systems using zonotopes. In: Morari, M., Thiele, L. (eds.) HSCC 2005. LNCS, vol. 3414, pp. 291–305. Springer, Heidelberg (2005). https://doi.org/10.1007/978-3-540-31954-2_19
22. Griesse, R., Volkwein, S.: A primal-dual active set strategy for optimal boundary control of a nonlinear reaction-diffusion system. SIAM J. Control Optim. **44**(2), 467–494 (2005)
23. Han, Z., Krogh, B.H.: Reachability analysis of hybrid control systems using reduced-order models. In: Proceedings of the 2004 American Control Conference, vol. 2, pp. 1183–1189, June 2004
24. Han, Z., Krogh, B.H.: Reachability analysis of large-scale affine systems using low-dimensional polytopes. In: Hespanha, J.P., Tiwari, A. (eds.) HSCC 2006. LNCS, vol. 3927, pp. 287–301. Springer, Heidelberg (2006). https://doi.org/10.1007/11730637_23
25. Kalise, D., Kröner, A.: Reduced-order minimum time control of advection-reaction-diffusion systems via dynamic programming. In: 21st International Symposium on Mathematical Theory of Networks and Systems, Groningen, Netherlands, July 2014, pp. 1196–1202 (2014)
26. Kalise, D., Kunisch, K.: Polynomial approximation of high-dimensional Hamilton-Jacobi-Bellman equations and applications to feedback control of semilinear parabolic PDEs. SIAM J. Sci. Comput. **40**(2), A629–A652 (2018)
27. Kapela, T., Zgliczyński, P.: A Lohner-type algorithm for control systems and ordinary differential inclusions. Discret. Contin. Dyn. Syst. B **11**(2), 365–385 (2009)

28. Koto, T.: IMEX Runge-Kutta schemes for reaction-diffusion equations. J. Comput. Appl. Math. **215**(1), 182–195 (2008)
29. Kühn, W.: Rigorously computed orbits of dynamical systems without the wrapping effect. Computing **61**(1), 47–67 (1998)
30. Kunisch, K., Volkwein, S., Xie, L.: HJB-POD-based feedback design for the optimal control of evolution problems. SIAM J. Appl. Dyn. Syst. **3**(4), 701–722 (2004)
31. Le Coënt, A.: OSLator 1.0 (2019). https://bitbucket.org/alecoent/oslator/src/master/
32. Le Coënt, A., Alexandre dit Sandretto, J., Chapoutot, A., Fribourg, L., De Vuyst, F., Chamoin, L.: Distributed control synthesis using Euler's method. In: Hague, M., Potapov, I. (eds.) RP 2017. LNCS, vol. 10506, pp. 118–131. Springer, Cham (2017). https://doi.org/10.1007/978-3-319-67089-8_9
33. Le Coënt, A., De Vuyst, F., Chamoin, L., Fribourg, L.: Control synthesis of nonlinear sampled switched systems using Euler's method. In: Proceedings of International Workshop on Symbolic and Numerical Methods for Reachability Analysis (SNR 2017), EPTCS, vol. 247, pp. 18–33. Open Publishing Association (2017)
34. Le Coënt, A., De Vuyst, F., Rey, C., Chamoin, L., Fribourg, L.: Guaranteed control synthesis of switched control systems using model order reduction and statespace bisection. In: Proceedings of International Workshop on Synthesis of Complex Parameters (SYNCOP 2015), OASICS, vol. 44, pp. 33–47. SchlossDagstuhl – Leibniz-Zentrum für Informatik (2015)
35. Lohner, R.J.: Enclosing the solutions of ordinary initial and boundary value problems. Comput. Arith. 255–286 (1987)
36. Lozinskii, S.M.: Error estimate for numerical integration of ordinary differential equations. i. Izv. Vyssh. Uchebn. Zaved. Mat. (5), 52–90 (1958)
37. Maidens, J., Arcak, M.: Reachability analysis of nonlinear systems using matrix measures. IEEE Trans. Autom. Control **60**(1), 265–270 (2014)
38. Mitchell, I., Bayen, A.M., Tomlin, C.J.: Validating a Hamilton-Jacobi approximation to hybrid system reachable sets. In: Di Benedetto, M.D., Sangiovanni-Vincentelli, A. (eds.) HSCC 2001. LNCS, vol. 2034, pp. 418–432. Springer, Heidelberg (2001). https://doi.org/10.1007/3-540-45351-2_34
39. Mitchell, I.M., Tomlin, C.: Overapproximating reachable sets by Hamilton-Jacobi projections. J. Sci. Comput. **19**(1–3), 323–346 (2003)
40. Moore, R.: Interval Analysis. Prentice Hall, Englewood Cliffs (1966)
41. Moura, S.J., Fathy, H.K.: Optimal boundary control & estimation of diffusion-reaction PDEs. In: Proceedings of the 2011 American Control Conference, pp. 921–928, June 2011
42. Moura, S.J., Fathy, H.K.: Optimal boundary control of reaction-diffusion partial differential equations via weak variations. J. Dyn. Syst. Meas. Control Trans. ASME **135**(3), 6 (2013)
43. Nedialkov, N.S., Jackson, K., Corliss, G.: Validated solutions of initial value problems for ordinary differential equations. Appl. Math. Comput. **105**(1), 21–68 (1999)
44. Nedialkov, N.S., Kreinovich, V., Starks, S.A.: Interval arithmetic, affine arithmetic, Taylor series methods: why, what next? Numer. Algorithms **37**(1–4), 325–336 (2004)
45. Pouchol, C., Trélat, E., Zuazua, E.: Phase portrait control for 1D monostable and bistable reaction-diffusion equations. CoRR, abs/1709.07333 (2017)
46. Reissig, G., Rungger, M.: Symbolic optimal control. IEEE Trans. Autom. Control **64**(6), 2224–2239 (2018)

47. Rungger, M., Reissig, G.: Arbitrarily precise abstractions for optimal controller synthesis. In: 56th IEEE Annual Conference on Decision and Control, CDC 2017, Melbourne, Australia, 12–15 December 2017, pp. 1761–1768 (2017)
48. Saluzzi, L., Alla, A., Falcone, M.: Error estimates for a tree structure algorithm solving finite horizon control problems. CoRR, abs/1812.11194 (2018)
49. Schürmann, B., Althoff, M.: Optimal control of sets of solutions to formally guarantee constraints of disturbed linear systems. In: 2017 American Control Conference, ACC 2017, Seattle, WA, USA, 24–26 May 2017, pp. 2522–2529 (2017)
50. Schürmann, B., Kochdumper, N., Althoff, M.: Reachset model predictive control for disturbed nonlinear systems. In: 57th IEEE Conference on Decision and Control, CDC 2018, Miami, FL, USA, 17–19 December 2018, pp. 3463–3470 (2018)
51. Söderlind, G.: The logarithmic norm. History and modern theory. BIT Numer. Math. **46**(3), 631–652 (2006)
52. Sontag, E.D.: Contractive systems with inputs. In: Willems, J.C., Hara, S., Ohta, Y., Fujioka, H. (eds.) Perspectives in Mathematical System Theory, Control, and Signal Processing. LNCIS, vol. 398, pp. 217–228. Springer, Heidelberg (2010)

Towards Formal Co-validation
of Hardware and Software Timing Models
# of CPSs

Mihail Asavoae[1], Imane Haur[1], Mathieu Jan[1(✉)], Belgacem Ben Hedia[1],
and Martin Schoeberl[2]

[1] CEA, List, Palaiseau, France
{mihail.asavoae,imane.haur,mathieu.jan,belgacem.ben-hedia}@cea.fr
[2] Technical University of Denmark, Lyngby, Denmark
masca@dtu.dk

Abstract. Timing analysis of safety-critical systems derives timing
bounds of applications, or software (SW), executed on dedicated platforms, or hardware (HW). The ensemble HW–SW features, from a timing perspective, two different types of computation – a SW-specific,
instruction-driven timing progression and a HW-specific, cycle-driven
one. The two timings are unified under a concept of *timing model*, which
is crucial to establish a sound and precise worst-case timing reasoning. In
this paper, we propose an investigation on how to systematically derive
and formally prove such timing models. Our approach is exemplified on
a simple, accumulator-based processor called Lipsi.

Keywords: Timing analysis · Timing model · Formal semantics ·
Chisel · HW/SW co-validation · Model checking

1 Introduction

Cyber-physical systems (CPSs) integrate computations running on embedded
platforms into physical systems that they interact with. This integration is
expressed through feedback loops between software and the physical environment and it may need to satisfy strong timing guarantees. To verify them, worst-
case timing analyses of safety-critical systems are combined. Such analyses cover
timing behaviors of computations (e.g., the worst-case execution time analysis,
WCET), communications (e.g., the worst-case traversal time analysis) or both
(e.g., the worst-case response time analysis). It is common to all these analyses that the applications semantics are projected on the timing behavior of the
underlying platforms. In this work, we focus on the computations, viewed as
a set of binaries (SW), i.e. sequences of instructions described at the instruction set architecture (ISA) level. On the side of the embedded platforms, i.e.
hardware level (HW), our inputs are register transfer-level (RTL) descriptions
of processors in a given hardware description language (HDL). We thus omit any
networking components and focus only on single-core or multi-core architectures.

© Springer Nature Switzerland AG 2020
R. Chamberlain et al. (Eds.): CyPhy 2019/WESE 2019, LNCS 11971, pp. 203–227, 2020.
https://doi.org/10.1007/978-3-030-41131-2_10

At these levels of design, a timing verification relies on a WCET analysis [41]. A WCET analysis computes safe and accurate timing bounds of a SW executed on a HW, where the HW is abstracted to micro-architecture elements (e.g., instruction and data caches, pipeline, speculation mechanisms, etc.). The workflow of the WCET analysis consists of a series of static SW- and HW-level analyses. A first analysis extracts the control flow graph (CFG) from the binary, with nodes being basic (single-entry, single-exit) blocks and edges safely representing the program flow. Then, the CFG is augmented with flow facts (e.g., loop bounds) and HW-related information (e.g., cache behavior). Finally, a path analysis, performed on the augmented CFG, determines the longest execution path which represents the WCET bound. In this workflow, a cache analysis reports that, for example, a basic block is classified as "always miss" in the cache and its timing behavior is a cache miss penalty, for example, 10 cycles. However, it is not always simple to establish such architecture-dependent bounds due to its complexity and unwanted timing phenomena [40]. WCET analyses require a proper timing model, whose correctness and accuracy ensure safe but also tight WCET estimations.

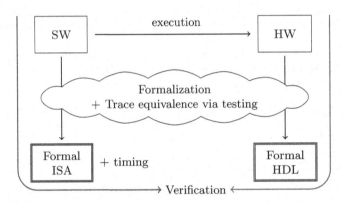

Fig. 1. General workflow for the HW/SW co-validation of timing models for CPS.

Even if formal verification of hardware design has been thoroughly studied (see [18] for a survey), it is mainly targeting the functional correctness. HW/SW co-verification also focuses on the functional side, as in [12], or interfaces between SW and HW as well as their temporal behavior [30], and thus not on extracting timing models of HW. In this work, we focus on building and validating such timing models for CPSs. Figure 1 shows our proposed general workflow that combines the formalization of the timing behaviors of both SW and HW sides. For the SW side, a timing model is added to an ISA formal description by relying on the input textual specification of the architecture. Both the functional and timing behaviors of this timing augmented formal SW model are tested, for confidence, against traces of actual code first over an instruction set simulator

(ISS) and then over a real execution. Note that by real execution, we mean traces generated by executing HDL code, i.e. the circuit, should be on an FPGA or by a cycle-accurate simulator. Similarly, on the HW side, a formal model is built which thus includes by construction a timing behavior. The confidence in this formal HW model is also verified by applying trace equivalence. Finally, the last step consists in the co-validation of these hardware and software formal timing models, i.e. verifying the consistency of their two timing models. More specifically, the instruction-level timing, from the SW model is encoded as a set of assertions, called *timing invariants*, in the formal HW model. A timing invariant identifies the hardware pattern, i.e. the sequence of updates on registers and wires that must be executed in x cycles, corresponding to the execution of an instruction in the timing augmented SW model in x cycles. We then prove the obtained timing model of a particular pairing of programs (SW) over a platform (HW) by model checking the formal HW model with these timing invariants.

To illustrate how this general approach can be used when designing CPS, we apply it over Lipsi processors [37]. Lipsi is a tiny sequential processor whose simplicity enables us to focus on building the complete approach for this HW platform. Lipsi comes with two components: an instruction-set simulator and the circuit, specified in Chisel [4]. We then build both HW and SW models using respectively the Temporal Logic of Actions (TLA$^+$) formal specification language [20] and the Sail formal language dedicated to express ISA semantics [1]. We detail these models, the simple timing model of Lipsi that we add in the SW model and how we add these timing invariants in the HW model of Lipsi. These timing invariants are then checked using the model-checker of TLA$^+$, called TLC. In the formalization phase, we discovered semantic issues between the intended behavior of Lipsi, from [37], and the actual Lipsi code. Finally, we report a possible use case for such verified timing models of CPS: the detection and minimization of memory interferences in a multi-core setting of Lipsi.

The remainder of this paper is organized as follows. Section 2 introduces the formal languages we rely on to build the HW and SW models of our general approach. It also provides an overview of the timing behavior of the Chisel language, from which the timing behavior of our HW model is constructed. In Sect. 3, we present the workflow for the HW/SW co-verification of timing models of CPSs. In Sect. 4, we apply the approach to a case study: the Lipsi processor. We provide concrete examples of the HW and SW formal models of Lipsi using TLA$^+$ and Sail languages. Section 5 reports and discusses the obtained results when considering this Lipsi case study. Section 6 presents related work, before concluding in Sect. 7.

2 Preliminaries

In this section, we briefly introduce two specialized specification languages we rely on to build the formal HW and SW models. To formally specify hardware behavior, we use the TLA$^+$ language [20,43], as it is a high-level specification language for modeling concurrent systems and comes with a model-checker.

On the SW side, we use Sail [1] to formally model programs as it is tailored for expressing Instruction-Set Architecture (ISA) semantics. It has been successfully applied to formalize various ISAs, such as ARM, RISC-V, and MIPS [1]. The K framework, which was recently used for a formal executable semantics of x86-64 ISA [10], is another option we have not yet considered so far [2].

Chisel. We first introduce the programming language we assume as input to perform hardware designs. We select the Chisel programming language [4] due to its current rising popularity in the hardware design community and its ability to reduce hardware design times. Chisel generates Verilog HDL, whose formal semantics has been studied in [11,27]. Compared to Verilog, Chisel provides some higher-level constructs to raise the level of hardware design abstraction, as it is embedded in the Scala programming language as a Domain Specific Language (DSL). Scala promotes functional-style programming and uses a strong static type system to facilitate concise and reusable code – some necessary attributes to address complex hardware designs. Chisel also supports testing through an internal cycle-accurate hardware simulator. We now briefly describe several language elements of Chisel, while more elaborate examples are presented in Sect. 4.3 when we formally specify the Lipsi processor from Chisel code.

Hardware designs are constructed on Chisel typed values that flow through wires, i.e. the combinational part of circuits, or held in state elements, i.e. the sequential part of circuits. The keyword `val` is used to declare variables whose values do not change. As basic datatypes, `Bool` represents the boolean values, `SInt` and `UInt` represent signed and respectively unsigned integers. For example, `val x = UInt(2)` declares x to be the unsigned int 2. The bit size of x is unspecified here, but could be inferred from the usage of x or specified to be 32-bit with `UInt(2, width=32)`. Simple combinational circuits are described using the `val` keyword. For example, `val land = a & b` has in `land` the bitwise and of a and b. Chisel uses registers for state elements, for instance, `val r = RegInit(0.U)` initializes r to 0. There are also conditional combinational circuits built with the class `Wire` and the conditional construct `when`. For example, `val x = Wire(UInt(0))` declares x to be an wire initialized to unsigned int 0 and modified to 1 as follows: `when (cond) { x := 1.U }`. The assignment operator `:=` connects the input of the left-hand side to the output of the right-hand side.

TLA⁺ is a modeling language proposing an advanced module system, untyped set theory and predicate logic, making it suitable to specification of complex computational systems such as computer architectures. TLA⁺ language is based on the notion of action (i.e., a transition predicate), which captures a state change as follows: an action `x' = x + 1` updates the next value, primed of x based on the current, unprimed value of x. If x is a record, its field f is accessed as `x.f` and a partial record update is expressed with `[x EXCEPT!.f = v]`, changing f to v and leaving the other fields of x unchanged. A module M having an action A could be referred in another module via the operator "!", as `M!A`. An instance of M could be created inside another module with the construct `INSTANCE M WITH`, with the state variables of M being initialized after the keyword `WITH`.

Abstraction and refinement are natural with TLA$^+$ and, supported by an explicit model checker called TLC, form a powerful formal specification and verification framework. It features stuttering invariance to reason about the specification paths at different levels of granularity and temporal existential quantification to slice away the unnecessary state elements. We elaborate more on the language and model checking of TLA$^+$ specifications in Sect. 4.3 where we present the case study of the Lipsi processor.

Sail is a first-order imperative language that comes with a type system for bit vector lengths and indexing to enables static checking. A Sail specification relies on the definition of an Abstract Syntax Type (AST) of the ISA of an architecture, i.e. a union of types with parameters. To each AST value, specific `execute` and `decode` functions are associated with respectively the sequential semantics of the instruction and the matching of its binary representation of its AST value. For readability and modularity, Sail supports the definition of scattered functions and unions allowing to group `decode`, `execute` and the AST value of an instruction in one place. The memory space and the registers of the architectural state of a processor manipulated by each instruction can also be specified to model data transfer paths. To this end, a specific `register` type is supported and it is possible to annotate functions with effects to describe their impact on either the declared memories or registers. From a Sail specification, both emulators and theorem proving definitions can be generated to support the fast execution of programs or deductive reasoning. In Sect. 4.2, we provide examples on how we use Sail to formally specify the ISA of the Lipsi processor.

3   Co-validation of Timing Models: General Approach

Typical CPSs are organized as networks of computational and communication elements that interact with the physical environment. CPSs are subject to various properties such as adaptability, autonomy, reliability, security or safety. From a structural point of view, a CPS features multiple components specified and implemented at different levels of details and using different modeling or specification languages. From a functional point of view, each such language comes with its semantics to address specific points. As such, the CPS semantics landscape includes hybrid approaches, synchronous data flow approaches, simulation or verification languages, general-purpose programming languages, such as C, etc. We thus abstract a CPS to ensembles of communicating binaries running of various platforms, as shown in Fig. 2. Heterogeneous computational and communicational components, $Comp_i$ are to be deployed for execution on various platforms, which is, in the general case, a many-to-many relation. For example, $Plat_3$ could be a multi/many-core system with applications from $Comp_{3-4}$ being executed in parallel. Also, different applications from $Comp_1$ could be executed on $Plat_1$ and $Plat_2$, whereas the applications of $Comp_2$ are executed only on $Plat_1$.

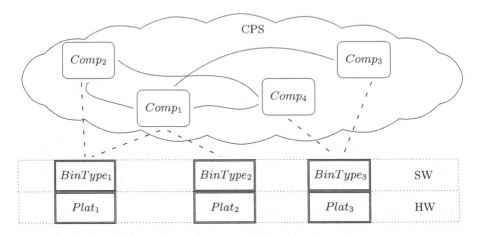

Fig. 2. Components $Comp_i$ of a CPS are classified based on their execution environments.

3.1 Motivations: Consistency of Timings

Let us elaborate on the semantics landscape of CPSs with concerning timing properties because well-defined timing is crucially important to ensure several of the aforementioned properties of CPSs. Timing models capture how software applications, or programs, are mapped on hardware resources when it comes to timing behavior. Timing models are necessary to perform timing analyses. A timing analysis needs to be safe and accurate and the most precise timing is to be found at the execution platform-level, i.e. the HW-level. To bridge the gap between HW-level timing and various ways of expressing timing at the application-level, i.e. the SW level, timing analysis is usually performed on binaries. From a semantic perspective, the working language is the assembly language specific to the execution platform under consideration, i.e. the ISA.

The high-level functional and temporal properties are however obfuscated or even lost when translated to this binary low-level, i.e. $BinType_{1-3}$ in Fig. 2. Let us consider a Model-Based Design (MBD) workflow, based on a synchronous language [7] as high-level programming language. The high-level specification is transformed into an intermediate language code, usually the C language, in a correct by construction way, ensured by the well-synchronized property of the high-level code. Then, a general-purpose compilation chain, in the absence of compiler optimization, could produce binaries that are traceable to the source code. However, the initial high-level timing properties can no longer be directly expressed at the binary level, as most ISAs simply do not include timing. A few exceptions exist, such as the PRET [26] and the Patmos [38] architectures that provide the `delay until` instruction that explicitly manipulates timing, i.e. the current hardware thread is stalled for a specified number of clock cycles. Even when it is up to the compiler to schedule instructions over a given hardware architecture, the defined timing behavior is limited to a single instruction in isolation. There is no way to impact the timing behavior of the whole architecture, as in PRET or Patmos. This prevents to implement in a proper way the initial high-level temporal properties, which thus simply disappear at the binary level. It is the goal of WCET analyses to recover them at this level.

When designing a hardware architecture, its timing behavior is in general not formalized. Besides, it remains to demonstrate, or at least show enough confidence, that the timings are correctly implemented by the circuit. Most formal verification of hardware designs focuses on the functional side of an implementation, for instance in Sect. 6, to cite an open-source tool/project. While the timing semantic of HDL languages has been the subject of various work (see Sect. 2), the timing behavior of a given micro-architecture is much more complex to identify and verify due to pipeline stalling, forwarding, interlocking, etc. The associated logic can be dispatched in different places of the design and mixed with rich low-level functionalities, such as the logic in charge of the functional part of the architecture. It is thus in general unclear to identify at the HDL level when an instruction terminates its execution. Appropriate abstraction and slicing are necessary to extract the timing model of a hardware design so that it can be used to perform WCET analyses, i.e. if the high-level temporal properties can be fulfilled over the given architecture.

3.2 Building Timing Models

In this work, we consider the pair SW and HW represented by $BinType_i$ and respectively $Plat_i$ in Fig. 2 and how models can be established between them. The SW model is supported by instruction-level simulation, sometimes with an ad-hoc cycle-level timing, whereas the HW model is a cycle-accurate execution. Now, a *timing model* in this context is a function between the time progression of SW, measured in executed instructions and the cycle-accurate timing, corresponding to HW. We thus propose a formal framework to construct and validate, from these HW and SW models, such *timing models* of CPS, abstracted as in Fig. 2. Note that this framework can either be used when designing new hardware architectures to provide to the SW the appropriate timing model, but also extract the timing behavior of existing hardware architectures.

Our framework relies on a combination of trace equivalences and model checking, as shown in Fig. 1. On the SW side, the steps of our workflow are thus the following:

1. We formalize the SW component by defining a formal executable semantics of $BinType_i$ ISA language.
2. This formal SW model is first tested, by comparing its output against traces generated from an Instruction Set Simulator (ISS), to gain confidence in the correctness of the functional part of the formal ISA model.
3. The formal SW model is then extended with timing behavior for each instruction. The augmented model is tested by comparing its output against traces from ISS, augmented with cycle-level timing behaviors, to gain confidence in the added timing model.

The result is a thoroughly tested formal SW model, though manually asserted, with a cycle-level timing behavior, i.e. formal ISA + timing in Fig. 1. Note that if a cycle-level simulator is not available, the timing behavior added in the above step (3) must be verified against traces from executions of the considered circuit. In all these steps, discrepancies can be identified either because of traces being not equivalent in steps (2) and (3) or simply when building the formal model at the step (1). In all cases, the origin of a discrepancy must be at least identified. While fixing an error in the formal model being built is, of course, possible, fixing erroneous simulators or the circuit depend on the availability of their source codes. When using a "black-box" circuit, its timing could thus be taken as the reference behavior. However, discrepancies could also come from the interplay of instructions at the micro-architecture level that the SW model cannot capture. This is the goal of the co-validation step, described in Sect. 3.3. Note that we assume that any input program described using our extended formal SW model is correct, i.e. correctness of programs is out of the scope of this work but, of course, not the correctness of the formal SW model. Finally, note that we can leverage existing formal SW models, such as [1] or [10] to avoid steps (1) and (2).

We propose similar steps to construct a formal HW model for $Plat_i$. Compared to the SW side of our workflow, a timing behavior already exists at the HDL level: we have to extract it. The steps on the HW side are thus the following:

1. We construct a formal executable HW model of the considered circuit. This is currently being done manually, automatically generating the HW model being a work in progress.
2. The built formal HW model is then tested, by comparing its outputs against traces from executions of the circuit, to gain confidence that it behaves as precisely as possible to the timing behavior of the HDL.

The result of these steps is a formal HW model with a cycle-accurate timing, denoted by formal HDL in Fig. 1. We assume that a description of the circuit in HDL or using a higher-level language, such as Chisel, is available. If it is not the case, a more abstract HW model can be built from the specifications of the data paths. The timing accuracy of such models is, of course, more limited. Note by executions of the circuit for step (2) on the HW side and step (3) on the SW side, we mean either the use of cycle-accurate HDL simulators, such as Verilator [42] or the built-in simulator of Chisel, or runs over an FPGA board. We ignore any timing inconsistency that may occur between considered simulation tools. We also ignore the impact of the environment, such as the temperature or the level of radiations, on the (functional and temporal) behavior of the HW, i.e HW fault-free conditions are assumed. Finally, the described steps in our framework are generic, i.e. they could rely on other toolchains than SAIL or TLA$^+$ to include timings in their formal models.

3.3   Verifying Timing Invariants

Following the aforementioned workflow, one may wonder why the timing behavior added to the formal SW model is not directly compared against such executions of circuits and thus considered as our timing model. These ad-hoc timings within the formal SW model are only compared to traces of an ISS augmented with cycle-level timing behaviors. The verification process would thus be limited to trace equivalence, with thus a limited coverage. While trace coverage can be easily computed on the SW side for the functional part, the diversity of timing behaviors on the HW side would be simply ignored.

The timing behaviors of the HW and the SW models must instead be verified together to establish the function which we name a timing model. Our verification thus proceeds as follows. The ad-hoc timings of the SW model are first encoded as *timing invariants* in the formal HW model. To achieve this, we identify for each instruction the sequence of hardware updates on the processor, such as changes on wires and registers. For a non-pipelined processor, a simple input-output relation is defined for each timing invariant. The input represents the instruction fetch, i.e. when the opcode is taken into account, whereas the output is instruction-specific, e.g., a memory load terminates with the correct value in the corresponding register, an ALU instruction modifies the accumulator register, etc. The input-output relation depends on the current clock cycle. A timing invariant should be read as follows: x cycles after an instruction is fetched, where x is given by the formal SW model, the instruction terminates its execution.

Let us denote a timing invariant by $TInv_i$, where i is an instruction from the language $\mathcal{L}$, $i \in \mathcal{L}$. A timing model for an architecture A is thus defined as:

$$TM_A = \left(\bigwedge_{i \in \mathcal{L}} TInv_i \right) \quad \text{-}$$

The corresponding assertions are then verified via model checking to establish the co-validation of the timing model. We expect these timing invariants to be useful in the context of WCET analyses and thus proving that high-level timing properties are fulfilled. However, we have not yet connected these timing invariants to any existing WCET tool.

4   Case Study: Lipsi Processor

We now illustrate our approach described in the previous section over a case study. We select a very simple processor, the Lipsi processor [37], to better illustrate the various steps of our approach. In this section, we thus first briefly describe the Lipsi processor. Then, we present its formal ISA and HDL models using, respectively, the Sail and TLA$^+$ languages.

4.1   Overview

Lipsi is a sequential 8-bit accumulator-based processor to be used in auxiliary functions or for teaching purposes. The ISA of Lipsi includes ALU operations using registers or immediate operands, load/store from/to the memory, unconditional and conditional branches, and an input/output (i/o) operation. A complete list of instructions and their encodings are shown in Table 1 of [37]. The Lipsi instructions are encoded using a single byte, except branch operations and ALU operations with immediate operands. For these instructions, a second byte is used to store either the address of the target branch or the immediate operand.

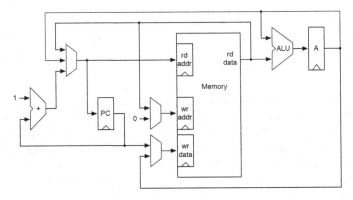

Fig. 3. The datapath of Lipsi, using an accumulator A, a single memory, an ALU and a program counter PC (extracted from [37]).

On the hardware side, Lipsi consists of an accumulator register (A), a program counter (PC), 16 additional registers and a single on-chip memory. Its datapath is shown in Fig. 3. Lipsi targets the use of a single block RAM in FPGA, which can be as low as 512 bytes. Addresses are thus 9-bits values. The memory is accessible through 2 ports: one for reads, the other one for writes. The lower half of the 9-bit memory space therefore stores up to 256 bytes of instructions, while the upper half stores first 16 additional registers ($R[x]$) followed by up to 240 bytes of data. $R[X]$ can be used to store intermediate results when performing ALU operations. The specification of Lipsi allows us to identify up to 16 different ports using bits [3:0] in the encoding of the i/o instruction. However, its current hardware implementation only uses 2 ports to exchange values with the accumulator A: one for outputting the value of A and the other one to load a new value in A. The hardware implementation of Lipsi is written in Chisel, and it has been synthesized to the Cyclon IV FPGA of the DE2-115 FPGA board. An Instruction Set Simulator (ISS), written in Scala, is also available.

The hardware implementation of Lipsi comes with a very simple timing model, as a single memory is connected to the processor. Two clock cycles are required to execute an ALU instruction: one for fetching the instruction and one for accessing the data and executing the ALU operation. Loading A with a value in $R[x]$ also takes 2 cycles while writing to $R[x]$ only takes 1 cycle due to the separated read/write ports to the memory. Updating $R[x]$ is performed while the next instruction is being from the read port. Memory store and load operations use the additional registers $R[x]$ to store the targeted memory address. Those operations thus perform three memory accesses: to fetch the instruction, to retrieve the memory address from $R[x]$, and finally to perform the memory operation at the specified memory address. A memory load thus takes 3 cycles, while a memory write takes only 2 cycles as the last access occurs meanwhile the next instruction is being fetched. Finally, the i/o operation takes 1 cycle.

4.2   Formal SW Model

We now present the formal SW model of Lipsi using the Sail language. We first define the architectural state of Lipsi, i.e. its accumulator A, its program counter PC and the ports used by the i/o instruction, i.e. din and dout for respectively the input and output ports. The nextPC register is used to store the address of the branch, i.e. the second byte of a branch instruction when it is decoded. All these variables are 8-bits registers, as in the hardware implementation of Lipsi.

```
type len_t = bits(8) /* 8-bit architecture */
register A : len_t /* Accumulator */
register PC : len_t /* Program Counter */
register nextPC : len_t /* For branch instructions */
register din : len_t /* For the i/o instruction, input port */
register dout : len_t /* output port */
```

Memory Model. The structure Memory represents the memory of Lipsi. It embeds respectively the instruction and data spaces, which are defined as a vector of bytes. These vectors are organized in downward memory addresses. Finally, a vector of registers Rs represents the additional registers $R[x]$ of Lipsi.

```
type memory_data = vector(256, dec, bits(8)) /* Data space */
type memory_inst = vector(240, dec, bits(8)) /* Instruction space */
struct Memory = { Inst : memory_inst, Data : memory_data }
register Rs : vector(16, dec, bits(8)) /* R[x] */
```

We now show the formal specification of the write operations, for both the memory space but also for $R[x]$. The function mem_write updates the content of Memory with the value v at the memory address adr. Either the instruction or the data vector of Memory gets updated, depending on the value of the Most Significant Bit (MSB) of adr, a 9-bit value. Note that the data vector is updated only if adr does not target Rs.

```
val mem_write : (bits(9), bits(8), Memory) -> vector(256, dec, bits(8))
function mem_write (adr, v, mem) = {
  if (adr[8] == 0b1) then {
    if (adrbits_to_adrno(adr[7..0]) >= 16) then
      plain_vector_update (mem.Data, length(mem.Data) - 1 - adrbits_to_adrno(adr
        ↪ [7..0]), v);
    else return mem.Data;
  } else {
    plain_vector_update(mem.Inst, length(mem.Inst) - 1 - adrbits_to_adrno(adr
      ↪ [7..0]),v);
}}
```

The function `reg_write` updates $R[x]$ and shares with the function `mem_write` a
similar signature. A string representing the name of the register, noted r, is
however used instead of a memory address. r is mapped into an offset in the
data vector using the functions `reg_name` and `regbits_to_regno`. X is the setter
function to update Rs with the value v, which uses the overload feature of Sail to
abstract read (not shown) and write accesses (function `wX`, signature not shown).

```
function wX (r, v) = if r < 16 then { Rs[15 - r] = v; }
overload X = {rX, wX}
val reg_write : (string, bits(8)) -> unit /* unit equivalent to void */
function reg_write (r, v) = {
  X(regbits_to_regno(reg_name(r)), v); }
```

Finally, the overload feature of Sail is used to abstract the organization of the
memory. Writing to $R[x]$ or the memory to implement the semantic of instruction
is performed by simply calling the function `lipsi_write`. Similar functions are used
for read operations (shown in the next paragraph).

```
overload lipsi_write = {mem_write, reg_write}
```

Instruction and Timing Models. We now present the part describing the
semantic of instructions. We have modeled in Sail all the ISA of Lipsi, as
presented in [37] (Table 1). We only show the use of Sail to decode and execute ALU instructions that rely on registers. First, the syntactic sugar of scattered definitions is used to group functions related to each instruction in one
place, i.e. AST union `ast`, mapping function `decode` and function `execute`. The
AST type `ALU_TYPE_REG` represents the considered ALU instructions. The mapping `encdec_alu_func_reg` matches a binary value to a constant value representing the requested ALU operation. The mapping `decode` matches the machine
code of instructions to the associated AST node within `ast`. The concatenation
operator @ is used to extract, from the input bit vector, the requested ALU operation (`func`) and the index of the additional register (`reg`). Finally, the function
`execute` implements the semantics of the instructions by first reading the value
from the specified additional register, i.e. `reg_val` and then performing the specified ALU operation on `reg_val` and A. `accureg` is an accessor to A, for reading or
writing.

```
scattered union ast
scattered mapping decode
scattered function execute

union clause ast = ALU_TYPE_Reg : (alu_func_reg, regbits)

mapping encdec_alu_func_reg: alu_func_reg <-> bits(3) = {
  LIPSI_ADD <-> 0b000,
  LIPSI_SUB <-> 0b001,
  ...
  LIPSI_XOR <-> 0b110,
  LIPSI_LD <-> 0b111
}
mapping clause decode = ALU_TYPE_Reg(func, reg) <->
      0b0 @ encdec_alu_func_reg(func) @ reg

function clause execute ALU_TYPE_Reg(func, reg) = {
  let reg_val : len_t = lipsi_read(regbits_to_regno(reg));
  let ret : len_t = match func {
    LIPSI_ADD => reg_val + accureg(),
    LIPSI_SUB => accureg() - reg_val,
    ...
    LIPSI_XOR => reg_val ^ accureg(),
    LIPSI_LD => reg_val
  };
  accureg(ret);
}
```

For the timing model, we simply use a register to represent clock cycles. This register is incremented by the clock cycles associated with each instruction being decoded. The formal SW model executes instructions in single steps, which is also equivalent to an instruction-level simulation of the input program. However, this clock register tracks in a cycle-accurate manner the timing behavior of each instruction.

4.3   Formal HW Model

We now present the formal HW model of the Lipsi processor specified in the TLA$^+$ language. We partially present the specification, using actual code snapshots of both TLA$^+$ and Chisel implementations, in Figs. 4, 5 and 6. Our presentation emphasizes the traceability between the two semantics representations. TLA$^+$ being a specification framework, it lacks program-specific infrastructure such as parsing, rich built-in libraries and AST manipulation. Hence, we also include several workarounds to preserve the traceability, such as convenient naming for instance. However, certain information is inevitably less obvious. For example, the type system of Chisel is abstracted in our TLA$^+$ model, and implicitly the type inference whose results are manually encoded in the corresponding TLA$^+$ specification. Our purpose is not to accurately provide a formal executable semantics of Chisel in TLA$^+$, but to specify, as precisely as possible, the Lipsi Chisel code.

We first present the memory model of the Lipsi processor, in Fig. 4, its integration in the datapath, in Fig. 5 and finally, in Fig. 6 a representative snapshot of the Lipsi processor. Our TLA$^+$ model of Lipsi is cycle-accurate and captures the execution of a Lipsi instruction through the circuit, with both combinational and sequential elements being encoded. The TLA$^+$ specification, LipsiSpec consists of the initial state, LipsiInit and the state transformer LispiTrans, the temporal operator "always", [] preceding the state transformer. It is applied on the system state LVars (i.e., the set of wires and registers):

$$\texttt{LipsiSpec == LipsiInit /\textbackslash\ [] [LipsiTrans]\_LVars}$$

Before detailing LispiSpec, let us present the specification of the memory model.

Memory Model. The TLA$^+$ specification of the Lipsi memory model, in Fig. 4, adheres to this specification style (e.g., with MemoryInit and MemoryTrans being presented). On the Chisel side, the Memory class declares a memory zone, mem, to store data of a total size 256 and elements of type unsigned int of size 8 (e.g., UInt(8.W)). data is used to access an element of mem and is initialized with the memory value at the address from the register rdAddrReg (a 9-bit address truncated to 8-bit as mem represents the data space of Lipsi). The equivalent TLA$^+$ code features the initialization, MemoryInit, of the state elements mem, data and rdAddrReg with their respective initial values. Note that mem_init, not listed, initializes mem with zeros. The Lipsi memory model features read/write memory operations, which are grouped in an interface io, whose fields are accessed using ".". For example, the Chisel code for a memory write at address io.wrAddr with value io.wrData is conditionally performed when the memory write is enabled, i.e. io.wrEna is true. Its equivalent transition in the TLA$^+$ specification updates primed mem with value io.wrData, only when the memory write is enabled (i.e., the predicate cond_io_wrEna tests if io.wrEna is true). Similarly, the new values, rdAddrReg' and data' are accordingly provided. Finally, class Memory is parameterized by prog, an input binary program, which is stored in a read-only memory. These details are omitted due to space constraints.

```
class Memory(prog: String) extends Module {
  val mem = Mem(256, UInt(8.W))
  val data = mem(rdAddrReg(7, 0))
  when(io.wrEna) { mem(io.wrAddr) := io.wrData } ...
}
```

```
MemoryInit == ... /\ rdAddrReg = 0 /\ mem = mem_init /\ data = 0
MemoryTrans == ...
  /\ mem' = IF cond_io_wrEna
              THEN [ n \in 0..255 |->
                IF n = io.wrAddr THEN io.wrData ELSE mem[n] ]
              ELSE mem
  /\ rdAddrReg' = io.rdAddr
  /\ data' = mem[rdAddrReg]
```

Fig. 4. From Chisel HDL to TLA$^+$ for defining the memory system of the Lipsi.

```
class Lipsi(prog: String) extends Module {
  val mem = Module(new Memory(prog)) ...
}
```

```
LOCAL Lmem == INSTANCE Memory WITH ..., rdAddrReg <- 0,
              data <- 0, mem <- [ n \in 256..512 |-> 0 ]

LipsiInit == LET memory_state_init == Lmem!memory_init (program) IN
               /\ ... /\ mem = memory_state_init.mem
LipsiTrans == LET memory_state == Lmem!update_memory_state (...) IN
               /\ ... /\ mem' = memory_state.mem
```

Fig. 5. From Chisel HDL to TLA$^+$ when integrating the memory system of Lipsi.

Figure 5 shows the integration of this memory model and how we preserve the modularity of the Chisel code in our TLA$^+$ specification. The class Lipsi instantiates a local state variable mem with the memory model from Fig. 4. The actual creation of the memory object in Chisel (using new) is translated to a local instance Lmem of Memory, using the construct INSTANCE WITH. LipsiInit can then use Lmem and apply the function memory_init to set its initial state. Similarly, LipsiTrans uses the function update_memory_state to apply the state transformer of the memory model. This updates at each cycle the memory system mem'. These two functions memory_init and update_memory_state are the equivalents of MemoryInit and MemoryTrans from Fig. 4, following a function-based integration approach possible in TLA$^+$. Finally, the parametrization, concerning the initial program, from Chisel is preserved in TLA$^+$ via the memory_init function.

Instruction and Timing Models. Figure 6 presents a snapshot of how Lipsi executes instructions. Compared to the formal SW model, an instruction is executed in potentially several clock cycles, i.e. cycle-level execution, by updating corresponding values in the wires and the registers of Lipsi. Lipsi is implemented with a Finite State Machine (FSM), whose states are first defined, represented as a list (Enum). The position in the list identifies the current state, captured in the register stateReg which is initialized to fetch (and equal to 0). Such states are encoded in TLA$^+$ as a sequence of LOCAL declarations with explicit assignments corresponding to their position in the list, while initializing stateReg to fetch in LipsiInit. Similarly, an exit flag (corresponding to the instruction exit in Lipsi ISA) is set accordingly in both Chisel and TLA$^+$.

The control logic of the FSM of Lipsi is handled by a switch statement over the current value of stateReg. When is(fetch) is true, the next state is by default set to execute (i.e., stateReg := execute) for the next cycle. However, any subsequent modification of stateReg, in the same clock cycle, overrides this modification, a behavior common to any HDL language. For example, if the instruction is an io (i.e., the opcode is equal to 0xf0.U), stateReg is reset to fetch for the next cycle (while copying the value of the accumulator, accuReg to outReg and setting enaIoReg to true). The timing model of the io instruction is

```
val fetch::execute::stind::ldind1::ldind2::exit::Nil = Enum(6)
val stateReg = RegInit(fetch)
val exitReg = RegInit(false.B)

switch(stateReg) {
  is (fetch) {
    stateReg := execute ...
    when (rdData(7) === 0.U) {... enaAccuReg := true.B ...}
      ...
    when (rdData === 0xf0.U) {
      outReg := accuReg enaIoReg := true.B stateReg := fetch }
      when (rdData === 0xff.U) { stateReg := exit }
    } ...
  is (stind) { wrEna := true.B stateReg := fetch }
  is (execute) { stateReg := fetch }
  is (exit) { exitReg := true.B }
}
```

```
LOCAL fetch == 0 ... LOCAL exit == 5

cond_rdData_eq_Bits0 (rddata) == b7(rddata) = 0
cond_rdData_eq_Bits0xf0 (rddata) == rddata = 240
cond_rdData_eq_Bits0xff (rddata) == rddata = 255

cond_stateReg_eq_fetch == stateReg = fetch
cond_stateReg_eq_stind == stateReg = stind
cond_stateReg_eq_execute == stateReg = execute
cond_stateReg_eq_exit == stateReg = exit
  ...
LipsiInit == ... /\ stateReg = fetch /\ exitReg = FALSE

LipsiTrans == ...
  /\ exitReg' = IF cond_stateReg_eq_exit THEN TRUE ELSE FALSE
  /\ outReg' =
      IF cond_stateReg_eq_fetch
      THEN IF cond_rdData_eq_Bits0xf0 (memory_state.io.rdData)
          THEN accuReg ELSE outReg
      ELSE outReg
  /\ stateReg' = ...
      IF cond_stateReg_eq_fetch
      THEN ... IF X_cond_rdData_eq_Bits0xff (memory_state.io.rdData)
              THEN exit ELSE fetch
      ELSE IF cond_stateReg_eq_stind
          THEN fetch ELSE IF cond_stateReg_eq_execute ...
```

Fig. 6. From Chisel HDL to TLA$^+$ for snapshot of Lipsi FSM.

thus one clock cycle. The other states are used to store the output of the decode when an instruction is fetched. For instance, is(stind) enables the memory write, i.e. the signal wrEna is set to true, while resetting stateReg to fetch. The timing model of a store instruction is thus one clock cycle, as the write occurs at the next cycle while the next instruction is fetched. Similarly, is(execute) resets stateReg, implying that execute represents the last stage in the timing model of some instructions. Finally, is(exit) signals the end of the program execution, represented in Lipsi by a specialized register exitReg. Therefore, exit takes three clock cycles. At the first cycle, the instruction is identified during is(fetch) based on its opcode 0xff.U and the next state of Lipsi set to exit. At the second clock cycle, exitReg is set to true, a change that would be visible at the third clock cycle. Contrary to other instructions, no further instruction can be fetched at this third clock cycle that we thus count in the timing behavior of the exit instruction.

The TLA$^+$ encoding of this code fragment is driven by a cascade of conditions on both the value of stateReg (e.g., cond_stateReg_eq_) and the instruction opcode (e.g., cond_rdData_eq_Bits). For example, exitReg' is set to true when the corresponding condition on stateReg is exit and outReg' is updated with the value in the accumulator, accuReg only when stateReg is fetch and the opcode is 0xf0 (i.e., cond_rdData_eq_Bits0xf0 is true). Otherwise it stays unmodified, as outReg. Similarly, stateReg' is updated with the corresponding value, capturing, in this way part of the timing model that we prove next.

5   Evaluation Results

We first report the semantic discrepancies we found between the SW and the HW models of Lipsi. These discrepancies concern not only the functionality but also the timing, justifying the need for formalization and verification of timing models. Finally, we present a potential application of such timing models - the detection of memory interferences in a multi-core context.

Semantic Discrepancies. We identified some semantics discrepancies when we performed the trace equivalence between traces from formal SW model and the simulators and the circuit (steps (2) and (3) on the SW side of our approach, see Sect. 3.2). First, the instructions sh and brl, specified in the Lipsi ISA, are not implemented in the Chisel hardware design of Lipsi. Next, the instructions adc and sbb produce outputs that are equivalent to respectively the add and the sub instructions. However, these implementation issues are known to the author of Lipsi.

A more interesting issue concerns the i/o instruction. Its specification allows the first 4 bits of its encoding to be used to specify the i/o ports. However, the hardware implementation of Lipsi only uses a single i/o port, the one with value index 0. Any non-zero index leads to a silent drop of the next instruction $(PC + 1)$, i.e. the execution continues at $PC + 2$. Even if this unprocessed instruction leads to be interpreted as an ALU operation (the default decoding), the value of the accumulator is not modified as it is guarded by a boolean value (not set by default). Note that contrary to the previous discrepancies, this difference was not explicitly documented in the hardware implementation of Lipsi.

Finally, while the instruction `exit` takes 3 cycles in the Lipsi circuit, it only takes 1 cycle in the Lipsi simulator. We reiterate that our goal is to detect timing problems and not to point out functionality issues in the considered design. However, such findings demonstrate that we can detect any kind of semantic discrepancy between the specified ISA and implementations of it.

Proving the Timing Model. We exemplify next the following timing invariants $TInv_i$ in Lipsi, with $i \in \{$ `exit`, `io`, `add`, `ld` $\}$ (`io` being the i/o instruction). We recall that the formal HW model of Lipsi is cycle-accurate and a cycle variable is incremented every time the system makes a transition. The opcode of the fetched instruction is stored in `curr_instr`. Also, for each invariant, we use a counter variable `x_`, which is initialized to 0 and incremented at each clock cycle. Then, this value is compared with the result of the augmented formal ISA to ensure that the timing on both SW- and HW-level are the same. Note that this counter variable is not necessary, but we opt to explicitly encode it for clarity (i.e., an alternative is to directly use the processor clock cycle).

Next, we present the invariant for the instruction `exit`, $TInv_{exit}$.

```
inv_exit (curr_instr) == curr_instr = 255 /\ exitReg /\ x_exit <= 3
```

Informally, it states that, whenever an instruction is an `exit` (its opcode is `0xff` or 255), the register `exitReg` becomes true 3 clock cycles later. This property follows the semantic of the Chisel code from Fig. 6, with `curr_instr` corresponding to `rdData`, the assignment `stateReg := exit` triggers at the next clock cycle the assignment to `exitReg` guarded by the condition `is(exit)`, with an observed result at the next clock cycle. The timing of instruction `exit` is thus 3 clock cycles (i.e., the condition `x_exit`) and proved using the TLC model checker.

The timing invariant of the instruction `io`, $TInv_{io}$, is presented next.

```
inv_io (curr_instr) ==
    LET val == curr_instr - 240 IN
        /\ curr_instr >= 240 /\ curr_instr <= 254
        /\ ((enaIoReg /\ val = 0) \/ not (val = 0))
        /\ io.dout = val
        /\ x_io <= 1
```

This instruction covers a range of opcodes, depending on the i/o port identifier. For example, the instruction `0xf1` is an `io` (opcode `0xf0` or 240) and the i/o port number 1. The variable `val` in $TInv_{io}$ represents the port number. Concerning i/o ports, the semantics of `io` is under-specified in [37]: the port number is not used by the instruction. Therefore, the implementation in the circuit only supports the use of port 0, i.e. `0xf0` is the only accepted opcode, as seen previously. The invariant captures the following hardware pattern: the instruction is identified as `io` and the port identifier is calculated in `val`, the register `enaIoReg` is updated to allow the actual port output. The timing of instruction `io` is proved to be 1 clock cycle.

Next, we present $TInv_{add}$, the timing invariant for instruction add.

```
inv_add (curr_instr, rddata) ==
   LET reg == curr_instr IN
      /\ curr_instr >= 0 /\ curr_instr <= 15
      /\ \/ (not (rddata = reg) /\ (not (reg = 0)) /\ enaAccuReg
         \/ not (res = reg)
      /\ x_add <= 2
```

Similarly to io, the opcodes for add include the value to be processed via the accumulator (i.e., the range is between 0x00 and 0x0f, according to Table 1 from [37]). The instruction add executes in two cycles. In the first cycle, the instruction is fetched and the flag register enaAccuReg is set to true. In the second cycle, the actual addition is computed, with the result stored in res. We use an auxiliary variable reg to distinguish between two cases, depending on if the operand is 0 or not (and if res remains the same, even after the addition is performed). $TInv_{add}$ does not include functional correctness, i.e. that the correct addition is performed, only that the accumulator is updated after two clock cycles. However, it could also be possible to have a functionality criterion included as well, as it is the case with the next timing invariant for a memory load instruction, ld.

The opcodes of ld are also in a range of values, the difference with 0x70 (or 112) being the target memory address. This address is represented by val. This instruction takes two cycles. The classical fetch first, followed with the actual memory read, stored in the accumulator, accuReg.

```
inv_ld (curr_instr) ==
   LET val == curr_instr - 112 IN
      /\ curr_instr >= 112 /\ curr_instr <= 127
      /\ accuReg = mem[val]
      /\ x_ld <= 2
```

We could also express $TInv_{ld}$ as $TInv_{add}$, i.e. without any functional checking, by replacing the actual functionality by only a check that the memory is accessed. The other timing invariants are expressed similarly.

The experiments are conducted on a quad-core Intel i7 at 2.8 GHz with 16 GB RAM and the TLA$^+$ Toolbox using the TLC model checker version 2.14. The results are presented in Table 1. The four lines show runtime and state space statistics for the timing invariants of instructions exit, io, add and ld. The results of a more general timing invariant for the instructions of type ALU reg (e.g., $TInv_{add}$ is part of this invariant) are shown in line 5. Finally, the timing model of Lipsi (i.e., without the instructions sh and brl which are not coded in the circuit) is verified in about 51 min and with a total size of the state space of about 34M (i.e., the last line in Table 1).

Detection of Interferences. We briefly illustrate a possible use of the proved timing model: the detection of memory interferences. We thus consider three different input binaries executed with our formal SW model of Lipsi, to represent a multi-core setting of Lipsi. Each Lipsi core is identified by an index. Besides,

Table 1. Proving the timing model of the Lipsi processor.

Timing invariant - $TInv$	Runtime (s)	State space size
$TInv_{exit}$	15	75K
$TInv_{io}$	67	197K
$TInv_{add}$	279	1.10M
$TInv_{ld}$	252	1.06M
$TInv_{ALU\_reg} = \left(\bigwedge_{i \in ALU\_reg} TInv_i \right)$	1538	18.87M
$TM_{Lipsi} = \left(\bigwedge_{i \in \mathcal{L}} TInv_i \right)$	3088	33.94M

as each Lipsi has its private memory, we rely on the i/o instruction to emulate the access to a shared device. Note that we only emulate the access to a shared device, not the device itself nor its arbitration policy. If two i/o accesses occur at the same time, we thus assume that the one coming from the Lipsi with the smallest index wins the access. The other Lipsi cores continue their execution as if their accesses were valid, as we are mostly interested in timing properties of programs not in their functional correctness.

For the input binaries, we reuse the same memory model for the spacing of memory accesses as in [14]. In this model, tasks or programs are represented as a sequence of memory requests separated by a given number of processor clock cycles, representing the amount of computation that is performed between two memory accesses. We assume a composable computer architecture [13], which ensures that the distance between requests is independent of the execution of other tasks. The only interference between the independent tasks thus stems from accesses to the emulated shared device.

The sequences of memory requests of our three input programs are: (A: $2, 24, 12$), (B: $14, 4, 2$) and (C: $26, 6$). The program A is made of 2 loops and thus generates i/o accesses at the (absolute) times 2, 26 and 38. The program B is made of a single loop and generates i/o accesses at the (absolute) times 14, 18 and 20. Finally, the program C is also made of a single loop and generates i/o accesses at the absolute (times) 26 and 32. It is then trivial to detect that an interference is going to occur at time 26 between program A and C. Our next step is to modify the input binaries, by adding appropriate nop instructions (ALU operations that do not change the current value of A) or by introducing a delay instruction, as in Patmos or PRET, to space out i/o accesses. While a straightforward algorithm can solve this problem for programs with a single path, the presence of multiple paths in input programs leads to an interesting optimization problem of minimizing the number of interferences.

6   Related Work

Traditionally, HW/SW co-verification methods [19,23,29,30] consider SW to be represented in higher-level languages than our low-level approach (which is characteristic of worst-case timing reasoning [40]) and HW to be based on HDL languages. These works use model checking techniques and focus mostly on proving functionality properties, while we propose advancements on the timing properties, also using model checking. For example, C code and Verilog designs are verified together via bounded model checking, in [30], similarly with the co-verification technique from [29], where model checking is used on C code and hardware abstractions based on push-down systems. High-level code is co-verified with HDL designs, in [19], by a combination of BDD-based model checking for HW and partial order reduction for SW. All these approaches consider an implicit interface between hardware and software (i.e., we presented this interface under the name of the hardware patterns). An explicit interface is expressed in [12] and integrated into the HW/SW co-verification procedure based on bounded model checking (i.e., as a side note, the application is considered at the binary level).

Our approach increases the confidence in the formal semantics of ISA with the help of an ISS, providing a de facto procedure to verify an ISS. There are several works [5,17], centered on the verification of ISS and its use in HW/SW co-verification. The ISS presented in [5] is symbolic and addresses both functional and timing properties in processors similarly using assertions with our procedure as another symbolic ISS, which is constructed over an instruction-level abstraction [17].

WCET analysis tools require a clear and explicit specification of timing models of architectures to estimate the WCET [40]. One approach is to rely on a product of timed automata to model the timing behavior of hardware elements, such as pipelines, caches, etc [6,9]. The WCET estimates are then obtained using the UPPAAL model-checker. However, in both cases, the timing accuracy of the hand-made models, which are difficult to design, is unclear and simplified compared to the underlying micro-architecture. Another approach is to automatically extract timing information from HDL processor designs, either using static analysis, as in [36] or aiming for patterns of pipelining using abstract simulation, as in [32]. Both approaches work directly on the processor code (in this case VHDL) as our approach. However, we differ in the formal technique: static analysis and respectively model-checking.

Another approach is to extend classical ISA-level Architecture Description Languages (ADLs) [28], such as ArchC or Sim-nML, to include the specification of timing models at the micro-architecture level. The OTAWA WCET analysis framework relies on an extended Sim-nML to specify timing models of pipelines by describing resource allocations of instructions over pipeline stages, functional units, and buffers [15]. In [24,25], the ADL Expression language is used to describe both ISA but also contention and parallelism relations at the micro-architecture, i.e. the timing model. Execution graphs are then generated on which WCET analyses are performed. The LISA ADL language [31] also enables the assignment of operations to pipeline stages, potentially with delays. Compared to timed automata models, the ADL-based approach enables the specification of timing models at a high-level description, from which a low-level network of timed automata can be generated. However, there is still no connection with the timing model at the HDL level and moreover, the timing anomalies are ignored.

Retargetable compilers have led to the design of processor models in order to extract instruction sets [8,21,33]. However, these compilers use a reservation table to describe the pipeline operations and these operations are not timing-accurate to model pipeline hazards.

In a different area, [16] proposes a timing-abstract behavioral model of pipelines to increase the instruction parallelism reuse and reduce bugs when optimizing implementations, for instance when performing logic retiming. Cycle-level details, such as pipeline staging, are generated from a concise specification through a process called timing augmentation.

7   Conclusion and Future Work

We proposed a general methodology to reason about the timing properties of CPSs by taking into account the interplay between HW and SW, both formally specified and verified. We also reported on how our methodology is applied on a simple processor called Lipsi towards defining and proving its timing model. Due to the formal nature of our approach we also discovered several semantic inconsistencies, both functional and temporal, between the specification and the implementation of Lipsi. Our methodology is demonstrated using a formal semantics of Lipsi ISA based on the Sail language and a formal specification of the corresponding hardware implementation in Chisel code, based on the TLA$^+$ reasoning framework.

We are currently pursuing several lines of research. First, we aim to automatically generate formal (TLA$^+$) models and the necessary timing invariants directly for the HDL code. Second, we have ongoing work targeting RISC-V designs, with complicated timing models due to pipelining, multi-level caches and speculation mechanism. Besides, since we use such timing models in worst-case reasoning to safely guarantee the timing behaviors, information on timing predictability [39] and timing compositionality [13] should also be verified. In other words, we are working to include the knowledge of timing anomalies [35] in our definition of a timing model to identify timing anomalies via model checking, as in one of our previous work [3]. Research communities on the WCET analysis [41] or synchronous languages [7] rely on traceability to transfer high-level semantics to low-level code [22,34]. We are interested in leveraging high-level timing properties and traceability enhancements within our HW and SW timing models. This includes the investigation of how these timing models could be used within a software compiler toolchain, such as LLVM, to include not only average case performance optimizations but also worst-case performance optimizations. Finally, we plan to address timing models for the communication part of the CPSs, which are currently abstracted away in our current work.

References

1. Armstrong, A., et al.: ISA semantics for ARMv8-a, RISC-V, and CHERI-MIPS. PACMPL **3**(POPL), 71:1–71:31 (2019)
2. Asavoae, M.: K semantics for assembly languages: a case study. Electr. Notes Theor. Comput. Sci. **304**, 111–125 (2014)
3. Asavoae, M., Hedia, B.B., Jan, M.: Formal executable models for automatic detection of timing anomalies. In: 18th International Workshop on Worst-Case Execution Time Analysis, WCET 2018, pp. 2:1–2:13 (2018)
4. Bachrach, J., et al.: Chisel: constructing hardware in a Scala embedded language. In: Proceedings of the 49th Annual Design Automation Conference, DAC 2012, pp. 1216–1225. ACM (2012)
5. Beatty, D.L., Bryant, R.E.: Formally verifying a microprocessor using a simulation methodology. In: Proceedings of the 31st Conference on Design Automation, pp. 596–602 (1994)
6. Béchennec, J., Cassez, F.: Computation of WCET using program slicing and real-time model-checking. CoRR abs/1105.1633 (2011). http://arxiv.org/abs/1105.1633
7. Benveniste, A., Caspi, P., Edwards, S.A., Halbwachs, N., Guernic, P.L., de Simone, R.: The synchronous languages 12 years later. Proc. IEEE **91**(1), 64–83 (2003)
8. Bradlee, D.G., Henry, R.R., Eggers, S.J.: The Marion system for retargetable instruction scheduling. SIGPLAN Not. **26**(6), 229–240 (1991)
9. Dalsgaard, A.E., Olesen, M.C., Toft, M., Hansen, R.R., Larsen, K.G.: METAMOC: modular execution time analysis using model checking. In: Lisper, B. (ed.) 10th International Workshop on Worst-Case Execution Time Analysis (WCET 2010). OpenAccess Series in Informatics (OASIcs), vol. 15, pp. 113–123 (2010)
10. Dasgupta, S., Park, D., Kasampalis, T., Adve, V.S., Rosu, G.: A complete formal semantics of x86-64 user-level instruction set architecture. In: Proceedings of the 40th PLDI 2019, pp. 1133–1148 (2019)
11. Gordon, M.J.C.: The semantic challenge of Verilog HDL. In: Proceedings of the 10th Annual IEEE Symposium on Logic in Computer Science, San Diego, 26–29, pp. 136–145 (1995)
12. Große, D., Kühne, U., Drechsler, R.: HW/SW co-verification of embedded systems using bounded model checking. In: Proceedings of the 16th ACM Great Lakes Symposium on VLSI 2006, pp. 43–48 (2006)
13. Hahn, S., Reineke, J., Wilhelm, R.: Towards compositionality in execution time analysis: definition and challenges. SIGBED Rev. **12**(1), 28–36 (2015)
14. Hebbache, F., Jan, M., Brandner, F., Pautet, L.: Shedding the shackles of time-division multiplexing. In: 2018 IEEE Real-Time Systems Symposium, RTSS, 2018, pp. 456–468 (2018)
15. Herbegue, H., Filali, M., Cassé, H.: Formal architecture specification for time analysis. In: Maehle, E., Römer, K., Karl, W., Tovar, E. (eds.) ARCS 2014. LNCS, vol. 8350, pp. 98–110. Springer, Cham (2014). https://doi.org/10.1007/978-3-319-04891-8_9
16. Hoover, S.F.: Timing-abstract circuit design in transaction-level Verilog. In: 2017 IEEE International Conference on Computer Design (ICCD), pp. 525–532, November 2017
17. Huang, B., Zhang, H., Subramanyan, P., Vizel, Y., Gupta, A., Malik, S.: Instruction-level abstraction (ILA): a uniform specification for system-on-chip (SOC) verification. ACM Trans. Design Autom. Electr. Syst. **24**(1), 10:1–10:24 (2019)

18. Kern, C., Greenstreet, M.: Formal verification in hardware design: a survey. ACM Trans. Des. Autom. Electron. Syst. **4** (2002). https://doi.org/10.1145/307988. 307989

19. Kurshan, R.P., Levin, V., Minea, M., Peled, D.A., Yenigün, H.: Combining software and hardware verification techniques. Formal Methods Syst. Des. **21**(3), 251–280 (2002)

20. Lamport, L.: Specifying Systems: The TLA+ Language and Tools for Hardware and Software Engineers. Addison-Wesley Longman Publishing Co., Inc., Boston (2002)

21. Leupers, R., Marwedel, P.: A BDD-based frontend for retargetable compilers. In: Proceedings the European Design and Test Conference, ED TC 1995, pp. 239–243, March 1995

22. Li, H., Puaut, I., Rohou, E.: Tracing flow information for tighter WCET estimation: application to vectorization. In: 21st IEEE International Conference on Embedded and Real-Time Computing Systems and Applications, RTCSA 2015, Hong Kong, China, 19–21 August 2015, pp. 217–226 (2015)

23. Li, J., Xie, F., Ball, T., Levin, V., McGarvey, C.: An automata-theoretic approach to hardware/software co-verification. In: Rosenblum, D.S., Taentzer, G. (eds.) FASE 2010. LNCS, vol. 6013, pp. 248–262. Springer, Heidelberg (2010). https://doi.org/10.1007/978-3-642-12029-9_18

24. Li, X., Roychoudhury, A., Mitra, T., Mishra, P., Cheng, X.: A retargetable software timing analyzer using architecture description language. In: 2007 Asia and South Pacific Design Automation Conference, pp. 396–401, January 2007

25. Li, X., Roychoudhury, A., Mitra, T.: Modeling out-of-order processors for WCET analysis. Real-Time Syst. **34**(3), 195–227 (2006)

26. Liu, I., et al.: A PRET microarchitecture implementation with repeatable timing and competitive performance. In: 2012 IEEE 30th International Conference on Computer Design (ICCD), pp. 87–93. IEEE (2012)

27. Meredith, P.O., Katelman, M., Meseguer, J., Rosu, G.: A formal executable semantics of Verilog. In: 8th ACM/IEEE MEMOCODE 2010, Grenoble, France, pp. 179–188 (2010)

28. Mishra, P., Dutt, N. (eds.): Processor Description Languages, Application and Methodologies. Systems on Silicon, vol. 1. Morgan Kaufman, Burlington (2008)

29. Monniaux, D.: Verification of device drivers and intelligent controllers: a case study. In: Proceedings of the 7th ACM & IEEE International Conference on Embedded software, EMSOFT 2007, pp. 30–36 (2007)

30. Mukherjee, R., Purandare, M., Polig, R., Kroening, D.: Formal techniques for effective co-verification of hardware/software co-designs. In: Proceedings of the 54th Annual Design Automation Conference, DAC 2017, pp. 35:1–35:6 (2017)

31. Pees, S., Hoffmann, A., Zivojnovic, V., Meyr, H.: Lisa-machine description language for cycle-accurate models of programmable DSP architectures. In: Proceedings 1999 Design Automation Conference (Cat. No. 99CH36361), pp. 933–938, June 1999

32. Pister, M.: Timing model derivation: pipeline analyzer generation from hardware description languages. Ph.D. thesis, Saarland University (2012)

33. Rau, B.R., Kathail, V., Aditya, S.: Machine-description driven compilers for EPIC and VLIW processors. Des. Autom. Embed. Syst. **4**(2), 71–118 (1999)

34. Raymond, P., Maiza, C., Parent-Vigouroux, C., Carrier, F., Asavoae, M.: Timing analysis enhancement for synchronous program. Real-Time Syst. **51**(2), 192–220 (2015)

35. Reineke, J., et al.: A definition and classification of timing anomalies. In: 6th International Workshop on Worst-Case Execution Time (WCET) Analysis (2006)
36. Schlickling, M.: Timing model derivation: static analysis of hardware description languages. Ph.D. thesis, Saarland University (2013)
37. Schoeberl, M.: Lipsi: probably the smallest processor in the world. In: Berekovic, M., Buchty, R., Hamann, H., Koch, D., Pionteck, T. (eds.) ARCS 2018. LNCS, vol. 10793, pp. 18–30. Springer, Cham (2018). https://doi.org/10.1007/978-3-319-77610-1_2
38. Schoeberl, M., Puffitsch, W., Hepp, S., Huber, B., Prokesch, D.: Patmos: a time-predictable microprocessor. Real-Time Syst. **54**(2), 389–423 (2018). https://doi.org/10.1007/s11241-018-9300-4
39. Thiele, L., Wilhelm, R.: Design for timing predictability. Real-Time Syst. **28**(2–3), 157–177 (2004)
40. Wilhelm, R.: Formal analysis of processor timing models. In: Graf, S., Mounier, L. (eds.) SPIN 2004. LNCS, vol. 2989, pp. 1–4. Springer, Heidelberg (2004). https://doi.org/10.1007/978-3-540-24732-6_1
41. Wilhelm, R., et al.: The worst-case execution-time problem - overview of methods and survey of tools. ACM Trans. Embedded Comput. Syst. **7**(3), 36:1–36:53 (2008)
42. Wilson, S.: Verilator 4.0 - open simulation goes multithreaded. In: The Open Source Digital Design Conference (ORConf), September 2018
43. Yu, Y., Manolios, P., Lamport, L.: Model checking TLA$^+$ specifications. In: Pierre, L., Kropf, T. (eds.) CHARME 1999. LNCS, vol. 1703, pp. 54–66. Springer, Heidelberg (1999). https://doi.org/10.1007/3-540-48153-2_6

Workshop on Embedded and Cyber-Physical Systems Education

A Remote Test Environment for a Large-Scale Microcontroller Laboratory Course

Manfred Smieschek, Stefan Rakel, David Thönnessen, Andreas Derks,
André Stollenwerk$^{(\boxtimes)}$, and Stefan Kowalewski

Informatik 11 – Embedded Software, RWTH University, 52074 Aachen, Germany
{smieschek,rakel,thoennessen,derks,
stollenwerk,kowalewski}@embedded.rwth-aachen.de
https://embedded.rwth-aachen.de

Abstract. We report on a remote test environment for a mandatory undergraduate lab course on microcontroller programming at RWTH Aachen University. Since the course is being attended by up to 320 students each semester, it is not possible to provide comprehensive supervised on-site access to the laboratory equipment during the preparation phase of the participants. To deal with this common scalability problem of lab courses we implemented a remotely and continuously accessible test pool with full feature support of the used microcontroller platform. The paper presents the architecture and the detailed implementation of the pool, and we provide an evaluation of its success based on usage statistics and student feedback.

Keywords: Computer science education · Lab course · Remote test environment · Operating system · Microcontroller · Remote access

1 Introduction

With rising student numbers in computer science at RWTH Aachen university (2.507 in winter term 2013/14; 3.405 in winter term 2017/18) [9], more students attend our lab course. These are in general harder to scale than traditional frontal teaching. We propose a remote scalable test environment to cope with the increasing number of computer science students in laboratory courses.

Our course was established from scratch in 2007 [11], and is mandatory in the second semester for every Bachelor student in computer science [8]. It consists of one voluntary experiment, in which the students are introduced to the used hardware and Integrated Development Environment (IDE). Afterwards, there are six mandatory experiments, in which a rudimentary operating system is developed. The experiments are carried out by the students in teams of two and take place every two weeks. Hence, the lab takes 14 weeks to complete. Each experiment takes three hours of on-site presence time with additional preparation time at home. The developed operating system consists of a bootloader, a scheduler

© Springer Nature Switzerland AG 2020
R. Chamberlain et al. (Eds.): CyPhy 2019/WESE 2019, LNCS 11971, pp. 231–246, 2020.
https://doi.org/10.1007/978-3-030-41131-2_11

with different scheduling strategies, static and dynamic memory allocation, and different communication protocols, like UART and SPI, to communicate with additional peripherals, e.g. a keyboard or touchscreen (TLCD). Until winter term 2018/2019 the course has been rated at 6 ECTS credits and since then at 8 ECTS credits.

The course not only teaches important skills in software engineering, but also how to work with real hardware and in a team. During the presence time the functionality of the newly developed part of the operating system is tested with software tests, which are made available to the students beforehand. An experiment cannot be passed by the students, if any of the software tests fails. As the presence time is strictly limited, the students have to prepare and test their implementation as much as possible beforehand, as coding and debugging would most probably not be feasible within the three hours of presence time. In the past, we used to only offer on-site consultation hours, during which students could use the lab rooms to program the same hardware as during the experiments and also run the provided software tests.

Our laboratory offers space for 12 teams simultaneously, and due to the increase of students to up to 320 per semester, we needed additional efforts to cope with their necessity of testing. We decided against a software emulator, as testing with an emulator is difficult and prone to errors. During a short evaluation phase, we experienced that an emulator would sometimes behave slightly different than the real hardware, which would be frustrating for students, as this might result in code that works perfectly at home with the emulator, but not during the presence time of the experiment. Therefore, we wanted to offer real hardware for testing, but with the advantage of working at home. Thus, we came up with the idea to build a remote microcontroller test environment (test pool), where the students can login, program real hardware, test their solution, and debug if necessary. The students can work around the clock from home without supervision from our side. Currently, the test pool consists of 26 test stations, which is already more than double the size of our laboratory. Additionally, the test pool can be expanded much easier than lab space, when student numbers keep increasing in the future.

2   Remote Access

A *test station* consists of a computer and a hardware assembly on which students can test their code. Part of the hardware assembly is a microcontroller, a remote webcam and dedicated hardware to simulate inputs. Test stations can be arranged in different hardware configurations, called *test setups* in the following, because the students need different hardware depending on the experiment. For example, there are experiments in which the students control a TLCD or others, in which a keyboard is controlled. For technical reasons, it is not possible to set up both configurations at the same time as they share mutually exclusive interfaces. Every test station is preconfigured to one test setup by us and made available to the students for their work. When accessing the test pool, the student can select the desired configuration and work on it.

2.1   User Scheduling

The test pool consists of 26 test stations. Each test station can be configured to one test setup. The test setups change over the different experiments of the lab course in one semester. The lab dates for different groups of students are distributed over a period of two weeks, so that the preparation time of the students for different experiments can overlap. Accordingly, the capacity of the test pool must be partitioned according to the test setups to be provided. However, the number of registrations for the lab can reach up to 320. Accordingly, there are significantly more students than there are test setups. To ensure fair access to the test pool, we have implemented a scheduling system for access requests.

Access requests are made initially via a dedicated web portal. This portal requires to log in with a unique student ID (single sign on). Once logged in, a so-called *session* can be requested for a test setup. The request puts the student in a queue that contains all test setups of the desired type.

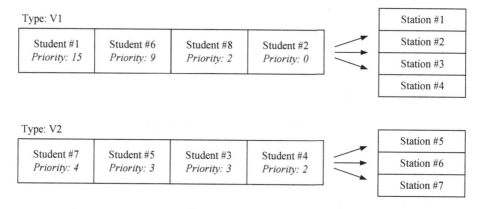

Fig. 1. Scheduling students to test stations using priority queues.

Figure 1 shows the schematic structure of the scheduling. The example shows two test setups "V1" and "V2" with four and three test stations, respectively. Currently there are eight students in the two queues. As soon as a station becomes available, the first student of the corresponding queue (rightmost position) is assigned to the free test station. The position of the students is first determined by the priority and, if this is not unique, by the time of entering the queue. The priority is determined by the duration the test pool has been used by the student in the past. At the beginning of a semester, all students have a priority of zero. With each use of the test pool, the priority increases by the duration of the session. This is to achieve a fair distribution of resources among the students. To prevent students from permanently blocking the test pool, the session time is limited. The maximum duration of a session is two hours. If the session is not closed by the user before the end of this period, it will be terminated by the system. As the user is disconnected from the test station and the computer is restarted, there is a risk of data loss of the students work. In order to prevent students from this, warning messages are issued to the user on the Graphical User Interface (GUI) of the test station starting 15 min before the end of a session.

2.2 Remote Control

After a session is assigned to a student, the corresponding Uniform Resource Locator (URL) of the test station appears on the screen and the firewall opens for the computer from which the session was requested. For security reasons, the test station cannot be reached from any other computer. The firewall also prevents students from accessing a test station without a session. Because the domain of a test station is static, students could access it without having a session if there was no firewall and they knew the address from a previous session.

The test environment of the test stations is Windows-based. Access to these is realized via Windows Remote Desktop which uses Remote Desktop Protocol (RDP) [1]. The users can enter the domain, which they received on the website, into a tool for Windows Remote Desktop and start a connection attempt. The computers' access is managed by an Active Directory [4], based on the universities identity management. Students can log in with their password like on any computer of the university.

3 Embedded Hardware

Stollenwerk et al. introduced a modular and robust microcontroller platform based on an ATmega [5,10], which we still use in our lab.

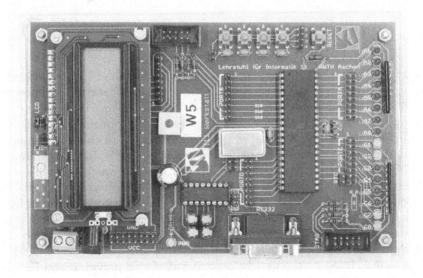

Fig. 2. The EVA Board which is used at the lab as well as the test pool.

Figure 2 shows the evaluation board, called EVA Board, which is programmed by the students during the course of the lab with different functionalities. Identical EVA Boards are also used in each test station of the test pool. Currently 26 test stations are available for the students. Each test station is associated with a Virtual Machine (VM). And each 13 of the VMs are operated by a VM host server. Thus, we are running two VM host servers for the moment.

We developed hardware and software to enable the students to remotely interact with the EVA Board like during presence time, called Remote Board and ATmegaRemote, respectively. To facilitate maintenance work, the hardware of the test stations is mounted in pairs in removable transportable boxes, see Fig. 3a. Each box is equipped with a power supply, two Remote Boards, two EVA Boards, two IP cameras, two JTAG ICE programming devices and LED lighting. A 5 V/12 V short-circuit-proof combi power supply provides energy to the EVA Boards, Remote Boards, cameras, LED strips for lighting and the USB hub via a DIN rail. An Edimax LAN IP camera is located above the EVA Boards, such that the complete work area can be displayed via our software ATmegaRemote, see Sect. 4.2.

(a) Top view of a box   (b) Side connectors of a box

Fig. 3. Sockets and top view of one of the modular transportable boxes containing two workplaces (based on the EVA Boards) for the students.

Due to the modular design, in the event of a fault or if the test setup has to be changed, only two test stations have to be withdrawn from the test pool. This is achieved by setting them to maintenance mode via our web portal. The maintenance mode assures that no new sessions are assigned to the affected test setups, as the user scheduling described in Sect. 2.1 can access the current mode of the test station. Afterwards, the regarding box can be brought to the workshop, where it is fixed or reconfigured to a new test setup. For transport, the front connector of the power supply, the network connectors of the cameras as well as the USB control of the Remote Boards are pluggable, see Fig. 3b. The Remote Board, see Fig. 4, purely serves as an interface between the user and the EVA Board.

Fig. 4. The Remote Board which serves as a mainboard for the expansion boards.

The Remote Board takes over the actions the user performs remotely on the hardware during a session. An ATmega2560 processes incoming commands from the ATmegaRemote software and sends them via extension boards to the EVA Board. The Remote Board is addressed via a pluggable FTDI USB interface. The easy exchangeability of the FTDI board allows easy troubleshooting in case of problems. The power supply is connected via a 4-pin Molex plug with reverse polarity protection. There are seven slots on the Remote Board for additional expansion boards. On both sides of each slot there are rails to hold the expansion boards firmly in place. The Remote Board is designed in such a way, that each two Input/Output (I/O) ports can be accessed individually via one slot. And each slot is configured to provide up to 16 I/O, and 5 V as well as 12 V to a pluggable expansion board.

For better maintainability, all functional components have been moved to these expansion boards. The Remote Board serves here as a pure mainboard and interface. The following extension boards can be plugged on to make the various practical experiments remote controllable: DAV6 Board: Generates analogue signals, SPI and UART connectivity available, see Fig. 5a and Sect. 3.1. Button Board: Simulates external buttons by two Darlington Driver ICs, see Fig. 5b and Sect. 3.2. JTAG and Supply Board: Controls power supply and JTAG connection of EVA Board, see Fig. 5c and Sect. 3.3.

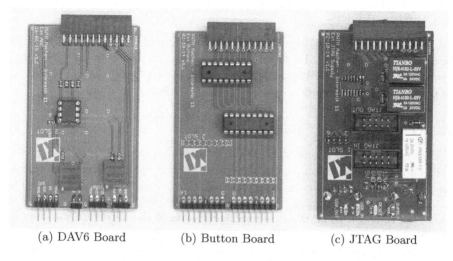

(a) DAV6 Board   (b) Button Board   (c) JTAG Board

Fig. 5. Different expansion boards for the Remote Board.

3.1 DAV6 Board

The DAV6 expansion board serves as a data interface between the EVA Board and the programming environment, and provides a DAC, a PWM output as well as an UART and an SPI interface. In various experiments offered during the practical course, an analog voltage is required, which has to be output digitally by the students on the one hand and used as an analog voltage reference in another experiment. On-site an external laboratory power supply is used, which provides the required variable voltage. The expansion board simulates the adjustable power supply with an amplified PWM output of the ATmega2560 of the Remote Board.

In another experiment of the course students have to read an RFID tag via an optional receiver board. The RFID tag is held by the student near the receiver board such that the ID of the tag can be read. The process of feeding the RFID tag near to the receiver board is performed by a servo in the remote workplace, which moves the RFID tag at a 90° angle to the board and away from the board. For direct control of the servo, the DAV6 Board offers a three-pole interface with a PWM output, 5 V and GND Pin connection. The PWM output is connected via the DAV6 Board and directly to the ATmega2560. The servo movement can be controlled via ATmegaRemote.

Students can connect a PS/2 keyboard to the EVA Board in another experiment and use the LCD as output for keyboard input using a program to be written. The UART interface is used to simulate the PS/2 keyboard. In ATmegaRemote the input is done via an on-screen keyboard, the processing is done by the Remote Board and the commands are sent via UART to the EVA Board. The SPI interface communicates with an externally connectable TLCD, see Sect. 4.1.

3.2 Button Board

The EVA Board provides four buttons which are used in the experiments for different input purposes. To be able to offer these buttons in the test pool, several I/O pins of the ATmega2560 are routed over a Darlington Driver IC of the Button Board and made available to the EVA Board as input pins.

3.3 JTAG and Supply Board

In practical operation it was shown that wrong programming of the microcontroller can cause connection problems between the microcontroller, the programming device JTAG ICE and the programming environment Atmel Studio. The viability of the system can at times only be achieved by the disconnection of all power supply poles. In addition, a long service life of the hardware can only be guaranteed if it is disconnected from the power supply when the workstation is not in use. For these reasons several relays are installed on this expansion board, which disconnects the USB voltage from the JTAG ICE, the 5 V as well as the 12 V power supply from the EVA Board, in order to separate the connected EVA Board from all power supply poles. The relays are controlled via a Darlington Driver IC from three digital outputs of the Remote Board and can be controlled via the ATmegaRemote interface of the respective VM. Another relay is used for remote triggering of the reset of the JTAG ICE to solve connection problems to the JTAG. The expansion board also provides the EVA Board with five Analog-to-Digital Converter (ADC) pins. These are looped directly through the ATmega2560 of the Remote Board. Hence, the slot of the JTAG and Supply Board is fixed to slot 1 on the Remote Board. Using these inputs, analog voltage values can be read in during an experiment and displayed via ATmegaRemote as a simulation of a multimeter.

4 Interface

As presented in Sect. 2, students connect to a test station via the Remote Desktop Protocol (RDP). Using RDP enables the students to see the desktop of the connected test station as well as control it by mouse and keyboard input. The test stations have all software installed needed for development, and to program and test software for the target hardware described in Sect. 3. Atmel Studio 7 [6] is used for the development and programming of the microcontroller. The programs developed by the students must change physical states of different connected hardware components like LEDs, an LCD screen or depending on the current experiment even a TLCD. Because of this it is necessary for the students to be able to visually verify these state changes. If for example a certain output on the LCD screen is requested the student must be able to verify the actual output. In addition, physical inputs like buttons connected to the hardware must be controllable by the user. For this the ATmegaRemote software stack and the Remote Board with its own software were developed. An overview of the architecture is shown in Fig. 6.

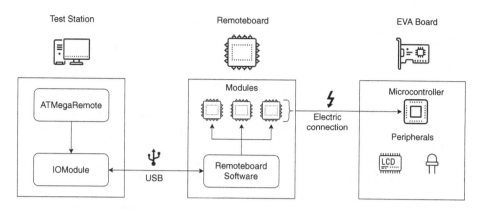

Fig. 6. ATmegaRemote architecture (Icons by https://icons8.com/).

The ATmegaRemote software, further described in Sect. 4.2, is the user interface showing a webcam image of the linked microcontroller and suitable controls for the current experiment and hardware configuration of the test setup. Input by the user is sent to the Remote Board by usage of a library called *IOModule*. The IOModule library communicates with the Remote Board hardware over an USB to UART connection utilizing FTDIs [2]. Communication is full duplex, i.e. both the IOModule and the Remote Board can transmit packages independently at the same time. The following subsections will detail ATmegaRemote as well as the IOModule by presenting their functionality on the example of the TLCD experiment.

4.1   Touchscreen Experiment

One of the experiments for the students involves a touchscreen (TLCD) which is connected as slave to the ATmega via a SPI bus [3]. The SPI bus is used to send image data to the display as well as receive touch data from the display. In addition, a *Sendbuffer Indicator* is connected. This is one pin connection which indicates to the master, in this case the microcontroller, if new touch data is available for collection. One goal of the remote microcontroller test environment is to run the software on real hardware as to eliminate possible errors resulting from simulations. Therefore, an actual TLCD is connected to the ATmega. Because developing and implementing a mechanical finger to operate the screen would be impractical, the touch events are generated by the ATmegaRemote software. As the remote implementation should be indistinguishable for the connected EVA Board the SPI bus needs to be taken over to transmit the touch events. For this purpose, the *Sendbuffer Indicator* is connected directly to the Remote Board. In addition, the three SPI wires are not connected directly to the EVA Board. Instead they are connected to a multiplexer [7]. However, the multiplexer is connected on the one side to the EVA Board and on the other side to the Remote Board. This enables the Remote Board to switch between connecting the TLCD to the EVA Board or to itself while sending simulated touch events.

4.2 ATmegaRemote

As shown in Fig. 7, the ATmegaRemote software presents a webcam view of the EVA Board to the student. The webcam view is overlaid with button graphics over the actual buttons. These can be clicked by the user to simulate a button press. Also shown are buttons to reset the EVA Board as well as zoom controls for the picture. Section 2 described the limited session time which is also displayed by ATmegaRemote. Furthermore, ATmegaRemote can present *Additional controls* depending on the configured experiment for this test station. This includes for example a voltage setting for an external voltage source, controls for a servo actuated RFID tag, and readouts like the current voltage measured by the Remote Board. Also implemented as additional controls is the TLCD, which can be seen in Fig. 7. As the actual screen content is shown on the actual TLCD, only an input area is presented. The user can draw on this area with his mouse. This input is then translated into relative coordinates of the TLCD and then transmitted to the EVA Board by the IOModule.

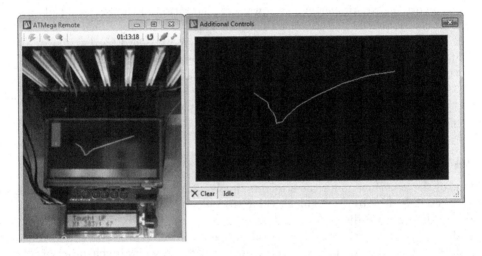

Fig. 7. The ATmegaRemote interface with TLCD controls.

In addition, ATmegaRemote incorporates a settings dialog only accessible by authorized users. The settings dialog is used to configure parameters like which additional controls to present or what part of the webcam's image to show. It also provides functionality to program predefined binaries onto the EVA Board to test and verify its functionality. This is for example used after a hardware fix or reconfiguration at the workshop.

4.3   IOModule

The IOModule library is written in C# and handles all communication with the Remote Board. This includes finding the connected Remote Board and establishing the communication. Further communication tasks like retransmitting lost packages are also automatically handled.

As described in Sect. 3 the Remote Board can be extended with different modules to interface with different parts of the EVA Board. These modules allow the Remote Board to be able to support experiments developed in the future. For every currently developed module the IOModule library provides a class. Creating a new instance of one of the module classes automatically sends initialization messages to the Remote Board. The Remote Board then registers the module on the specified slot and performs necessary initialization for the module. Every module class also provides member functions, which correspond to the functionality provided by the hardware module.

Every information sent is packaged in a *Message*. A Message consists of the following fields:

bool   System Message
byte   Module Index
bool   Answer
bool   Fault
byte   Message ID
byte   Size
byte[]   Data

The *System Message* flag indicates whether the message is intended for a module or for the Remote Board itself. System messages would for example be messages that instruct the microcontroller to reset or add a module to a specified slot. The *Module Index* field is only used if the message is for a specific module. In this case the field holds the slot index of the module as a unique identifier to address it. The slot index is assigned when the module is created and corresponds to the slot on the hardware. The *Answer* flag indicates whether this message is an original message or an answer to a previous message. To provide robust communication with the Remote Board, every Message must be acknowledged by the receiver. For this the original message is copied, the *Answer* field set to true and the *Data* field set to zero. If the message was handled correctly the *Fault* flag is set to false, otherwise to true and then sent back to the sender. To be able to identify messages the *Message ID* field is populated with a unique id for every message. The id is simply generated by counting up. As messages from the IOModule library and the Remote Board can be distinguished simply by who is receiving it, the counters do not need to be synchronized. The *Size* field holds the size of the *Data* field in bytes. Finally the *Data* field holds the payload data for the message. This data depends on the module the message is sent to and every model defines its own protocol for the data. The *DAV6* module class for example provides these methods for the TLCD experiment: TLCD_Activate, TLCD_SendEvent and TLCD_TriggerSend.

The TLCD_SendEvent function is used to simulate a touch event, which is added to a queue on the Remote Board. This queue is sent to the EVA Board by the Remote Board when the TLCD_TriggerSend function is called which sends a corresponding *TriggerSend* message. The TLCD_SendEvent function takes the coordinates of the touch as well as whether it was a touch down or touch up event as arguments and sends this information to the Remote Board. The IOModule library then creates the following message to be sent over USB to the Remote Board:

System Message: false
Module Index: 1
Answer: false
Fault: false
Message ID: 42
Size: 6
Data: [TLCD_SEND_EVENT, true, x, y]

Where TLCD_SEND_EVENT is the constant indicating to the *DAV6* module the kind of message sent, in this case a touch event message. The **true** indicates that this touch event is a down event, i.e. the finger is pressed down. Finally the x and y are the coordinates of the touch event. Each is 2 bytes long which gives the size of 6 bytes as is also indicated in the *Size* field.

4.4   Remote Board Software

The software running on the Remote Board mirrors the communication functionality by the IOModule library. It is implemented in C and therefore does not present the modules as classes. Instead, a struct is defined for every module which holds all necessary information about the state of the corresponding module. All module information structs are kept in a global array so the software can dispatch received messages accordingly. For each module implementation a create, a destroy and a dispatch method is defined. The create method initializes the peripheral, while the destroy method shuts the peripheral down and cleans the state. The dispatch method is called with received messages as argument that are intended for this module.

The Remote Board software initializes the communication automatically and waits for a connection by the IOModule library. It also initializes all common peripherals like the clock and watchdog timers. The watchdog timer ensures the software does not hang by resetting the microcontroller if the timer has not been reset in a defined amount of time. When the software receives an initialization message for a module it creates the corresponding struct. After the struct is created the correct initialization function for the module is called to ensure a defined state. Every module can also define a loop function which is registered in the create function and then continuously run by the software. This is achieved by implementing a scheduler on the Remote Board which in turn runs all loop functions for a defined amount of time before scheduling the next function.

The loop functions are used if the peripheral connected needs ongoing operations to be performed. The TLCD for example defines a loop which sends the current touch event queue received from the IOModule if no further event was received for one second.

In the TLCD example the Remote Board software receives the message sent by the IOModule library. The software first checks the *System Message* flag to determine if the message needs to be handled by itself or by a module. As the message is intended for the *DAV6* module it is dispatched to its dispatch method `dav6_dispatch`. This method inspects the first byte and detects if it is a touch event message in case the first byte has the `TLCD_SEND_EVENT` value. The rest of the payload is then extracted and added to the touch event queue to be sent later to the actual EVA Board. Sending of the queue is triggered either by the timeout in the loop method or by a `TLCD_TRIGGER_SEND` message. The sending process is then automated and performs the following steps:

1. Switch the multiplexer from the TLCD to the Remote Board.
2. Indicate new touch events with the *Sendbuffer Indicator* wire.
3. Respond to communication requests by the EVA Board until the communication is terminated by it.
4. Switch the multiplexer back to the TLCD.

5   Evaluation

The described lab consists of one voluntary and six mandatory experiments. After participating at each experiment the students are encouraged to leave anonymous feedback on our website. That way we can get experiment specific feedback, which helps us to improve each description of the building block of the implemented operating system. Besides, the RWTH Aachen University evaluates each course. We perform this evaluation at the end of the semester with the help of anonymous real-paper survey forms. The survey forms are distributed during one of the last lectures or experiments, respectively. Thus, the participation rate is quite high. In winter term 2018/2019 76.5% (202/264) of the students filled out a form. The overall rating of the lab was 1.7 (where 1 is the best and 5 the worst grade). The free text part of the survey often contained very positive feedback about the remote test environment. Students appreciate the convenience to work from home at any time of the day.

Looking back 10 years, during winter term 2008/2009, when no remote test environment was present, the overall rating of the lab has been 2.7 and the students sometimes mentioned in the comments that on-site consultation hours collided with other courses they had to attend or at other times where overrun by students. Of course, during these 10 years the class material has been improved and several minor changes have been applied. Therefore, the overall increase of the class rating cannot solemnly be attributed to the remote test environment, but the overwhelming positive feedback of the students highly suggests that it had a very positive effect in the students' perception of the lab.

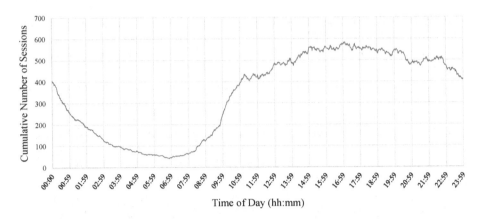

Fig. 8. Cumulative usage of the test environment in winter term 2018/2019.

As described in Sect. 2, the students request a session for a test station and after they are granted one, they are able to connect to the test station for the next two hours. We log these connections to create usage statistics and to plan further extension of the test pool, if necessary. In the 14 weeks of the course during winter term 2018/2019, the 264 participating students requested 8898 sessions, which results in an average of around 34 sessions per student, or roughly one session per student every three days. We identified 227 unique users among the students who requested at least one session, but as two students always work as a team, it is possible that only one login of the team was used to access the test environment. The average and mean length of a session was roughly 55 min and 44 min, respectively. The distribution of the session lengths is U-shaped, with high peaks at both ends. Namely, there were 2586 sessions (29.1%) shorter than 15 min. We expect students to have used these short sessions to flash the microcontroller with their code, run the provided tests, and if necessary, perform a little bit of debugging to narrow down possible errors before they terminated the session, and revised their code locally. This procedure is recommended and highly advised by us as the capacity of the test pool is not sufficient for all students to work online simultaneously. We communicate this fact openly and appeal to fair use, such that every team has the opportunity to test their code on real hardware before the date of their experiment. In addition, we make technical efforts to ensure this by prioritizing session requests from students with the fewest cumulative hours spent connected to the test pool, see Sect. 2.1. Nevertheless, there were also 2372 sessions (26.7%) longer than 1 h and 45 min. Remember, sessions are terminated after two hours, with warnings issued 15 min beforehand, as described in Sect. 2.1. These longer sessions are an indicator for us, that the test pool is not only used for test execution, but also for in depth debugging, and probably as well for implementing some of the required functionalities. These sessions also show, that the test pool must be convenient to use and is highly accepted among students.

The total duration of all sessions was about 8293 h, which corresponds to about 345 and a half days. During on-site consultation one student assistant supervises a maximum of six teams, therefore the usage of the test pool corresponds to around 1382 manpower hours, if realised by on-site consultation. Figure 8 shows the cumulative usage of the remote test environment for each minute of the day. The peak usage was at 17:07 with a cumulative 584 sessions during the 14 week period. This means, that during the 98 days of the course, at 17:07 of each day there were on average six sessions active. The theoretical maximum with the current setup of 26 test stations would be 2548 (26 stations · 14 weeks · 7 days in a week).

6   Conclusion

Laboratory courses in computer science are difficult to scale to large student numbers. We presented a remote microcontroller test environment, which helps to cope with the students' need to test their implementation. In the past, only on-site consultation hours could be offered. However, these are labour intensive and restricted in a timely manner to usual times of the day. Our test pool is accessible around the clock and compared to emulators much less likely to behave differently than the hands-on hardware during the experiment, as identical hardware is used in the test setup.

Students' evaluation with survey forms showed that the rating of the lab improved after the introduction of the test pool. In the free text section of the survey forms it is often mentioned very positively. Additionally, usage statistics is the best indicator that the acceptance of the test pool is remarkably high among students. Around 86% (227/264) of the students used it at least once. With over 345 days of cumulative session duration within a 14 weeks period, the test environment has become an essential part of the lab. Moreover, to enable this amount of testing on-site at least 1382 manpower hours would have been necessary for supervision.

References

1. Deshpande, S.G.: Remote desktop protocol compression system, 30 January 2007. US Patent 7,171,444
2. FTDI: FT230X – full speed USB to basic UART. https://www.ftdichip.com/Products/ICs/FT230X.html. Accessed 12 June 2019
3. Leens, F.: An introduction to I2C and SPI protocols. IEEE Instrum. Measur. Mag. **12**(1), 8–13 (2009). https://doi.org/10.1109/MIM.2009.4762946
4. Lowe-Norris, A.G., Denn, R.: Windows 2000 Active Directory. O'Reilly & Associates Inc., Sebastopol (2000)
5. Microchip Technology: Atmega644. https://www.microchip.com/wwwproducts/en/ATmega644. Accessed 12 June 2019
6. Microchip Technology Inc.: Atmel Studio 7—Microchip Technology (2019). https://www.microchip.com/mplab/avr-support/atmel-studio-7. Accessed 12 June 2019

7. ON Semiconductor: Mc14551b: Quad 2-channel analog multiplexer/demultiplexer. https://www.onsemi.com/pub/Collateral/MC14551B-D.pdf. Accessed 12 June 2019
8. RWTH Aachen University: Studiengangspezifische Prüfungsordnung für den Bachelorstudiengang Informatik der Rheinisch-Westfälischen Technischen Hochschule Aachen. http://www.rwth-aachen.de/global/show_document.asp?id=aaaaaaaaabcejid. Accessed 12 June 2019
9. RWTH Aachen University: Zahlenspiegel (2017). https://www.rwth-aachen.de/global/show_document.asp?id=aaaaaaaaabajkbe. Accessed 12 June 2019
10. Stollenwerk, A., Derks, A., Kowalewski, S., Salewski, F.: A modular, robust and open source microcontroller platform for broad educational usage. In: Proceedings of the 2010 Workshop on Embedded Systems Education, p. 8. ACM (2010)
11. Stollenwerk, A., Jongdee, C., Kowalewski, S.: An undergraduate embedded software laboratory for the masses. In: Proceedings of the 2009 Workshop on Embedded Systems Education, pp. 34–41. ACM (2009)

An Embedded Graduate Lab Course
with Spirit

André Stollenwerk[(✉)]

Informatik 11 – Embedded Software, RWTH Aachen University,
52056 Aachen, Germany
stollenwerk@embedded.rwth-aachen.de

Abstract. In this paper, we give an overview of aspects a graduate lab course should cover for didactic success. As worked example, we present an interdisciplinary lab course for computer scientists and engineers with the goal to automatically controlled distill wine to brandy. We present the developed automation hardware, with respect to the features allowing for a sound lab course performance. We also illustrate the affected organizational structure and the associated blended learning capabilities. These allow for an efficient carrying out of the course. Beyond, we give information on the special boundary conditions from regulatory and safety departmental side for this special example. Yet, the presented work can be used as template for inspiration up to a blueprint when designing a graduate lab course.

Keywords: Embedded systems education · Model-based engineering · Graduate lab course · Blended learning

1 Motivation

During graduate studies at a university, generally spoken lots of theoretical knowledge is imparted. Nevertheless, to a certain degree the practical application of this knowledge is also needed to steady the knowledge. This may be addressed by exercises going along with lectures, but also lab courses, which can easily cover the fields of more than one lecture. Therefore, in computer science and engineering education, we offer lab courses in which the students can work on real-life challenges in a hands-on manner [1]. From our perspective to be fertile, such a course needs to fulfill some basic requirements, which are elaborated in the next paragraph. In the next section, we propose a lab course we implemented fulfilling these needs and give some practical aspects in order to give a best practice template.

Lab courses in embedded systems engineering allow for the reinforcement of already acquired knowledge. However, they should address particular aspects in order to be of didactic value:

© Springer Nature Switzerland AG 2020
R. Chamberlain et al. (Eds.): CyPhy 2019/WESE 2019, LNCS 11971, pp. 247–263, 2020.
https://doi.org/10.1007/978-3-030-41131-2_12

Challenge

In order to motivate students one should keep in mind different facets that should challenge them. The subject of a lab course should allow students to identify themselves with the subject and in addition gain motivation out of it. Each individual student should be able to recognize his individual contribution to the final solution. The general subject should build on existing knowledge, but nevertheless some details of the given task should lead beyond their major field of study.

Creativity

Within a lab course the tutor always has to ponder on the interaction between an easily maintainable course, during which the students execute one explicitly given task after the other and a openly formulated definition of their task which allow for different final solutions. This challenge for the students creativity can result in motivation if periodically achievements can be obtained throughout.

Modularity

The modularity of the given task as well as the tools offered to fulfill the given task is of importance to the didactically success of a lab course. Beside the already mentioned aspect of creativity, furthermore the modularity of a task allows for partitioning of a task and therefore better planning and supervision. Offering a modular choice of tools to achieve the defined goals will allow for new creative solutions to come up. Of course, if speaking of hardware, specific interfaces should be defined in order to allow for quick interconnection and to minimize interconnection issues. These pieces of hardware, which are mostly embedded, need to be robust in everyday usage for the students. Talking of modularity of the given task small sub-tasks enable the individual student to identify with his own contribution to the overall solution of the team. Which goes in hand with the aspect of gaining motivation out of a challenging task.

Results-oriented

The general problem given for a lab course should be addressable in a results-oriented manner. It is crucial for the motivation of the participating students to see first results of their effort already during early stages and continuously throughout the course.

After the elaboration of the above stated aspects for a pedagogic effective lab course, we also kept in mind soft-skills to be made subject of the discussion. First of all, working as a team with the need of communication and a certain level of project management is to be named. Hence, from our point of view an interdisciplinary topic of a lab course should be chosen. In our case of embedded systems education, we wanted to address computer scientists as well as engineers.

2   Automated Control of Distilling Spirit

Like motivated, a graduate lab course should challenge students while offering freedom for creativity. Joining this with the need for a manageable basic complexity, we identified a control problem, being solved by a reactive system to be suitable to impart the envisaged competences for both, computer scientists as well as engineers.

Hence, we developed a lab course in which the students should automate the process of distilling wine into brandy. The very basic setup consists of a heating mantle, the distilling apparatus, some temperature sensors and a weighting scale. We supply the students with a microcontroller-based hardware to interconnect the stated setup. The used microcontroller, an ATmega, is known to all computer science students who did their bachelor at RWTH Aachen University, due to a mandatory lab course in the third bachelor semester. In this third semester course, the students have to implement a basic operating system on an ATmega microcontroller [2]. Besides the existing experience of the students with the device the second asset of the presented setup is the ease of the components which allows the students within some hours of work to see first results in terms of measuring temperatures or controlling the heating up of water.

Generally spoken, the distillation of wine can be automated by the means of e.g. a closed-loop PID controller [3]. This allows an early feeling of success for the students. Nevertheless, more sophisticated control techniques like optimal control (e.g. a model-predictive controller) or intelligent control (e.g. fuzzy logic) have been designed and implemented by the students attending this course.

2.1 Structure of the Lab Course

Students in teams of five people attend the lab course. These teams generally are equally staffed with computer scientists and engineers. Students from the majors electrical engineering or automation engineering to be more specific. The odd number of persons per group allows for compensation if e.g. some of the computer scientists have a minor in engineering or vice-versa.

The lab course starts with an introductory meeting, all participating students of the course need to attend. After this introductory meeting, individual weekly meetings with the teams are arranged. During the introductory meeting, organizational aspects are treated and general questions are discussed. The organizational aspects cover the forming of the teams of 5 students each, explaining the legal context, filling out of the documentation needed for the regulatory restrictions, explaining the given overall time window and giving hints for getting started. The experience over the years showed some aspects need to be explicitly stated, like the need to work in interdisciplinary pairs. During the first weekly meeting, we hand out the available hardware to the students. In general, during the weekly meetings the status with respect to the schedule is reviewed. Furthermore, the recent problems worked on and the next steps are discussed.

There are only very little predefined work packages to the students. One is, for each team, to work out a specific time-plan with a weekly granularity. This helps the students to manage the evolving sub-tasks for the distillation automation and prevents from losing track on progress. Within the teams as a next work package, the students have to assign some specific roles to team members for the course of the semester. This is the appointment of a team leader, a software architect and a systems architect, where each roll has to coordinate its specific field and be a responsible contact to other team members. Especially when decisions have to be made, they are responsible for the coordination. The team leader furthermore has to coordinate the team-internal progress and if necessary the assignment of sub-tasks. Both architect roles are bound by education, software architect to computer science students and systems architect to engineering students. In addition, the team leader owns the work package to prepare a brief written status report prior to the weekly meetings with referencing the time-plan. These kind of organizational structures for the management of a project should also prepare the students for the industrial needs [4]. Despite the already mentioned work packages only two additional ones are defined, all other obligations needed for project progress are self-defined by the teams. Namely one work packages is to elaborate a first brief automation concept, which is refined over the courses of the weekly meetings.

In the end of the semester every team has as their last work package to give a presentation of 5 to 7 min covering either a problem they solved in a very elegant manner from their perspective or a problem which kept them busy for a while. Here the students are explicitly motivated to include fail reports and lessons learned out of errors, in terms of a fail culture.

2.2   Offered Hardware

For the time-span from the first individual team meeting until the end of the semester, we lent the students various hardware in order to enable them to automate the distilling process. In general, this hardware can be clustered in four different classes:

1. Distilling Apparatus (laboratory glassware),
2. Sensors,
3. Actuators and
4. Embedded Hardware for controlling the distillation process,

which will be explained in detail in the following. For all of the described hardware we hold spare parts in case something breaks (especially the glassware). Hence, reordering usually takes some weeks.

Distilling Apparatus. The distilling setup is available in a small and a large size setup. Each team retains an individual small size setup (see Fig. 1a). This shall help them during model design of the distillation process. The large size setup is available only once and hence, intended for shared use (see Fig. 1b). The large size setup is meant for productivity purposes when trying to produce lager volumes of spirit. Speaking in general, both setups consist of comparable elements. Therefore, the findings from the small setup can be transferred to the large setup.

Round-Bottomed Flask
  Both setups comprise of a round-bottomed flask. In case of the small setup the flask has a volume of 500 ml and 10, 000 ml for the large setup respectively.

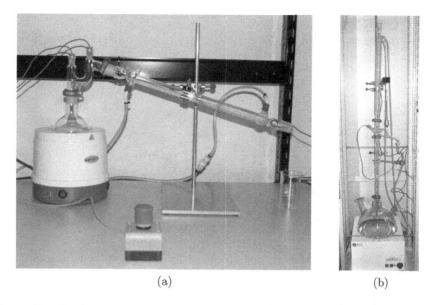

(a)   (b)

Fig. 1. Completely assembled of the 500 ml small size setup (a) and the 10 l large size setup with a Vigreux column (b).

Condenser

In the small setup for condensing the evaporated liquor a Liebig condenser is used. For the large setup we use a Widmer condenser, due to the higher thermal capacity of this layout in order to procure the higher energy supplied to the 10,000 ml round-bottomed flask.

Claisen Tower

In the small setup the connection between the round-bottomed flask and the condenser is done using a Claisen tower.

Reflux Separator

In the large setup the connection between the round-bottomed flask and the condenser is established using a reflux separator (see Fig. 2). The reflux separator introduces a valve to the setup, which enables us to turn off the outflux when the feint would start. The feint contains a higher amount of fusel alcohols and is the part of the outflux following to the actual brandy. Therefore this output of the distillation process is unwanted in the final product.

Rectification Glassware

For rectification within the large setup we offer a Vigreux column and a Hempel column. Rectification means the successive separation in several distillations. Within this columns the evaporated liquor will condense and due to the following vapor getting evaporated again. Yet, this enables multiple distillations in one run/rectification of the educt.

The Hempel column in addition enables to add (essential oils as) flavor carriers to the process. In detail, e.g. parts of a fruit can be added to the steam

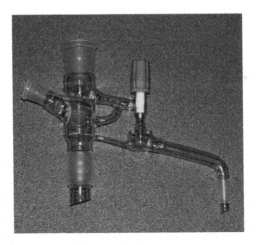

Fig. 2. The reflux separator used for the outflux control of the large setup

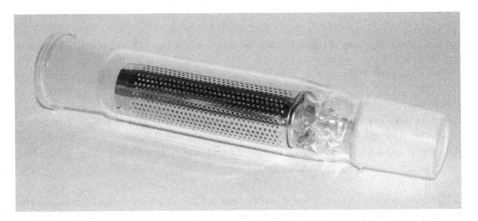

Fig. 3. The smallest size of Hempel column with a stainless steel tea filter for hosting of flavor adding additives

phase, which imprints this flavor to the final product. We are using stainless steel tea filters here to prevent fruits from obstructing the column when getting slushy with the progression of the distillation (see Fig. 3). A whole distillation run on the large setup takes several hours while a distillation on the small setup takes up to one hour including heating up and cooling-down.

Sensors. For the distillation process, the students are offered two different types of sensors:

Temperature Sensors

At different points of the setup the temperature needs to be measured. This is at least at the flask and at directly prior to the condenser. Depending on the implemented algorithm also the ambient temperature is of importance. Therefore, the students get offered four PT1000 (platinum based) temperature sensors, which have a IP68 rating and accordingly are suitable for continuous immersion in a liquid.

Weighting Scale

The outflux of the distilling apparatus is caught in a beaker. To quantize the outflux the students get a scales with a resolution of 0.1 gramms, on which the beaker can be placed. This scales has a serial RS232 interface. Therefore, the readings can be processed electronically and the mass flow can be calculated online.

Actuator. The presented distilling process has two different actuators:

Heating Mantle

With respect to the two different sizes of the round-bottomed flasks (500 ml and 10,000 ml) there are also two different heating mantles with a heating capacity of 250 W and 1,400 W respectively.

Both models of heating mantles were chosen paying attention to not having a thermal control within the mantles itself, since this would be a disturbance for the control the students have to implement. We only were able to find heating mantles that incorporate different duty cycles and two heating zones. The students are elucidated on these settable variables. Usually, these are set both to maximum. For safety reasons in addition, the heating mantles are operated with an incorporated residual-current circuit breaker.

Valve of the Reflux Separator

Like already explained the reflux separator has a valve which can stop the outflux of the distillation process (green cylinder in Fig. 2). This is used to stop the distillation at the transition to the feint. This valve is connected via a flexible extension to a stepper motor. The flexible extension absorbs lateral forces to the valve and hence, prevents the glass from braking. We offer the students off-the-shelf wine from a supermarket. Doing so, we can assure the absence of methanol and hence do not need to separate the very first outflux.

Embedded Hardware. The described sensors and actuators are interconnected via a set of self-designed printed circuit boards (PCBs). These PCBs can be interconnected in a modular way, which offers a wide variety of possible configurations, and therefore empower the students' creativity. The available PCBs are described in the following:

Main Board

The core of the embedded hardware is a main board which holds an ATmega2650 microcontroller (see Fig. 4). On this main board there are four general connection slots which provide each

- Supply Voltage,
- two 10 Bit Analog-to-Digital-Converter Inputs,
- a SPI interface with two Chip-Select Lines,
- one general-purpose Interrupt Line and
- eight general I/O lines.

In addition to these general connection slots there is one slot dedicated for a power board controlling the heating mantle and the stepper motor. Besides the mentioned connection slots, the main board takes care of the power supply for all the hardware and offers two serial interfaces. One RS-232 interface for the interconnection of the scale and one virtual COM-Port based USB connection for data transmission to and configuration from a computer.

Fig. 4. Main Board of the supplied Embedded Hardware with voltage supply, communication interfaces, four general connection slots and an additional slot (5) specially for the power board.

Analog Temperature Board

The analog temperature board connects two PT1000 temperature sensors via a Wheatstone bridge and operational amplifiers for buffering and amplification, of the analog voltage signal, proportional to the temperature, to one of the internal 10 Bit Analog-to-Digital-Converter (ADC) inputs of the microcontroller each. Via some jumpers the students can decide, if they want to use the PT1000 sensors in 2, 3 or 4 wire connection. An other jumper allows for the decision if the signal shall be amplified or the signal from one side of the Wheatstone bridge, which than is a simple voltage divider, shall be directly connected to the ADC input.

Digital Temperature Board

The digital temperature board holds a dedicated Analog-to-Digital-Converter Chip (AD7792), which is connected via the SPI interface to the microcontroller. This chip has a resolution of 16 Bit, three input channels, noise filtering (50/60 Hz rejection) and a current source. The current source enables for direct resulting voltage measurement. We use two of the input channels for the measurement of two PT1000 temperature sensors, respectively. The third available channel is used to measure a reference resistor with a very high accuracy to be able to eliminate measurement noise. At the digital temperature board, again, the students can configure via jumpers, if they want to use the PT1000 sensors in 2, 3 or 4 wire connection. Additionally, the measurement of only one temperature sensor can be configured via a jumper.

Display with Connection Board

Coming along as two boards, we have a converter board fitting in the general connection slots, which is translating the SPI bus to a low voltage differential signaling (LVDS) interface and a compatible LED Display board. The translation to LVDS was introduced due to the first experiences with the SPI interface in conjunction with the electromagnetic induction during the switching of the heating mantle to a cable carrying the SPI signal. Here we are now using CAT 5 Ethernet cables. This interface is connected to a second PCB which holds 16 seven-segment-display digits. These LEDs are driven by a MAX7221CWG chip. On this PCB the LVDS is converted to SPI again. Furthermore, this board also has two buttons which can be used as general purpose user interface.

Power-Board

The power board holds besides the stepper motor drivers and the control connection for a switching power socket a safety circuit (which is explained in more detail in the next sub-section). The switching power socket is controlled via a 5 V signal, which is the logical *and* conjunction in hardware of a GPIO pin of the microcontroller and the result of the safety circuit.

Aluminum Housings at Distilling Apparatuses

Each student team (consisting of 5 persons) receives at the beginning of the semester a hardware set consisting of

- one main board,
- two analog temperature boards,
- two digital temperature boards,
- four temperature sensors,
- one display board and one SPI-LVDS adapter,
- one power board,
- one heating mantle,
- one switching power socket,
- one 500 ml round-bottomed flask and
- one Claisen tower.

This hardware is handed out as bare printed circuits boards. For the three above mentioned dedicated productive distilling spaces for a big volume setup and twice a small volume setup all the PCBs have an aluminum housing (see Fig. 5). This is done on the one hand to enhance robustness due to the fact that the students are working with a liquid and on the other hand for shielding with respect to electromagnetic induction. Furthermore, to the list of hardware, which is handed to each student's team, mentioned before, at the productive distilling spaces the parts which are still missing, but already described, are made available to the students. Which are in detail

- different kinds of rectification glassware,
- a condenser,
- a reflux separator at the big volume setup,
- a scales and
- a stepper-motor to control the valve of the reflux separator,
- some safety sensors which are given in detail in the next sub-section.

Fig. 5. Aluminum housings used at the distilling apparatuses equiped with two temperature boards, two vacant general connections slots and the power board.

Additional Debugging Hardware

Besides all the described hardware, we also offer some dummy temperature sensors. The students can configure them with a jumper to a defined resistance and hence simulate a temperature sensor at a specific temperature. This is very helpful for debugging. As last to mention PCB we offer a test board. This board can be inserted in one of the general connection slots and sends out defined patterns at all connection pins in a high frequency. Moreover, the ADC inputs are also assigned with different analog voltages throughout the whole voltage-range of the setup (i.e. 0; 1.25; 2.5; 3.75; 5 V). This board in combination with a software we provide to the students, helps for finding hardware issues like bad solder joints, short circuits or lost contacts. The experience over the different runs of the course showed that these kinds of hardware errors happen every now and then if the students are working with the PCBs all the time.

Safety Related Aspects of the Hardware. When preparing this lab course we had several discussions with the safety department of the university. This resulted in some general rules, the students have to comply with some constructive and electric safety measures. From the constructive point, we introduced a safety screen in front of the distilling apparatus. In addition, we needed to assure the cooling water circuit having a sufficient throughput and hence the evaporated liquor being adequate cooled, when heating the distilling apparatus. Therefore, like already introduced, the power board comprises a dedicated safety circuit. The safety circuit supervises

- a mushroom emergency stop button,
- a flow sensor on the return line of the cooling circuit,
- a temperature sensor supervising the temperature of the outflux and therefore double-checking on correct cooling and
- a microswitch supervising if the additional safety screen is installed.

If and only if all of the above-mentioned measures hold the switching power socket can conduct energy to the heating mantle. For the stepper motor only the emergency stop button is considered. Finally, the result of the safety circuit is given back to the microcontroller for information purposes. Here a diode prevents the microcontroller from being able to override this safety signal by misconfiguration. The used flow sensor emits impulses for a specific volume of measured water. Hence, to guarantee a specific cooling we need a minimal number of impulses per time-interval. To supervise this signal we used a modified NE555 based monostable multivibrator, which requires the user to manually press a button to enable the measurement. This prevents from unwanted heating. Once the cooling water flow was too low and this deficiency was fixed the user needs to press the button again.

2.3   Regulatory Affairs

In Germany, the distilling of spirits is subject to the supervision of the customs office [5]. Therefore, each semester the course is offered, first of all we need to apply for a certificate of exemption. In addition, every time wine shall be distilled into liquor the appointment has to be notified to the customs office 14 days in advance. All distilling actions need to be documented and all distilling results need to be stored in appropriate containers. Some kind of plastics can be dissolved by ethanol and are therefore not suitable for holding liquor.

For the collecting of brandy, one room at our university was declared as a customs quarantine store [6]. At this store, we are allowed to produce and keep untaxed liquor. If we want to withdraw some of the liquor out of the quarantine store, we have to announce this to the customs office and pay the taxes before doing so.

We are subject to unannounced checks by the customs surveillance unit throughout the whole semester.

3   Blended Learning Aspects

The theoretical parts of the presented lab course are organized in a flipped classroom way. There are different videos with a duration of 5 to 14 min each [7]. The students get communicated different milestones until which a specific set of videos need to be watched and understood. These milestones are:

– the introductory meeting,
– the first individual meeting,
– the individual meeting prior to the first time distilling on the small setup and
– the individual meeting prior to the first time distilling on the big setup.

During the mentioned respective meetings, possible questions are clarified and the resulting next steps for the further approach are discussed. The flipped classroom format allows the students for a straightforward repetition of specific topics in an independent and individual manner. One of the benefits of a practical lab course, the practical application of theoretical knowledge, goes in hand with the drawback, that sometimes one recognizes not having understood the theory in the moment when trying to apply it. Here the students have the chance to watch the according parts of the videos again. Breaking the whole theory in small chunks of less than 15 min allows for having the full attention, when watching these videos. In general, the videos for the lab course cover the following topics in one or several videos for each topic:

– regulatory affairs,
– organizational aspects,
– the general distillation process,
– the provided distillation apparatuses,
– safety measures,
– the supplied embedded hardware,
– measurement of the brandy for the documentation,
– known problems,
– hints on the quality of distilled brandy,
– basic control theory: the design and configuration of a controller and
– basics on embedded software engineering.

In addition to these videos the students are granted access to an additional set of ten videos produced for a lecture on basic control engineering aspects for computer science students. The first run of this course showed these additional optional videos to be very fruitful for the interdisciplinary communication. In this additional set of videos basic aspects on modeling, parameterization of a model and the design of a basic PID-controller is given.

4   Control Engineering Aspects

The distillation of wine can be treated with a very basic control approach, in first instance. One has to heat up the wine until the wine starts boiling. After this point, only a very reduced amount of energy needs to be fed to the system to receive a slightly decreasing outflux as a quite fair result. This enables the students to archive at a very early stage first positive results. Nevertheless, all phases of the distillation can be improved to a far more sophisticated way.

The heating up process can be optimized for fast heating without an overshoot. Here a well parameterized model with an e.g. PI-controller works fine. For the distillation process itself, we have to have a slightly deeper look at the process.

During the distillation the concentration of alcohol in the round-bottomed flask continuously decreases, which results in an increasing temperature at the round-bottomed flask, if the mixture is still distilled. Figure 6 shows the boiling-point diagram for the intermixture of water and ethanol. The lower curve describes the boiling properties. With decreasing ethanol the temperature increases in a non-linear manner. Hence, more energy is needed to keep this temperature. Furthermore, water has a way higher evaporation enthalpy than ethanol. Thus, the feed energy needs to be increased over the course of the distillation process, if the outflux shall be constant. A constant outflux is stated as overall optimization goal in literature [8].

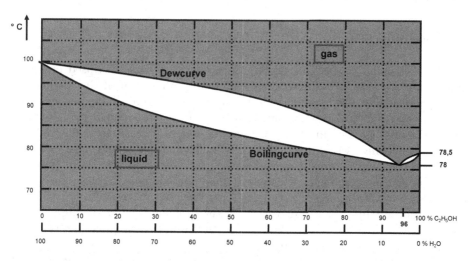

Fig. 6. Dew-Boiling-Diagram of an ethanol water intermixture with the vapor–liquid equilibrium at 95.6% ethanol (modified from [9]).

There are different time delays and dead times to be dealt with: From the heating mantle as only process-controlling actuator to the different temperature sensors and the scales.

So far, the different teams of students came up with distinctly varying solutions to control the distilling process. This was enabled by the modular setup of the hardware and the very open formulated definition of the lab courses goal. Besides the very basic solution of a PI-Controller, we have seen Smith Predictors to overcome some of the time constants, different implementations of a fuzzy control and various implementations of physically motivated model based control algorithms. Mostly in a gray box manner.

There was e.g. a particle simulation, in which a process model and the current status was used to simulate the outcome of the next time-step. The simulation results were afterwards used to find the set-values for the next time-step. In another approach, the students parameterized a look-up-table which was used to run and supervise the distillation process. The supervision included a possible recalculation of the look-up-table, if the systems behavior deviated too much from the model.

Finally, there was also one team with a not very embedded solution: Since the distillation process itself is very slow (the set value of the heating mantle is usually changed in the dimension of one change per minute), the hard real-time constraints to be fulfilled are in the same dimension of at least some seconds. Therefore, a communication with a Windows-based PC was established, which feed a artificial intelligence algorithm to find an optimal solution with the help of a neuronal network on a high performance computing cluster the university offers to the students. Nevertheless, this exhibits again the individual creativity on the student's side.

5 Evaluation

The presented lab course was offered three times up to now. Based on these experiences we also introduced some evolution in the setup of the distillation apparatus and the hardware that is given at the disposal of the students. In detail we faced several times issues resulting out of electromagnetic induction when switching the heating mantle. Hence e.g. the LVDS transceivers and the aluminum housings were introduced. The additional debugging hardware was developed a year ago, since we experienced students spending lots of development time put into problems, which were finally based on broken hardware. The debugging hardware offers the students some efficient tools to identify hardware errors. Additionally they can determine, if the problem they are facing is based on their software or the provided hardware. In this paper, we presented the final version of the setup and the hardware.

The proposed video-based blended learning aspects within the course not only allow the students for a re-view of the applicable video prior to specific actions like starting to work with a specific piece hardware or the first distillation on the small or large setup, respectively. In addition, this also reduces supervision effort. In the first year, prior to having videos, the tutors were experiencing to explain nearly all major relations at least twice to each team. Now, in general they only need to talk about specific questions which may have come up while watching the videos. Up to now in the beginning of each semester the course was offered in, we updated some of the videos, but not all, based on the questions which came up in the previous run of the course. In general the needed effort in average is about an hour per team and per week. Of course, this is varying over the semester. e.g. when the students are working the first time with new hardware or start distilling there are more questions, which result in a higher demand of supervision than in the other weeks.

The introduced setup was chosen with respect to allow for a maximum in modularity. Furthermore, the conceptual formulation of the overall task was intentionally done in an ambiguous way. Like explained before, this leads to a wide variety of different solving strategies. Hence, the students felt challenged in developing a solution, which reflects their knowledge and puts this into effect. Besides the already depicted creativity with respect to the control strategy we also have to mention efforts like the development of a droplet counter or various aspects of additional human-machine-interfaces and cloud-based control apps, which we saw over the years. These are again explicit results of the encouraged creativity of the students.

Though first achievements can be gained in a very early stage of the semester the problem of automatically distilling wine has many facets such that the lab course is challenging over the whole coarse of the semester. Besides all the knowledge-based experiences, the students also gain soft-skills throughout this lab course. To solve the given problem in an adequate manner they need to work in interdisciplinary teams. This is one of the aspects explained to the students within the introductory meeting. Yet, regularly some teams at some point in the semester report on trying to work solitary. This usually resulted in a way higher time consumption for the addressed sub-task or even failing in solving the sub-task. The participating students regularly point out project management and interdisciplinary cooperation as some of the gained key competences during the presentations in the end of the semester or the subsequent discussion.

Obviously, there is a risk of having the students copy the code of some last years class fellow students. However, this did not really happen. On the one hand all different majors of students in the course are not familiar with the details about the distillation process. Hence they need to familiarize themselves with distilling as process, which is the real effort. The other way round, when copying over they would not be able to explain their approach. On the other hand, during the intense weekly discussions the students also have to explain details of their solution. Therefore a copy-over of previous solutions could not be experienced. Since this a masters course we explicitly do not put any effort in plagiarism identification, which would be possible though [10].

5.1 Survey

At our university, we evaluate every course with a survey based on a fixed questionnaire within the semester. The questions are predefined on basis of the type of the course (here lab course). Therefore, not all of the results are given here, only the relevant ones. Over the three runs of the lab course 73 out of 90 students participated in the surveys. The evaluation surveys are conducted in an unsolicitous and anonymous way.

The *practical concept* was evaluated a mean 1.3 over the three runs of the course, where 1 is "very good" and 5 is "poor". The average over all lab courses of the department was 1.6.

The mean answer to the question *I find the course interesting* was answered a mean 1.29 with a department's mean of 1.7, where 1 is "strongly agree" and 5 is "strongly disagree". The question *The trials improve my experimental skills* had a mean answer of 1.26 with an overall department's mean of 1.7 and the same scale as before. Stated on the hardware the statement *The materials provided are helpful* was evaluated a 1.4 with a department's average of 1.8. The second statement in the section hardware, *There is enough equipment available*, scored a 1.4 with a department's mean of 1.6.

All but one student perceived the group size as appropriate. The one student would have favored smaller groups. The majority of the students, with 25.9%, state that they invest 3–5 h per week to the lab course. The other classes in this assessment were assigned: 1–3 h per week with 10.0%, 5–7 h per week with 20.1%, 7–3 h per week with 24.2% and more than 9 h per week with 19.8%.

In addition to the given questions there were comment boxes. These comments were not always filled in. However, we summarize some of the main statements. Mostly the students appreciated the offered autonomy towards the given implementation tasks they needed to do. The blended learning concept allowed the students for a very independent time management. Due to the special kind of project, they on the one hand have to work together in an interdisciplinary way, which was often gratefully appreciated at the end of the course, on the other hand they were able to gain applied insights to many project management aspects. Finally, the students regularly mentioned the practical *relevance* of the course.

Yet, with the presented lab course, we did not only receive very good evaluation results, but were also in all points significantly better than the department's average.

These good evaluation results lead to the point that the presented lab course was nominated and obtained the teaching award of the computer science department of RWTH Aachen University in 2018 with the inscription "dedicated to the lab course *automation of a distillation plant* which connects the application of embedded systems and control theory with an enthusiastic spirit". This prize is awarded once a year for a single course.

6   Conclusion

In this work, we stated general requirements to an embedded systems lab course and presented a concept for a lab course to apply the knowledge gained in control and embedded software engineering lectures in an interdisciplinary way. The worked example was the automation of distilling wine into brandy. Besides the theoretical demand, we also examined on the practical aspects of the realization. This gives a blueprint for the development of comparable interdisciplinary masters' lab courses. We put an emphasis on the autonomy-enabled creativity of the students participating in the lab course.

In particular, we also put emphasis on the specific characteristics of the automation of distilling brandy, which results in a template for an instantiation at other universities. Besides commenting on the organizational structure and the features of the elaborated circuits, we also commented on the regulatory affairs applying for us (in Germany) and gave best practice for the cooperation's results with the safety department.

In the evaluation, the course proved to be outstanding with respect to other lab courses in our department. The concept of the lab course was therefore awarded the teaching award of the department computer science of RWTH Aachen University.

References

1. Wade, J., Cohen, R., Blackburn, M., Hole, E., Bowen, N.: Systems engineering of cyber-physical systems education program. In: Workshop on Embedded Systems Education, WESE 2015, Amsterdam, Netherlands, pp. 0–7. ACM, New York (2018). https://doi.org/10.1145/2832920.2832927
2. Stollenwerk, A., Jongdee, C., Kowalewski, S.: An undergraduate embedded software laboratory for the masses. In: Workshop on Embedded Systems Education, WESE 2009, Grenoble, France, pp. 34–41. ACM, New York (2009). https://doi.org/10.1145/1719010.1719017
3. Wescott, T.: Applied Control Theory for Embedded Systems. Elsevier, Amsterdam (2011)
4. Törngren, M., Herzog, E.: Towards integration of CPS and systems engineering in education. In: Workshop on Embedded Systems Education, WESE 2016, Pittsburgh, Pennsylvania, USA, pp. 6:1–6:5. ACM, New York (2016). https://doi.org/10.1145/3005329.3005335
5. Malle, B., Schmickl, H.: Schnapsbrennen als Hobby. Verlag Die Werkstatt, Rastede, Germany (2016). ISBN 978-3895334115
6. European Parliament and Council Regulation: the Union Customs Code, No. 952/2013
7. Velegolt, S., Zappe, S., Mahoney, E.: The evolution of a flipped classroom: evidence-based recommendations. Adv. Eng. Educ. 4(3), 1–37 (2015)
8. Yorke, C.: Home Distilling Handbook. Mason Creek Publishing, La Center (2017). ISBN 978-1978458109
9. Chemie Uni Münster. https://bit.ly/2TsCGw1. Accessed 12 Aug 2019
10. Prechelt, L., Malpohl, G., Philippsen, M.: Finding plagiarisms among a set of programs with JPlag. J. UCS 8(11), 1016 (2002)

Competence Networks in the Era of CPS – Lessons Learnt in the ICES Cross-Disciplinary and Multi-domain Center

Martin Törngren[1(✉)], Fredrik Asplund[1], Tor Ericson[2],
Catrin Granbom[3], Erik Herzog[4], Zhonghai Lu[1], Mats Magnusson[1],
Maria Månsson[5], Stefan Norrwing[1,5], Johanna Olsson[1],
and Johnny Öberg[1]

[1] KTH Royal Institute of Technology, 100 44 Stockholm, Sweden
martint@kth.se
[2] ÅF Digital Solutions AB, 169 99 Stockholm, Sweden
[3] Ericsson AB, Torshamnsg. 21-23, 164 80 Stockholm, Sweden
[4] Saab Aeronautics, 581 88 Linköping, Sweden
[5] Prevas AB, 12030 Stockholm, Sweden

Abstract. Cyber-Physical Systems (CPS) are evolving to become more intelligent, autonomous and collaborating, playing an important role in societal infrastructure. The amount of knowledge required in developing and managing future CPS will be unprecedented, leading to stronger needs for collaboration, competence provisioning, continuous learning and renewal of education. This is where "competence" (or learning) "networks" involving academia and industry play an important role. We elaborate and discuss needs, lessons learnt and challenges for such competence networks in the context of CPS. We draw upon our experiences gained from ICES - the KTH-industry cross-disciplinary and multi-domain competence network which in 2019 has been operational for 11 years, growing from 6 to more than 30 participating organizations. The ICES network focuses on activities to support students, industrial engineers and managers, and academic faculty, acting as a network, catalyst and competence provider directed towards these stakeholders. We elaborate challenges faced during the operation of ICES including the lack of prioritization of competence networks and education, the paradox with strong needs for competence networks but perceived lack of time, the challenges of reaching out to stakeholders, and fragmented efforts addressing competence provisioning. We finally discuss ways forward. In conclusion, we believe that the ICES type of network could be relevant in many other areas characterized by complex systems.

Keywords: Cyber-Physical Systems · Embedded systems · Competence networks · Learning networks · Industry-academia collaboration · Engineering education · Technological paradigm shifts · Life-long learning · Science outreach

© Springer Nature Switzerland AG 2020
R. Chamberlain et al. (Eds.): CyPhy 2019/WESE 2019, LNCS 11971, pp. 264–283, 2020.
https://doi.org/10.1007/978-3-030-41131-2_13

1 Introduction and Motivation

Enabled by continued technological advances, Cyber-Physical Systems (CPS) are evolving to become more intelligent, autonomous and interconnected, and with an increasing collaboration with other systems. As a result, CPS are being (and will be) deployed in all kinds of applications in society, playing an important role in societal infrastructure. These trends represent what many see as a socio-technical paradigm shift in which present engineering methodologies and legal frameworks will have to change to accommodate for the new systems built. And paradigm shifts do take time [30]! A typical example is that of intelligent transportation systems involving highly automated vehicles. For such systems, neither engineering methodologies to ensure safety and availability, nor societal frameworks (e.g. for liability, homologation and insurances) are in place. New ground has to be broken [1, 2].

The corresponding capabilities and complexity of future CPS will generally demand much more from various stakeholders, in particular concerning CPS development, operational management and maintenance. This will involve more and more experts and knowledge. Even large organizations will face challenges in incorporating all expertise needed, implying that the CPS supply chain and usage will evolve further towards sophisticated networks of collaborating organizations, ranging from customers to CPS component manufacturers.

The engineering of CPS has always been a multidisciplinary endeavor. However, there is a growing scope of concerns that needs to be addressed, such as sustainability, complex unstructured environments, technological content (e.g. AI and cloud connectivity), systems of systems collaboration, system change (due to updates and learning), and new and changing risks (e.g. cyber-security, safety and privacy concerns).

These new trends, supply chains and concerns, paired with a faster development speed, result in a situation in which competence provisioning and life-long learning for organizations working with and using CPS becomes crucial. The need for what we refer to as competence or learning networks is therefore growing. With a competence network, we refer primarily to non-profit collaborations to promote learning and knowledge creation. While the concept of a competence network is general, we use it here in the specific context of the engineering of CPS and related education and research.

We elaborate and discuss needs, lessons learnt and challenges for such competence networks in the context of embedded and cyber-physical systems. We draw upon our experiences gained from ICES (*Innovative Center for Embedded Systems*) - the KTH-industry cross-disciplinary and multi-domain competence network. In 2019 ICES has been operational for 11 years, and has during this period grown from 6 to more than 30 participating organizations [3, 4]. The ICES network focuses on activities to support students, industrial engineers, managers, and academic faculty as key stakeholders. The network further has a focus on shared concerns among members across industrial domains – it acts as a network, catalyst and competence provider directed towards the key stakeholders, while collaborating with other networks.

The paper is organized as follows. In Sect. 2 we briefly review the state of the art on competence networks and other initiatives with a flavor of "competence network". In Sect. 3 we describe the ICES competence network and its developed practices. In Sect. 4 we highlight lessons learnt, aspects that we believe are important in organizing and operating competence networks. We correspondingly then in Sect. 5 turn to challenges that we have identified over the years – issues that need to be handled and overcome for a competence network to function. In Sect. 6 we discuss the findings and their potential generalization - the relevance of the identified lessons learnt and challenges in other settings. Finally, in Sect. 7, we present conclusions and ways forward.

2 State of the Art and Other Networks

In this section we first describe research that relates to competence and learning networks. We then briefly outline a number of existing initiatives with some ingredients of competence provisioning.

2.1 Competence Networks: State of the Art

There is no extensive discourse on competence networks, or non-profit collaborations to promote learning, per se. However, there exists a wider discussion on (public-private) networks and the future of engineering education.

As knowledge can be seen as a resource that enables firms to stay competitive [15], network cooperation can be seen as beneficial by generating complementarities and inter-firm learning [16, 17]. It is typically also an efficient way to share knowledge as the associated breadth of competencies can be exploited over a long time period. In regard to different types of networks those that contain both industry and academia are often of special interest, as firms can use them to access new technology and specialized consultancy [18]. However, academic institutions can also benefit from such networks when covering the whole state of the art of a topic area is beyond any single institute – they allow academics to identify important topics [19], and to understand exploitation better [20].

As far as the state of the art is concerned there is thus a heavy emphasis on studies concerning knowledge transfer from, or services provided by, academia to industry. The implications of this relationship on academia as a whole has not received as much attention.

However, these interactions are not effortless. Organizations do not have an easy time engaging with organizations that are not similar to them due to difficulties to identify and absorb knowledge that is different from their own [21]. This is by necessity the case for academic institutions and firms. At the same time, firms typically do not get as much value capture (in terms of innovations, as represented by e.g. patents) from cooperation with academia when they also invest heavily in internal scientific research [22, 23]. Academic institutions are similarly negatively affected – the broader a university's collaboration breadth, the more negative increasing cooperation with industry reflects on academic innovation [20].

The cost of engaging in a competence network might thus be considerable, while potentially neither resulting in a direct monetary benefit to industry nor academia. However, if a firm and academic institute are indeed closely aligned, the former's recruitment of employees should regardless benefit from a close cooperation.

On that note engineering programs are currently tasked with fostering new skills, such as cultural awareness, sustainability, innovativeness, entrepreneurship, etc. [24]. This is driven by demand from firms and the opening up of new career paths [25]. However, with engineering curricula already stretched to their limits, the introduction of new content is difficult. Both new teaching practices and learning environments have been suggested as solutions to this dilemma [24]. However, while teachers in higher education might not be outright dismissive of these suggestions, they often have a blind spot in regard to them. This is unfortunate, as new learning environments can lend themselves naturally to new pedagogies. A solution to this problem might be an increased societal support for lifelong learning, where the professional environment of learners can be matched to new learning approaches.

The challenges of creating viable lifelong learning opportunities will still be significant [25]. However, even if firms do not see direct payback in the form of innovative products from their cooperation with academia, they could thus benefit from forming alliances to coordinate lifelong learning. If they can match their specific internal context to the right pedagogies, then they could ensure that new employees had a natural way of progressing from novice to the type of expert they need.

Furthermore, curricula are affected by occurrences at the societal level [26]. Downey and Lucena for instance mention the active push by engineering reformers in the US to increase the importance of scientific skills in engineering education following the Sputnik incident [27]. This revamping of US engineering education was at least partly to maintain the status of engineering. The emergence of the European Higher Education Area (EHEA) also strongly emphasized supporting peaceful interaction between societies, democracy building and academic freedom [28]. It was stressed that education should not be considered merely a servant to the purposes of political or economic power. This perspective was challenged during the end of the 1980's when the cooperation between European universities was being framed as vocational training. This prompted the signing of the Magna Charta Universitatum by heads of universities from all over Europe and beyond [29].

Clearly the business needs of engineering firms can be both synergetic and in opposition to the wider role of academia. Competence networks could be a more neutral type of cooperation than those focused strongly on value capture, functioning as so called communities of practice, see e.g. [33, 34]. This could allow industry and academia to achieve a mutual understanding of each other's motivations more easily.

Research centers can also act as competence networks as described in the Berkeley research center experience, highlighting success stories from several research centers with success factors including multidisciplinary (and regionally local) collaboration involving demonstrators [32].

2.2   Other Related Initiatives/Networks

The need for sharing and improving competence is acknowledged and supported by many organizations. In the scope of CPS, we have identified several types of initiatives. The list is not intended to be exhaustive, but to provide representative examples in an attempt to relate ICES to other efforts.

A distinguishing characteristic of ICES in relation to the listed initiatives is that both engineering and PhD students are found among ICES' stakeholders. This enriches the interactions with the other groups of stakeholders. Most of the other efforts focus on engineers and/or faculty. ICES is also characterized by its regional scope and by being based at a University.

We identified the following types of initiatives, here characterized in terms of primary stakeholders, activities and scope:

- Academic disciplinary communities, for example represented by ESWeek and CPSWeek:
  - Primary stakeholders: Academic faculty
  - Activities: Academic conferences
  - Scope: Worldwide
- Communities for open source software and software forums:
  - Primary stakeholders: Practicing engineers
  - Activities: Shared software and discussions hosted by IT platforms.
  - Scope: Worldwide
- Social and networks, e.g. Linkedin and Meetup:
  - Primary stakeholders: Anyone
  - Activities: Dialogues and information sharing hosted by IT-platforms.
  - Scope: Worldwide
- Professional associations, e.g. INCOSE and IEEE:
  - Primary stakeholders: Association members, typically including industry and academia.
  - Activities: Workshops, meetings, roadmapping and project funding (e.g. Artemis-IA/ECSEL).
  - Scope: Depends on the scope of the association, e.g. worldwide or Europe.
- Company internal competence networks:
  - Primary stakeholders: Company employees
  - Activities: Courses, workshops and demonstrator projects.
  - Scope: Organization (e.g. company)
- Innovation activities such as EC funded projects, training networks and strategic innovation programs:
  - Primary stakeholders: SMEs, innovators, innovation hubs, academia and industry.
  - Activities: Innovation projects (acting as "program offices" for setting up projects) and "Innovative Training Networks" (a type of EU funded project that funds PhD students in multiple countries, involving academia and industry collaboration as well as mobility).
  - Scope: According to program/project scope.

- Networks of excellence (e.g. those previously funded by the EU):
  - Primary stakeholders: Academic faculty
  - Activities: Workshops, conferences, roadmaps and information provisioning.
  - Scope: The network and affiliated partners.
- Traditional research centers hosted by universities:
  - Primary stakeholders: Academic faculty and industrial partners (if any).
  - Activities: Research projects and workshops.
  - Scope: According to center scope.
- Educational initiatives such as Udacity, and EdX:
  - Primary stakeholders: Anyone (e.g. students and practicing engineers)
  - Activities: Online courses
  - Scope: Global

3 The ICES Competence Network

In 2006 discussions to improve collaboration in the area of embedded systems started within the KTH faculty. Fragmentation was identified during these discussions, in particular in terms of non-collaborating research groups (see Fig. 1) with piecewise contacts to industry in different industrial domains. There was no focused embedded systems program and industry seeking contact with experts had problems finding their way into KTH.

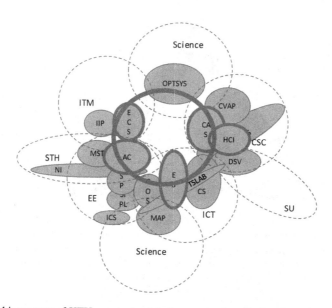

Fig. 1. Initial inventory of KTH groups (and their organizational belonging - the acronyms refer to schools/departments/divisions at KTH in 2008), working with some aspects of embedded systems – illustrating the fragmented situation before ICES.

Key Stakeholders and Role of the Network: In discussions involving industry, the suggested solution was to gather resources from all relevant areas in KTH and companies with an interest in research and education in the area of embedded systems as a KTH center. At KTH, a "center" is an entity typically used to cater for cross-school collaboration that also involves external organizations. When ICES was created, the needs and concerns of the various partners and research groups were elicited. This resulted in the realization that while faculty wanted to do research, the industrial partners stated clearly that their main problem was in competence provisioning in a broad sense. They wanted to recruit students, and get access to KTH faculty. As a result, the center was formed as a "competence network", with the purpose to create a platform for contacts among faculty, students and industry. This would allow for exchanging experiences, agreeing on challenges and developing cooperation projects to influence research and education. The key stakeholders of ICES and their identified concerns are shown in Fig. 2.

Thematic Focus and Goals: The need to understand what the various organizations and researchers considered as relevant topics in the scope of embedded systems surfaced early. After multiple workshops, a view of shared concerns for embedded systems was created. This view has since then been revised and updated, with the current state illustrated in Fig. 3. Only minor Changes had to be made during the updates. The changes included introducing more industrial domains (as represented by the larger set of member companies) and a larger thematic scope (from embedded systems to encompassing software-intensive CPS). Within this scope, the guiding vision of ICES is to *achieve a prospering eco-system for industry and academia, catalyzing world-class education, research and innovation.*

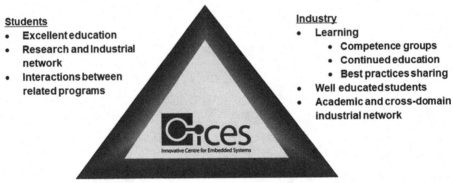

Students
- **Excellent education**
- **Research and Industrial network**
- **Interactions between related programs**

Industry
- **Learning**
  - **Competence groups**
  - **Continued education**
  - **Best practices sharing**
- **Well educated students**
- **Academic and cross-domain industrial network**

Academia:
- **Knowledge and insight in state of the art industrial challenges**
- **Supporting educational improvement and renewal**
- **Opportunities for forming research projects and their funding**
- **Multidisciplinary research and industrial network, Impact in society**

Fig. 2. ICES key stakeholders and their needs

The Vision and Goals document has been revised several times over the years [4]. It forms an important element of the network. The document describes the long- and short-term goals of ICES, including vision, strategic objectives and operational goals. The strategic objectives include (i) a focus on key concerns that are shared among members across industrial domains (recall Fig. 3), (ii) acting as a network, catalyst and competence provider directed towards the key stakeholders of the center (recall Fig. 2), and (iii) creating synergies and leveraging existing efforts, including with related KTH research centers and other organizations.

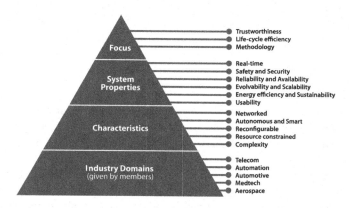

Fig. 3. Thematic focus of the ICES competence network

Operational goals and KPIs have been defined within the areas that correspond to the workgroups based on these strategic objectives [4].

Network Evolution and Management. The network was officially inaugurated on September the 1st, 2008, with KTH, ABB, ÅF, Ericsson, Enea, Scania, and Stoneridge as initial members.

During its 10 years of operation, the ICES center has grown, and now has more than 30 companies as members. It has a track-record of actually "improving the lives" for its stakeholders. As a KTH center, ICES has a board, a director, a co-director and an administrator. Student representatives (from selected, relevant KTH programs) are part of the board to strengthen the bi-directional interactions with students (student representation is quite common at KTH, but this case is special with its connections to multiple programs). The center is funded by the members (roughly 50% of the turnover), innovation project funding (roughly 25%), and by KTH (roughly 25%). The turnover is in the order of 200 kEUR, which is used to fund the ICES office (roughly one FTE) and ICES events. The actual turnover is much larger considering the in-kind efforts, which are at least in the same order of magnitude as the direct funding. Moreover, there is value created by catalyzed spin-off research projects, improvements in education, and other secondary effects caused by the networking.

ICES distributes a newsletter to some 1500 receivers and arranges a number of events each year. Most events are open. Some are free and some have a differentiated fee (with rebate for members). Generally, the fees are low and only covers the cost of the events.

The Competence and Work Groups. A central part of the network is the industrial competence groups where industrial experts and KTH faculty meet, organize activities (such as workshops), and exchange experiences on topics of common interest (cmp. Fig. 3) and/or on education and continued education.

The current competence groups are as follows:

– Artificial intelligence and machine learning
– Autonomous systems and platforms
– Embedded real-time systems
– Interoperability
– R&D Managers
– Safety
– Security
– Testing of embedded systems
– Systems engineering

A new competence group usually starts by a stakeholder raising a need, followed by one or more workshops where the group is formed. This includes identifying an (initial) core team (usually composed of a mix of people from academia and industry), and deciding on an (initial) focus. The competence groups have slightly different profiles in terms of the types of activities they have chosen to organize. For example, the Safety group has emphasized the organization of a relatively new Scandinavian Conference that provides a venue for cross-domain industrial interactions and for meeting academia. The systems engineering group has instead focused on introducing systems thinking and systems engineering into a capstone course at KTH with industrial engineers as teachers. It has also organized workshops, such as on how systems engineering can deal with the complexity of future CPS.

The competence groups receive administrative support from the ICES office and a small budget. The competence groups are in turn expected to organize a few events and meetings each year and report back to the ICES board. The results from the groups are made available to the network through workshops, seminars, courses and conferences.

Another central part of the network is the workgroups. Management and development of the network takes place through the following workgroups:

– Education and student interaction (improving current engineering education, and creating contacts)
– Continued education (creating and hosting courses adapted for industry)
– Marketing and member involvement
– Competence groups (as described above)
– Learning network (supporting, managing and creating new competence groups)
– Interactions and catalyzing (research/innovation) projects
– Management of the center

As an example group activity, the continued education task force has been investigating prioritized thematic topics by industry, funding, and models for implementing flexible and part on-line courses. A course is now being developed in system safety and cyber-security as a collaboration between faculty from computer science and industrial engineering. This type of course is largely lacking both in engineering and continued education today.

Achievements. Among the achievements, the ICES network has catalyzed multiple research projects[1], a new research center[2], and annually organizes more than 20 events. As examples of such events we present an overview of events that were organized during 2017:

- Two conferences: The ICES annual conference with a focus on "DevOps for CPS", and the 5th Scandinavian Conference on System and Software Safety. Both conferences had roughly 100 participants from industry and academia each (some 60% from industry, with a good spread across industrial domains and academic disciplines).
- 50 work group and competence group meetings corresponding to about 3–4 meetings/year.
- Multiple efforts to promote student-industry interactions, including dedicated MSc thesis fairs, study visits, and industry involvement in teaching (e.g. guest lectures).
- 7 workshops, for example on the topic of CPS foundations and trustworthiness, Systems engineering and CPS education needs in collaboration with INCOSE, and Innovation in CPS and IIoT (featuring funding opportunities and information from innovation support organizations).
- Several special ICES events, including the then newly started "coffee with an expert series" (featuring e.g. prominent guest professors and industrial experts), a meeting with the Swedish minister on Research, and an M.Sc. thesis fair.
- Several other events with ICES involvement, including Embedded Conference Scandinavia and the Cybersecurity and Privacy (CySeP) Summer School (co-funded by ICES).

As a further example of achievement, ICES paved the way for the international master-level program in Embedded Systems at KTH. Given that KTH already had many programs, the industrial support for launching a new program was decisive in motivating its launch. The program was designed as a collaboration between four schools, each providing their "best courses" to the program. The interest in the program has grown from its start in 2011. 2019 the program had about 700 applicants world-wide, with 335 having the program as its first priority. To maintain top quality, the number of students has been limited to about 50–70 per year. The program scores well in course evaluations and is highly appreciated by the industrial partners in ICES.

---

[1] Examples of catalyzed projects include the European projects iFEST (ARTEMIS-project initiated through ICES), MBAT (ARTEMIS project with ICES initiated Swedish sub-consortium) and SCOTT (ECSEL project with ICES initiated Swedish sub-consortium), each larger 3-year research projects involving multiple ICES stakeholder organizations.

[2] The TECoSA research center was recently approved and is scheduled to start early 2020. https://www.vinnova.se/en/news/2019/06/efforts-on-world-class-research-environments/ (accessed Oct. 2019).

4 Lessons Learnt

In operating the ICES network for more than 10 years we have designed, introduced, revised and observed a number of practices that we have found especially important for the long-term evolution, growth and efficient operation of the network. These are here summarized.

Stakeholders. ICES early on spent an effort in identifying key stakeholders and their needs, recall Fig. 2. While the needs have been revised, this early effort has been instrumental in providing the relevant "services" for the stakeholders, thus creating interest in ICES. For example, it is clear that there is a large demand for CPS engineers – thus creating strong incentives for industry to engage with universities[3]. The paradigm shift motivates extra efforts for revising education programs. Indeed, university educators are actively engaged in discussing how to reform programs to educate the CPS engineers of tomorrow, see e.g. [6–8] – and here it is beneficial with university and industry interactions to better understand the needs for how such new programs could be formed.

Vision and Goals. In ICES, the Vision and goals document has been jointly elaborated, followed-up and improved. The operational goals, concretely drive work towards the vision and goals. Over the years, the role of ICES as a competence network has been strengthened by the insights and experiences in designing and redesigning activities to create value for the stakeholders. The name of ICES stands for Innovative Center for Embedded Systems, with "Innovative" indicating the purpose to be innovative and learning in the way the center is organized. Accordingly, we have continuously had a dialogue with stakeholders and attempted to improve a practices as well as introducing new ones.

Agreement. In the set-up of ICES, various types of agreements were considered. Eventually it was decided to not use (complex) agreements. Instead ICES relies on a code of conduct (including that the network cannot be used for marketing purposes) and the understanding that aggressive competitors are not included. However, it must be noted that many of the partners are indeed competitors (e.g. multiple consultancy companies, Scania and Volvo) but here the benefits of long-term competence development are seen as more important. Generally, information that partners bring to the network is considered to be open. This approach can be compared with research projects with rather complex contracts and with results that are not generally and widely shared. Agreements come into play for example when ICES catalyzes a research project. Such projects will then be separate from ICES with their own agreements, but can still benefit from ICES as a vehicle for bi-directional communication.

---

[3] According to an investigation by ARTEMIS and ITEA2, the global market of Digital Technology (encompassing software, embedded software, IT services, internal IT and hardware) was estimated to USD 3,300 billion, corresponding to approximately 50 million jobs, predicted to have continued strong growth, [5].

Board Composition, Management and Decentralized Organization. The ICES board has generally been rather large, involving "gold member" representatives, as well as representatives from the involved schools at KTH, with the purpose to engage the organizations and to spread information. Moreover, with the various groups, the organization is decentralized, engaging multiple persons that contribute in various ways. The management is divided further into a director and co-director, and a management team, creating robustness in the organization.

Stakeholder Engagement. As part of the key stakeholders, we would like to explicitly mention the involvement of student representatives in the board and in some of the work groups. The students currently represent three relevant master programs at KTH. The students provide valuable insights into how they see the current education and improvement potential, communicate ICES activities to students, and facilitate student interactions with industry as well as with academic faculty. As a further example, one of the competence groups is dedicated to R&D managers so that managers with similar technology challenges but in different industry domains meet 3–4 times a year – providing interactions that are perceived as valuable by the participating managers as well as for enriching the ICES network.

From Disciplinary to Multidisciplinary. Based in a university, it is important to be aware of the difficulties in trying to create integration across academic disciplines, departments and schools. Universities have deep traditions and have slow time constants; for example, it will take more than one year to launch a new program and after its launch there will be several more years before the first students exit the program.

Moreover, there is a lack of incentives to integrate across disciplines. As opposed to a company that needs product integration, academic faculty are usually directly rewarded by specialization, depth and in staying within their discipline. While there might be large potential in multidisciplinary work, it takes time, is risky and sometimes even counter-productive in that funding schemes may make it difficult to include more than one discipline or more than one group from a university. Competence provisioning in the era of CPS is thus challenged by the current disciplinary university system and the growing amount of knowledge – resulting in fragmentation across disciplines, experts, groups, etc. The disciplinary setting makes it more difficult to provide new bridging competences required for future CPS and there is a corresponding lack of T-shaped educators [9]. Similarly, academic teachers often lack first-hand experience with industrial applications, creating a gap between the taught theory vs. concerns of real CPS.

We believe that competence networks can at least partly help in addressing these problems. Establishing collaboration between academia and industry, can help to bridge the gap between theory and real-world CPS, and also incentivizes creating bridges between disciplines. ICES has contributed to improved contacts to industry for both faculty and students, and we have through the collaboration also been able to integrate industry taught modules. The purpose here has been to bring in industrial competence related to complex engineering issues that are not (readily and typically) taught at a university, complementing traditional academic courses. This has for example included the introduction of an industry taught module on systems engineering as part of a capstone course at KTH [10].

A competence network, with opportunities for contacts with industry and for catalyzing research projects thus helps in providing incentives towards integration. ICES has catalyzed several research projects that involve more than one research group and discipline at KTH. The era of CPS also provides new opportunities to promote multidisciplinary research since the needs are becoming much more apparent – for example, when equipping cars with various artificial intelligence (AI) techniques, safety concerns become relevant for the AI community.

Collaboration with Other Networks. In the area of CPS, and especially in the midst of a socio-technical paradigm shift, a huge number of efforts and centers are devoted to various aspects that relate to CPS. ICES has evolved into a networking center, establishing strategic collaboration with other initiatives as one way to deal with this plethora of initiatives. As examples of successful collaboration we would like to highlight the tradition of co-organized events with the Swedish chapter of INCOSE, and the KTH membership in ARTEMIS-IA. Currently, ICES is offering collaboration to other KTH centers that in some way relate to software-intensive CPS. The potential arises since most other centers are focused on research while ICES is a competence network. ICES also collaborates with THINGS – a KTH based CPS/IoT incubator, bringing startups and small SMEs closer to the ICES network, and thus to larger companies, KTH faculty and students.

Neutral Ground and Regional Focus. We have noticed that having a university to host a competence network will have some form of trust enhancing effect – with the university seen as more neutral compared to many other stakeholders. ICES has further traditionally had a regional focus (the larger Stockholm area), facilitating for stakeholders to physically engage in the network.

5   Challenges

During the operation of the ICES network we have encountered several challenges. We here highlight what we consider as key challenges that are relevant when setting up a competence network, especially considering hosting at a University.

Competence Networks and Education Are Not Prioritized. At universities, research merits are generally driving promotion (e.g. along tenure track schemes), and education has a much lower status; this is also true for continued education [6, 11, 12].

This somewhat chocking reality has a further implication that adoption of best practices in education is progressing very slowly – much university education is still using passive learning through traditional lectures whereas there is clear scientific evidence of much improved education when active learning is adopted [13].

Universities are typically given the task to communicate and share knowledge to a broader audience, referred to as public or science outreach, or the third mission of a university. Unfortunately, the third mission is vaguely defined and not incentivized. As a result, academic researchers – who are generally busy doing research within their specific discipline, will not prioritize competence network initiatives since it draws their attention from their research. When enthusiasts are recruited, on the other hand, activities may become dependent on them, making it difficult to provide continuity.

The lack of priorities for competence networks is seen for example in the lack of funding to support such activities; while research is funded, dissemination of research and exchange of best practices from industry are also not prioritized (typically with smaller short-term efforts as part of research projects). Another indication is the funding struggles we have had with ICES. Most of the centers at KTH are research centers, with larger but time-limited funds provided by e.g. public funding. For such centers, a standard model will provide funding support from the university. ICES is on the other hand a competence network that operates on lower budgets and with no clear time limit. While research centers deliver tangible research output, ICES output is often more subtle or indirect, with for example work to improve the engineering education, catalyzing new research projects and through other effects that we may not even be aware of. Capturing and estimating the corresponding indirect value is difficult. A competence network thus often represents an "odd-bird" at a university. We therefore believe that there are strong needs to balance the priorities; given the importance of competence, regions that emphasize this are likely to become winners!

More recently, the funding situation has improved due to the involvement of ICES in EU innovation projects and a Nordic academic network on the industrial internet of things [14]. As a related opportunity and centered in ICES, a Digital Innovation Hub on Industrial Digitalization was recently formed [31].

The Paradox with Strong Needs but (Perceived) Lack of Time. Industrial companies would generally agree that competence networks are increasingly important. However, at the same time, most industrial stakeholders and experts in the field perceive themselves as very busy. This is quite natural during a paradigm shift. It is however likely to create an imbalance in addressing short-term vs. long-term needs (this balance relates closely to the previous challenge, the lack of prioritization). Because people are so busy, it becomes more difficult to engage people in various competence network activities. We also see this issue with trends such as breakfast seminars, lunch meetings, webinars etc. – trying to grab the small free slots available and resorting to shorter "doses" of interactions. As a consequence, a competence network may need to spend more time on management and work to make seminars and workshops worthwhile to attend. It becomes imperative to consider the needs of stakeholders and design activities to give value to the attendees. We further believe that it is essential to develop a culture and schemes to promote the longer-term perspective, for example, by having companies invest in their employees continued education by engaging in suitable competence networks.

Communication. In these days of communication overflow, finding the right channels and being able to actually get the attention of stakeholders is becoming increasingly challenging. People are already overloaded with information, very busy (cmp. previous bullet), and various hypes makes it even more difficult to penetrate the ether. Just using email is no longer good enough. Moreover, different organizations use different IT-tools and this makes it more difficult to create for example useful forums or wiki like information exchange. ICES is currently using multiple modes of communication, including through the contacts created in the network, a newsletter, social media, and a web page where presentations, recordings, contacts etc. are made available. A special challenge is to reach out to companies which are new to CPS. Developing and implementing clear communication strategies is essential and further work is needed.

Fragmented Efforts Addressing Competence Provisioning. Different aspects of competence networks are today addressed by many initiatives and organizations. These efforts are however fragmented, there is a lack of coordination and overview of who does what, and the sharing of best practices is limited. As one remedy, ICES has initiated dialogues with other initiatives and engaged in several collaborations with other associations as described in Sect. 4.

6 Discussion

In this section we discuss our findings by relating ICES to the state of the art as described in Sect. 2.1, and by elaborating on the generality of our findings.

6.1 Relating ICES to the Discourse on Learning Networks

We relate back to the Prioritization and "Paradox" challenges identified in Sect. 5 and then further discuss purposes of University and academia collaboration.

Prioritization. Related to the lack of prioritization, the incentives and evaluation of Universities today to a very little extent encompasses the third mission. Universities are today mainly evaluated as individual organizations – not relating to their interactions with other organizations, implying that University accomplishments that relate to their collaboration with companies and other external actors are likely to be unnoticed. For individual researchers, their research production represents the main incentive. For the University as a whole, the main incentives in Sweden today include funding related to the educational output ("finished students") and the "ranking" which is geared towards research performance.

With respect to companies, they often invest too little in competence development and instead focus on having a higher employee turnover to "shift competences". In reality this is most likely quite costly, but it is easier to argue inside a firm that new employees with desired competence should be hired while others lacking the right knowledge and skills should be laid off than to argue that employees need a budget for lifelong learning. One reason for this may be that central HR takes much of the costs for hiring and firing, whereas continuous competence development is typically carried out by the business units, resulting in unbalanced incentives. Companies need to consider the real costs of updating competences as compared to hiring new people, and maybe also policy makers need to create incentives for lifelong learning inside companies, not only support activities for the ones who have been found to have outdated knowledge and consequently have lost their jobs.

Paradox and Communication. During the years with ICES, we see a lot of potential for even more engagement by the involved companies. Apart from "the lack of time" that we perceived, the state of the art provides an additional explanation – the cost of interacting with others with a different background. Without the strong motivation that comes from working towards direct value capture or knowledge creation the participants thus struggle to find the time to engage continuously. The paradox also relates closely to the positioning and culture within the company (as just discussed under priorities) – and this requires some level of management support and a way of operating the network, and of course, interest by people.

The barrier for engaging may also relate to the fact that competence networks constitute unusual entities (i.e. "odd birds" as noted in Sect. 5) in the world of academia, Comparing with traditional research centers, ICES offers a slightly more complicated mode of engagement. In the setting of a research center, a company pays money to the center, and is typically in return invited to a few workshops per year and a committee for deciding on projects. ICES on the other hand offers rich opportunities for interactions in terms of the work groups and competence groups, the board, workshops, conferences, and other activities. To access the network thus requires an initial effort in understanding what the network and groups are about, and then further time (and prioritization) in actually engaging.

The paradox further relates to the challenge of communication. To reduce the barriers, there is a need for efficient communication. We believe that IT-support in various forms (from webexes, recorded talks, forums etc.) have a role to play but deploying and getting the network to adopt the right tools also introduces another potential barrier so this requires careful considerations. W.r.t. communication we have noticed that our reach within some of the larger company members is somewhat limited. To spread information in such large companies, we believe it is beneficial to tap into their communication structures. Such efforts have been attempted and will be continued in ICES.

A competence center can in many ways be seen as a "community of practice" as it is based on some important pillars: a shared view of its purpose (learning), mutual trust (making it possible to reveal both strengths and weaknesses), efficient communication through specialized language (jargon), a strong focus on knowledge (meritocracy) rather than power stemming from hierarchical positions, and a network-based organization. In order to function as a community, it cannot be expanded to a very large group of people as this will undermine all the above pillars, and consequently this type of community has to be established and managed locally in a bottom-up way (not excluding support from university and funding bodies, but these should ideally not come with too much demands and limitations).

Purposes of University and Academia Collaboration. The role of academia in supporting industry and society encompasses education, research and outreach.

Ensuring a continued flow of possible recruits with the right knowledge is in itself a strong motivator for public-private cooperation. Our experiences from ICES suggest that this type of cooperation can also affect the involved stakeholders in other ways than e.g. cooperation focused on innovation: understanding each other, achieving a common vision and finding a neutral common ground was strongly emphasized among the stakeholders.

Interactions taking place in competence networks provides information about graduates' needed competences and skills as this is made explicit by industry representatives, making it possible to adjust curricula accordingly in order to increase employability and reduce the time needed for graduates to find suitable employment. The high cost of misalignment between supply and demand for university-developed knowledge and skills could thus be reduced by access to more relevant and updated information about needs and development trends. In our experience, this type of collaboration has a strong potential since in the era of complex CPS – insights into technology, engineering complex systems and science will all be required. The collaboration has to respect the integrity of the involved organizations, and balance short vs. long term as well as between science, engineering and technology.

6.2   Generality of Findings

If one would like to replicate the ICES competence network – how would that work in other regions and countries, i.e. what might be specific for the regional context of ICES?

The operation of the ICES competence network has evolved in Sweden in the larger Stockholm area. We believe that many of the experiences are valid also in other settings, although differences in regional needs, constraints and culture needs to be considered in attempting to draw upon the findings from ICES.

The Swedish setting is characterized by free university education, a strong multi-domain industry, and a tradition of governmental sponsoring of research and education (with little corresponding direct industrial sponsoring of such activities). In addition, Sweden is known to be home to a collaborative culture. Moreover, the use of the university as neutral ground, the policy to avoid fierce competitors, and the regional scale have most likely been important in creating an environment of trust, where no agreements are needed and where people are still participating and sharing information.

Thus, while we do believe that many of the ingredients and effects as discussed in Sects. 4 and 6.1 should be relevant in other regions with other characteristics, the element of building trust will be important for setting up a competence network also in other contexts.

We note that the trends and challenges with CPS are not specific to any region. The industrial presence and the types of domains related to a region could however vary. A broader spectrum of CPS application domains – such as we are fortunate to experience with ICES, certainly implies that it should be easier to set up a competence network. Engaging in a network to share experiences, may be easier across domains since there is less competition. However, even with a smaller number of domains, the needs for competence networks are still strong.

Many other areas are also characterized by complex systems and paradigm shifts, involving a range of stakeholders. We believe that the experiences from the ICES network could be relevant in other domains, beyond CPS. For example, considering the transitioning to sustainable and circular systems, it would be highly beneficial to establish collaboration – e.g. in the form of a competence network – involving for example stakeholders representing economy, management, material scientists, experts in sustainability (e.g. life-cycle analysis), industrial manufacturing, systems engineering, and digital technology experts.

7   Conclusions and Ways Forward

The amount of knowledge required in developing and managing the CPS of tomorrow is unprecedented and requires grasping a broader area of concerns and a corresponding availability of experts in these areas. This leads to strong needs for collaboration.

Competence networks address the needs for CPS involved organizations to continuously learn within and across organizations, to get access to experts and recruit competent people, in sharing experiences and best practices, and working to re-shape the engineering education to better meet the needs for engineering future CPS, including developing life-long learning through continued education for the existing work-force.

We have described the ICES competence network involving academia and industry, lessons learnt and challenges faced during the operation of the network. There are several important ways forward:

- Competence networks ought to be recognized as important mechanisms for spurring regional innovation. In order to accomplish this, incentives, funding, KPIs and evaluation schemes need to be made available. The EC initiative on digital innovation hubs could here correspond to one useful mechanism forward.
- Companies needs to recognize the importance of internal competence development, and here collaboration with universities in the form of competence networks represents one promising way forward.
- As well recognized, but still pertinent to this paper, there is a need to provide incentives for life-long learning and to raise the status of education.
- Gathering, investigating and disseminating best practices on competence networks. We believe that further work is needed in this direction, including addressing the identified challenges.

In conclusion, our experience is that the ICES type of competence network fills an important role as information carrier and collaboration mechanism in our regional setting with cross-industry domain and academia collaboration. The network is perceived as important by the involved stakeholders, and would be relevant to introduce also in other areas involving complex systems.

Acknowledgments. This work has been supported by FED4SAE (H2020 Innovation action), HI2OT (supported by NordForsk's Nordic University Hubs programme, grant agreement no. 86220) and ICES at KTH. We greatly acknowledge the contributions of the many persons and organizations that have engaged in ICES or otherwise supported ICES since its start in 2008!

References

1. Thompson, H., et al.: Platforms4CPSKey Outcomes and Recommendations, 1st edn. Steinbeis-Edition, Stuttgart (2018). Report from the Platforms4CPS project (H2020 project Grant Agreement No 731599). ISBN 978-3-95663-184-9
2. Törngren, M., Grogan, P.T.: How to deal with the complexity of future cyber-physical systems? J. Des. **2**(4) (2018). https://doi.org/10.3390/designs2040040

3. ICES: www.ices.kth.se. Accessed 12 Aug 2019
4. Törngren, M., et al.: ICES - VISION and GOALS. ICES Working Document, February 2018 [3]
5. ITEA ARTEMIS-IA High-Level Vision 2030: Opportunities for Europe, Autumn 2013. https://itea3.org/publication/download/itea-artemis-ia-high-level-vision-2030-v2013.pdf. Accessed 12 Aug 2019
6. Törngren, M., Bensalem, S., McDermid, J., Passerone, R., Sangiovanni-Vincentelli, A., Schätz, B.: Education and training challenges in the era of cyber-physical systems: beyond traditional engineering. In: Workshop on Embedded and Cyber-Physical Systems Education (WESE) at ESWEEK 2015, Amsterdam (2015). http://dl.acm.org/citation.cfm?id=2832928
7. First Workshop on CPS Education, 8th April 2013, Philadelphia, PA (part of CPSWeek 2013) – accessible at. http://cps-vo.org/group/edu/workshop. Accessed July 2015
8. Workshop on Embedded and Cyber-Physical Systems Education (WESE) 2015, Organized as a part of Embedded Systems Week. http://www.emsig.net/conf/2015/wese/
9. Törngren, M., Herzog, E.: Towards integration of CPS and systems engineering in education. In: 12th Embedded System Week Proceedings 2016 Workshop on Embedded and Cyber-Physical Systems Education, Pittsburgh, October 2016
10. Herzog, E., Larsson, Å.N., El-Khoury, J., Törngren, M.: Experience from introducing systems engineering in an academic environment using an industry training course. In: INCOSE International Symposium, vol. 28, no. 1, pp. 245–259 (2018)
11. Debate article in Dagens Nyheter (Swedish newspaper) by Swedish University Chancellor Harriet Wallberg, 04 August 2014 on "Unacceptable de-prioritization of the higher education system" (article in Swedish). http://www.dn.se/debatt/oacceptabel-bantning-av-undervisning-pa-universitet/. Accessed August 2019
12. Chalmers, D.: Progress and challenges to the recognition and reward of the scholarship of teaching in higher education. High. Educ. Res. Dev. 30(1), 25–38. https://doi.org/10.1080/07294360.2011.536970
13. Prince, M.: Does active learning work? A review of the research. J. Eng. Educ. 93, 223–231 (2004)
14. http://www.nordic-iot.org/. Accessed August 2019
15. Grant, R.M.: Toward a knowledge-based theory of the firm. Strateg. Manag. J. 17(S2), 109–122 (1996)
16. Ozman, M.: Inter-firm networks and innovation: a survey of literature. Econ. Innov. New Technol. 18(1), 39–67 (2009)
17. Pyka, A.: Innovation networks in economics: from the incentive-based to the knowledge-based approaches. Eur. J. Innov. Manag. 5(3), 152–163 (2002)
18. Ankrah, S., Omar, A.-T.: Universities–industry collaboration: a systematic review. Scand. J. Manag. 31(3), 387–408 (2015)
19. Mansfield, E.: Academic research underlying industrial innovations: sources, characteristics, and financing. Rev. Econ. Stat. 77, 55–65 (1995)
20. Lin, J.-Y.: Balancing industry collaboration and academic innovation: the contingent role of collaboration-specific attributes. Technol. Forecast. Soc. Chang. 123, 216–228 (2017)
21. Cohen, W.M., Levinthal, D.A.: Absorptive capacity: a new perspective on learning and innovation. Adm. Sci. Q. 35(1), 128–152 (1990)
22. Hess, A.M., Rothaermel, F.T.: When are assets complementary? Star scientists, strategic alliances, and innovation in the pharmaceutical industry. Strateg. Manag. J. 32(8), 895–909 (2011)
23. Soh, P.-H., Subramanian, A.M.: When do firms benefit from university–industry R&D collaborations? The implications of firm R&D focus on scientific research and technological recombination. J. Bus. Ventur. 29(6), 807–821 (2014)

24. Jamieson, L.H., Lohmann, J.R.: Innovation with impact: creating a culture for scholarly and systematic innovation in engineering education. American Society for Engineering Education, Washington (2012)

25. Kasworm, C., Hemmingsen, L.: Preparing professionals for lifelong learning: comparative examination of master's education programs. High. Educ. **54**(3), 449–468 (2007)

26. Seely, B.: Patterns in the history of engineering education reform: a brief essay. In: Educating the Engineer of 2020: Adapting Engineering Education to the New Century, pp. 114–130. The National Academies Press, Washington (2005)

27. Downey, G.L., Lucena, J.C.: Knowledge and professional identity in engineering: code-switching and the metrics of progress. Hist. Technol. **20**(4), 393–420 (2004)

28. Corbett, A.: Principles, problems, politics … what does the historical record of EU cooperation in higher education tell the EHEA generation? In: Curaj, A., Scott, P., Vlasceanu, L., Wilson, L. (eds.) European Higher Education at the Crossroads, pp. 39–58. Springer, Dordrecht (2012). https://doi.org/10.1007/978-94-007-3937-6_3

29. The Magna Charta Observatory: Magna Charta Universitatum. Bologna University, Bologna (1988)

30. Simon, H.A.: The steam engine and the computer: what makes technology revolutionary. Comput. People **36**(11–12), 7–11 (1987)

31. The KTH Innovation Hub of Digital Industrialization - https://s3platform.jrc.ec.europa.eu/digital-innovation-hubs-tool/-/dih/5792/view. Accessed 12 Oct 2019

32. Patterson, D.: How to build a bad research center. Technical report UCB/EECS-2013-123, EECS Department, Univ. of California, Berkeley, June 2013 (2013). http://www2.eecs.berkeley.edu/Pubs/TechRpts/2013/EECS-2013-123.html. Accessed 12 Oct 2019

33. Brown, J.S., Duguid, P.: Organizational learning and communities-of-practice: toward a unified view of working, learning, and innovation. Organ. Sci. **2**(1), 40–57 (1991)

34. Wenger, E.: Communities of practice and social learning systems. Organization **7**(2), 225–246 (2001)

Author Index

Printed in the United States
By Bookmasters